Handbook for Sexual Abuser Assessment and Treatment

Edited by
Mark S. Carich, Ph.D.
Steven E. Mussack, Ph.D.

Safer Society Press
PO BOX 340 • BRANDON • VT 05733
A program of The Safer Society Foundation, Inc.

Production management: Jenna Dixon
Copyediting: Linda Lotz
Proofreading: Beth Richards
Design and composition: Jenna Dixon
Index: Barbara DeGennaro
Printed in the United States of America by Malloy Lithographing.

Chapter 12, Working with Culturally Diverse Populations, was previously published in *Cultural Diversity in Sexual Abuser Treatment: Issues and Approaches* (© 1998 The Safer Society Press/Safer Society Foundation, Inc.). Reprinted by permission.

Library of Congress Cataloging-in-Publication Data

Handbook for sexual abuse assessment and treatment / edited by Mark S. Carich, Steven E. Mussack.
     p.   cm.
Includes bibliographical references and index.
ISBN 1-884444-58-X (alk. paper)
    1. Sex offenders—Mental health services—Handbooks, manuals, etc. 2. Sex offenders—Rehabilitation—Handbooks, manuals, etc. I. Carich, Mark S., 1957-   II. Mussack, Steven E., 1953-

RD560.S47 H355 2000
616.85'83—dc21   00-055375

Safer Society Press
A program of The Safer Society Foundation, Inc.
PO Box 340
Brandon, Vermont 05733 USA
(802) 247-3132

ISBN 1-884444-58-X / $28.00 / Bulk discounts available

In memory of Steven Fischer, LCSW, who died on August 5, 1995, and was an esteemed colleague and friend.

I am dedicating this book to the following: My immediate family, wife Audrey and daughters Andrea and Cassie; my parents Dr. Pete and Mary Carich for their continuous support and encouragement and from whom I derived a great deal of motivation; and to the Joe/Jan Verbeck family (Joe, Jan, Jody, Gina, and Jason) for their continuous warmth and support in my writing endeavors throughout the years. I also appreciate the support throughout the years of an esteemed colleague and friend, Dr. Don Wahl.

Special thanks goes to my coeditor for his effort, time, and editorial skills, without which this book would be a much rougher document. I appreciate Robert Freeman-Longo's support and belief in me, in developing both this book and *The Adult Sexual Offender Assessment Packet.* I also appreciate the support of Euan Bear on this book.

Mark S. Carich

Also, in special memory of Fay Honey Knopp who has inspired so many of us to greater dedication to this field and to Robert Freeman-Longo who has taken up Honey's banner and served as a mentor to me when I entered this field and as a friend for many years.

I am dedicating this book to my wife, Alice, my children, Amber and Jordan, my father, Paul who dusted off his skills as an English teacher to review each chapter; and my mother, Marlene, for patiently giving him the time to do so. I also dedicate this book to the sexual offenders who have allowed me to enter their lives in a quest to make society safer and to all of you who read this book and join me in this quest.

Steven E. Mussack

Contents

Foreword, Stephen M. Hudson   vii
Preface   ix
About the Contributors   xi

Introduction   1
1   Sexual Abuser Evaluation   11
    Steven E. Mussack & Mark S. Carich

2   Program Development: Key Elements
    and Staff Management   37
    Gary Lowe

3   Working with Denial in Sexual Abusers:
    Some Clinical Suggestions   47
    Laren Bays

4   Cognitive Distortions and Restructuring
    in Sexual Abuser Treatment   65
    William D. Murphy & Mark S. Carich

5   Relapse Prevention and the Sexual Assault
    Cycle   77
    Mark S. Carich, Alison Gray,
    Sacha Rombouts, Mark Stone &
    William D. Pithers

6   Using Behavioral Techniques to Control
    Sexual Arousal   105
    Robert J. McGrath

7   The Sex Abuser Treatment Group
    Process   117
    Peter Loss

8   Empathy Training   141
    William Marshall & Y. M. Fernandez

9   Enhancing Social and Relationship
    Skills   149
    William Marshall

10 Family Treatment of Adult Sexual
    Abusers   163
    Jerry Thomas & C. Wilson Viar III

11 Assessment and Treatment of Intellectually
    Disabled Sexual Abusers   193
    Emily M. Coleman & James Haaven

12 Working with Culturally Diverse
    Populations   211
    Alvin D. Lewis

13 Aftercare Programming   225
    Steven E. Mussack & Mark S. Carich

14 Perspectives on the Future   237
    Steven E. Mussack & Mark S. Carich

Index   241

Foreword

To say that sexual abuse is a public health problem of almost epidemic proportions has become almost a cliché, and like most clichés, it expresses a truth. The pioneers in sexual abuser treatment — some of whom are represented in this volume — were courageous enough to begin to work with these men and women even though the conventional wisdom was that they could not be treated. Gradually, we have come to understand that for many abusers, treatment works — if we can find the right combination of approaches and a way to reach beyond their defenses, remediate their social and emotional deficits, and teach them socially benign ways to cope with inevitable life stresses.

Sexual abuse treatment is still a comparatively young field; its issues and approaches are still open to dispute and investigation. Although no "handbook" issued at this point can hope to be so authoritative that it is without controversy, the points of view represented here support the urge of treatment providers to keep looking for more effective approaches, while providing a firm basis in current practice and the history of the field. The chapters reveal the twin origins of sexual abuser treatment — criminal justice/corrections and psychotherapeutic practice — and its recent movement into the arena of public health concerns. Although we've come a long way from the days when the public's attitude veered from "boys will be boys, no real harm done, she asked for it," to an image of child molesters as "dirty perverts in trenchcoats loitering in playgrounds" to "lock 'em up and throw away the key," we must remain ever on guard against public pressure for the easy answer, the urge to extract revenge for the pain caused to victims and families, and the rupture of the societal fabric of trusting interaction.

We do little to justify our responsibility to the men, women and children who will be abused if we behave as if we have all the answers to the complex set of puzzles posed by sexual abuse. Editors and authors Mark Carich and Steven Mussack have sought to create a reference that is practitioner oriented and at the same time refuses to shy away from healthy disagreement. They describe their own practices extensively and collect the experiences of a wide variety of knowledgeable, experienced clinicians on how to treat sex offenders within a contemporary framework. The editors also make some excellent suggestions about program content and raise fundamentally important issues in the introductory sections, such as treatment-induced change in level of risk and amenability to treatment.

The Handbook for Sexual Abuser Assessment and Treatment provides the basic outline of treatment approaches and their justifications, the "how" and "why" of current practice. It is an invaluable resource for any agency treating sexual abusers and taking on new practitioners. This is challenging work, particularly our role of encouraging the abusers we work with to give up behaviors associated with pleasure or at least with the reduction of emotional pain. Both the abusers we work with and we ourselves need all the support available, as contributor Gary Lowe emphasizes in his chapter on building a program.

Another challenging notion addressed here is that therapists should accept and work with the certainty that not all facts will be disclosed at the initial assessment. Given the likelihood that an abuser has been mandated into treatment and the fact that this gives the therapist a great deal of power over the client, how can the abuser-client be expected to trust the therapist immediately? Mark Carich, Steven Mussack, and Laren Bays point out such dynamics, Mussack and Carich in their practical chapter on assessment, and Bays in his thought-provoking discussion of breaking through denial by encouraging us to consider how we would react — or have reacted in the past — when we have been caught doing something we might be ashamed of. These suggestions highlight the need to be firmly humane in our approach to incremental disclosure and breaking through denial. Modeling respect for persons (not for their harmful actions) in interactions with abusers, even those who have committed heinous crimes, is one of the surest ways to teach it.

The book also seeks to cover practical issues in a practical fashion. Lowe's comments concerning the need to be transparent with the media are well taken, as are his comments about the community context of setting up a program.

The need for a benign treatment climate, staff adherence to the program's model, and watchful respect for the clients cannot be overstated. The chapters on the fundamental treatment components of in any program — cognitive distortion, empathy, social skills, denial, cultural considerations, offending processes, family therapy, and aftercare — are characterized by practical suggestions and clinical vignettes so useful for practitioners. With the development of multicultural awareness reflected in Alvin Lewis's chapter and the realization of the importance of involving and treating the families of sexual abusers shared by Jerry Thomas and C. Wilson Viar III, the *Handbook for Sexual Abuser Assessment and Treatment* shows that our field has begun to mature beyond its early punitive and ethnocentric origins.

Many of these areas are contentious, for example, what offending processes actually look like and how best to conceptualize them, the necessity of aftercare, and how to deal with the conceptual interface of cognitive distortions, empathy deficits, and issues of victim harm. However, as the editors intend, debate can only stimulate more effort, which in turn can only enhance our ability to assist the men and women who are entrusted to our care. Translating this opportunity into fewer victims in the future is what we are all about.

Stephen M. Hudson, Ph.D.
University of Canterbury,
Christchurch, New Zealand

Preface

This book is designed to be practitioner oriented. Our goal is to provide both new and experienced sexual offender treatment providers with information that can be directly applied in either community-based or inpatient treatment programs. This handbook is organized around the continuum of treatment spanning initial assessment to aftercare and discharge planning. Theories, guidelines, strategies, and, in some cases, specific outlines concerning effective assessment and treatment methods are included. Each chapter is written with a separate focus by experienced therapists in the field, many of whom are well known as national and international trainers and researchers.

This handbook is also intended to challenge the reader and provoke thought. No handbook in this field can be considered definitive, as sexual offender treatment is in constant evolution. It is expected that readers may find aspects of this book with which they disagree. We support such disagreement as the foundation of constructive debate and further research, which serve to enrich our field. It is our hope that you will take the information provided in these pages as encouragement to add to our base of knowledge in the field of sexual offender treatment.

About the Contributors

Mark S. Carich, PhD, is coordinator of the Sexually Dangerous Persons Program (civil commitment sex offenders) with the Illinois Corrections at Big Muddy River Correctional Center. He is on both the teaching and the dissertation faculties of the Adler School of Professional Psychology in Chicago. With Mark Stone, he coauthored the *Sex Offender Relapse Intervention Workbook* and coedited *Offender Relapse Prevention*. With Donya Adkerson, he coauthored *The Adult Sexual Offender Assessment Packet*. Dr. Carich has been a prolific writer, coauthoring or creating numerous treatment and assessment inventories, articles, and chapters, and conducting training workshops nationwide. His clinical research interests include contemporary sex offender treatment processes, cognitive restructuring, victim empathy, covert arousal control, the assault cycle, relapse prevention, assessment, and recovery.

Steven E. Mussack, PhD, is a licensed psychologist in Oregon and has provided treatment to sexual abusers in community settings for 19 years. He currently directs the CHOICES Sexual Offender Treatment Program in Eugene. In addition, he serves as a consultant to the Sexual Abuse Treatment Project at the Eugene Center for Family Development and provides clinical training in sexual abuser treatment at the Eugene Family Institute, a community-based training clinic. Dr. Mussack is a member of the Oregon Psychological Association Professional Ethics Committee and a past board member of Oregon Mental Health Associates. He is a cofounder and past board member of the Association for the Treatment of Sexual Abusers.

Laren Bays, MS, ND, works with the Correctional Treatment Services of the Oregon Department of Corrections and has worked with adult male sexual abusers for 16 years. He is a coauthor of the Safer Society Press sex offender workbook series and works as a Zen Buddhist priest.

Emily M. Coleman has over 20 years of clinical and research experience in the assessment and treatment of sexual offenders. After earning her master's degree in behavior modification from Southern Illinois University in 1975, she worked on the first federally funded grant to research the treatment of sexual offenders. Ms. Coleman developed and directed sex offender treatment programs for the Colorado Department of Corrections and the Bronx-Lebanon Hospital Forensic Clinic in New York City. Since 1986, she has been the director of the Sex Offender Program at Clinical and Support Options, Inc., a community mental health center in western Massachusetts. Her most recent publication, coauthored with James Haaven, is "Adult Intellectually Disabled Sex Offenders: Program Considerations" in *The Sourcebook of Treatment Programs for Sexual Offenders* (Plenum, 1998). She lectures throughout North America, specializing in the assessment and treatment of intellectually disabled sexual offenders. Ms. Coleman is on the board of the Association for the Treatment of Sexual Abusers and Stop It Now, a national organization focusing on the primary prevention of sexual abuse. She lives in the country with three dogs, two horses, one cat and her partner.

Y. M. Fernandez, MA, graduated with a BA (Hons.) in 1994, earning her master's in 1996 from Queens University in Kingston, Ontario, Canada. She is currently in the fourth year of a PhD in clinical/forensic psychology at Queens University under the supervision of Dr. William Marshall. In addition to her studies, Ms. Fernandez is a therapist for the Sexual Offender Program at Bath Institution, a medium-security federal penitentiary. She is an active researcher who currently has done several presentations at international conferences and 17 publications, including two books she coauthored or coedited. Ms. Fernandez anticipates successful completion of her doctoral program in 2001 and hopes to continue working in the field of sexual offender treatment and research.

Alison Gray, MS, is a project officer in the Child Health Outcomes Unit of the Queensland Department of Health, where she develops and implements departmental policies on the prevention and treatment of child abuse and neglect. Prior to immigrating to Australia, she served as the coprincipal investigator and program director on a grant examining children with sexual behavior problems. She has published widely on children with sexual behavior problems and adolescent sexual abusers. Ms.

Gray created statewide networks of adolescent treatment providers in Oregon and of treatment providers for children with sexual behavior problems in Vermont.

James Haaven, MA, is director of the Social Rehabilitation Unit at Oregon State Hospital in Salem. He has been treating the sexual offending behavior of adult males with developmental disabilities for the last 20 years. Mr. Haaven is coauthor of *Treating Intellectually Disabled Sex Offenders: A Model Residential Program* (Safer Society Press) and other publications; along with other staff and residents, he is the subject of the video *An Introduction to the Assessment and Treatment of Intellectually Disabled Sexual Offenders*.

Alvin D. Lewis, MSW, EdD, is a faculty member at Pima Community College and is in private practice in Tucson, Arizona. For several years he was the associate clinical director of a residential treatment program for juvenile sex offenders. He is a returned Peace Corps volunteer and has presented papers throughout the United States on diversity and multiculturalism. Dr. Lewis received his MSW from Temple University and doctorate from Nova Southeastern University.

Peter Loss, MSW, ACSW, has treated adult and juvenile sex offenders, victims, and families in community and correctional settings and provided training and consultation to other professionals in the sexual assault field since 1978. He has also directed the Sex Offender Treatment Program under contract with the Rhode Island Department of Corrections since 1987 and is currently a member of the Rhode Island Board of Review of Sexually Violent Predatory Behavior ("Megan's Law"). With Jonathan Ross, MA, Mr. Loss coauthored "Assessment of the Juvenile Sex Offender" in *Juvenile Sexual Offending: Causes, Consequences, and Correction*, edited by Gail Ryan and Sandy Lane.

Gary Lowe, MSW, LCSW, retired from youth and adult corrections in California in 1999 after 30 years of service specializing in sex offender treatment and community supervision. While working in corrections, Mr. Lowe also developed community-based treatment programs for victims of sexual assault. He has served on the board of directors of the State Coalition on Sex Offending and the California Sexual Assault Investigators Association. He was a participating member of the National Task Force on Juvenile Sexual Offenders. He is a consultant to and instructor for the California Peace Officers Standards and Training and the Pressly Institute of Criminal Investigation, specializing in sex crime investigation and officer wellness. He has written numerous articles for professional publications. Gary Lowe and his wife Nancy reside in Sacramento, California. They have four sons and five granddaughters.

William Marshall, PhD, is a registered psychologist in Ontario, Canada. He is a professor of psychology and psychiatry at Queen's University, Kingston, Ontario, and director of the Bath Institution Sex Offenders' Program. Dr. Marshall has researched and treated adult male sexual abusers for over 30 years and has published over 200 journal articles and chapters and six books. He is the lead author of *Cognitive Behavioral Treatment of Sexual Offenders.*

Robert J. McGrath, MA, is the clinical director of the Vermont Department of Corrections' network of programs that provide treatment to sex offenders at two prisons and 11 outpatient sites. He has served as a consultant to the National Institute of Corrections since 1989 and to the Center for Sex Offender Management since 1998. He has provided training on sex offender assessment, treatment, and program development to corrections, mental health, victim advocate, and judicial groups throughout the United States and Canada. He is a former chairperson of the Board of Directors of the Safer Society Foundation.

William D. Murphy, PhD, received his BA in psychology from Southern Illinois University in 1971, his MS and PhD in clinical psychology from Ohio University. He is currently a professor in the Department of Psychiatry at the University of Tennessee in Memphis. Since 1986, he has served as the coordinator of the University of Tennessee Professional Psychology Internship Consortium and is director of the Special Problems Unit, a sex offender treatment program operated by the university. He has presented over 75 workshops and papers at regional and national meetings and has published over 40 book chapters and journal articles on sexual offending. He is a past president of the Association for the Treatment of Sexual Abusers and serves on the editorial boards of a number of journals.

William D. Pithers, PhD, is an associate professor and director of clinical psychology at Griffith University, Gold Coast, Australia. Dr. Pithers is widely recognized for his adaptation of relapse prevention for use with sexual abusers. His work on empathy building with sex offenders has been reviewed in the *New York Times* and is mentioned in Daniel Goleman's *Emotional Intelligence.* He received the Significant Achievement Award from the Association for the Treatment of Sexual Abusers and has been both a board member and president of ATSA. Most recently, with Alison Gray, Aida Busconi, and Paul Houchens, he has conducted groundbreaking research on children with sexual behavior problems and their caregivers.

Sacha Rombouts, B Psych (Hons), is a doctoral candidate in the clinical psychology program at Griffith University, Gold Coast, Australia. He is also a registered practicing psychologist currently facilitating groups of adolescent survivors of sexual abuse. His primary research interest is in the area of criminal personality profiling of sexual abusers, and he maintains an interest in the study of assessment and treatment of both adolescent and adult sexual abusers.

Mark Stone, EdD, PsyD, ABPP, is a provost and professor at the Adler School of Professional Psychology in Chicago, Illinois. He has been a substance abuse treatment supervisor and counselor and a supervisor of sex offender treatment programs. He has been in private practice as a licensed psychologist for 25 years.

Jerry Thomas, MEd, has been active for many years on the local, state, and national levels as an advocate for state-of-the-art treatment services for children. She is a member of the National

Task Force on Juvenile Sexual Offending, the National Adolescent Perpetration Network, the Child Welfare League, APSAC, AACRC, NAPTC, and ATSA. Her professional background includes counseling in a crisis shelter; providing family therapy in a hospital program; and being the administrator of a residential treatment center, the clinical coordinator of a full-service psychiatric hospital, and a program specialist for a private corporation developing sex offender programs. She authored "Family Treatments of Juvenile Sex Offenders" in *Juvenile Sexual Offending: Causes, Consequences, and Correction*, edited by Gail Ryan and Sandy Lane, and is currently the principal of J. Thomas Consulting and Training Services in Memphis, Tennessee, providing clinical consultation and training.

C. Wilson Viar III has earned multiple bachelor's degrees in psychology, sociology, and creative writing and has done extensive graduate study in a variety of fields, ranging from law to child and family development. He identifies himself as an information broker and has provided research and writing services to a variety of child treatment professionals for over 15 years, concentrating almost exclusively on juvenile sexual offender treatment for the last 10. Mr. Viar has worked closely with J. Thomas Consulting and Training Services since its founding. Among his publications are "Estimation of length of stay" (1996), written with Jerry Thomas and published in *Interchange*, and a wide range of program, staff, and training manuals and materials produced by J. Thomas Consulting and Training Services.

Introduction

Steven E. Mussack
Mark S. Carich

Over the past 20 years, sexual offender treatment has been gaining acceptance as a mental health discipline. The number of sexual offender treatment programs in the United States has increased from a handful in the early 1970s to well over 2,700 currently. Freeman-Longo, Bird, Stevenson, and Fiske (1995) received 1,784 responses during a nationwide survey of treatment programs, which represented only 65 percent of the number of programs identified.

The development and growth of the Association for the Treatment of Sexual Abusers (ATSA) have been natural extensions of this expansion of sexual offender treatment programs. ATSA was founded in 1983 in Salem, Oregon, by a small group of professionals who were interested in promoting quality research and effective treatment of sexual abusers. ATSA is now an international organization headquartered in Beaverton, Oregon, with membership of over 2,000 and affiliations around the world. As a result of the growth in this discipline, there is a consistent need to gather and disseminate up-to-date information concerning the assessment and treatment of sex offenders. This handbook is an effort to meet that need.

The purpose of this handbook is to provide treatment professionals with concise information concerning how to treat sex offenders within a contemporary framework. We focus on four specific areas:

1. introduction to treatment
2. program development, treatment strategies, techniques, and skills development
3. working with selected populations
4. aftercare and follow-up

Each chapter focuses on a specific area considered critical in the assessment and treatment of sexual offenders. Topics include assessment, program development, group therapy, cognitive restructuring, development of victim empathy and remorse, social skills and relationships, assault cycles and modified relapse prevention strategies, family therapy, therapeutic strategies for dealing with denial and resistance, special considerations when treating intellectually disabled offenders, culturally diverse populations, and aftercare programming.

The constructive value of the evaluation and treatment of sexual abusers, in terms of economic, community safety, and emotional considerations, has been effectively addressed in the available literature. The scope and purpose of this handbook are to provide the practitioner with guidelines, strategies, and methods for evaluating and treating sexual abusers. This is a hands-on book filled with practical applications used by some of the leading authorities in the field.

BASIC ASSUMPTIONS

The chapters in this book are predicated on the following basic assumptions:

1. Sexual abuse is a learned, habituated behavior and is not curable. The potential to sexually abuse is much greater for someone who has already exhibited such behaviors than for someone who has not sexually abused anyone. Sexual deviancy is, however, controllable, and such controls can remain in effect throughout an abuser's lifetime if an effort is made to keep them in place.

2. Sexual abusers are more likely than non-abusers to commit sexual crimes, even when long periods — up to several years — have elapsed since the last offense. Time, in and of itself, does not "heal" the abuser of perpetrating behaviors (e.g., cycles, urges, fantasies).

3. Sexual abusers falling within the same category have motivational, behavioral, psychological, historical, and personality characteristics in common that, when identified, aid in effective diagnosis and treatment. The intensity of these characteristics and the extent to which they are manifested differ among abusers within each subtype and across categories. Effective assessment identifies both these common characteris-

tics and individual differences, as part of the development of a comprehensive intervention plan.

4. The act of committing sexual abuse results from a series of thoughts, feelings, and behaviors that become patterned and predictable as the specific abuse behavior is repeated, resulting in an identifiable sexual abuse cycle. Identifying these patterns is necessary to effectively interrupt the offense pattern, as well as to develop and implement a relapse-prevention plan.

5. A sexual abuser often exhibits more than one type of sexually abusive behavior that may manifest serially or concurrently. An abuser with multiple *serial* sexually abusive behaviors typically engages in a single type of behavior for an extended period, often stopping the previous behavior before beginning another type. For example, an abuser may engage in voyeurism of adult females for several months or years, discontinue that behavior and begin engaging in exhibitionism to adult females, then discontinue the second behavior and begin sexually abusing female children. An abuser with multiple *concurrent* sexually abusive behaviors typically engages in more than one type of behavior at the same time. For example, an abuser may engage in exhibitionism to adult females, interspersed with voyeurism of adult females and abuse of female children. Thus, an abuser may have more than one type of victim (adult females and female children), demonstrate sexual arousal to several deviant categories of stimulus, and engage in several discrete patterns of sexual assault (sexual assault cycles).

6. An abuser is best served in a therapeutic environment that holds the abuser fully accountable for his or her harmful sexual and assaultive behaviors.

7. Any sexually abusive behavior may have its genesis in a wide range of circumstances and events, including genetic abnormality, posttraumatic repetition of early experi-

ence, accidental pairings of events, seeking of support or nurturance from inappropriate sources, or purposeful expression of power or control, among many others. Sexually abusive acts become self-reinforcing because they temporarily meet a variety of psychological and/or emotional needs and because of the gratification aspects of sexual behavior, including orgasm.

DEFINING SEXUAL ABUSERS

A sexual abuser or offender is commonly thought of as an individual who sexually violates or exploits another individual through the initiation of unwanted or nonconsensual sexual contact. Sexual violations or sexual transgressions against others encompass a variety of behaviors ranging from sexual harassment, exhibitionism, and pedophilia to forcible rape and sexual homicide. No age, socioeconomic, gender, racial, ethnic, or religious profiles have been identified as specific to sexual abusers. Clusters of psychosocial and developmental factors have been identified as common to specific categories of sexual abusers, and these can be used to develop effective intervention strategies.

Many individuals engaging in sexually abusive behaviors present with one or more of the paraphilias, or sexual behavior disorders, as defined in the *Diagnostic and Statistical Manual of Mental Disorders* (*DSM-IV*; American Psychiatric Association, 1994). Two notable exceptions are rapists and incest abusers. There is no clearly defined paraphilia for some types of rapists, and there is reason for debate concerning the appropriateness of diagnosing many incest abusers with pedophilia. Other sexual abusers may have engaged in sexually abusive acts but may not meet the diagnostic criteria for a particular paraphilia. For example, an individual may have sexually abused an unrelated child as a single act with no previous history of similar behaviors or fantasies. Such an act is clearly sexually abusive and appears pedophilic in nature, but it does not meet the specific criteria for a diagnosis of pedophilia.

Although all sexual abusers exhibit sexually deviant behaviors, not all sexually deviant individuals fit within the classification of sexual offender. For example, an individual who engages in transvestite fetishism is not a sexual offender unless illegal activity accompanies the fetishistic behavior (such as theft of clothing). An individual who engages in self-mutilation or pain induction as part of private masturbatory acts has done nothing illegal and thus is not a sexual offender. An adult male or female may engage in ongoing masturbatory fantasies involving sexual interactions with children, to the point of defining prepubescent children as a sexual preference, yet he or she has never had direct sexual contact with a child or sought out child pornography. Any of these individuals is potentially diagnosable with a paraphilia but does not fall into the category of sexual offender. Such considerations point to the need for thorough assessment and diagnosis. Mussack and Carich discuss methods of gathering necessary information in chapter 1 of this handbook.

There are also situations in which individuals are misdiagnosed as having a paraphilia. Such misdiagnoses are often found in the population of developmentally disabled individuals. These individuals may engage in sexual behaviors in inappropriate ways simply due to a lack of information, or in inappropriate places due to a lack of suitable locations. Coleman and Haaven, in chapter 11, discuss special considerations in the assessment and treatment of this population.

Another essential component of identifying a sexual offender is the presence of a victim. Victims of sexual offenders are defined as recipients of nonconsenting or exploitive verbal or physical sexual behavior. Nonconsent is defined in terms of an individual's direct indication of a lack of desire or of an unwillingness to engage in sexual activity; failure to provide overt consent; inability to give consent due to intoxication, physical infirmity, or unconsciousness; and/or inability to provide consent by virtue of lack of specific or appropriate information on which to base a decision regarding consent due to age, maturity level, or mental, emotional, or physical disability.

DEFINING SEXUAL ABUSER TREATMENT

KEY AREAS AND ELEMENTS OF TREATMENT

Most sexual abuser treatment programs have several key elements, including identfiable structure, consistency, a problem-resolution component, skills training in a broad range of areas, and a high level of intensity. It appears that abusers respond well to structure, even though problems or conflicts with authority figures surface initially. Within the structure, personal responsibility is encouraged. The treatment structure or regimen is based on consistency of rules, consequences for rule infractions, and repetition. Although sexual abuser treatment is offense specific, it also needs to be holistic, addressing a wide range of issues beyond the specific focus of sexual abuse.

ATSA outlined several key components of treatment in its 1997 handbook. Some of these components include cognitive therapy (cognitive restructuring), interpersonal relationships and social skills, marital and family therapy, victim empathy, relapse prevention skills, and behavioral therapy (reconditioning arousal patterns or sexual interests, and reducing deviant arousal).

The modality forming the strong foundation of sexual abuser treatment is group therapy. Individual and family therapy may also be provided alongside sexual abuse treatment. Behavioral interventions focused on sexual arousal reconditioning, when employed, are generally conducted individually in a behavioral laboratory and/or private setting.

Early sexual abuser group therapy encompassed a harsh, confrontational approach ("gestapo therapy" or "pound therapy") that appeared to be adapted from the Synanon model

for drug abuse treatment (Baker & Price, 1997). Such approaches can result in the revictimization of the abuser and promote the maintenance of characteristics that support abusers in victimizing one another. Both these outcomes can result in the furthering of abuser pathology. Many intensive sexual abuser treatment programs now provide a measure of nurturance and the consistent demonstration of respect, while continuing to hold the abusers fully accountable for their sexually deviant and assaultive behaviors.

During the last 20 years, sexual abuser treatment has largely been based on cognitive-behavioral approaches centering around group therapy. Although cognitive-behavioral approaches remain a foundation of contemporary sexual abuser treatment, more holistic approaches have recently been added. These approaches include modalities covering a variety of dimensions (e.g., cognitive, affective, behavioral, physiological, social, familial, contextual, biological).

Freeman-Longo et al. (1995) surveyed 1,740 treatment programs concerning their models of treatment. Nine different treatment models were identified. Forty percent of the respondents identified cognitive-behavioral treatment as their foundational model. Murphy and Carich discuss cognitive restructuring, a component of that model, in chapter 4. Another 37 percent of the respondents identified relapse prevention as their primary treatment model. Inclusion of the relapse prevention model as a core component of sexual offender treatment is discussed in chapter 5.

COMMON TREATMENT OBJECTIVES

The sexual abuser treatment programs represented by the contributing authors and editors of this handbook adhere to a common central goal of enhancing safety in our communities by reducing sexual abuse perpetration. Although methods of treatment may differ, each program seeks to accomplish this goal through effective behavioral management and monitoring of the abusers treated, reduction in the overall intensity of an abuser's sexually deviant urges (see chapter 6), and ongoing efforts to improve the effectiveness of intervention methods.

Some specific objectives to consider when providing a comprehensive sexual offender treatment program include requiring the offender to:

- develop motivation and commitment toward recovery

- develop personal accountability, empathy, remorse, and an appropriate sense of guilt concerning abusive behaviors at both emotional and intellectual levels

- develop and adopt the general notion of social interest

- develop a clear understanding of his or her sexual abuse cycle, the emotional satisfaction gained from offending, and healthy alternatives to identified dysfunctional behavioral, physiological, cognitive, and affective components

- reduce deviant sexual arousal and interest and clarify his or her sexual identity

- develop a comprehensive relapse prevention plan

- develop appropriate and healthy functioning relationships, resolving such issues as possessiveness, jealousy, isolation, overattachment, and inappropriate use of power and control

- develop healthy alternatives to other dysfunctional behaviors

- understand thoroughly the impact that developmental experiences, including personal victimization, have had on current belief and value systems and establish healthy alternatives to any that are dysfunctional

- learn to both assertively and appropriately express emotions

- learn and demonstrate effective stress management skills

- develop an appropriate sense of self-worth

- identify and constructively change any other methods employed to avoid responsibility and/or enable an offending behavior

Some of these objectives may not be fully obtainable by abusers with specific disabilities or other limiting factors.

HOW SEXUAL ABUSER TREATMENT DIFFERS FROM OTHER THERAPIES

The sexual abuser presents unique problems for both the evaluator and the therapist. Consequently, new therapeutic approaches had to be developed and older approaches adapted to the special needs of this population. Issues of community protection, previously within the purview of corrections and courts, became a focus of therapy to a degree never before necessary.

Sexual abuser treatment differs, in many ways, from what might be considered traditional therapies. An initial difference is in the nature of the client and his or her presenting problems. The sexual abuser presents the same range of psychological and emotional problems as the general clinical population, compounded by the presence of sexually deviant patterns of behavior. Sexual abusers employ the same kinds of psychological defensive coping strategies (e.g., denial, rationalization, minimization, repression) with an added intensity fueled by fears of criminal prosecution; loss of employment, family and friends; and community ostracism and perhaps by conflicts with their own morals and values. General population clients may present with one or two of these fears but rarely the entire constellation.

Many clients seeking psychotherapy do so under some form of mandate or demand by others that, if not adhered to, may result in either no change in their current status or relationship loss. In addition, a sexual abuser generally faces intensive and intrusive mandates imposed by the criminal justice system. The criminal justice system can dictate with whom and where they reside, with whom they can have contact, and in what daily activities they may engage, in addition to requiring participation in sexual abuser treatment. Should the sexual offender fail to follow through with such legal requirements, a further loss of freedom, through incarceration, can result.

Sexual abusers often enter therapy in fear of other sanctions that may be imposed. They may present denial to avoid further sanctions. They are also often angry and focused on their feelings of being treated unfairly due to the shame of public exposure or the losses or sanctions they have already experienced.

Sexual abusers in community-based treatment also present a potential risk to the community. The therapist is placed in a position of accepting two clients, the offender and the community. The initial focus, especially in community-based sexual abuser treatment, is on the development of attitudes and behaviors that will make the community safer. Consequently, sexual abuser treatment is more directive, structured, confrontational, and authoritarian than other types of therapy.

Trust is an important issue in all therapeutic settings and is the foundation of facilitating therapeutic change. This creates a dilemma for the sexual abuser treatment professional. A balance of respect and trust with healthy skepticism and thorough monitoring may best serve both community and client concerns. Sexual abusers frequently have a view of themselves and the world that is enshrouded in secrecy, distortions, and lies, which is brought into the treatment setting. Abusing behavior is also often strongly habituated. Thus, even if the abuser believes in his or her own safety and ability not to reoffend, the abuser can fall prey to preexisting distortions and faulty beliefs, placing both the community and the abuser at risk.

These issues create a significant dilemma for the therapist. If trust is the foundation of an effective therapeutic relationship, but trusting the abuser may not be in the abuser's best interests, how can effective therapy occur? An initial focus of effective sexual abuser therapy is the development of trust, mediated by skepticism and clarified through external validation of abuser statements and self-observations. External validation of an abuser's self-report is necessary and should be obtained whenever possible, if cognitive distortions are to be effectively identified; effective, ongoing assessment of progress is to occur; and treatment is to be completed. Polygraphic assessment is being used in some sexual abuser treatment programs as part of an effort to externally validate sexual abusers' statements.

Supportive confirmation is the basis for eventual trust on the part of the therapist and is a necessary part of the initial phase of sexual abuser treatment, with a certain amount of skepticism being maintained throughout treatment. If a therapist demonstrates a lack of trust with disdain and denigration, the therapeutic relationship necessary for effective treatment is not likely to develop. If the development of trust is presented as a mutual goal for both client and therapist, then an effective therapeutic alliance can be established.

Sexual abusers employ patterns of cognitive distortions, commonly called thinking errors, to ward off psychological and emotional discomfort (empathy, guilt, and shame) that they might otherwise experience about their victimization of others. This pattern of distortions is one of the greatest obstacles to effective treatment of sexual offenders. Whereas other clients often seek therapy because they are experiencing psychological or emotional pain, abusers use cognitive distortions to avoid psychological or emotional pain. One of the first tasks in treatment is to help abusers relinquish their use of cognitive distortions so that the experience of discomfort with current and past beliefs and behaviors can begin. This discomfort can then become a source of internal motivation for change.

RECOMMENDATIONS FOR THERAPISTS WORKING WITH SEXUAL OFFENDERS

Working with sexual offenders requires therapists to change many of their traditional approaches to and attitudes toward psychotherapy. Carich and Adkerson (1995) created an outline of basic recommendations for therapists engaged in sexual offender treatment. In this volume, Mussack developed the following modification and expansion of this outline:

SET THE STRUCTURE. Many specific treatment goals are predefined as part of the program structure. Each client's strengths and weaknesses in predefined areas are evaluated as part of developing an individualized treatment plan. Each client is expected to either possess or gain proficiency in all areas, as well as to complete other individually defined treatment goals. An abuser's accomplishment of, and compliance with, these predefined goals is one of the keys to successful treatment.

KNOW YOUR MATERIAL AND CLIENT. Therapists need to be well educated with regard to both abuser characteristics and the skill areas they are attempting to help their clients master. A thorough individual assessment is an important part of any intervention process.

FOCUS ON BOTH STRENGTHS AND PROBLEMS. An initial focus on problems is necessary in developing an intervention plan that ensures community safety and, in turn, client safety. Decisions about the therapeutic venue — inpatient versus outpatient — are also based on this focus. Identification of strengths is necessary to develop intervention strategies that are usable and that the abuser can understand. Initial interventions that build on an abuser's strengths is a common approach that provides opportunities for the abuser to experience success early in the treatment process. Providing positive, constructive therapeutic experiences early in treatment can do much to encourage the abuser to join in the therapeutic process and begin to set his or her own goals.

EMPHASIZE WHAT OVER WHY. Developing a factual picture of the client's history of sexual abuse, what offenses the client has committed, is an important initial step in confronting both denial and cognitive distortions. Police reports, other investigative reports, and statements by victims or family members can be extremely useful in developing an effective treatment plan. The answer to why someone offended is often multifaceted and may never be truly determined. The answers to questions that focus on what has occurred assist the client in becoming fully accountable for his or her abusive history. These answers also provide the foundation for developing a comprehensive understanding of the offender's sexual assault cycle and an effective relapse prevention plan. Exploration of the motivational aspects of offending and the contributing developmental and experiential factors is also important.

JOIN THOUGHTS AND BEHAVIORS WITH FEELINGS. A sexual abuser typically has difficulty identifying emotions with specific thoughts and behaviors. Abusers' misidentification and misattribution of both their own affective states and the emotional experiences of their victims are intrinsic components of many sexual assaults. Learning appropriate affective attributions is necessary if abusers are to develop empathy and to meet personal needs in a nonabusive manner.

FOCUS INITIALLY ON FACTS AND BEHAVIORS OVER WORDS. Abusers employ cognitive distortions both during the process of offending and during nonoffending periods to justify their actions and/or to prevent being overwhelmed by negative emotional states. Any description of internal states and external behaviors an abuser provides, especially during the early phases of treatment, may differ remarkably from what the therapist or others observe. Providing consistent, factual feedback to the abuser can begin the development of cognitive dissonance, the presence of two competing ways of understanding the same event, within the client. This dissonance can provide the therapist and the client with the "crack in the armor" needed to begin the process of long-term change.

DEPERSONALIZE INTERACTIONS. Abusers may try to manipulate therapists to put them on the defensive. Abusers may attack therapists verbally or act in a manner that would provoke confrontation or verbal attack out on the street. Therapists can remind themselves that these actions are often attempts to change the focus of the interaction and deflect attention from the sexually abusive behavior. They may also represent efforts to discredit therapy and reinforce the clients' cognitive distortions. Abusers may also be habituated to confrontational interactions due to historical life experiences and social skills deficits.

Therapists may feel strongly invited to take personal offense at these clients' statements or actions, but of course, accepting such invitations would effectively obstruct therapy. To cope with the risk of this kind of negative countertransference, therapists working with sexual abusers should be in ongoing consultation with supervisors and peers to maintain their effectiveness.

REINFORCE NEW LEARNING WITH REPETITION. Patience and repetition are two of the most important resources a therapist can bring to sexual abuser treatment. Much of what an abuser needs to gain through therapy is new information in his or her life. Providing repeated opportunities for learning and integrating this new knowledge, with varied presentation methods and practical rehearsal situations, increases the chances of therapeutic success.

USE EXAMPLES AND SPECIFICS. Providing multiple examples of concepts and specific applications increases client learning and understanding. Abusers are often vague about details in describing their thoughts, feelings, and behaviors and the situations leading up to their offenses. They usually minimize what they've done and the reactions of their victim as a primary defensive coping strategy. Requiring clients to be extremely specific about their abusive behaviors, in terms of their own thoughts, feelings, and actions, is an effective method of confronting cognitive distortions and help the clients understand the destructiveness of their behaviors. Requiring abusers to give specific descriptions of victims' experiences can also assist empathy development by increasing clients' understanding of the impact of abuse.

USE PRESUMPTIVE QUESTIONING. Presumptive questions are a useful vehicle when interacting with an offender. A presumptive question such as "When did you touch his genitals?" often elicits much more information than a yes-or-no question such as "Did you touch his genitals?"

The client often assumes that the therapist already has information or will correct a mistaken assumption by providing useful alternative information.

MAINTAIN CLEAR THERAPEUTIC BOUNDARIES. Even more so than with most clients, the therapist needs to maintain clear boundaries and limits throughout the therapeutic process. Dual relationships are destructive to any therapeutic process and are particularly destructive in sexual offender treatment. Dual relationships can be exploited by the abuser to maintain a deviant lifestyle and, consequently, reoffend. An effective therapist demonstrates consistent respect, adheres to relationship boundaries, and expects the same from the offender.

The issue of self-disclosure by therapists has been the subject of ongoing debate within the context of therapy. Many therapeutic disciplines discourage any therapist self-disclosure, regardless of clinical focus. Concern about this question increases in sexual abuser treatment, because many abusers seek out therapist vulnerabilities as a way of avoiding self-examination or redirecting the focus of therapy. Therefore, therapist self-disclosure in this context needs to be considered with even greater caution.

There is also a role for nurturance in sexual offender treatment. Many abusers have had little or no nurturance, particularly during early developmental stages. This deficit results in the development of a destructive sense of entitlement, a belief or feeling of constant deserving to offset the feeling of deprivation, a feeling that life "owes" the abusers something to make up for the lack. These feelings provide a rationale for the abusers to take from others, regardless of the consequences, contributing to the development of a sense of self-worth that can be reinforced and maintained only by engaging in abusive behaviors.

Therapeutic nurturance needs to be provided within a context of the therapist's intention and ability to:

- consistently recognize the abuser's positive value

- identify and create opportunities for the abuser to make positive contributions to others

- recognize these contributions and influence others to recognize them also

- consistently discriminate between the abuser's worth as a human being and the destructiveness and wrongfulness of his or her offending behaviors

- hold consistent expectations of the abuser to make positive efforts

- hold consistent expectations of the abuser to remain fully accountable for his or her current choices, both constructive and destructive

This approach begins the development of *constructive* entitlement: a sense of having something positive to contribute to the well-being of others, that it is in his or her best self-interest to do so, and that there is intrinsic value in doing so. This process contributes to the development of self-worth that is reinforced through refraining from abusive behaviors.

It is our goal to provide readers with current information on methods that have been found to be effective in both community-based and institutional-based sexual abuser assessment and treatment. We also hope to provoke a measure of thought and debate that will promote expansion and improvement in this difficult field.

Useful information on different aspects of treatment can be found in the following: ATSA (1997b); Barnard, Fuller, Robbins, and Show (1989); Bays and Freeman-Longo (1989); Calder (1999); Carich and Adkerson (1995a); Haaven, Little, and Petre-Miller (1990); Knopp (1984); Laws (1989); Marshall, Laws, and Barbaree (1990); Mayer (1983, 1988); Salter (1988); and Schwartz and Cellini (1988, 1995, 1997).

REFERENCES

American Psychiatric Association. (1994). *Diagnostic and statistical manual of mental disorders* (4th ed.). Washington, DC: Author.

Association for the Treatment of Sexual Abusers. (1997a). ATSA ethical principles and standards of practice. Beaverton, OR: Author.

Association for the Treatment of Sexual Abusers. (1997b). *Membership list.* Beaverton, OR: Author.

Baker, D., & Price, S. (1997). Developing therapeutic communities for sex offenders. In B.K. Schwartz & H.R. Cellini (Eds.), *The sex offender: New insights, treatment innovations and legal developments: Vol. 2* (pp. 19-1–19-4). Kingston, NJ: Civic Research Institute.

Barnard, G.W., Fuller, K.A., Robbins, L., & Show, T. (1989). *The child molester: An integrated approach to evaluation and treatment.* New York: Brunner/March.

Bays, L., & Freeman-Longo, R. (1989). *Why did I do it again? Understanding my cycle of problem behaviors.* Orwell, VT: Safer Society Press.

Calder, M. (Ed.). (1999). *Assessing risk in adult males who sexually abuse children.* Dorset, England: Russell House.

Carich, M.S., & Adkerson, D. (1995a). *Adult sexual offender assessment packet.* Brandon, VT: Safer Society Press.

Carich, M.S., & Adkerson, D. (1995b). *Guidelines in sex offender assessment.* Unpublished manuscript.

Freeman-Longo, R., Bird, S., Stevenson, W., & Fiske, J. (1995). *1994 nationwide survey of treatment programs and models.* Brandon, VT: Safer Society Program and Press.

Haaven, J., Little, R., & Petre-Miller, D. (1990). *Treating intellectually disabled sex offenders: A model residential program.* Orwell, VT: Safer Society Press.

Knopp, F.H. (1984). *Retraining adult sex offenders: Methods and models.* Syracuse, NY: Safer Society Press.

Laws, D.R. (Ed.). (1989). *Relapse prevention with sex offenders.* New York: Guilford Press.

Marshall, W.L., Laws, D.R., & Barbaree, H.E. (Eds.). (1990). *Handbook of sexual assault.* New York: Plenum Press.

Mayer, A. (1983). *Incest: A treatment manual for therapy with victims, spouses and offenders.* Holmes Beach, FL: Leanies Publications.

Mayer, A. (1988). *Treating child sex offenders victims: A practical guide.* Beverly Hills, CA: Sage.

Salter, A.C. (1988). *Treating child sex offenders and victims: A practical guide.* Beverly Hills, CA: Sage.

Schwartz, B.K., & Cellini, H.R. (1988). *A practitioner's guide to treating the incarcerated male sex offender.* Washington, DC: NIC.

Schwartz, B.K., & Cellini, H.R. (Eds.). (1995). *The sex offender: Corrections, treatment, and legal practice.* Kingston, NJ: Civic Research Institute.

Schwartz, B.K., & Cellini, H. (Eds.). (1997). *The sex offender: New insights, treatment innovations and legal developments: Vol. 2.* Kingston, NJ: Civic Research Institute.

1 Sexual Abuser Evaluation

Steven E. Mussack
Mark S. Carich

Psychological evaluation is a process of gathering behavioral, sociological, medical, legal, and psychological information about an individual. This information is collected through a number of methods, including clinical interviews, collateral interviews, review of previous evaluative and investigative reports, behavioral observations, and medical and psychological testing. The information is then compiled to provide a comprehensive, narrative picture of the client's current status, to develop and support both *DSM-IV* (American Psychiatric Association, 1994) and other differential diagnoses, and to provide a foundation for the development of an appropriate treatment plan. No assessment instrument or method is completely valid or reliable. Reliance on any single assessment tool increases the likelihood of invalid assessments. The utilization of multiple assessment tools and methods is likely to increase both the validity and the reliability of any assessment and the resultant recommendations.

As a discipline, we are growing beyond the more generic treatment approaches of the past. Much of this growth is the result of research that has improved our ability to develop accurate differential diagnoses. Effective evaluation and differential diagnosis have gained increasing support in the professional literature as essential components of sexual abuser treatment (Dougher, 1988; Freeman-Longo & Bays, 1995; Groth & Birnbaum, 1981; Groth, Hobsen, & Gary, 1982; McGovern, 1991; McGrath, 1990, 1993). Research has effectively demonstrated discrete psychological and characterological differences among sexual abusers (Gebhard, Gagnon, Pomeroy, & Christiansen, 1965; Hall, 1989; Hall, Graham, & Shepherd, 1991; Knight & Prentky, 1990; Malcolm, Andrews, & Quinsey, 1993; O'Brian & Bera, 1986). These noted differences have prompted a greater focus on individualized treatment planning and exploration of intervention strategies specific to offender characteristics. This increased focus on evaluation has resulted in more comprehensive and flexible interventions, enhancing program adaptability and effectiveness.

A comprehensive sexual abuser evaluation has goals similar to those of any other form of psychological evaluation, depending on its type and scope. These include:

- identification of mental disorders experienced by the client

- identification of medical and other disorders or disabilities that have a significant impact on the client

- identification of risks or impediments to treatment, if any, posed by identified disorders or disabilities or the client's experience of such disorders

- identification of strengths and resources brought to the therapeutic process by the client

- clarification of the least restrictive environment in which the offender can be treated without significant risk to client or community

- determination of the nature and availability of support systems

- development of accurate diagnoses

- assessment of the client's amenability to treatment

- development of a specific treatment plan

The clinical evaluation of sexual abusers differs from other types of evaluations by its extensive focus on the client's sexual deviancies, current sexual interests, and sexual history. Such evaluations focus on the impact of developmental, environmental, sociological, relational, medical, and psychological factors on the development of sexually deviant thoughts and behaviors. Other data gathered, which are unique to the evaluation of sexual abusers, can include sexual arousal and interest patterns and, in some programs, data concerning the veracity of client self-report through polygraphic assessment. Conducting a sexual abuser evaluation also requires the clinician to accept a significant level of responsibility for community safety.

The purpose of this chapter is to provide an overview of the components of a comprehensive psychosexual evaluation. Two components, the risk assessment and the treatment amenability assessment, need to be repeated at intervals during the course of treatment to evaluate ongoing progress. Treatment progress evaluations form the basis for decision making concerning client transitions from inpatient to outpatient care, from active treatment to aftercare, and from aftercare to the end of treatment involvement. Specific guidelines for the completion of a comprehensive initial psychosexual evaluation and the evaluation of client progress are presented, including recommended components, data to be gathered, and interviewing methods. Risk assessment and treatment amenability criteria are also discussed.

COMMON ASSUMPTIONS IN SEXUAL OFFENDER ASSESSMENT

Some basic assumptions about sexual offender assessment are summarized below:

- A thorough evaluation is necessary to the development of an effective treatment plan.

- It is unreasonable to expect a sexual abuser to fully disclose his or her entire history of sexually deviant behaviors during an initial assessment. Further disclosures are likely during the course of therapy if intervention is at all effective.

- The greater the level of disclosure at the initial evaluation stage, the more rapidly the client will effectively engage in treatment.

- Most sexual abusers have a history of multiple paraphiliac behaviors (Abel, Becker, Mittleman, Cunningham-Rathner, and Rouleau, 1987; Abel & Rouleau, 1990).

- It is not appropriate to assume that all sexual abusers have diagnosable personality disorders. Although many sexual abusers do have diagnosable personality disorders, paraphilias can exist independently of a personality disorder in a given sexual abuser.

- Paraphilias are diagnosable mental and emotional disorders for which there is no known cure. There is, however, the potential for effective control with appropriate clinical interventions.

- Effective assessment of historical and current psychosocial environments and experiences can have a significant bearing on the interventions recommended.

- During the course of an evaluation, it is important to identify any nonparaphiliac mental or emotional disorders experienced by the abuser. Once identified, their relationship to the paraphiliac behaviors and/or their potential impact on intervention efforts must be assessed in order to make appropriate recommendations for interventions.

- The inclusion of *collaborative* data is essential for an effective evaluation. An abuser is likely to attempt to avoid disclosing or to misrepresent some or all of the information provided.

- Reliance on a single source of information or testing modality increases the likelihood that assessment errors will occur.

- Throughout treatment, periodic reassessment is needed to make valid and reliable statements about a client's progress.

- Conclusions drawn from an assessment must fit the data available and be based on information gathered by the evaluator. It is both inappropriate and unethical for an evaluator to make definitive diagnostic statements about an individual who has not been interviewed directly by the evaluator.

SPECIALIZED ASSESSMENT METHODS

Among the many types of assessments, some may be completed as part of the initial evaluation and repeated throughout the course of therapy to assist with client progress and risk assessment. These can include psychophysiological arousal assessments of sexual interests, updated psychological assessments, and polygraphic assessments. (For listings and information on various instruments used to assess sexual abusers, see Calder, 1999, and Prentky and Edmunds, 1997.)

ASSESSMENT OF SEXUAL INTERESTS

Assessments of sexual interests are efforts to gather data about the abuser's sexual arousal and interest patterns, both deviant and nondeviant. Initially, such data are usually gathered through clinical interviews and review of data describing an abuser's sexual offense history. A structured interview with the abuser exploring a full range of nondeviant and deviant sexual behaviors is part of an initial evaluation. Freeman-Longo, Bird, Stevenson, and Fiske (1995) found that approximately 30 percent of all adult programs responding to their survey use "sexual arousal measures/phallometry."

PSYCHOPHYSIOLOGICAL AROUSAL. Psychophysiological arousal assessments using a penile plethysmograph are another method of assessing sexual arousal and interest patterns. This assessment procedure attempts to measure a client's physiological sexual arousal response when presented with specific deviant and nondeviant potentially sexually arousing stimuli. Physiological assessments of sexual interests (phallometry) often help identify areas of deviant sexual arousal and interest that the client is either aware of and denying or may not be consciously aware of because of his or her cognitive defense mechanisms. Research by Abel, Becker, Cunningham-Rathner, Mittleman, and Rouleau (1988) found that it is common to identify four or more paraphilias coexisting in an abuser. Both deviant and nondeviant sexual arousal patterns are evaluated.

For a male client, the phallometric assessment requires him to place either a mercury-in-rubber strain gauge or a Barlow gauge (attached by a wire to a computer and printer that will record changes in circumference) around his penis while sitting or lying in a private room. The client is then exposed to potentially sexually arousing stimuli in audio, video, or 35mm slide formats. As the offender experiences sexual arousal, the circumference of his penis increases, which stretches the gauge. The stretch in the gauge causes a change in the resistance to a microamperage electrical current being passed through it. This change is recorded by the plethysmograph on a strip of graph paper much like the recording of an electrocardiograph. A professional trained to evaluate these tracings can determine the offender's sexual arousal and interest patterns.

A photoplethysmograph, a small glass or plastic device about the size and shape of a tampon, can be used to assess the sexual arousal and interests of female offenders. In a private room, the client places the instrument in her vaginal canal. As the client experiences sexual arousal when exposed to stimuli, changes in vasoconstriction (blood flow) occur in the walls of her vaginal canal. The photoplethysmograph measures these changes, which are recorded on graph paper by the plethysmograph and evaluated by a trained professional.

ABEL ASSESSMENT FOR SEXUAL INTEREST. Abel (1996) developed the Abel Assessment for Sexual Interest, which is described as a "computer-driven psychology test" that provides "an objective reaction time measure of deviant sexual interests."

CARD SORTS. Card sorts are another method for assessing sexual interests. A card sort usually consists of a deck of 50 or more 3-by-5 inch cards, each containing a short description of a deviant or nondeviant sexual activity. The client is asked to sort the cards into several piles from most to least preferred sexual activities, with one neutral pile (Laws, 1986). The client's choices provide information about his or her sexual interests patterns. Abel has created one set for adults that has been used by many clinicians (Abel et al., 1988).

POLYGRAPHIC ASSESSMENT

Polygraphic assessment is becoming increasingly accepted as a useful tool in sexual abuser treatment. Mussack (1993) reported conducting full-disclosure polygraphic assessments as a part of the initial evaluation and then twice-yearly follow-up assessments with all abusers in a community-based treatment program.

The polygraph measures changes in physiological parameters, including galvanic skin response, respiration, heart rate, and/or blood pressure, in response to specific and carefully worded yes-or-no questions. When a client gives a response, measurable changes in these autonomic functions are recorded on a continuous strip of graph paper, allowing a trained professional to determine, with a significant degree of certainty, whether the client is being truthful or deceptive.

COMPREHENSIVE PSYCHOSEXUAL ASSESSMENT

Elements of a complete sexual offender assessment are outlined and discussed in this section. These elements include:

- purpose of the evaluation
- demographics
- psychosocial history
- military history
- criminal history
- drug and alcohol use history and assessment
- medical history and biological assessment
- sexual history
- mental status, psychological assessment, and testing results
- diagnoses
- risk assessment

- treatment amenability
- recommendations

Each of these elements includes multiple areas of additional inquiry. A reproducible evaluation outline is provided in the appendix of this chapter, adapted and expanded from Mussack and Grapp (1992). Many of the same issues and concerns are discussed in separate areas of the evaluation and assessment. Since evaluation is a process that may take several meetings over weeks or months, such repetition can elicit new information or a fuller, more detailed response as the client becomes more comfortable with the interviewer and the process. If different parts of the assessment are being conducted by different agencies or individuals, comparison of answers to similar questions can provide insight into the abuser's perceptions, distortions, and attitudes toward offending and treatment.

It is important to understand that the following information applies to the evaluation of adult sexual abusers. For adolescent abusers, issues of marital and work history are generally irrelevant, and additional emphasis is placed on academic, family, and peer relational histories. The evaluation of preadolescent abusers is not addressed in this chapter.

Components of a thorough sexual offender evaluation include the following.

INTRODUCTION

BIOGRAPHICAL INFORMATION. Biographical information includes current age, date of birth, race, marital status, educational level, and the like (Carich & Adkerson, 1995a). These brief details are elaborated in the psychosocial history section.

PURPOSE AND METHODS OF EVALUATION. The evaluator should explain to the client the purpose of the evaluation and should provide in the evaluation report a description of the client's level of understanding of this purpose, his or her level of cooperation, and the methods employed to gather data.

PSYCHOSOCIAL HISTORY

FAMILY OF ORIGIN. This section describes the client's family of origin, including number, sex, birth order, age differences, and general relationships of siblings. The overall quality of family relationships, economic level, and geographic stability are also explored, as well as employment histories of both parents; the quality of the relationship between the parents; the nature, frequency, and types of affection and discipline provided by each parent; the impact these had on the client; and sex roles within the family. The impact of any separations, divorces, remarriages, substance abuse, prolonged absences, or deaths should also be evaluated. Information regarding the involvement of parental surrogates in the client's development can provide clues concerning home environment, external support networks, and possible history as a victim of neglect or of physical, emotional, or sexual abuse. Investigating a client's status as a natural, step, foster, or adopted child is also important to provide information concerning his or her experience of attachment during crucial developmental periods.

EXTENDED FAMILY HISTORY. The extended family history encompasses family members outside the immediate family. The involvement of and roles played by extended family members can provide salient information, including meaningful relationships during the developmental years with aunts and uncles, grandparents, cousins, and other significant relatives. Exploring the nature and availability of these relationships also provides information concerning the client's values development and his or her attachment, abuse, discipline, love, and support experiences.

ROLE OF RELIGION. We have found that sexual abusers frequently use a distorted view of religion to avoid dealing with their problems or to justify their sexually abusive acts. Many abusers seem to have "spiritual conversions," especially when involved in the legal system. Assessment of the role of religious involvement in a client's upbringing and current life can provide additional information concerning home environment, commitment, and overall accountability. Understanding how religion was viewed in an abuser's family of origin might provide insight into one or more distortions the abuser may now employ in his or her religious involvement.

Religious involvement can be an invaluable resource or an impediment, depending on many variables. Specific data to gather include type of religion, dates of practice or membership, level of participation, current interest and degree of participation, stability of beliefs, inconsistency or consistency of beliefs, religious view of sex and gender issues, access to victims through religious activities, whether offending involved religious activities or occult or unusual practices (level of violence, sadism, sexual behavior, aggression, and secrecy), religious community support or role in enabling denial or minimization by the abuser, and overall views of treatment. Thorough understanding of these issues can be important in developing an effective treatment plan.

GEOGRAPHIC STABILITY. A client's history of geographic stability, both as a child and as an adult, can provide information concerning the type and quality of extrafamilial relational experiences and academic experiences and their effect on the client's emotional and psychological development. This information can provide important clues to a client's current need for help in the development of effective relationship skills and general capability of forming age-appropriate affiliations.

ACADEMIC HISTORY. A client's level and quality of education, adaptation to the academic environment (including compliance with behavioral norms and rules or aggressive behaviors and sanctions), behavioral and learning difficulties, and participation in normal academic developmental experiences should be evaluated. The number of schools the client attended, the length of his or her attendance, and the reasons for moving from school to school can provide information concerning the client's development of peer relational skills, adaption skills, attachment, and self-sufficiency. Feelings of belonging or experiences of ridicule provide infor-

mation concerning peer-based acceptance. Participation in extracurricular activities can give indications of interests and ability to function in group settings. The quality and types of affiliations and experiences can uncover information concerning the client's current beliefs about himself or herself in relation to others.

WORK HISTORY. Thorough exploration of work history furnishes additional information about a client's general stability within a community, ability to deal with stressors, and ability to be self-sustaining and self-motivating. Information concerning childhood and adolescent work history can provide data about values development and social development and further information about intrafamilial relationships. Other important aspects of work history include numbers of jobs held, frequency of and reason for job changes, consistency of employment, and whether the employment has been career focused as opposed to pickup work. For clients with histories of multiple job changes, exploring their understanding of the reasons for such changes supplies information about their level of personal accountability and common cognitive distortions. Additional factors to consider include offense behaviors at work, sexual harassment, disciplinary measures, potential access to victims, and sexual behaviors at the work site (Carich & Adkerson, 1995a).

MARITAL AND SIGNIFICANT RELATIONSHIP HISTORY. Evaluating a client's marital and relationship history provides information about age-appropriate affiliative needs and skills. The length and quality of relationships, as well as the reasons for their dissolution and the length of time between relationships, are all important issues. If the client has children, his or her present and past relationship with them, their ages, and their current placement may demonstrate the client's degree of loyalty, parenting ability, and willingness to be responsible. Factors such as frequency of arguments, presence of violence, perception of who is or was responsible for difficulties, and presence of any substance use or abuse provide information concerning impulsiveness, relational problem-solving skills, and self-control. Investigating an abuser's loyalty within the relationship, his or her perception of ability to satisfy a partner sexually, engagement in extramarital (or extra–primary relationship) sexual affairs, and general perception of what constitutes an effective working partnership can shed light from another angle on a client's affiliative needs and skills, cognitive distortions, and personal and moral value systems.

CURRENT SOCIAL RELATIONSHIPS AND ACTIVITIES. The quality and nature of the offender's current social relationships and activities provide additional insight into affiliative skills, interests, and involvement in the community. This provides information about current support systems, their availability for involvement in offender treatment, and the extent to which they provide support for offender pathology.

MILITARY HISTORY. Important questions include branch of service, whether voluntary enlistment or draftee, dates of service (and age of client during service), location of service, duty in active combat zones, disciplinary actions, rank at discharge, reason for discharge, levels of authorized and unauthorized violence, and types of sexual experiences. Additionally, any psychological problems stemming from military service need to be assessed. This information can provide insight into the client's adaptability to authority and, if in combat, to severe stressors. It can also reveal the client's ability to achieve advancement and his or her methods of decision making concerning the future.

CRIMINAL HISTORY

Criminal history refers to documented and undocumented crimes, both as a juvenile and as an adult. Information to be gathered includes types of criminal activity, dates and ages when the crimes were committed, whether they were gang related, weapon use and levels of aggression involved, sanctions experienced (including incarceration, probation, or parole), outcome of sanctions, current legal status, and description of the current offenses. For clients who have been in-carcerated, it is important to gather information concerning adaption, treatment, and sexual and nonsexual activities while in custody. When possible, information concerning a client's motivations and cognitive distortions during criminal behavior should be obtained.

GANG HISTORY. Exploration of an offenders's involvement in gang activities can provide information concerning values, morals, and sexual and criminal history. Some gangs condone sexual violence; others do not. Important aspects to investigate include name of the gang, type of gang, rules, client's position or rank, duties, attitudes, ages when involved, reasons for joining, reasons for terminating involvement (if it has been), how the involvement was terminated, current gang status (if any), current level of participation, level of allegiance and loyalty, and types of sexual offenses and relationships and activities that earn status in the gang (Carich & Adkerson, 1995a).

SUBSTANCE USE OR ABUSE HISTORY

Sexual abusers are often more willing to discuss their substance use or abuse history than their sexual offense history. Abusers often use alcohol or other drugs when offending and provide them to their victims; they are likely to have a history of substance abuse. The continued use of such disinhibitors can increase the risk of reoffense. Details of the abuser's drug and alcohol history provide information concerning impulse control, patterns of cognitive distortions, addictions, and current treatment needs. Specific information to gather includes substances used, age of first use or abuse, frequency, consequences, motivations, and rationalizations for substance use or abuse. It is also important to clarify levels of prescription medication use, since some abusers may rely on these medications as disinhibitors rather than on so-called street drugs.

OTHER ADDICTIONS AND INDULGENCES. Offenders may have other addictions and indulgences, such as gambling, dangerous behavior, sex, and so forth.

MEDICAL HISTORY

Gathering a medical history provides information about current and past medical problems to be considered when making treatment recommendations. Medical histories include any major medical problems and hospitalizations, current physician supervision, current or frequent use of prescription and nonprescription medications, surgeries, diseases (including sexually transmitted diseases), head trauma, serious accidents, birth defects, chronic pain, and any other potentially significant medical conditions. Information on diet, caffeine intake, and exercise provides some insight into the quality of the offender's self-care.

SEXUAL HISTORY

Obtaining information about the offender's sexual history is critical. This information should include dates of events (such as earliest remembered sexual experience); age and gender of individuals involved; how and why partners were chosen; types of sexual activity; the general nature, duration, and quality of relationships; and the client's perceptions of these sexual events. This discussion must be specific and detailed in order to be useful in the assessment process.

DEVELOPMENTAL SEXUAL EXPERIENCES. Early sexual experiences are a foundation for later sexual behavior. Longitudinal data about an offender's sexual development and sexual experiences, deviant and nondeviant, provide a clear picture of the client's sexual information, attitudes, experiences, and beliefs. Information on the client's sexual development addresses the availability and types of sexual information in the family home, other sources of sexual education and information, and preadolescent sexual experiences. Early masturbatory behaviors, exposure to pornography, sexual victimization, and age-inappropriate sexual behaviors are investigated. The client's perceptions of these early experiences may differ considerably from information gathered through collateral resources, and the differences may be instructive

in terms of understanding the client's perceptions and/or cognitive distortions.

Similar information is gathered for all developmental stages through the present. Areas covered include:

- primary sexual orientation and sexual experiences outside the client's orientation
- frequency of sexual experiences
- sexual activities involved
- number of partners
- involvement with prostitutes or engaging in prostitution
- affairs
- frequenting of strip bars
- ongoing pornography use and type used
- frequency of masturbation, location, and methods
- content of sexual fantasies and intrusiveness

SEXUAL DYSFUNCTION. Many sexual abusers experience premature ejaculation, inhibited orgasm, or impotence. Sexual dysfunction can have a significant impact on an offender's perception of his or her ability to engage in age-appropriate, consensual sexual behavior. It can also indicate medical and/or psychological problems.

HISTORY OF PARAPHILIAC AND OTHER SEXUALLY DEVIANT BEHAVIORS. This information provides clarity regarding the extent of an abuser's sexually deviant behaviors or patterns. The client should be nonjudgmentally questioned regarding any involvement in the full range of paraphilias listed in DSM-IV. Additionally, involvement in bondage, dangerous autoerotic behaviors, group sex, and other high-risk or unusual sexual activities can be further explored in this section.

SEXUAL ABUSE/ASSAULT PROFILE. The sexual abuse/assault profile involves identifying characteristics of the abuser's assaultive behavior and history of sexual aggression. Carich

(1994c) outlines multiple factors that facilitate a thorough assessment of an assault profile. These factors have been adapted and expanded by the authors for this publication.

1. Victimology: Victimology is the documented and nondocumented history of the client's sexual assaults and victims. Typically, sexual abusers have committed many offenses that are not documented. Different formats for gathering this information have been provided (Carich & Adkerson, 1995a; Gray & Wallace, 1992; Mussack & Grapp, 1992).

2. Victim profile and selection process: The victim profile identifies the characteristics of victims that are significant to the abuser. The victim selection process involves the specific methods used by the abuser to select and gain access to his or her victims. Information gathered includes:

   • gender preferences and choices

   • age range and ideal age of victims

   • preferred physical characteristics and dress of victims (e.g., hair color and length, eye color, body morphology, short dresses or shorts)

   • relationship of abuser to victim

   • locations and methods of victim access, stalking and searching patterns, specific victim vulnerabilities

   • the client's perception of the victims' response and the victims' actual response

3. Deviant fantasy profile: This section explores how the content, frequency, and timing of the client's sexual assaults relate to his or her abusive sexual fantasies. Further information about an abuser's masturbatory history is also gathered at this time. The Sexual Offender Fantasy Assessment, by Mussack and Gray (1992), provides a structured format for assessing this. Key characteristics to evaluate include:

   • frequency, location, and duration of fantasies, both deviant and nondeviant

   • ideal or most frequent deviant fantasy content or themes

   • victim characteristics, including type of responses fantasized

   • masturbatory patterns, methods, and locations

4. Violence profile: The violence profile evaluates the levels, types, and patterns of threatened or actual physical force involved in the abuser's sexual offending. It is also valuable to investigate the presence of such behaviors in sexual activities the offender considers "normal" or "consensual." Evaluation of an offender's level of aggression in nonsexual activities may reveal sadistic themes important to the overall evaluation. Several key factors include:

   • type and frequency of violence

   • age at which the client began using violence

   • the client's arousal to violence

   • age and gender of target victims

   • any history of the client's witnessing or experiencing violence

5. Sexual offense cycle: Thoughts, feelings, behaviors, and experiences prior to the offense (precursors) and the events afterward that lead to a period of emotional and psychological stabilization make up the abuser's sexual offense cycle. Sexual offending occurs in patterns or recurring cycles without a specific time frame. Two models for analyzing sexual assault cycles are provided by Carich and Stone (1993) and Bays and Freeman-Longo (1990). Key elements include:

   • trigger events

   • enabling behaviors

   • cognitive distortions (thinking errors)

- primary defense mechanisms
- mood states
- isolation and fantasies, cognitive rehearsal
- victim-grooming behaviors
- use of disinhibitors (such as drugs or alcohol)
- methods of avoiding responsibility or coping with negative emotional states after the assault

6. Offending paraphernalia: Offending paraphernalia refers to specific people, equipment, and items that are either directly part of the sexual abuse or used by the abuser to advance through an assault cycle in preparation to commit a sexual assault. Areas to investigate include:

- group or gang involvement either during the assault or as part of preparing to assault
- use of pornography before or during an assault
- use of drugs or alcohol before or during an assault or provision of drugs or alcohol to victim
- vehicles used
- bondage materials
- disguises
- materials used to dispose of physical evidence
- weapons used

7. Sexual orientation and identity: Further exploration of the offender's sexual orientation is conducted in this section when needed. Relationships between the offender's age-appropriate sexual preferences and offending behaviors are assessed. Issues of sexual identity confusion and distress, transvestism, transsexualism, and body dysmorphism are evaluated. Also of concern are issues of self-mutilation, sadism,

masochism, and ritualized sexual behaviors that may not have been discovered to this point.

8. Psychophysiological sexual arousal and interest patterns: The assessment of psychophysiological sexual preferences involves interviewing the client about experienced interest in and sexual arousal to a broad range of deviant and nondeviant categories. Specific testing methods employed to augment the information gathered through the interview process were discussed previously in this chapter.

PSYCHOLOGICAL ASSESSMENT

The goal of psychological assessment is to determine a client's current mental status and to identify any enduring psychological, psychosocial, intellectual, neurological, and characterological issues that may affect the client's need for, amenability to, and ability to benefit from particular types of treatment. The psychological impact of known medical conditions is often considered. Any suicidal and homicidal ideation or intent is also examined. A complete psychological assessment can consist of multiple clinical interviews, psychological testing, and a medical assessment, along with interviews with significant others.

Psychological assessment is also an ongoing part of sexual abuser treatment. Repeated measures offer both the client and the therapist measures of client change, adaptation, and accommodation. Change will occur in the areas in which the abuser is able to develop new skills, attitudes, and beliefs. Accommodation is needed when a client is unable to constructively reorient his or her abusive sexual interests. It is also needed when negative characterological or personality traits are so deeply ingrained that the best a client can do is to accept that such traits exist and develop constructive compensatory behaviors to manage a reoffense-free life.

MENTAL HEALTH STATUS. The mental health status assessment evaluates an offender's current and past mental functioning. Key elements include:

- orientation in time, person, and place
- speech patterns (logical, coherent, circumstantial, tangential, slurred)
- current reality testing/contact
- functioning of immediate, recent, and remote memory
- concentration
- mental processing strengths in concrete and abstract realms
- ability to generate similarities and differences and make appropriate comparisons
- presence of organic psychopathology
- presence of hallucinations or delusions
- history of difficulties with comprehension or understanding of verbal or written language or other identifiable information processing strengths or deficits at an intellectual level (IQ)
- current or historical suicidal or homicidal ideation or attempts

NONSUICIDAL SELF-DESTRUCTIVE HISTORY. This area of assessment focuses on high-risk masochistic and self-mutilating behaviors that do not appear as overtly suicidal.

PRIOR TREATMENT AND PSYCHIATRIC HISTORY. Treatment, prior mental health evaluations, major mental illnesses, hospitalizations, and prescription of psychiatric medications are explored in this section. Specific data include dates, locations, diagnoses, ages of occurrences, types of interventions and outcomes, any offenses committed while in treatment, and so on.

PSYCHOLOGICAL TESTING. It is common to employ psychological testing as part of a psychological assessment. Areas tested can include personality/psychopathology, mood/affect, relationships/family, beliefs/attitudes, neuropsychological concerns, and cognitive functioning/intellectual level and abilities.

Results of psychological testing are necessarily included in the psychological assessment. Such testing can both validate clinical observations made during the assessment interviews and raise additional questions. A discussion of the outcome of such testing and whatever validations and questions are raised is an important part of this section. Specialized training is generally required to interpret the results of such tests.

SKILLS AND KNOWLEDGE TESTING. Skills and knowledge testing is increasingly being employed as a measure of progress in sexual offender treatment. Many programs use entrance and exit exams as concrete measures of change in an abuser's knowledge base. Areas assessed often include knowledge of personal offending patterns, empathy development, and integration of concepts that are important in the maintenance of a long-term relapse prevention process.

SOCIAL INTEREST. The assessment of social interest focuses on the offender's general care and concern for others. Data gathered provides information concerning the offender's:

- experience of belongingness within the world
- ability to understand, experience, and express empathy; *victim empathy* is defined as the comprehension of and compassion for the abuse experience of victims
- experience and expression of remorse for the harm caused others; *remorse* is defined as the painful regret and appropriate sense of guilt for harming others
- overall levels of self-pity and feelings of personal victimization due to the client's current situation
- desire to contribute constructively to others
- accountability for sexually abusive or assaultive behaviors
- level of spontaneous emotional expression about and involvement with others

RESPONSIBILITY AND DISOWNING BEHAVIORS. Responsibility is shown when clients hold themselves accountable for and own up to their behaviors. Disowning refers to any method employed by clients to avoid taking responsibility for their behaviors or that is used to enable the commission of a sexual assault (Carich, 1994a).

Offenders' responses during evaluation interviews range from total denial to full admission and acceptance of responsibility. Typically, abusers use a number of methods to avoid accepting full or even partial responsibility for their sexual offending behaviors. Many of these methods involve cognitive distortions (e.g., justification, denial, blame, minimization, lying, rationalization, entitlement, personalization/depersonalization).

Attending to the client's utilization of cognitive distortions provides significant information concerning his or her primary defensive coping strategies, ability and willingness to cope with emotional and psychological stressors, self-image, self-respect, and overall respect for others. An abuser may display disowning behaviors in all life areas or only with regard to his or her sexual offending. It is important to note the abuser's responses to questions and the style of response used to describe the offenses.

RELATIONSHIP DYNAMICS. Information concerning relationship dynamics is gathered throughout the evaluation process. Relationship dynamics refers to both constructive/supportive and destructive/exploitive affiliations. Assessment of these dynamics through each developmental phase of the client's life, including the present, provides information concerning an abuser's overall psychology. Key factors to consider include:

- length, frequency, and quality (superficial versus intimate) of relationships

- loss, abandonment, infidelity, rejection, alienation, isolation, and withdrawal

- boundaries within relationships (enmeshed, healthy, disengaged)

- dependence versus independence

- age appropriateness

- exploitation, possessiveness, jealousy

- sexual satisfaction and focus on sexual interactions

- communication and participation style (assertive, passive, passive-aggressive, aggressive)

Each of these areas provides important information concerning the client's ability to form and maintain age-appropriate, supportive relationships. They also provide information concerning affiliative needs that the offender may have been attempting to meet through sexual victimization.

GENERAL PERSONALITY CHARACTERISTICS. The broad range of information gathered during the interview process provides the evaluator with diagnostic information concerning the likelihood of the client's having a diagnosable personality disorder, the presence of which would have significant implications for the client's treatment. A personality disorder is defined as "an enduring pattern of inner experience and behavior that deviates markedly from the expectations of the individual's culture, is pervasive and inflexible, has an onset in adolescence or early adulthood, is stable over time, and leads to distress or impairment" (American Psychiatric Association, 1994, p. 629).

The presence of a personality disorder has serious implications. Treatment often needs to focus on helping the client adapt to the disorder as a permanent disability that must be consciously compensated for, much like a paraphilia. A personality disorder diagnosis may be confirmed or augmented through paper-and-pencil tests such as the Minnesota Multiphasic Personality Inventory (MMPI) and the Millon.

RISK ASSESSMENT

Risk assessment is the evaluation of the likelihood that an individual will commit a new offense and the conditions that influence that likelihood (McGrath, 1991, 1992). The initial assessment aids the evaluator in making recommendations concerning the appropriateness of inpatient or community-based treatment modalities. Subsequent risk assessments focus on the current and future dangerousness of the offender and are employed to assess both progress in treatment and the appropriateness of transferring the client from one treatment modality to another.

McGrath (1992, p. 6) outlines five specific questions to consider when conducting a risk assessment:

1. What is the probability of reoffense?

2. What degree of harm would most likely result from a reoffense?

3. Under what conditions is a reoffense most likely to occur?

4. Who would be the likely victims of a reoffense?

5. When is a reoffense most likely to occur?

Doren (1999) compiled a list of 30 different risk assessments (Carich 1994b, 1994d; Carich & Adkerson 1995b; Carich, Fischer, & Campbell, 1999; Carich, Metzger, & Campbell, 1999; Carich & Steckel, 1994; Freeman-Longo & Bays, 1995; Hanson, 1997; Hanson & Bussiere, 1998; Hanson & Thornton, 1999; McGrath, 1991; McGrath & Hoke, 1995). They examine factors believed to increase the risk of sexual reoffense, including:

- denial about offense history

- history of multiple victims

- history of multiple victim types

- diagnosis of multiple paraphilias

- extensive history of offending

- extensive history of nonsexual criminal behavior

- history of abusing prepubescent or younger victims

- extensive history of violence, with increased risk if violence was part of the sexual abuse

- extensive history of substance abuse, with increased risk if substance abuse was involved in the sexual abuse

- offense behaviors involving rituals

- use of pornographic or nonpornographic materials depicting behaviors similar to the abuser's offending history, with increased risk if the abuser masturbates while viewing these materials

- lack of remorse or empathy

- no sexual offender–specific treatment or failure to successfully complete treatment or aftercare

- failure to develop or maintain an age-appropriate relapse prevention network

- presence of a thought disorder that has not been effectively treated and was present at the time of initial offending

- failure to successfully complete probation or parole requirements

- presence of a significant personality disorder for which the offender has not established constructive adaptations

- presence of other mental or emotional disorders that have not responded positively during clinical intervention

- presence of many ingrained antisocial features or characteristics

- history as a victim of extensive sexual abuse, characteristics of which are mirrored in the abuser's offending behavior

- presence of cognitive distortions and defensive coping mechanisms used to deny or minimize responsibility for sexually abusive acts

Hanson (1997) and Hanson and Harris (1998) differentiated two basic types of risk factors: (1) static or nonchangeable (historic in nature) and (2) dynamic or changeable behavior. Hanson and Thornton (1999) composed a list of the following statistically significant static risk factors: prior sex offense charges and convictions, prior sentencing dates, convictions for noncontact offenses, index nonsexual violence, prior nonsexual violence, any unrelated victims, any stranger victims, age under 25 years, and single. In the same document, they discuss Hanson's (1997)

Rapid Risk Assessment for Sex Offence Recidivism (RRASOR) and Thornton's structured Anchored Clinical Judgment risk assessment instruments.

Carich (1997, 1999) and Carich, Fischer, and Campbell (1999) made a distinction between initial versus recovery-oriented risk assessments by placing significant importance on the variable of treatment. An initial risk assessment is made prior to an abuser's receiving any treatment. A recovery-based risk assessment takes into consideration an abuser's participation and performance in sexual offender treatment. Recovery-based assessments are repeated throughout the treatment process, creating an opportunity to assess the impact of treatment and the longevity of gains made during the treatment process.

Care must be taken when conducting risk assessments, because risk assessment is inherently a probability-based process. The presence or absence of any single factor or cluster of factors does not guarantee that a given individual will not offend or reoffend.

ASSESSMENT OF AMENABILITY TO TREATMENT

Assessing amenability to treatment involves evaluating the likelihood that an offender will constructively benefit from treatment once an appropriate modality is determined. Decisions concerning amenability are based on many of the same factors involved in risk assessment, including levels of resistance to treatment and the degrees of denial and accountability expressed by an offender. However, evaluators must expect some level of resistance and denial in most abusers during the initial evaluation and early in treatment.

Freeman-Longo and Bays (1995) identified several criteria they consider important in assessing amenability to treatment. These include:

- level of denial

- motivation for treatment (i.e., need for treatment)

- level of anger or rage

- dangerousness level

- level of disclosure and admission of previous offenses

- level of victim awareness (i.e., empathy, remorse)

- other factors, including literacy, prison or jail behavior (compliance with institutional requirements), history of quitting, or lack of history of completing difficult tasks

Carich (1993) lists several factors that make treatment more challenging: extensive psychopathology (e.g., psychosis, organicity, low IQ); high levels of antisocial, narcissistic, schizoid, or borderline behaviors; and extensive victim history.

The question of whether an abuser who maintains complete denial of an offense can or should be treated is the subject of ongoing discussion. Many programs, both inpatient and community based, are now accepting offenders who initially display complete or near complete denial of their offenses. Such decisions are based on the assumption that if the offender is ever to relinquish his or her denial, treatment is necessary.

Initial treatment plans for such clients include specific timelines within which the abuser must begin accepting responsibility for the offenses or be discharged from treatment. Some programs have expressed a willingness to provide a complete treatment program to offenders who maintain their denial throughout the course of treatment, but for others, the issue is allocation of scarce resources to those most likely to benefit. This issue continues to be the subject of debate.

DIAGNOSES

The inclusion of diagnoses provides the foundation for conclusions and treatment recommendations. The *DSM-IV* (American Psychiatric Association, 1994) is the current standard for developing and reporting mental health diagnoses. It outlines a five-axis diagnostic method, with multiple entries possible for the first four axes. Although *DSM-IV* is considered the authority on the diagnosis of paraphilias, sexual abusers may have other coexisting mental health issues and diagnoses as well. The reader is referred to this manual for further information.

SUMMARY, ASSESSMENT, AND RECOMMENDATIONS

This section is the final and most important portion of the evaluation. All data gathered are summarized, an initial risk assessment is completed, amenability to treatment is assessed, and a recommended initial treatment plan, if appropriate, is written.

GUIDELINES AND TACTICS FOR INTERVIEWING SEXUAL OFFENDERS

Evaluators frequently find themselves receiving implicit invitations to engage in power and control struggles when interviewing sexual abusers. Clients are often vague and/or evasive as they attempt to cope with high levels of fear and shame when asked to discuss the details of their deviancy and other life experiences.

Mussack and Stickrod (1988), McGrath (1990), Gray and Wallace (1992), and Carich and Adkerson (1995a) have each published guidelines for interviewing offenders. We have adapted and expanded on these guidelines below to provide a foundation for conducting effective clinical evaluation interviews with this difficult population.

1. Review all available legal, investigative, and evaluative documents prior to the assessment. This preassessment preparation provides an opportunity to assess similarities and differences among the data gathered during the evaluation and collateral information.

2. Inform the client of costs, legal aspects, and confidentiality limitations at the beginning of the first interview.

3. Review with the client the evaluation process at the outset. Describe the evaluation methods, including any testing; clarify the approximate length of time for each part of the evaluation; and outline the topic areas so the client knows what to expect. Outlining the topic areas gives the offender time to think about these issues between interviews. Explain the difference between an evaluation interview and a therapy interview. It is important that the client understands that the goal is to develop information about his or her current status and needs. Further explain that you will be making recommendations concerning appropriate interventions and that you will not be providing therapy during the interviews.

4. Ask the client to describe his or her understanding of the nature of the current situation, any criminal charges or allegations he or she faces, and the reason he or she is participating in the evaluation. Provide the client with your understanding of each of these areas, clarifying areas of concurrence or difference.

5. Take and maintain control of the interview, consistently providing structure. Remain comfortable and relaxed, avoiding power struggles. When necessary, remind yourself that you are the expert, reinforcing your confidence. In situations in which the client invites power struggles or goes off on a tangent, it is often helpful to respectfully remind the client, while appreciating his or her concerns, that the time available is limited. Firmly explain that you need to move to another topic or back to the one at hand if you are going to complete a useful evaluation.

6. Always conduct the interview in a respectful manner. Refrain from using intimidation or other potentially abusive methods of maintaining interview control. When a

client refuses to provide information, explain to the client its importance to the evaluation process. If the client continues to refuse or to respond in an overly vague manner, simply note it and continue with the interview. Often a significant amount of information can be obtained through what the offender does not say.

7. Be observant of the client's behaviors and affect throughout the interview process. Attend to any incongruencies and note them. Also note topic areas that elicit highly emotional responses. Be careful to identify items that may have cultural significance and differences from mainstream Anglo-American cultural expectations.

8. Remember, the assessor's job is to be an investigator who is respectfully curious and not judgmental. The assessor must avoid forming opinions about the client until all the data have been gathered so as to prevent biasing queries or missing valuable information because the assessor has assumed the offender's response. Any clue as to the assessor's opinions may also provide cues to the offender about how to answer questions.

9. Trust is not a factor in the evaluation process. Both the assessor and the client have agendas. The assessor's is to develop information, through interviews, observation, and testing, in an unbiased manner that supports objective clinical opinions and recommendations. The client may have one of many agendas, depending on his or her circumstances. The client may make efforts to present in an unrealistically positive or negative light or may supply accurate information. Remaining objective allows the evaluator to provide accurate, useful clinical observations, diagnoses, and recommendations.

10. Create opportunities for the client to ask questions during the interview process. Encourage the client to ask for clarification or restatement of any query, as it is impor-

tant that all questions be fully understood. Allow opportunities for the client to ask the purpose of a question. If you cannot explain its purpose, the question is likely of little value. Also, periodically check the client's understanding of a question. This will help you word questions in ways that the client can understand. Confusing responses may be the result of poor understanding rather than avoidance or other uncooperativeness.

11. Consciously separate the individual from his or her offending behaviors. This simple method of conveying respect reduces client defensiveness.

12. Avoid displaying shock or disgust as an abuser describes his or her offense history. This form of unconditional acceptance facilitates disclosure, thus furthering the goals of the evaluation. Intermittent empathy-based statements and statements of appreciation for the client's participation and efforts also do much to facilitate client responsiveness and candidness.

13. Avoid keeping secrets and/or colluding with the offender. Be clear with the offender that information discussed during the evaluation will be included in your report.

14. Ask who, what, where, when, and how questions. Questions involving why often elicit both unuseful responses and frustration on the part of the offender. Employ open-ended questions that are difficult to answer with a yes or no response. For example, presumptive questioning, questions beginning with "When have you...?" often elicit significant amounts of information. Questions beginning with "Have you...?" invite yes or no responses and often facilitate denial-based answers. However, too-frequent use of presumptive questions can unintentionally convey bias and accusation, eliciting frustration from the client.

Effective interviewing of sexual abusers requires practice, patience, and skill. It is strongly recommended that practitioners who have never conducted such assessments, even though they may have experience conducting other types of psychological evaluations, initially do so under the supervision of a practitioner who is experienced in sexual offender evaluation.

PROGRESS ASSESSMENTS

The progress assessments that have been referred to throughout this chapter should be conducted at least every 90 days. Progress assessments compare the client's current status with the treatment completion goals outlined in the treatment plan. They also assess the abuser's current risk for reoffense through the examination of several variables, including compliance with program requirements, stability in the community, substance abuse, deviant sexual arousal control, honesty during treatment, impulse control, criminality, and self-motivation. Variables evaluated when assessing stability in the community include community ties, economic stability and employment, self-sufficiency, and the availability of effective support systems (relapse prevention networks). Metzger and Carich (1999) provide a more thorough review of different variables in their eleven-point treatment plan.

COLLATERAL INTERVIEWS

Comparing offender and victim versions of offense behaviors provides important information about the sexual abuser client. Interviews and consultation with family members are another important source of information concerning an abuser's honesty and progress in treatment. Inclusion of such interviews also lays the foundation for the ongoing participation of family members and other significant persons in the client's treatment. Mussack (1993), in a 20-month community-based study, found that

86 percent of offenders whose family members were involved in their treatment program continued in treatment over the period of the study. Conversely, 65 percent of offenders without family members involved in their treatment left during the period of the study.

CONCLUSION

The assessment of sexual abusers is a complex and challenging process. Practitioners who accept this challenge take on a measure of responsibility for the safety of the community that is beyond the expectations we have of most mental health professionals. Such assessments are complex, difficult, and emotionally demanding. The information gathered extends well beyond that gathered for most other psychological assessments. The potential gravity of the conclusions drawn and recommendations made can have an immense impact on the client, the family, and the community.

REFERENCES

Abel, G. (1996). *Therapist product information: Abel Assessment for Sexual Interest.* Atlanta, GA: Author.

Abel, G., Becker, J., Cunningham-Rathner, J., Mittleman, M., & Rouleau, J. (1988). Multiple paraphiliac diagnoses among sex offenders. *Bulletin of the American Academy of Psychiatry and the Law, 16*, 153–168.

Abel, G., Becker, J., Mittleman, M., Cunningham-Rathner, J., & Rouleau, J. (1987). Self-reported sex crimes of nonincarcerated paraphiliacs. *Journal of Interpersonal Violence, 2*, 3–25.

Abel, G., & Rouleau, J. (1990). The nature and extent of sexual assault. In W. Marshall, D. Laws, & H. Barbaree (Eds.), *Handbook of sexual assault* (pp. 9–21). New York: Plenum Press.

Allen, C., & Lee, C. (1992). Family of origin structure and intra/extra familial childhood sexual victimization of male and female offenders. *Journal of Child Sexual Abuse, 1*(3), 31–45.

American Psychiatric Association. (1994). *Diagnostic and statistical manual of mental disorders* (4th ed.). Washington, DC: Author.

Barnard, G.W., Fuller, A.K., Robbins, L., & Shaw, T. (1989). *The child molester: An integrated approach to evaluation and treatment.* New York: Brunner/Mazel.

Bays, L., & Freeman-Longo, R. (1990). *Why did I do it again? Understanding my cycle of problem behaviors.* Brandon, VT: Safer Society Press.

Calder, M. (Ed.). *Assessing risk in adult males who sexually abuse children: A practitioner's guide.* Dorset, England: Russell House.

Carich, M.S. (1992). Categories of behavioral characteristics of sex offenders based upon lifestyle/personality disorders, from a linear view. *INMAS Newsletter, 5*(2), 22–25.

Carich, M.S. (1993). Elements of sex offender assessment and evaluation. *INMAS Newsletter, 6*(1), 12–14.

Carich, M.S. (1994a). Basic types of distorted thinking and behavior. *INMAS Newsletter, 7*(3), 10–11.

Carich, M.S. (1994b). List of risk factors used in risk assessment. *INMAS Newsletter, 7*(2), 9.

Carich, M.S. (1994c). Nine-factor assault profile or typology. *INMAS Newsletter, 7*(4) 10.

Carich, M.S. (1994d). A review of different risk factors. *INMAS Newsletter, 7*(4), 3–10.

Carich, M.S. (1997). Towards a concept of recovery in sex offenders. *The Forum, 9*(2), 10–11.

Carich, M.S. (1999). Evaluation of recovery: 15 common factors or elements and 15-factor sex offender recovery scale. In M. Calder, A. Hampson, & J. Skinner (Eds.), *Assessing risk in adult males who sexually abuse children* (pp. 279–287). Dorset, England: Russell House Publishing.

Carich, M.S., & Adkerson, D. (1995a). *Adult sexual offender assessment packet.* Brandon, Vermont: Safer Society Press.

Carich, M.S., & Adkerson, D. (1995b). Carich-Adkerson sex offender risk assessment scale. In M.S. Carich & D. Adkerson (Eds.), *Adult sexual offender assessment packet* (pp. 81–84). Brandon, VT: Safer Society Press.

Carich, M.S., Fischer, S., & Campbell, T. (1999). Recovery risk assessment scale. In M. Calder (Ed.), *Assessing risk in adult males who sexually abuse children* (pp. 290–291). Dorset, England: Russell House.

Carich, M.S., Metzger, C., & Campbell, T. (1999). Risk assessment checklist scale. In M. Calder (Ed.), *Assessing risk in adult males who sexually abuse children* (pp. 274–276). Dorset, England: Russell House.

Carich, M.S., & Steckel, S. (1994). Factors used in risk assessment for recovery. *INMAS Newsletter, 7*(1), 6.

Carich, M.S., & Stone, M. (Eds.) (1993). *Offender relapse prevention.* Chicago, IL: Adler School of Professional Psychology.

Doren, D. (1999). *Using and testifying about sex offender risk assessment instrumentation.* Unpublished handout.

Dougher, M.J. (1988). Clinical assessment of sex offenders. In B. Schwartz (Ed.), *A practitioner's guide to treating the incarcerated male sex offender* (pp. 77–84). Washington, DC: NIC.

Freeman-Longo, R., & Bays, L. (1995). Evaluation of dangerousness for sexual offenders. In M.S. Carich and D. Adkerson (Eds.), *Adult sexual offender assessment packet* (pp. 88–93). Brandon, VT: Safer Society Press.

Freeman-Longo, R., Bird, S., Stevenson, W.F., & Fiske, J. (1995). *1994 nationwide survey of treatment programs and models.* Brandon, VT: Safer Society Press.

Gebhard, P., Gagnon, J., Pomeroy, W., & Christiansen, C. (1965). *Sex offenders: An analysis of types.* New York: Harper & Row.

Gray, A.S., & Wallace, R. (1992). *Adolescent sexual offender assessment packet.* Brandon, VT: Safer Society Press.

Groth, A.N., & Birnbaum, H.J. (1981). *Men who rape: The psychology of the offender.* New York: Plenum Press.

Groth, A.N., Hobsen, W., & Gary, T. (1982). The child molester: Clinical observations. *Journal of Social Work and Human Sexuality, 1,* 129–144.

Hall, G., Graham, J., & Shepherd, J. (1991). Three methods of developing MMPI taxonomies of sexual offenders. *Journal of Personality Assessment, 56,* 2–13.

Hall, R.L. (1989). Assessment and diagnosis. In G.W. Barnard, A.K. Fuller, L. Robbins, & T. Shaw (Eds.), *The child molester: An integrated approach to evaluation and treatment.* New York: Brunner/Mazel.

Hanson, R.K. (1997). *The development of a brief actuarial risk scale for sexual offense recidivism* (User Report 97-04). Ottawa: Department of the Solicitor General of Canada.

Hanson, R.K., & Bussiere, M.T. (1998). Predicting relapse: A meta-analysis of sexual offender recidivism studies. *Journal of Consulting and Clinical Psychology, 66*(2), 348–362.

Hanson, R.K., & Harris, A.J.A. (1998). *Dynamic predictors of sexual recidivism* (User Report 1998-01). Ottawa: Department of the Solicitor General of Canada.

Hanson, R.K., & Thornton, D. (1999). *Static 99: Improving actuarial risk assessments for sex offenders* (User Report 1999-02). Ottawa: Department of the Solicitor General of Canada.

Hare, R. (1985). *The psychopathy checklist.* Department of Psychology, University of British Columbia, Vancouver, BC.

Knight, R., & Prentky, R. (1990). Classifying sexual offenders: The development and corroboration of taxonomic models. In W. Marshall, D. Laws, & H. Barbaree (Eds.), *Handbook of sexual assault* (pp. 23–52). New York: Plenum Press.

Laws, R. (1986). *Sexual deviance card sort and sexual deviance audiotape scripts.* Unpublished manuscript.

Malcolm, P., Andrews, D., & Quinsey, V. (1993). Discriminant and predictive validity of phallometrically measured sexual age and gender preference. *Journal of Interpersonal Violence, 37,* 138–157.

McGovern, K.B. (1991). The assessment of sexual offenders. In B. Maletzky (Ed.), *Treating the sexual offender* (pp. 35–66). Newbury Park, CA: Sage.

McGrath, R.J. (1990). Assessment of sexual aggressors: Practical clinical interviewing strategies. *Journal of Interpersonal Violence, 5*(4), 507–519.

McGrath, R. (1991). Sex offender risk assessment and disposition planning: A review of empirical and clinical findings. *International Journal of Offender Therapy and Comparative Criminology, 35*(4), 328–350.

McGrath, R. (1992). Assessing sex offender risk. *American Probation and Parole Association Perspectives, 16*(3), 6–9.

McGrath, R.J. (1993). Preparing psychosexual evaluations of sex offenders. *Journal of Offender Rehabilitation, 20*(1/2), 139–158.

McGrath, R., & Hoke, S.E. (1995). Vermont assessment of sex offender risk. In M. Carich & D. Adkerson (Eds.), *Adult sexual offender assessment packet* (p. 72). Brandon, VT: Safer Society Press.

Metzger, C., & Carich, M.S. (1999). The eleven-point treatment plan for sex offender programs. In M. Calder, A. Hampson, & J. Skinner (Eds.), *Assessing risk in adult males who sexually abuse children* (pp. 292–311). Dorset, England: Russell House.

Mussack, S. (1993). *The impact of family involvement on sexual offenders' treatment participation.* Paper presented at the annual conference of the Association for the Treatment of Sexual Abusers, San Francisco, CA.

Mussack, S., & Grapp, P. (1992). *Psychosexual assessment outline.* Unpublished manuscript.

Mussack, S., & Gray, A.S. (1992). *Juvenile sexual offender fantasy assessment.* Paper presented at the Oregon Adolescent Sex Offender Treatment Network, Medford, OR.

Mussack, S., & Stickrod, A. (1988). *Juvenile sexual offender assessment.* Unpublished manuscript.

O'Brian, M., & Bera, W. (1986). Adolescent sexual offenders: A descriptive typology. *Preventing Sexual Abuse, 1*(3), 1–4.

O'Connell, M.A., Leberg, E., & Donaldson, C.R. (1990). *Working with sex offenders.* New York: Sage.

O'Donohue, W., & Letourneau, E. (1992). The psychometric properties of penile tumescence assessment of child molesters. *Journal of Psychopathology and Behavioral Assessment, 14*, 123–174.

Perry, G.P., & Orchard, J. (1992). *Assessment and treatment of adolescent sex offenders.* Sarasota, FL: Professional Resource Exchange.

Prentky, R., & Edmunds, S.B. (1997). *Assessing sexual abuse: A resource guide for practitioners.* Brandon, VT: Safer Society Press.

Quinsey, V., Rice, M., & Harris, G. (1995). Actuarial prediction of sexual recidivism. *Journal of Interpersonal Violence, 10*(1), 85–105.

Rice, M., Quinsey, V., & Harris, G. (1991). Predicting sexual recidivism among treated and untreated extrafamilial child molesters released from a maximum security psychiatric institution. *Journal of Interpersonal Violence, 5*, 434–448.

Richardson, J., Loss, P., & Ross, J.E. (1988). *Psychoeducational curriculum for the adolescent sex offender.* Unpublished manuscript.

Ross, J., & Loss, P. (1991). Assessment of the juvenile sex offender. In G.D. Ryan & S. L. Lane (Eds.), *Juvenile sexual offending: Causes, consequences, and correction* (pp. 199–251). Lexington, MA: Lexington Books.

Schwartz, B. (1988). Decision-making with incarcerated sex offenders. In B. Schwartz (Ed.), *A practitioner's guide to treating the incarcerated male sex offender* (pp. 43–49). Washington, DC: NIC.

Simnon, L., Sales, B., Krazniak, A., & Kahn, M. (1992, June). Characteristics of child molesters: Implications for the fixated-regressed dichotomy. *Journal of Interpersonal Violence, 7*(2), 211–225.

APPENDIX
PSYCHOLOGICAL/PSYCHOSEXUAL SEX OFFENDER EVALUATION PROTOCOL

Generally the evaluation involves:

1. Four to five hours of data collecting; can be as little as two to three hours

2. Clinical observations (functioning, coping skills) and diagnosis

3. Use of Mr., Mrs., or Ms. to address client; use of the victim's first name only

4. Informed consent for evaluation and/or treatment

Note the presentation of the client during interviews:

- Defensive/open
- Vague/clear
- On time for appointments
- Grooming
- Eye contact
- Current legal status
- Desire/willingness to participate in therapy
- Level of understanding of the purpose of the interview

I. HEADINGS

- Client's name
- Date of birth
- Interview date
- Evaluation methods:
  - clinical interviews, collateral interviews
  - all sources of information, which could include police, child protective services, and other investigative reports; prior evaluations; and prior treatment summaries
  - mental status and psychological assessment
  - intellectual functioning
- personality assessment
- social skills assessment (assertiveness and self-esteem)
- psychological and other testing used, which could include MMPI, MCMI, Projectives, Beck, Shipley, and/or others; sexual history inventory; psychophysiological arousal assessment of sexual interests; polygraph; others
- Evaluation by
- Date of report

II. PURPOSE OF EVALUATION

A. Reason for referral, both from referral source and client version

B. Demographics: name, age, marital status, education level, race, developmental disabilities

C. Purpose and methods of evaluation, including client's statement of understanding

D. Client's dress, appearance, self-presentation, and general approach to the evaluation (defensive, cooperative, etc.)

III. PSYCHOSOCIAL HISTORY

A. Family members: include relatives' ages, birth order, specific relationship (step, adoptive, extended family members in the home or having significant influence)

B. Relationships with family and parents, including siblings, surrogate parental figures/caretakers, important extended family; strengths and problems in the family

C. Structure/environment in family of origin

- Economic level/parental employment
- Parental relationships

- General sense of involvement within the family
- Sex roles in family
- Parental divorce and remarriage (dates, contact after, impact)
- Parental availability and mode of nurturing available (verbal, physical contact, frequency) from parents
- Parenting style/discipline (type, frequency, and by whom) either described as or apparent abuse
- Parental and sibling substance use or abuse and impact on client
- Death of parent or other family member and impact on client
- Role of religion
- Family moves (number, beginning, and effects)

D. Foster/adoptive care
- Number and quality of placements and reasons for initial placement and any moves
- Structure, environment, religion
- Discipline: type and by whom
- Display of nurturing (verbal, physical contact)
- Sexual or physical abuse/violence
- Alcohol/drug use
- Other victimization

E. Significant extended family history

F. Client's childhood:
- Sense of self-worth, trust
- View of self
- Trustworthy adults
- Pets
- Peer relationships
- School completion, problems, performance, extracurricular activities

G. Client's adolescence:
- School completion, problems, performance, extracurricular activities
- Runaway or dropout
- Aggressive patterns (temper, cruelty)
- Legal problems
- Employment

H. Higher education/special training:
- Intellectual ability
- Leadership, discipline problems, attendance
- Academic performance, behavior
- Successes, failures, problems
- Extracurricular activities
- Friendships, isolation, peer group (inadequate? isolated? fantasies? popular? ostracized?)
- Self-image, self-worth

I. Client's employment history:
- Types of employment, vocational preference
- Satisfaction/dissatisfaction
- Frequency of job changes/employment (length)
- Reasons for changes
- Any difficulties with authority, suspicion, relationship with supervisors
- Welfare involvement
- General level of financial responsibility, frustration, tolerance
- Overall financial status

J. Significant relationships and marriages:
1. Complete relationships, bonding history:
   - Parental, extended family, siblings, and other significant others
   - Girlfriends/boyfriends

- Hurts, rejection experiences
- Anger, feelings of inadequacy
- Willingness and apparent ability to approach age-appropriate partners
- Current available support

2. Number of marriages:
   - Age of client and partner at time of marriage
   - Duration
   - Reasons for divorce/separation
   - Children, stepchildren, adoptive children
   - Past divorce or separation: contact with children, apparent effect on client
   - Welfare, child protective services, criminal justice involvement
   - Sexual relationship quality (self and partner)

3. Children:
   - Current number
   - Custody
   - Visitation
   - View of roles
   - Supervision and sleeping arrangements in the home

4. General tone about relationships and marriage:
   - Sexual relationship (type, quality)
   - Disagreements, content
   - Mutuality or manipulative
   - Anxious and inadequate, jealous, passive, dependent, possessive
   - How adult needs met and by whom

K. Current social relationships: general quality (disengaged, superficial, intimate) and activities (sexual and nonsexual)

IV. MILITARY HISTORY

- Active duty in war zone
- Discharge date, type, and reason
- Discipline problems
- Difficulty with authority
- AWOL
- Responsibility for actions
- Observer/participant in violent behavior against women/men and children in battle

V. GANG HISTORY

Include type, position, rank, ages, why entered and terminated, allegiance, participation, sexual activity, activities to earn status.

VI. CRIMINAL HISTORY

- Any sexual and nonsexual criminal history
- Arrest history/convictions
- Driving under the influence (DUI)/other driving arrests (e.g., reckless driving)
- Outcome (juvenile and adult) of events/litigation of cases
- Use of violence or weapons
- Current legal status
- Prior incarceration, probation, parole; adaptation and outcome

VII. MEDICAL HISTORY/LIFE STRESSES

A. Stressors:
   - Before and during time of sexual abuse (employment, legal, financial, relational, health)
   - Current (isolation, health, diet, employment, legal, relational)
   - Accomplishments and failures: current and historical

B. Medical:

- Major illness or injury history
- Chronic or severe physical problems or disabilities
- Current medical treatment, historical severe medical problems, prescriptions
- Sexually transmitted diseases
- Tobacco, caffeine use; exercise; vitamins
- Biological testing results

VIII. SUBSTANCE ABUSE AND ADDICTION HISTORY

- Types of substances used
- Age at first use
- Age at first intoxication
- Frequency of use
- Age at significant change in use
- Frequency and quantity of use over past 3 years
- Most recent use and quantity

IX. SEXUAL HISTORY

A. Stated sexual preference: heterosexual, homosexual, bisexual

B. Sex education: family attitude toward sexuality, explanations, attitudes, behaviors; discussions about boundaries, anatomy, values in the family

C. Complete history of sexual experiences[†] (*sexual* is broadly defined as kissing, petting, fondling, overt sexual acts, abuse), chronological time between experiences, typical age, satisfaction, complaints, mutuality/manipulative, impulsive, heterosexual/homosexual

D. Masturbatory history: first time, historical and current, frequency, fantasy content, where learned, locations

E. History of paraphilia and unusual sexual behaviors: fantasies of children, voyeurism, exhibitionism, bestiality, necrophilia, coprophilia, urophilia, cross-dressing, transport, frottage, force, rape, rituals, sadism, masochism, obsessive-compulsive acted out, with or without masturbation, with or without consenting/nonconsenting partner, other

F. Pornography utilization, first exposure, ongoing use, types, locations, frequency, themes

G. History of personal sexual abuse:

- Details, description—current or past
- Length, frequency, quality of relationships
- Use of force, threats, trickery, bribes, confusion, weapons, drugs

H. Attitude toward sexuality:

- Male/female prerogative
- Lack of information
- Male/female stereotypes, attitudes and cognitive distortions, objectification
- Cognitive perceptions about children's sexual behavior

I. History of sexual dysfunction:

- Types
- Self-esteem
- Fear in approaching age-appropriate sexual partners
- Feelings of sexual adequacy/inadequacy

[†] In the sexual history, begin with the first sexual experience and include type of sexual interaction, age of those involved, any victimization, feelings of guilt, rejection, or satisfaction, and so forth. Note affairs, prostitution use (frequent, episodic, ongoing), frequenting of strip bars, and any unusual sexual experiences (e.g., multiple partners). Attach additional pages as necessary. Note attitudes toward women, men, and children; feelings of entitlement, adequacy, inferiority, conquest; respectful, supportive, nurturing behavior; sexual objectification; views of women or men as controlling, withholding, rejecting.

J. Most recent or current sexual satisfaction/ behavior:

- Compulsive, impulsive, obsessive, or preoccupied
- Drive, body image
- Forced sex (forced can include no = yes), exploitation, manipulation
- Extramarital relationships
- Client's definition of sexual satisfaction

K. History of sexually abusive behaviors:

1. Types: hands-on or hands-off offenses, exhibitionism, voyeurism, rape, pedophilia, nonrape pedophilia, incest, hebephilia (teens), sadism, masochism, necrophilia, frottage, rape (anger, power, sadistic), transvestism, fetishes, sexualized fire setting, sexualized animal torture, animal sex, group sex, hurt/humiliation, cross-dressing, pornography, prostitution, peeking, chronic masturbation, pornography addiction, sexual addiction

2. Details of current and past abuse/ deviant behavior:

- Description, length, frequency
- Early offending history
- Use of alcohol and drugs, for victim or self
- Circumstances of abuse when depressed, angry, high, impulsive, compulsive; influence of life stresses, motivation, emotion, relational difficulties
- Methods of gaining access and engaging and maintaining silence: weapon use, intimidation, coercion, trickery, games, bribery, assault, guilt
- Use of pornography before or during offense
- Progression to more frequent, elaborate, sophisticated, intrusive offenses
- Group-based or solitary offending

- Methods of preventing victim disclosure
- Beliefs about victim's experience
- Attitudes and reactions regarding the victim's behavior (sorry, aware of effect, empathy with victim)
- Consistency of multiple victim characteristics
- Content and frequency of deviant sexual fantasies and temporal relationship to sexual assaults
- Sexual offense cycle: the events prior to the offense—thoughts, feelings, behaviors, and experiences (precursors)—and the events afterward that lead to a period of emotional and psychological stabilization
- Methods of evidence disposal
- Willingness/unwillingness to accept professional help/responsibility
- Family reaction to disclosure
- Current sexual alternatives other than children, teens, other victims

3. Other factors:

- Cognitive distortions that indicate psychology: interpersonal dysfunction—affiliative, dependency, intimacy, inadequacy, power and control concerns, emotional immaturity
- Verification of description of offense (police report, victim's and victim's parents' statements, offender's version)
- Level of consistency among the various reports
- Details and patterns, including behavioral description of offenses, age and sex of victims
- Degree of acceptance of responsibility for current (or past) situations (none to full)

- Response to current situation
- Empathy for victim, understanding of or concern for impact of behavior on victims and others

X. PSYCHOPHYSIOLOGICAL AROUSAL ASSESSMENT OF SEXUAL INTERESTS

XI. POLYGRAPHIC ASSESSMENT

XII. PSYCHOLOGICAL ASSESSMENT

A. Psychiatric/Psychological History/Mental Status (discuss relational/familial, sexual, and social histories as they relate to the client's present psychological status):

- Any prior therapy, treatment, hospitalization; reason, diagnosis, outcome
- Contact with reality, adult world
- Depression history
- Borderline traits
- Paranoia exhibited
- Personality disorder apparent
- Delusions, hallucinations, other abnormal psychopathology
- Compulsions, obsessions
- Central nervous system impairment
- Memory, short and long term
- Reasoning or conceptual problems (abstraction, concrete, other)
- Awareness of time, place, person
- Organicity
- Obsessive-compulsive behaviors (e.g., gambling, drugs)

B. General social competence (the interviewer may reference presumed or apparent functioning in these areas):

- Adjustment to authority
- Cognitive functioning

- Self-concept (relationships to others, social abilities, assertiveness)
- Anxiety, social anxiety
- Self-expression, fear of negative evaluation
- Social avoidance/distress
- Realistic goals
- Leader, follower, loner
- General self-presentation: appearance, timeliness for appointments

C. Communication: Obvious strengths, deficits

- Voice quality and eye contact
- General self-presentation, affect
- General appropriateness of verbal content
- General stream of consciousness
- Social skills
- Language impairment
- Educational deficits/strengths
- Listening skills deficits/strengths

D. Discuss psychological significance of all items in sections III and IX

E. Psychological test results (watch for impulsive, rigid, obsessive modes of coping and problem solving; depression, suicide potential; antisocial behavior; thought disorder)

XIII. DIAGNOSIS

Five-axis DSM-IV

XIV. SUMMARY, ASSESSMENT, AND RECOMMENDATIONS

A. Summary of evaluation findings

B. Risk assessment (danger to self or others):

- Honesty, openness, strengths and weaknesses, coping skills, attitudes, responsibleness
- Risk factors around children or preferred victim categories (anger, depression, substance abuse, contact availability, obsessiveness, compulsiveness)
- Available supervision, family involvement, relapse prevention network
- Overall level of stability
- Other risk factors

C. Amenability to treatment

D. Recommendations
- Specific treatment needs
- Inpatient or community based
- Restrictions

2 Program Development: Key Elements and Staff Management

Gary Lowe

States rarely have the luxury of a legislative mandate to develop a treatment program with the complementary sums of money to establish a state-of-the-art treatment center. Treatment programs for sexual abusers usually develop when an innovative and motivated mental health professional who recognizes the need sets out to create a program on his or her own. Advances have also been made when a correctional or mental health institution struggles to manage this problematic population of clients more effectively. With little or no resources, "within an existing budget," innovative pioneer programs have grown to become state of the art, though not without adversity. The public's skepticism and unwillingness to "give" anything to perpetrators of heinous crimes, coupled with the doubts of treatment critics, ensure that programs and budgets for this unpopular client population undergo tight scrutiny.

Administrators and managers continually have to legitimize their efforts. As an administrator or manager of a sex offender program, you must be aware that sex offenders reoffend after the worst of treatment and after the best of treat-ment. Preparing yourself in advance during early program development to handle these adversities is extremely important. Because such events are always in the eye of the media, the public's response to a sex offender's recidivism is often a highly charged outcry for a legislative investigation. Positive media relationships, community networking, and comprehensive program outcome evaluation can help immensely in these least optimal of times.

PRE-IMPLEMENTATION CONSIDERATIONS

If your program is to be within an institution or is community based, the need for administrative and community support is paramount. Of course, if you have an administrative or legislative mandate or a community initiative to develop a treatment program, you are well along in the search for initial support for program development and operation. For most of us, a primary task is finding this direction and support, which many times means having to convince one or two high-level administrators or community leaders of the need.

Developing an understanding of the sex offender population and surveying treatment programs, treatment approaches, and the results of program evaluations will put you in a better position to convince the most skeptical of administrators. Be prepared to answer the following questions:

- Why not just lock them up?

- Does treatment "cure" a sex offender?

- Have sex offender treatment programs in institutions and in the community been successful?

- Can every sex offender be treated successfully?

- What kinds of staff work best with sex offenders?

- What techniques are used in sex offender treatment programs?

- What will a sex offender treatment program cost?

- Are there less expensive alternatives?

- Should sex offenders be housed in a separate therapeutic living unit or in the general population within an institution?

- How long should the treatment be?

- Do sex offenders have a legal right to treatment?

- Does the treatment program assume any liability as a result of treatment methods used?

- Is the state, an institution, or an agency liable if a sex offender commits a sex offense after completing treatment?

Additional questions a new manager should address with regard to residential treatment program management include:

- What services are available after clients leave the treatment setting?

- Can I influence or, ideally, manage the aftercare, so that a level of continuity and continuum of treatment exists?

- For those who need the intensity of a residential program, should the money be spent when there is no aftercare?

The manager of a treatment program for sexual abusers needs to be prepared to educate the funding agents that such treatment is cost-effective over the long term and that there is no quick fix for an abuser.

Developing the program evaluation component prior to program implementation is very important. The manager should be aware that during the first year, the growing pains of program implementation are at their height, and the initial program design on paper seldom looks much like the program in operation a year later. Consequently, adaptations to the initial evaluation structure will be needed as the program matures.

IMPLEMENTING THE PROGRAM

PROGRAM GOALS AND DIRECTION

The immediate program objective should be to modify the offenders' criminal and antisocial behavior, with the goal of reducing the likelihood of that behavior recurring. A long-range objective is to improve upon the state of the art in the treatment of these abusers by developing and testing innovative approaches. Within the framework of this objective, the program needs to provide answers to the following questions:

- Can treatment reduce the incidence of recidivism in this population? If so, what treatment components appear to be the most effective, and should they be included in other programs for these abusers?

- Are these treatments more effective with some types of offenders than with others?

If so, what demographic, historical, and clinical factors are related to amenability?

- What factors are the best predictors of recidivism?

- What factors are best predictors of successful community adjustment?

Given the seriousness of the impact on society, as well as on the victims of violent, heinous crimes against children, can intervention techniques be developed that will, at a minimum, reduce the kind and/or degree of violence even if the abuser fails to maintain a crime-free life?

CLIENT POPULATION

The next step is to determine the client population your program can serve, given budgetary restraints and program location. In some systems, that issue has already been decided or determined.

The question of who to treat is vital. Realistically, some offenders are too dangerous to treat in the community, and other abusers who are less dangerous do not need the level of supervision and intensity provided by institutional or residential treatment. Treatment amenability is also an issue. Experience tells us that those who are most in need of intensive treatment are often the least amenable, and those who are most amenable often need less intensive treatment. It follows that offenders who are most amenable to treatment generally experience better treatment results, whereas treating a less amenable population necessitates longer treatment time and more intensive resources. Although offenders who are more amenable to treatment generally need less time in treatment and less intensive resources, the question remains: Are we treating the population that is most in need?

So who can we treat? We can limit our abilities to work with different offender populations, or we can to take risks with different populations of sex offenders and not discount our abilities to work with them. As sex offender therapists, our ability to successfully treat a difficult abuser is often limited by our unwillingness to risk being innovative in our approaches to treatment. I am not advocating taking risks that put either the community or the abuser in jeopardy, but rather risks that involve the employment of therapeutic strategies in ways that you may not have considered previously. Sometimes you can be surprised. It always amazes me how creative, innovative, and successful we become when my staff and I have to work with a denying, resistive, highly aroused predatory offender population.

VOLUNTARY OR INVOLUNTARY PARTICIPATION

Referral sources often dictate whether a program accepts offenders for treatment who are voluntary, involuntary, or both. The program manager needs to consider this issue as part of program design. When making this decision, the manager needs to consider many factors, including:

- Voluntary clients will probably be more amenable to treatment, but may not be the most in need.

- Voluntary clients will probably show a higher success rate on outcome studies.

- Voluntary clients can sometimes help engage involuntary clients in treatment.

Many times, the major difference between a voluntary and an involuntary client presenting for treatment relates to the client's level of denial. Voluntary clients, for the most part, are in less denial of their offending behavior than involuntary clients, who are often in rigid denial. Assessing both the degree of denial and the reasons for it is an important aspect of offender assessment. Some common reasons for denial are:

- They didn't do the offense.

- Court action is pending, and they see it as being in their best interest to remain in denial.

- They have a fear of treatment, and their denial is a way of staying away from it.

Denial prevents the offender from experiencing additional feared consequences. Such fears often focus on abandonment concerns, especially by family and friends; job loss; or additional legal expense. Helping an offender relinquish denial, often called "breaking through denial," is a process that involves the development of trust and feelings of safety and security in the treatment environment — feelings that these clients have little experience with. These clients can be expected to take risks and disclose more as they find the environment less hazardous than anticipated.

CONFIDENTIALITY

The issue of confidentiality is somewhat controversial. In some state and private agencies, confidentiality is covered by legal statutes and policies. When this is not the case, I prefer to have a "no confidentiality" policy. That is, whatever is said or divulged will be provided to anyone who needs to know. With adolescents especially, whatever is disclosed is eventually communicated to someone within a system of agencies and individuals that constitute the treatment team. These clients have lived in a world of secrets, and they don't need any additional ones within their treatment milieu.

When a sex offender treatment program is housed within a larger institutional setting, a question may arise concerning the importance of protecting the client from being identified by other residents as a sex offender. This "protection" may be important in some correctional environments. I have found that this protection of identity is more of an issue with institutional staff than with the client population. It has been my experience that most of the client populations in these settings already know which inmates are sex offenders. Such a focus on the maintenance of confidentiality may, in some instances, have a negative impact on our efforts to further legitimize our work. Each program manager needs to examine his or her policy on confidentiality closely. The more we can do to legitimize our field, the greater the likelihood that we will be able to continue to provide needed services.

ASSESSMENT ISSUES

Once the population has been identified, the next step is for the manager to do a cursory assessment of the common needs of the identified population (see chapter 1). For example, a program with a primary population of highly aroused predatory pedophiles may need to emphasize behavioral intervention, whereas a program with a primary population of incest offenders may need to emphasize relapse prevention and coping skills. Reviewing state-of-the-art treatment for specific sex offender populations can give the manager insight and direction in developing the program; it can reveal which specific treatment interventions have proved to be the most beneficial, as well as the field's limitations.

It is important not to presume to understand the population after the initial assessment. We find ourselves continually assessing our clients. At the outset, you may have a general idea of who the population is, but the more you understand the nature of their problems, the better able you are to develop program resources to meet their needs. The nature and needs of client populations change over time. To be successful, your program should always be in the process of change, both as you learn more about your population and as you develop new treatment interventions. The program's goal should be to meet the needs of the client population rather than requiring the clients to fit the program.

Initial assessments of new clients involve the consideration of demographic, historical, and clinical factors. At the same time, we need to be careful not to identify so many problem areas needing intervention that the client feels overwhelmed. We have found that beginning with a step-by-step, gradual identification of problems, then expanding into more intensive and thus more risk-taking interventions, is successful. The first steps the client takes in the new growth process should be ones that allow the client to experience fairly immediate success — it is simply confusing and ineffective to teach algebra before the student has learned arithmetic.

As clients move through stages of growth and treatment, corresponding treatment phases can be developed that relate to the growth demonstrated, and expectations can be increased with each phase of growth. Sex offender treatment is not a short-term process. When we are dealing with trust issues, levels of denial, levels of deviance, and criminality, as well as diverse ethnic, cultural, and religious backgrounds, growth and change don't happen overnight.

CREATING THE ATMOSPHERE FOR CHANGE

It is a program manager's responsibility to create an atmosphere that is safe and secure, where the client can take the risks needed for change to occur. The considerations and decisions involved in developing this atmosphere are just as important as those involved in developing the treatment model. It will not matter what the treatment model is or that it has tools the client population can use to make the needed changes in their overall functioning or even that you and your staff have the requisite skills to effect client change if the general atmosphere of the program does not provide safety and security for the clients. Additionally, it is crucial that the staff demonstrate their commitment to the treatment model and that their beliefs are conveyed to the client population. In my experience, safety, security, and commitment to the model are what make treatment work.

Most programs attempt to create a therapeutic milieu by initially selecting clients who appear to be the most amenable. This process allows for the development of a core group of clients who adopt a set of values that support the treatment program goals. New clients who are less amenable are then more easily indoctrinated by the "cultural influence" generated by the core group, aiding staff in maintaining a safe, secure environment that nourishes change.

STAFF SELECTION AND TRAINING

The selection and training of staff competent to explore and understand the uniqueness of individual sex offenders are important initial endeavors for the manager. Staff personality and ego strengths must be adequate to listen to clients' reports of deviant behavior without overreacting. When interviewing potential staff members, I look for the following:

- an appreciation for the dignity and worth of the abuser separate and apart from what he or she has done or what they do (respect)

- a force of presence, self-confidence, a conviction in the helping process, and a command of self (potency)

- healthy coping strategies for dealing with stress

- experience with sexual abuse, both as treatment professionals and personally

- creativity, innovation, and the ability to work independently.

- use of problem-solving techniques; types of thinking processes used

Education is also an important factor, but I have found that staff who demonstrate these qualities, even though they may not have a great deal of education or professional experience, can be trained to be competent, skilled, and energetic helpers with a commitment to the treatment model.

TRAINING

Staff need some minimum training at the onset of program development and continual and more intense training as the program unfolds. As one of my administrators said to me many years ago, "Training is the lifeblood of a treatment program, and program success is based a great deal on it." Initial training should include the following:

- normal range of human sexuality, as a reference for measuring the degree of deviance and as a basis for setting rehabilitative goals

- clear descriptions and definitions of abusive and victimizing sexual behaviors

- how to recognize signs of victimization

- an explanation of the obsessive, compulsive qualities of many of these behaviors

- descriptions and definitions of sociopathic, predatory exploitation behaviors

- patterns of criminal thinking

- current treatment interventions in programs for sex offenders

As always, additional, ongoing training is a necessary component of developing a treatment program that effectively evolves with the changing needs of the clients and innovations in the field.

BURNOUT PREVENTION

In any treatment program, it is important to create an atmosphere in which the client population can grow. It is equally important to create an environment in which staff can grow. Treatment of sexual abusers involves a high risk of staff burnout. The work is exhausting and draining. Treatment is a slow, long-term process with fewer apparent rewards and significantly more stress than in many other mental health professions. Staff members and treatment professionals often have fewer collegial resources; are more reluctant to discuss their work with spouses, friends, and social contacts; and may experience covert or overt community disapproval (Edmunds, 1997).

GROUP STRUCTURE AND CONTENT

Ideally, regardless of the setting, programs should attempt to provide from one to three weekly, ongoing sex offender treatment groups, supplemented by a variety of related psychoeducational groups, skill-building sessions, and task groups whenever possible. In some settings, especially residential and secure settings, such educational information may be available in the form of job interview training, social skills training, relapse prevention, victim empathy, cognitive restructuring, daily management skills, and sex education. For specific details on group structure, content, and group process, see chapter 7.

If staffing or funding limits the program's ability to provide separate group sessions, providers may elect to schedule ongoing treatment groups and convert the content of those groups to an educational or skill-building format. In residential or correctional sex offender treatment programs, offenders living in various areas can assemble at a central location for their group sessions. Optimally, sex offenders are housed separately in a facility expressly designed for their ongoing specialized treatment.

SPECIAL TASK GROUPS

A portion of the psychoeducational forum can be devoted to developing task groups. A task group is made up of a group of abusers who focus on a variety of broader legislative, correctional, or educational issues (see chapter 7 for a more detailed discussion of task groups).

GROUP STAFFING PATTERNS AND INTEGRATING COOPERATION

Each ongoing treatment group requires shared responsibilities between two providers. Cotherapists must obviously work well together and embrace the program philosophy equally. Two providers are necessary to manage the various responsibilities incumbent upon a group leader; for example, one provider functions as a clinical observer while the second provider directly addresses group issues.

The group structure and process also require constant management, including the processing of assignments and goals and the examination of offending and personal histories. On a personal level, two providers can give each other moral support in this difficult work, as well as affirm or critique each other's group facilitation.

Treatment providers need time to prepare, plan, and maintain a record of each group's activities, assignments, and attendance. A review of a group's statistics at this time is recommended to assist providers in this preparation. Documentation of attendance is important for reporting to probation or parole and other authorities, and explicit recording of assignments and issues promotes continuity. The co-providers pool information gathered from family sessions and educational or other corollary classes, as well as from probation or parole officers, police departments, and school, line, or unit staff. The staff decide during this preparatory time which one will address any conflicts or issues with the group member and the approach used to manage the problem.

Programs should equally divide the authority roles between male and female providers to avoid stereotypical sex roles, despite the fact that they may have an employer-employee relationship outside the group. Unequal group leader relationships encourage splitting and manipulation by group participants. During the group session, the file should be documented and, at the conclusion of the session, both providers should review the dynamics of the group, provide constructive criticism to each other, and plan for the next scheduled session.

The co-providers should ideally be a male and female team in order to accomplish the following objectives: (1) redefine and model appropriate sex role characteristics; (2) address offender issues with female authority figures, especially with rape offenders; and (3) provide the offenders with a woman's perspective on relationships, communication, parenting, sexuality, or intimacy. In many cases, when offenders have various control issues relating to women, these issues surface only after facing a female authority figure—in this case, a treatment provider—in an intimate group setting. Female authority figures tend to elicit responses associated with past offender-client dysfunction such as intimidation, controlling behavior, and fear of intimacy. With a female co-therapist, these issues can be openly examined. Although a program can operate with two men or two women, the male-female combination is preferable.

It may be stating the obvious, but staff leading sex offender treatment groups require experience in treating sexual abusers. Similar experience in treating domestic violence offenders, substance abusers, or other criminal offenders can provide a therapist with a foundation of clinical experience that, with proper supervision and training, can be developed into sex offender treatment skills. If one therapist has specific sex offender treatment experience, the second co-therapist could be a carefully selected line staff member, probation or parole officer, corrections officer, or other appropriate law enforcement or child protection professional, provided that legal liability and ethical concerns are addressed. In this case, the second provider receives responsible supervision.

Treatment providers working with sexual abusers must have some skill in maintaining personal control of interviews and sessions without abusing their power. They need to embody the balance of control and collaboration with clients that is present in any healthy authority role. Providers should be able to employ a range of supportive and confrontational verbal skills and be able to set and enforce clear, reasonable limits. In addition, providers should be approachable and willing to self-examine when faced with constructive and detailed criticism, including that which is offered in good faith by other professionals and by offenders in treatment. Providers should, in other words, listen and negotiate when flexibility is appropriate, and stand firm when such personal strength is warranted.

The provider generally assumes the role both of ally and adversary throughout treatment. The goal of stopping destructive patterns and replacing them with healthy ones underscores the importance of treatment providers' modeling the characteristics of pseudoparental authority figures. Authority issues and figures are usually objects of distrust and resentment for many offenders due to negative parental and family experiences. Treatment providers therefore have the unique opportunity to use their clinical skills to replace those dysfunctions with the demonstration of appropriate authority roles and behaviors.

Sex abuser group treatment should be directly coordinated with other individuals or agencies with a legitimate role in treatment, security, and supervision. The dynamics of group treatment cannot be discussed without considering the valuable roles of such extragroup practitioners. Probation and parole officers, line and educational staff, parole and classification bodies, police and protective services workers, corrections officers, and victim treatment providers are other professionals who are considered treatment team members. These individuals are critical to the safety of the offender and the success of the group, providing treatment in the form of support and authority even though they may not provide a direct therapy intervention. Extragroup practitioners in many cases can also directly reinforce positive values about safety, treatment, and recovery discussed during group sessions.

These professionals should be notified of or notify treatment providers about relevant offender behavior or risk issues, and offenders should be made aware of their roles and boundaries. The type of information provided must generally be about risk and cooperativeness. Private communications about personal issues not involving potential risk to others should be kept private. Information covered by the previously mentioned waiver of confidentiality is defined as that involving potential risk to others or recent unreported sexual assaults or violent crimes, and is not to be held private. Such information should be reported directly and immediately to authorities, including reports made

under the mandatory child abuse reporting laws.

In residential and correctional settings, the more the line staff is involved in the direct provision of treatment services, the more treatment information is exchanged with line staff. For example, line staff on a smaller unit may provide and receive detailed information about offenders' treatment goals and other treatment information. In a larger correctional setting, where line staff may not be directly involved in treatment, staff may receive and give general reports about institutional behavior, cooperation with treatment, and specific instances of risk to others. In community sex offender treatment settings, probation and parole officers, police, and child protective services personnel may exchange information regarding cooperativeness and risk level. It has become an indispensable tool to include probation and parole officers, protective services workers, line staff, police, correction officers, and others directly in treatment sessions when a problem arises with a particular offender.

Abusers must always be visually and verbally reminded about their accountability as offenders and about the supervisory and criminal aspects of their treatment. Criminal justice and corrections agencies have a legitimate public safety interest in the dynamics of specialized treatment.

Interagency and interdisciplinary collaboration reduces the likelihood of offender manipulation of agencies and promotes the success of sex offender treatment itself. Sex offender programs with strong support from other agencies are more likely to facilitate offender cooperation or rapid responses to ensure community safety when offenders do not cooperate. Program success rates should be defined not only by the number of offenders remaining offense free and making positive changes but also by the number of offenders removed from treatment and incarcerated or denied parole. Both are measures of success, because they promote public safety.

TREATMENT CONTRACTS

Specialized sexual abuser treatment can be structured by using a treatment contract specifically designed for sex offenders, such as the Adult Offender Treatment Contract, the Adolescent Offender Treatment Contract (Loss & Ross, 1987), or the Correctional Sex Offender Treatment Agreement (Loss 1994; Loss & Ross, 1987). Such agreements outline the safety and behavioral rules for offenders who participate in the program. The contract is first discussed in the latter part of the psychoeducational phase of the program and is generally used throughout treatment (see chapter 7 for suggested contract provisions).

Contract conditions are specific and detailed. Concrete regulations ensure that clients understand and are then less likely to manipulate and distort program rules. For example, abusers typically distort the rule forbidding contact with victims to mean that they cannot have body contact but may call, write, or have visual contact with the persons they victimized.[†]

STAFF SELF-CARE AND PROFESSIONAL SUPPORT

Program managers must be sensitive to the potential impact of this work on staff members. Emotional, behavioral, and physical symptoms caused by work-related stress can range from isolated reactions to combinations of symptoms. The duration, frequency, and intensity of symptoms indicate the extent to which the individual staff member is suffering.

Emotional signs of burnout include apathy, anxiety, depression, irritability, fatigue, preoccupation, and inability to concentrate. Sometimes a person may overwork to exhaustion, retreat into withdrawal, or become argumentative

and even hostile. Behaviorally, staff may neglect specific responsibilities. They may misdirect their attempts to cope through alcohol abuse, drug abuse, or compulsive gambling. Occasionally, poor physical appearance and tardiness are signs of burnout. Physical effects range from recurring minor ailments to long-term illnesses. Staff members may complain of being exhausted during the workday. Headaches, nausea, and weight loss or gain are other physical symptoms in reaction to stress.

Preventive strategies for staff who are experiencing burnout due to stress may be to limit direct exposure to or clinical involvement with clients. They can find support through networking with colleagues. Taking a vacation or a "mental health" day off can be helpful. Humor is one of the better ways to deal with stress. Involvement in physical fitness programs that advocate exercise, proper diet, and sufficient sleep is also valuable. Personal recognition, especially from supervisors and administrative staff, is always important.

Viewing sex offender treatment as a prevention effort that translates into fewer victims can also be a major support for staff. It is also crucial, for the wellness of program staff, that they know that their efforts will receive continued support, in spite the inevitable treatment failures. As with any stress-related illness, the earlier burnout is identified and treated, the better the prognosis for renewal.

REFERENCES

Carkhuff, R.R., & Berenson, B.G. (1976). *Beyond counseling and therapy.* New York: Holt, Rinehart & Winston.

Edmunds, S.B. (Ed.). (1997). *Impact: Working with sexual abusers.* Brandon, VT: Safer Society Press.

Farrenkopf, T. (1992). What happens to therapists who work with sex offenders? *Journal of Offender Rehabilitation, 18*(3/4), 217–223.

Knopp, F.H. (1984). *Retraining adult sex offenders: Methods and models.* Syracuse, NY: Safer Society Press.

Krauth, B., & Smith, R. (1988). *An administrator's overview: Questions and answers on issues related to the incarcerated male sex offender.* Washington, DC: U.S. Department of Justice, National Institute of Justice.

[†] An explicitly worded no-contact rule is necessary to make it clear to abusers the various types of contact they are required to avoid.

Loss, P. (1994). *Correctional sex offender treatment agreement.* Unpublished manuscript.

Loss, P., & Ross, J. (1987). *Adult and adolescent offender treatment contracts.* Unpublished manuscript.

Lowe, G. (1987). *Oak specialized counseling program casework procedures manual.* Ione, CA: Preston School of Industry.

The revised report from the National Task Force on Juvenile Sexual Offending of the National Adolescent Perpetrator Network (1993). *Juvenile and Family Court Journal, 44*(4).

Schwartz, B.K. (1988). *A practitioner's guide to treating the incarcerated male sex offender.* Washington, DC: U.S. Department of Justice, National Institute of Justice.

3 Working with Denial in Sexual Abusers: Some Clinical Suggestions

Laren Bays

Merriam *Webster's Collegiate Dictionary* (1996) defines denial as "refusal to admit the truth or reality." We all do it. Our world is permeated with denial. Popular magazines have acknowledged that denial is a national problem that affects families, schools, neighborhoods, towns, and the nation. *Newsweek* magazine has called our country a "nation in denial." Even *Cosmopolitan* magazine (Gross, 1994) writes about the necessity of "facing up to the dreadful dangers of denial." The *National Catholic Reporter* (McCarthy, 1994) says that our society is "in denial, addicted to violence and losing its soul." Denial is a problem even in relatively healthy parts of our society. It can be crippling when found in mentally or physically ill, addicted, or criminal populations.

Denial is a common defense against fearful or unwanted information. Its spectrum ranges from healthy to pathological. Healthy denial allows us to function, such as when we ignore the possibility of a car wreck while speeding at 65 miles per hour on the freeway. Pathological denial allows problems to multiply and become increasingly destructive. It leads to more pathology, as in the alcoholic who denies drinking or the sexual abuser who denies abuse he or she has committed. Anyone who avoids unhealthy

Editors' note: Denial occurs along a conscious-unconscious continuum, often containing elements of both. Cognitive distortions (see chapter 4) can reduce conscious recognition of "truth" or "reality" because the offender does not recognize that he or she is employing distortions. A sexual abuser, in rare instances, may have fully unconscious denial because his or her sexually abusive behavior is so abhorrent or traumatic that conscious recall is too painful. Denial, as a defensive coping strategy, is a self-protective process. Conscious denial involves overt recognition of the truth or reality of an event and a purposeful choice not to acknowledge the event's existence (e.g., a person who has full memory of sexually abusing a child states that the report is false and no such action occurred). Unconscious denial involves a failure to overtly recognize truth or reality, which, in the extreme, leaves an individual unable to acknowledge the event's existence because no conscious memory of the event is retained (e.g., a man who acknowledges fondling his daughter but is firmly convinced that the child's statement that he committed cunnilingus is false because he has no memory of it, but it is later found that he had dissociated this event using unconscious denial). The denial discussed here is conscious denial. — *S. Mussack*

47

denial can more directly and firmly deal with life's problems.

WHY IS DENIAL A PROBLEM?

Denial hides, distorts, misrepresents, and falsifies problems. The first step in treatment is finding out what is true and real about a problem. To be useful, an assessment or diagnosis has to be based on accurate information. Denial prevents the client, the healthcare worker, or the counselor from gathering the essential information needed for successful treatment. Not knowing the true nature of a problem means not finding the solution. Knowing only part of a problem leads to a partial solution. A problem can be accurately defined, assessed, and treated only when there is minimal denial.

However, even if a problem is diagnosed correctly, unless the client acknowledges its truth, the very basis for a therapeutic relationship does not exist. Both the mental health treatment provider and the client must have some agreement about the diagnosed problem, especially in correctional settings, for effective therapy to occur. No therapy can occur, much less progress in therapy, if the treatment provider thinks that criminal behavior is the problem and the client denies that it exists. For example, therapy is impossible if a treatment provider perceives the real problem as greed, lack of empathy, and distorted thinking, while the client's perception of the problem is that he is being set up by a hostile system. Or, to use a medical analogy, if a physician diagnoses the problem as type II diabetes but the patient thinks the problem is depression and refuses medication or changes in lifestyle and diet, a return to health will be virtually impossible.

Until there is some degree of mutual agreement about the nature of the problem to be addressed in therapy, the mental health professional's only alternative is to try to educate the client. Education can occur despite denial; it is one way to bring both sides closer to agreement. In the medical analogy, when there is agreement

that the problem is diabetes, the diabetes can be managed. The physician and patient can work together. The physician can prescribe medications, and the patient can engage in diet control and exercise. Likewise, when an abuser admits that he or she has harmed others and has the potential to do so again, a therapist can help the abuser identify risk situations and avoid potential victims. In this case, therapy can begin, and progress is made.

Denial is ubiquitous and unavoidable. In one study, 55 percent of a sample of acute admissions to a psychiatric ward denied that they had any mental health problems (Perkins & Moddley, 1993). We collude with one another in our denial and get upset when someone goes outside our area of comfort or disagrees with us. Our denial allows us to act as though we will not die, will not become helpless with age, will never be diagnosed with a terminal illness, do not have the potential for violence, or are not in danger when exceeding the speed limit in our cars. We are comfortable with speeders as long as they don't go much faster than we do. Most of us avoid the thought of dying and don't have wills.

Our denial is activated when we are afraid. Denial is a defense mechanism that allows us to disavow thoughts, feelings, needs, or circumstances that cause us to feel anxiety. Denial is the first of Kubler-Ross's (1969) five typical steps in the dying process. When we face the fear and admit that someday we will be old, weak, and sick, we can make reasonable plans for retirement and care. If we can break down our own denial, then we can realistically expect clients to break down theirs.

SEXUAL ABUSERS' DENIAL

A sexual abuser's denial is unhealthy, but not surprising. The abuser often denies having deviant sexual desires or committing criminal acts and does not acknowledge the effects of his or her crimes. There are strong social and personal reasons that encourage and support the abuser's use of denial. Admission of sexually deviant behavior is not without potentially severe consequences. The fear of incarceration and of the loss of respect, money, and family causes anxiety and leads to denial. After adjudication, the offender is afraid of other inmates, new criminal charges, and stricter probation sanctions. For the abuser, the shame and humiliation he or she experiences from violating personal, familial, religious, or social mores can be severe. These pressures can be so intense that even the most moral and sincere abusers will retreat into denial. Sex offenders typically have two basic unhealthy defenses to avoid the dangers of reality: They pretend that the reality of a crime doesn't exist by denying or partly denying it, or, they make a partial admission and then offer excuses to mitigate their culpability. Either strategy seems to buffer them from the consequences of truth. Most offenders use elements of both defenses.

Though it is essential for personal change, relinquishing denial doesn't always help. Some same-sex pedophiles fully admit being sexual with boys, but their admission often has little or no effect on their deviant behavior or their motivation to change because their cognitive distortions are so strong (see chapter 4 for a discussion of the sex offender's use of cognitive distortions in the service of maintaining denial); their denial is of any harm resulting from their actions. In fact, some pedophiles enjoy the opportunity to discuss their crimes; they get pleasure from it. When pushed, other offenders admit to committing serious sex crimes, but they later compartmentalize their disclosure so that it has little impact on their thinking or behavior. Still other offenders move into and out of denial whenever it appears to benefit them.

Denial means hiding from or avoiding what is true and real. From an abuser's perspective, he or she is not employing denial; by the abuser's criteria, it is the therapist who is in denial about the truth. One technique for dealing with this type of discussion is to never debate an abuser about who is right or wrong. Instead, the therapist identifies for the abuser the social and legal standards for appropriate sexual behavior as part of the initial psychoeducational process (which can be provided to the offender even though strong denial is in place). Then, the therapist uses these standards as criteria to assess, either with or for the abuser, his or her current level of denial and the cognitive distortions being employed to maintain the denial.

UNDERSTANDING DENIAL

The better we understand something, the more effectively we can deal with it. Part of the justification for group therapy with abusers or addicts is that group members have similar experiences. Knowing what the experience feels like from the inside, they can better speak the language and evaluate the honesty of other participants. For therapists to help abusers face and break through their denial, it is important for therapists to understand as much as possible about their own use of denial. One way for professionals to do this is to remember how we reacted when faced with accusations against ourselves or close family members: a speeding ticket, shoplifting, an affair, wasting money needed for household bills, and so on. If the consequences were not severe, or we were too young to know what they were, we may have openly admitted our guilt and responsibility. But what if the consequences could have been severe, such as losing a job or a license, being left by a spouse, being arrested, being sued, and so on? When confronted, it is unlikely that we were immediately open and completely honest about what we had done. In such cases, like most people, we were probably tempted to plead ignorance, minimize the harm (and thereby our culpability), or blame someone else. How many of us have said something like, "But officer, there wasn't a yield sign there." "But officer, that traffic light was green, not yellow, and certainly not red!" "What's the matter, didn't you make your quota yet?"

Imagine being in a sex abuser–client's position. Most of the time you are not thinking clearly, are full of anger, shame, fear, and guilt.

You are being coerced to go to an evaluation or treatment because you committed a sex crime. Rightly or wrongly, your freedom, family, and job, everything you think is important in life, are likely to be lost. The therapist begins asking you question after question about what you have done. With each answer, you fear that you may be closer to going to prison; yet you must answer. If you tell the truth, it is likely to be doubted; if you lie, you are likely to be accused.

How would you react in a similar situation? Probably you would do exactly what sex offenders do and fall into denial and excuse making. When we understand what leads to denial, we have taken an important step toward learning how to break denial.

RELINQUISHING DENIAL

Here's the bottom line: No one relinquishes denial before weighing the possible outcomes and deciding, at some level, that the truth is to his or her advantage. Denial is employed at all points of an abuser's association with the criminal justice system: when first contacted, during questioning, in court, in prison, and in treatment. In the offender's mind, it serves many functions. Denial is employed as a form of self-protection against real and perceived dangers. Sex offenders, particularly during early stages of treatment, generally feel in jeopardy of experiencing more suffering, more demands, more punishment, more shame, more loss, and so on. Often, such fears are realistic.

In the short term, coming out of denial may harm the abuser as well as help him or her. The criminal justice system is unpredictable; individuals within it with whom the offender comes in contact will respond idiosyncratically to disclosures. A sexual abuser who tells of additional anonymous victims is immediately under greater suspicion, is viewed as more dangerous, may be kept from his or her family longer, and may be disliked so much that the interviewer or therapist finds an excuse to place him or her back in prison. In prison, admitting to being a sex offender is likely to result in being harassed and possibly harmed.

Many individuals let go of their denial only when they feel that they have nothing left to lose. Only a courageous individual (with a worldview that it is somehow to his or her advantage to tell the truth) is able to be honest when there are potentially fearful consequences to honesty.

Denial may be rewarded in minimal consequences. If an abuser can deny convincingly, he or she is more likely to be treated better than one who openly admits offenses. A primary foundation of the criminal justice system is being convinced that someone is guilty "beyond a reasonable doubt." Anytime an offender can create reasonable doubt, the consequences are mitigated. Avoiding denial and admitting guilt open an offender to the full consequences of his or her behavior. Abusers can be expected to use some aspect of denial to create doubt about an aspect of the crime or the whole crime in an effort to mitigate culpability and potential suffering. Consider how differently we treat someone who misses work intentionally versus someone who misses it because of illness. A malingerer knows that by denying health he can intentionally avoid some of the apparent consequences of not working. An offender who can skillfully or convincingly deny completely over time is almost always viewed as less culpable than he or she actually is (unless there is ongoing contact with the victim) and much less culpable than an abuser who admits guilt.

Denial helps some people feel safer and helps others be safer. All of us deny, to some extent, whenever we are afraid. But when we do, it can be like a child hiding under the covers at night. It does not protect the child or solve any problem; actually, hiding under the covers makes the child more vulnerable because he or she can no longer see and respond appropriately to any supposed threat. But the child *feels* somewhat better. For abusers, denial may truly make them safer. Denial protects abusers from hostile feelings and actions, especially when they are first accused of a crime and in prison. During an investigation, offenders may create doubt through denial, which may help them avoid years of prison or unwanted therapy. Prison inmates are often warned by authorities to deny being sex offenders while incarcerated.

Denial also functions to minimize the consequences of feelings of self-condemnation and unworthiness and their effects. By denying weakness, ineffectiveness, criminality, and moral poverty, an abuser can maintain a counterfeit sense of positive self-worth or confidence. It is a tactic that seems to be successful, as it is used universally. In one study, only 14 percent of offenders reported feeling any remorse for their offense (Marshall, 1994). Continued denial allows the offender to begin believing his or her lies, to focus on feelings of mistreatment by the "system" rather than on accountability and the need for change, and it further diminishes negative self-judgments. Feeling that one is more victim than perpetrator often fuels a righteous anger, giving one a sense of power. In prison, denial of being a sex offender allows some inmates to gain power that would otherwise be impossible. Publicly opposing therapists or supervisory personnel within a treatment group in order to thwart treatment is another method by which a guilty offender may employ denial to gain status or power.

Denial about sex crimes sometimes allows abusers to more easily continue deviant behavior. Many abusers feel that sex is the most important thing in their lives; they are loath to give it up. It is often their major form of excitement and pleasure. Denying that such behavior harms anyone, that it is sexually abusive, or that they feel guilty about their deviancy is a mental trick to allow the behavior to continue. Many abusers think that being happily deluded is far preferable to the reality of their behavior.

Some abusers who have been through the criminal justice system or who are smart businesspeople seem to enjoy playing a game with police, parole or probation officers, and therapists. They know what the interviewer wants, and they enjoy seeing him or her try to get it from them. Anything they can successfully get

away with gives them satisfaction and a sense of one-upmanship.

Denial can allow offenders to avoid responsibility and unwanted effort. If offenders can convince themselves and/or those around them that they did not do something, then they do not need to correct it or do the hard work of therapy. If offenders can convince themselves or others that they didn't do the crime, then they are not responsible for making any effort to change or relieving the victims' pain and remediating the effects on their families and friends. Most importantly, abusers believe that if they are not culpable, they will not have to pay as much. Denial can reduce demands for money, which in our society, is often viewed as the way to make restitution. Many civil lawsuits are attempts to gain compensation for harm done. Guilty abusers are in therapy longer, pay more restitution, are civilly liable, must pay for the victims' therapy or education, and so on.

Lastly, denial helps some abusers keep the support and love of family and friends. Strong denial by young adults or adolescents often brings parents to their defense in a way that they have never experienced before. An incest offender who convinces his wife that he has been unfairly accused may gain emotional and financial support. An offender who regularly attends church may gain a congregation of allies through denial. Coming out of denial can turn rescue, protection, and help into anger, accusation, and rejection.

COMMON PATTERNS AND METHODS OF DENIAL

Denial is always a complicated phenomenon. Though there are common patterns and methods, denial can be as unique as each offender. Denial takes many forms, depending on an offender's history and circumstance. One British study (Kennedy & Grubin, 1992) of a heterogeneous group of sex offenders categorized four basic patterns of denial: rationalizers, externalizers, internalizers or disassociators, and absolute deniers.

RATIONALIZERS. These offenders have the least overt denial and almost always are pedophiles and/or incest offenders. Rapists, sadists, exposers, or fetishists are much less likely to employ this form of denial. Rationalizers often admit their crimes but explain away their behavior as either harmless or genuinely good for the victim. In their minds, they are not incorrect in their sexual behavior; society is hung up on Puritanical values and rules. They frequently cite historical evidence that sexual behavior with children is natural and only contemporary society's perspective and paranoia are wrong. Frequent excuses include: "I was only putting on her medicine." "He was lonely and I was the only person who really cared about him; I gave him counseling, support, and attention." "Sex is one of our most important behaviors, so he needed to learn about sex. I was teaching him a much needed skill."

EXTERNALIZERS. These offenders are often angry and hostile. They feel that they were "set up" and are being persecuted by law enforcement and the legal system. They often identify a specific person who personally hates them and wants to destroy them. They use their persecution fears as a way to reinforce their denial. They project a belief that they are innocent. It is the system that is bad. When externalizers are resourceful enough, they often band together and find solidarity and comfort in groups that attack children's protective services, the police, or even the whole idea of child sexual abuse. The government, they might say, invented child sexual abuse to confiscate children from their natural parents and raise them in state schools and daycare; it's all a communistic government plot to brainwash the children. In their minds, the intensity of their anger and attacks is inversely proportional to their innocence. These abusers usually label the victims and the victims' parents as vindictive. They may try to prove their innocence by accusing victims of provocative behavior or of having unsavory sexual reputations. With older victims, abusers may accuse them of saying yes, enjoying the experience, and later lying about being coerced.

INTERNALIZERS OR DISASSOCIATORS. Frequently these abusers are intrafamilial abusers who have personal feelings or responsibility for their victims. They have learned that admitting the abuse is helpful to victims, is spiritually efficacious, and may get them leniency in the courts. They deny full responsibility by blaming the crimes on an abnormal state of mind. They deny being responsible for this abnormal state and usually blame it on drugs, alcohol, extreme stress, desperate loneliness, severe depression, unbearable financial pressure, or incapacitating health problems. They may indirectly place responsibility for the problem on other family members, such as a sexually unresponsive or abusive spouse. As with all denial, they try to prove that they are not fully culpable and therefore should not be fully punished or held accountable. When they get into therapy, these abusers often use the excuse of having an unhappy and abusive childhood (an excuse they are less likely to use in court) in an effort to find a more sympathetic listener.

Both externalizers and internalizers often try to avoid culpability by denying that they made any decisions. They deny making the choice to continue offending at each step of the crime. Usually they say, "I had no choice." When looked at closely, this really means, "Of the possible choices I had, the sex crime was the most appealing or seemed the safest." This type of abuser usually attributes the cause of his or her crime to compelling outside forces that made him or her commit the crime, such as a woman who says that her boyfriend forced her to have sex with a young boy; a man who says, "Satan made me do it"; a boy who says that he had to do it as a gang ritual; and all abusers who say that the victim made them do it.

An extreme form of such denial is employed by an abuser who denies even being in control of his or her body; for example, he may say that he was asleep and his daughter got into bed and put his hand between her legs. Essentially, this abuser tries to convince the listener that the victim molested herself using his body. Many times these abusers deny that choosing *not* to do something is as much a decision as choosing to do it. For example, the abuser who finds his niece in bed with him denies that he *chose* not to get up and leave. Because these abusers deny making a choice, they rationalize that they are not guilty of any crime. They somehow disassociate and deny that what their body is doing has anything to do with themselves.

ABSOLUTE DENIERS. These abusers are often angry, frequently intelligent, and full of reasons why they could not have committed such a heinous crime. Many adult rapists, those who use violence in their crimes, and most abusers from ethnic minority groups are likely to use complete denial. Adult rapists frequently try to appear strong, "macho," and in control. Complete denial helps them build this image, whereas admission of guilt does not. Men who come from ethnic cultures that are sexually conservative or mother-centered or who do not have an honesty ethic are likely to deny all sex crimes.

Eminent researcher Howard Barbaree (1991) distinguishes patterns of denial differently. He considers that there are three types of denial about sex offenses:

1. complete denial

2. admission of action but denial that it was an offense

3. admission of action but denial of sexual components

He further differentiates between denial and minimization and has identified three types of minimization about sexual offenses: minimizing harm, minimizing extent, and minimizing responsibility. These categories are similar to those identified by Anna Salter (1988) and both have been used to research the efficacy of the group process to break denial and minimization.

RATIONALE FOR BREAKING THROUGH DENIAL IN THERAPY

Virtually every therapy program regards denial as the single largest impediment to sex offenders' progress in therapy. Offenders must come out of denial, to some degree, for treatment to occur. Maintaining denial negates an important premise of therapy: that an individual with a problem would like to solve it and works with a therapist to that end. There are several other reasons why breaking denial is important.

HELPING VICTIMS. An abuser who admits to committing a crime helps the victim. A clear acknowledgment can remove the implied accusation that the victim is lying about what happened. It also can reduce the victim's guilt and/or stigmatization by others by clearly attributing responsibility.

WILLINGNESS TO CHANGE. Coming out of denial shows that the abuser is willing to change. Denial is a kind of resistance. Ending resistance to interventions is essential if there is to be any progress in therapy. Coming out of denial allows the abuser's motivation for treatment to be enhanced. The further out of denial the abuser comes, the more willing he or she is to participate in treatment.

ADMITTING NEED FOR HELP. An offender who admits his or her crime also begins the process of admitting that he or she needs help. The personal weaknesses, addictions, emotional instability, lack of social skills, and irrationality that nourish the cycle of deviance begin to be revealed. Once an abuser admits the offense, the details of how he or she got to that point and what must be done to avoid repeating the action become available. This process is the first step toward asking for and admitting the need for treatment and help.

STANDARD FOR EVALUATING PROGRESS. Breaking through or dissolving an offender's denial gives the therapist a concrete way to evaluate the offender's progress and the efficacy of the treatment plan.

ASSESSING DENIAL

Treatment depends on accurately assessing the range and depth of denial, which can be done in many ways. The least reliable source of information is the abuser. However, he or she is also the most convenient, inexpensive, and readily available source. Although it may be unreliable in any specific case, clinical judgment based on long experience of typical sex offender characteristics and patterns of denial is a useful rule of thumb. For example, if a 30-year-old same-sex pedophile says that he has picked up "no more than 10 boys" for sex, based on experience with other offenders and the literature, the therapist can assume that this is an incomplete and inaccurate accounting. Until abusers are engaged in therapy, there is rarely any compelling reason for them to tell the whole truth. As denial is being assessed, the default position should be, "Yes, he is in denial." Though abusers' reports are sometimes helpful, for more exact clinical, legal, or other formal use, there are more reliable, valid, and consistent methods of assessing denial.

When evaluating denial, the first rule is to collect information from as many sources as possible, although, given the cost and time it takes to gather information from disparate agencies, an extensive information-gathering process is not always practical. Any source that provides relatively objective information can be useful. Direct comparison between the abuser's statements and the police report, child protective services files, and victim statements is the first reliable step in estimating the extent of denial. However, all these sources depend on an accurate, true, unembellished statement by the victim. Unfortunately, the victim's trauma, fear, or confusion may distort his or her statement. In intrafamilial sex abuse, the consequences to the victim or family of a conviction for a sexual offense may be severe and may influence the victim to deny or minimize the crime. At the other extreme, when there are potential benefits of an arrest or conviction (such as in contested divorce or child custody proceedings), the criminal behavior may or may not be exaggerated. Although a cli-

nician must take such circumstances and their possible effects into consideration, unless there are solid grounds for suspicion (not generated by the offender), it is best to assume that the victim's version is accurate.

A number of inventories, scales, or measures attempt to evaluate denial. The Clarke Sex History Questionnaire (Langevin, Paitich, Russon, Handy, & Langevin, 1990), Multiphasic Sex Inventory (Social Sexual Desirability Scale) (Graham, 1987; Marshall & Hall, 1995), and MMPI-2 (Lie Scale) (Simkins, Ward, Bowman, & Rinck, 1989) have all been used for this purpose. All objective measures of denial, in essence, provide a structured way of comparing offenders' self-reports about their thinking and behavior with the crime reports, documented sexual histories, or victim statements. None of them is capable of detecting the extent of a sex offender's denial by itself. They are unable to distinguish between an offender who is denying specific sexual acts and someone who has never committed such acts.

The best way to evaluate denial with adult abusers in treatment is to take a complete relationship and sexual history (see chapter 1 for guidelines on gathering this information). Such histories must be detailed to be useful, and detail takes time. It is helpful to prepare yourself by reviewing all the objective and third-party statements. As the offender speaks, note all the details and, when they contradict other sources, come back to the points and ask for an explanation. Additional useful information is almost always revealed. Begin with the abuser's first relationship and first sexual experience. Most abusers will talk openly about events with ex-wives, children, or other victims if they think that these events are outside the statute of limitations or are irrelevant to the current offense. Abusers often enjoy relating what good lovers they are and how many sexual partners they have had. They will readily tell you what their ex-wives were like, the terrible things those women did to them, and how they got even. Though this kind of background information does not tell you directly about a current, relevant offense, it clearly shows the abuser's pattern of behavior over many years. If an abuser tells you about years of inappropriate sexual and relationship behavior and then tells you that it had all changed by the time of the offense, this is a good suggestion of the extent of denial. How an abuser has acted for 20 years paints a clear portrait of how he acted in the 21st year and how he is likely to act in the 22nd year.

Although the primary focus of assessing denial is past sexual behaviors, sexual preferences may be indicative of potential future behaviors. Objective testing through phallometry and potentially the Abel Screen II (G.G. Abel, personal communication, October 1996) is the only way to objectively assess sexual preference. It must be noted, however, that such phallometric assessments are never properly used to indicate guilt or innocence in relation to a particular sexual offense.

BREAKING THROUGH AND EMERGING FROM DENIAL

No one comes out of denial until the benefits outweigh the risks. Abusers come out of denial only when they are convinced that it is better for them to do so. At some level, the abuser must hope that he or she will experience less guilt, less anger from others, less fear, and less chance of punishment or that there will be less suffering for the victim. The abuser may hope for an immediate release of anxiety and pressure. The abuser may also look for the realization of some long-term benefit, such as admission to and insight from therapy (many treatment programs exclude abusers who are in denial). The abuser may have been convinced by a therapist that relinquishing denial is necessary to gain the trust needed to end curfew or to visit his or her children. Sometimes, an intrafamilial abuser weighs the benefits of denial against the potential benefits of a better relationship with his or her spouse. In a few cases, an abuser may actually trust a therapist's intentions enough to come out of denial.

Knowing that denial is a protective mechanism is helpful when trying to get an abuser to stop denying. Taking away all hope for freedom or release is seldom helpful. Give an offender hope that things will improve with his or her admission. If the abuser is convinced that he or she will get more respect and less hassle, save money, and so on, he or she is more likely to come out of denial.

To understand how to work with sex offenders' denial, it is first important to know how to work with and understand our own. Few people, criminal or noncriminal, disclose their full sexual histories without a great deal of leverage or incentive being applied. University students and healthy, sexually active women were both confidentially asked to anonymously disclose the details of their sexual histories. Neither group did so consistently (Anderson & Brofitt, 1988). If even healthy noncriminal populations do not disclose fully, how can we expect sex offenders, with all the pressure of the criminal justice system on them, to make full admissions immediately after entering treatment or during the initial evaluation?

It is helpful to reflect on how many embarrassing or shameful things in our lives we have not told our spouses, family members, or intimate friends. It is easy to hide or try to rationalize away even noncriminal behavior. Typical things that noncriminal people might hide include past sexual partners, behavior during a divorce, excessive discipline or emotional abuse of children, severe arguments or vengeful actions, gambling debts, drug use, and so on. A healthy, rational, intelligent person would be willing to disclose details of his or her past if there were clear reasons or situations requiring it. Thinking about what conditions would be compelling enough for us to disclose all the details of our past is helpful in trying to figure out how to encourage a sexual abuser to disclose.

An abuser usually comes out of denial in stages. Ironically, by the end of an effective treatment program, an abuser has often revealed so much that he or she looks more dangerous than when treatment began. An abuser who entered treatment having disclosed only a few victims often reveals many more. The process of moving from minimal admission to full disclosure and acceptance of responsibility for his or her life may happen over many years. Although each abuser is unique, in general abusers often follow similar stages of increasing disclosure:

1. disclosing noncriminal information: name, marital status, vocation, children, and so on

2. recounting daily events and problems: frustrations at work, problems with spouse, money, and so on

3. admitting things for which there is hard evidence: parts of the instant offense, past criminal record, and so on

4. nominally accepting responsibility for life: admitting his or her role in the deviant cycle, his or her half of arguments, and so on

5. admitting social and intellectual inadequacies: acknowledging failing, feeling weak, feeling stupid, and so on

6. admitting anonymous criminal behavior: revealing past undisclosed crimes that cannot be traced

7. accepting responsibility for crimes more completely: acknowledging that he or she made a choice to do crimes and could have stopped them

8. admitting destructive emotional, verbal, and controlling behaviors and hidden family secrets

9. admitting profound personal vulnerability and perhaps terror: deep fears of life, death, and powerlessness

10. fully admitting and accepting personal responsibility for all aspects of life and crimes: empowerment

These stages are not absolute, and some are repeated over and over as personal confidence and the offender's trust in the professional grows.

SPECIFIC TECHNIQUES

There are many methods for encouraging disclosure (see chapter 1 on evaluation). Methods discussed here range from the coercive, which play on fear and anxiety, to the persuasive, which try to convince the abuser that disclosure is in his or her best interests. There are several specific times when strong interrogation of an abuser is effective. Typically, strong interrogation is most useful when there is only one opportunity to get an admission from an abuser, such as when conducting an evaluation with little background data on a convicted offender or interviewing a suspect about a crime. Any leverage the therapist or investigating officer has, such as witness reports or a failed polygraph, makes this task easier.

The strategy for this type of interview is often different from that used when the therapist and client have a longer relationship. There are two ways to approach the interview, and the approach employed depends on the therapist's personal style. One is to make the abuser feel anxious, tense, or uncomfortable and to let that feeling build until it can be easily relieved by an admission. In this technique, the investigator asks for immediate answers, tells the abuser the worst possible outcomes of denial, and questions the abuser vigorously and specifically about the crime. The abuser should not be given time to reflect on excuses. The other approach is to be the offender's most understanding and best friend. If the investigator is warm, cheerful, comforting, and understanding amd makes up excuses about why the abuser had to do what he or she did, many abusers will open up and reveal further details. Because many abusers are used to shutting down when dealing with hostility, including recent interrogation by the police, this softer method often works best. Such interview methods may be construed by some as manipulative or clinically inappropriate. As with any clinical work with clients, the therapist must remain aware of ethical boundaries.

When a therapist has a longer time with the offender, he or she must be empathetic and reasonable most of the time. Falling into a habit of anger, rage, reactive blame, constant criticism, and/or indifference often exactly reflects the problems the abuser has and his or her way of dealing with them. Stable emotions and balanced honesty are essential. Balanced honesty, being able to acknowledge both good and bad, avoids the error of thinking that criticism and negative feelings are the most honest feelings. As professionals, we must model truth-telling, respect, and ethical behavior. If we don't, how can the people we work with ever learn it? During the process of unraveling an offender's denial, professionals must remain clearly in charge. They need to establish a working therapeutic relationship with the offender, based on respect for healthy behavior, without forgetting that the client is a sexual abuser who has hurt many people and is likely to do so again. The more experience and techniques the therapist has available, the more possible it is to achieve this difficult balance.

Following are some techniques that are useful in breaking through denial. Each of them has advantages and disadvantages and is applicable at different times.

CONFRONT THE OFFENDER DIRECTLY ABOUT THE SPECIFIC SEXUAL ACTS. Being asked embarrassing questions about the details of sexual acts and criminal behavior is uncomfortable to many offenders. Socially, even in criminal circles, there are topics or ways of speaking about topics that are not generally acceptable. Be very direct and specific about behaviors: "Show me how far you put your finger in." "What position were you in?" "Where were your pants when your penis was in her?" "How did it taste?" Using visual and tactile descriptors rather than professional language may help: "What color was her anus?" "What was her expression?" "What temperature did it feel like?" "Tell me about the smell." Often, when questions are asked in unordinary ways, abusers do not have ready answers. When they are caught off guard and must answer quickly, the truth comes to mind more readily, requiring less effort than fabricating a lie.

DIRECTLY CONFRONT LIES AND CONTRADICTIONS. If the abuser's response goes against your experience with a particular type of offender or contradicts the victim's statement, the police report, or the abuser's earlier statements, immediately confront him or her. State that you think he or she is lying, and push the abuser to give you a more "reasonable and honest" explanation. Unless the abuser is a true psychopath, each clarification reveals a bit more information. Even if he or she responds with more lies, through consistent and respectful confrontation and specific questioning, eventually the abuser's web of deceit becomes so complex that he or she cannot remember or sustain it.

DEMYTHOLOGIZE STEREOTYPES ABOUT SEXUAL ABUSERS. Many clients believe that if they admit to a sexual offense they are admitting to certain social stereotypes as well. Admitting to committing a sex crime is hard, but admitting to being a "dirty old man" or an emotionally depraved, foaming-at-the-mouth sex maniac who commits crimes is far harder. Try to dispel some of these concerns by talking about how typical abusers present themselves and act.

SUPPORT AN ABUSER'S GENUINE RELIGIOUS BELIEFS. Offenders frequently become interested in religion after they have been apprehended or incarcerated. Sometimes, this new interest is just an excuse to continue denial, but there may be a core of genuine belief on which to build. Emphasize that confession of sin is important for forgiveness. In every major religion, being honest and helping others, especially victims or families, are foundations for healthy spirituality. Discuss that everything we do, feel, say, and think, whether positive or negative, has some consequence.

MAKE FUN OF AN ABUSER'S EXCUSES FOR THE CRIME (but without shaming him or her). Many abusers try to explain what happened with fantastic stories or rationalizations that reflect cultural myths and prejudices. A 160-pound offender who says that a 9-year-old girl "made me do it" can be kidded about how weak he is. A same-sex pedophile who picks up young boys "only to give them a lift" can be laughed at for thinking that he can fool the assessor. Use anything respectful that will keep the offender off balance so that he or she does not have time to reconstruct excuses.

OFFER TWO INCRIMINATING CHOICES. Of the two ways to do this, the more effective is to offer two choices for the offender's motivation. Make sure that one is more socially undesirable. For example, "Did you do it because you hated her, or were you just terribly confused?" Follow this with a suggestion that the real motivation was the more socially acceptable one: "I'll bet that everything was going wrong in your life and your mind was just confused. Isn't that right?" The other option is to offer two equally guilty choices, such as, "Did you touch your niece first on the clitoris or the anus?" "Did you expose yourself because you needed to pee or because you were sexually aroused?" "Was she more comfortable when you did it in her room or in your room?" "Were you drinking or not when you molested her?"

ASK SPECIFIC DETAILS OF THE CRIME. Ask such questions as: "Exactly what time did you arrive?" "What exactly did you do next?" "What did you say? What words did you use?" "Where did you go, and by what route did you get there?" As you compile the list of details, if the abuser is lying, he or she will not be able to keep them all in mind while under pressure. As you note discrepancies, keep them in mind and come back to them later.

DON'T ALLOW TIME FOR CAREFUL REFLECTION. If the abuser has to come up with an answer quickly, it is more likely to be the truth than a fabricated story (mentally, the truth takes less energy and time than the act of creating a factitious story). Don't let him or her have any time to review or create the details of a false story.

SEE DENYING CLIENTS AT THE END OF THE DAY. Tell the abuser that he or she is the last client and that the session will last as long as it takes to hear the truth. Don't let the abuser see a clock to keep track of time. An abuser who thinks that he or she can't outlast the therapist is more likely to tell the truth by the end of the session.

ASSUME THAT THE COURT'S VERDICT IS CORRECT. If the offender has been adjudicated, don't retry him or her in your mind. Offenders frequently try to change the focus from their crimes to the inconsistencies of the criminal justice system. Talk to the abuser as though he or she is guilty. Therapists can do this best when they know the statistics on typical numbers of sex crimes, nonsex crimes, and modus operandi (MO). Speak with confidence about how his or her pattern is similar to that of the average abuser. Don't show doubt. Confidently assume that he or she has done outrageous things (the offender can then correct you and tell you that it wasn't as bad as that).

GET A DETAILED SEXUAL AND RELATIONSHIP HISTORY. Often, if the therapist shows great interest in their exploits, abusers will tell many details, giving the therapist a clear understanding of what kind of people they are and their likely MO in the instant offenses. When there is some question of culpability, abusers' histories provide plenty of reasons to be in therapy and may allow abusers to work on current issues by admitting to similar problems in the past.

BE SYMPATHETIC AND UNDERSTANDING. Listen well, ask reflective questions, and be accepting of both the client and what he or she says, while taking detailed notes of everything that is said. Convince the client (if you really believe it, given this situation) that telling the truth is the best way to help himself or herself. Help the offender to relax and let down defenses, without getting into a victim-stance saga. If the abuser is allowed to spin out a story of denial and injustice, he or she will feel too committed to the story to change position during the interview. Don't acknowledge his or her denial; sidestep it.

GIVE THE ABUSER EXCUSES FOR DOING THE CRIME. When the primary purpose of an interview is to break through denial, take any small admission and support it with reasons why the abuser had no choice but to do what he or she did. Help the offender acknowledge the behavior, even if he or she denies motivation or culpability. Later, come back to the admission and dissect the chain of cause-and-effect decisions that led up to the crime. For example, an abuser admits that she molested her niece but insists that it was the victim's fault. Accept the admission without worrying about the thinking or attribution errors; support them even temporarily. Later, use the admission to assist the client in accepting culpability. The offender may try to retreat into denial, but insist that the admission was true.

Typical examples of distortions to temporarily support an abuser, in order to gain an admission, might include acknowledging that the offender didn't have any choice, given the situation: "You were in a gang and had to go along and rape the woman, or you would have been attacked." "You couldn't help it. You were asleep and your nephew came into the bed and started giving you fellatio before you fully woke up." "Your daughter said that you had to touch her friend or she would tell her mother about you touching her." Another temporary distortion would be to let the offender blame others: "She seduced me. I was out for a hike in the woods and came upon a woman who gave me some beer and seduced me." "She always walked around the house with no underwear on. She intentionally turned me on and had to bear the consequences." "The mother did not control the girls. They were wild and blackmailed me into having sex with them." Later, you can confront the offender with his or her admission and begin to help him or her accept culpability.

BALANCE POSITIVE AND NEGATIVE FEEDBACK. Positive feedback about what a good job the client is doing by admitting guilt and how much courage it takes is important. Convince the abuser that each step out of denial is a step toward a more healthy, satisfying life. Some abusers take positive feedback as a sign that they have given you enough and stop revealing. With them, appropriate use of criticism or derisive humor about the extent of their disclosure is important. "What a minute, I don't think you are dumb enough to think I would believe that." "You're just continuing to lie. I'll have to report that you are incorrigible." With both positive and negative feedback, emphasize how the abuser's behavior will affect his or her case, family, victim, future disposition, or mental health.

OTHER TECHNIQUES FOR BREAKING THROUGH DENIAL

GROUP PRESSURE

Use group pressure to confront denial. Group pressure works after the abuser has been in the group for two or three weeks, perhaps longer — long enough to know the other group members but not long enough for them all to have met afterward and collude in denial. Use group disclosure as a modeling technique by having each person in the group make some confession, with the denier going last. The more positive feedback each disclosing group member gets for disclosure, the more likely it is that the denier will make some admission. Later, encourage the admitting group members not to let the denier get away without telling the truth. Emphasize that the revealing group members have to bear the consequences of admission and that the denier should not be excused. Other group members' righteous indignation is strong fuel for breaking down denial. However, the therapist can't allow anger and criticism to become common behavior for the group. Use caution, assist group members in providing positive support, and convey the benefits that each has experienced by relinquishing denial as a positive model for the newer group member (see chapter 7 for more on group process).

AVERSIVE BEHAVIORAL REHEARSAL

An extremely intrusive method for gaining more details about sexually abusive behavior (and decreasing its attraction) is aversive behavioral rehearsal (ABR).[1] ABR requires the offender to publicly act out the behavior in front of the therapist and/or the treatment group. This technique is effective with abusers who partially admit their offense. Having them act it out while verbalizing their thoughts requires them to fill in many details. Ask questions such

[1] ABR has been constructively employed in both inpatient and outpatient settings. The description offered here is not sufficient for a clinician inexperienced with this method to safely and effectively implement it. As indicated, ABR is extremely intrusive and can involve significant risk if improperly implemented. Prior to attempting this intervention, the therapist should review available literature, seek specialized training, and conduct the intervention only when knowledgeable consultation and supervision are available.

as: "How did you get her pants off?" "Exactly what position was she in?" The ABR may be videotaped, watched by a group or family, or done only with a therapist present. To break through partial denial, conducting ABR alone with a therapist is most effective. The more people who watch it, the more shame and resistance the offender feels. To achieve the abuser's maximum aversion toward the behavior, a larger group is best.

DENIERS' GROUP

Groups or classes composed of sex abusers in denial can be very effective. The purpose is to reduce fear and convince offenders that they are better off telling the truth. A pretreatment deniers' group should be limited to about 10 sessions. It should have two specific goals: to break through denial and to provide motivation to participate in therapy. When abusers feel they are not alone with their problems, that they are recognized and can be helped, they are much more likely to come out of denial. The main approaches that have been shown to be effective are (1) repeated group disclosure and confrontation combined with victim empathy and (2) a structured deniers' group. The structured deniers' group is less dependent on the composition of the group and the personality of the therapist. Typical subjects for a deniers' group include:

- **EFFECTS OF VICTIMIZATION.** Providing denying abusers with clear, specific information concerning the impact of sexual victimization can be effective in confronting their distorted beliefs that no harm was done by the abuse or that the victim actually derived some benefit from it. Such information may explain abusers' feelings, beliefs, and attitudes maintained from earlier years if they were sexual abuse victims themselves. Such information, provided in an educational format, often results in a relinquishing of denial without more overt confrontation.

- **IRRATIONAL BELIEFS ABOUT SEX CRIMES.** A didactic presentation concerning irrational beliefs, combined with methods to alter such beliefs, may provide abusers with information and skills they did not previously possess. These skills are needed to identify and alter cognitive distortions.

- **SEXUAL ABUSE IN THE CONTEXT OF HEALTHY SEXUAL AND RELATIONSHIP BEHAVIOR.** Such information can clarify for abusers how their failed or dissatisfying relationships are directly related to their sexually deviant behavior, rather than being attributable to other causes. This information can create an opportunity for offenders to recognize that there is hope for positive relationships and that specific behaviors can be learned and implemented to make positive changes.

- **ASSERTIVENESS SKILLS.** Deficits in communication skills and difficulties in getting personal and relational needs met are common among sexual abusers. Assertiveness training frequently results in immediate positive communication experiences, which can lead abusers to accept the idea that therapy can have positive benefits.

- **HOW THERAPY WORKS.** Many, perhaps even most, abusers have never participated in any form of therapy. Thus, some of their guardedness may simply be due to lack of information. Providing specific information makes abusers feel less out of control, anxious, and fearful of the unknown.

POLYGRAPHY

A polygraphic assessment, or lie detector test, can be an extremely useful tool for breaking through denial. Research by Humbert (1990) supported the use of this technology as an adjunct to therapy and recognized that it can result in a significant increase in offense disclosures during the course of treatment. More admissions come through its effective use than by any other method. Skillful use of the polygraph requires a trained specialist. When using the polygraph, take the following steps:

- Prepare the abuser by telling him or her well in advance that he or she will be taking a polygraph.

- Emphasize that the test is accurate (it is especially accurate when evaluating truth telling).

- Tell the abuser that this is an opportunity to prove how honest and reliable he or she is.

- Tell the abuser that it will confirm all that he or she has been telling you and that you will then regard the client as a much more sincere person.

- Tie passing the polygraph to some positive benefit, such as removing a curfew, allowing a visit with a child, receiving an out-of-state travel permit, increasing other visitation, and so on. Likewise, set up negative consequences for failing the polygraph.

- Use a detailed pretest interview.

During the pretest interview, ask specific questions about sexual history and behavior. This should be the longest and most complete part of the exam. All the abuser's answers should be recorded. After the pretest interview, ask specific questions for the actual polygraph. Among these questions should be general questions about the truthfulness and accuracy of responses given during the earlier pretest interview.

Conduct a posttest interview. If the abuser failed any of the polygraph questions, review them and ask for an explanation. Note everything the offender says. Implement the appropriate positive or negative consequence.

When the polygraphic assessment is completed in this way, the pre- and posttest information is most important. If done correctly, the

questioning will reveal details about the offender's crime, current behavior, and sexual history without the offender's being hooked up to the instrument. Remember that this information is what the offender admits without an evaluation for honesty. This procedure sidesteps all the issues of reliability and validity.

VIDEO OF VICTIM'S STATEMENT

It may be determined during the victim's therapy that making a video describing the details of the sexual abuse or its effects on her or him may be of benefit to the victim. If such a resource is available, it can be very effective when shared with the perpetrators of intrafamilial sex crimes. Fathers are especially affected when they see their sons or daughters crying, angry, or depressed while talking about what was done to them. This technique often leads to tearful admissions of guilt if the father has genuine feelings of concern for the child.

PHALLOMETRY

Results of phallometry can be used to confront abusers about denial. Knowing an abuser's true sexual preference allows comparison with what he or she admits. It is helpful in assessing denial and useful in encouraging additional disclosure. In one study (Abrams, 1991), even experienced interviewers with consistent procedures were able to determine only 50 percent of offenders' deviant sexual preferences. Being able to show exactly how much an offender is aroused and by what helps him realize that he is not fooling anyone with his denial. In another study (Abel, Rouleau, & Cunningham-Rathner, 1985), 55 percent of 90 offenders disclosed additional paraphilias, and 62 percent made more admissions of deviant behavior after phallometric data were shown to them.[2]

[2]As with any assessment tool, it is important not to place excessive reliance on penile plethysmography, nonphallometric sexual interest screening such as the Abel Screen, or the polygraph. Although it is clear that such technology is a valuable addition to sexual offender treatment, each can be susceptible to falsifica-tion or error to varying degrees. Using these tools increases the amount of information gathered about the offender, assisting in more effective treatment planning and progress and risk assessment. See chapter 1 for additional information on phallometric and polygraphic assessment.

EMERGING FROM DENIAL: AN ONGOING PROCESS

When denial is defined broadly (not just as "yes, I did it" or "no, I didn't"), abusers emerge from denial slowly, in stages. It is as though light penetrates through layers of darkness and deceit one layer at a time. Each admission and acknowledgment of responsibility allows the next layer of lies to be exposed and worked with. For abusers in therapy, there are two practical ways of measuring progress out of denial. The first, and most pivotal, level is a basic admission of "Yes, I did it." Even if it is done with many reservations, excuses, and denial of responsibility, it is an essential step. The second perspective on denial is to monitor whether the abuser is continuing to become more honest over time.

When an abuser is progressing in therapy, gaining a degree of mental health and becoming a less dangerous person, each few months of therapy should result in a reduction of denial and a greater acceptance of responsibility for his or her life. Even when a client is in therapy for a few months and remains in denial, he or she may gain some useful skills and may come out of denial in the future. The choice to keep an offender in therapy or not must be based on the availability of resources and patience.

Fundamentally, coming out of denial is the initial focus of therapy. In therapy, a central theme is to claim successes and admit failures, accept weaknesses and celebrate strengths, and acknowledge that only each individual can make the choices necessary to live his or her life healthfully. Denial should be an underlying concern in every interaction with an abuser. The degree of an abuser's denial is probably equal to his or her resistance to leading an honest life. It can be used as an indicator of prognosis and amenability to treatment.

Denial is normal. Its presence is not a reason to refuse therapy initially. It can be changed and/or decreased in many abusers. If it cannot be dissolved or continues to increase, then denial becomes a good criterion on which to base a decision that an abuser is not amenable to treatment.

REFERENCES

Abel, G.G., Cunningham-Rathner, J., Becker, J.V., & Mchugh, J. (1995). *Motivating sex offenders for treatment with feedback of their psychological assessment.* Paper presented at the World Congress of Behavior Therapy (1983), Washington, D.C. Quoted in B.K. Schwartz & H.R. Cellini (Eds.), *The sex offender: Corrections, treatment and legal practice* (pp. 12–5, 12–6). Kingston, NJ: Civic Research Institute.

Abel, G.G., Mittelman, M.S., & Becker, J.V. (1985). Sex offenders: Results of assessment and recommendations for treatment. In M.H. Ben-Aron, S.J. Hucker, & C.D. Webster (Eds.), *Clinical criminology.* Toronto: M & M Graphics.

Abel, G.G., Rouleau, J.L., & Cunningham-Rathner, J. (1985). Sexually aggressive behavior. In W.J. Curran, A.L. McGarry, & S.A. Shah (Eds.), *Forensic psychiatry and psychology: Perspectives and standard for interdisciplinary practice* (pp. 289–313). Philadelphia: F.A. Davis.

Abrams, S. (1991). The use of polygraphy with sex offenders. *Annals of Sex Research, 3*(3–4), 239–263.

American Psychoanalytic Association. (1990). Denial. In E.M. Burness, & B.D. Fine (Eds.), *Psychoanalytic terms and concepts.* New Haven, CT: Yale University Press.

Anderson, B.L., & Brofitt, B. (1988). Is there a reliable and valid self-report measure of sexual behavior? *Archives of Sexual Behavior, 17,* 509–525.

Barbaree, H.E. (1991). Denial and minimization among sexual offenders: Assessment and treatment outcome. *Forum on Corrections Research, 3,* 30–33.

Graham, J.R. (1987). *The MMPI: A practical guide* (2nd ed.). New York: Oxford University Press.

Gross, L. (1994). Facing up to the dreadful dangers of denial. *Cosmopolitan, 216*(3), 180.

Hanson, K.R., Cox, B., & Woszczyna, C. (1991). Assessing treatment outcome for sexual offenders. *Annals of Sex Research, 4,* 177–206.

Humbert, P.E. (1990). The impact of polygraph use on offense history reporting. *The ATSA Professional Forum, 4*(3), 20.

Kennedy, H.G., & Grubin, D.H. (1992). Patterns of denial in sex offenders. *Psychological Medicine, 22,* 191–196.

Kiechel, W. (1993). Facing up to denial. *Fortune, 128*(9), 163.

Knopp, F.H. (1984). *Retraining adult sex offenders: Methods and models.* Orwell, VT: Safer Society Press.

Kubler-Ross, E. (1969). *On death and dying.* New York: Macmillan.

Laflen, B., & Strum, W.R. (1994). Understanding and working with denial in sexual offenders. *Journal of Child Sexual Abuse, 3*(4), 19–36.

Langevin, R., Paitich, D., Russon, A., Handy, L., & Langevin, A. (1990). *Clarke sex history questionnaire for males manual.* Etobicoke, Ontario: Juniper Press.

Marshall, W.L. (1994). Treatment effects on denial and minimization in incarcerated sex offenders. *Behavior Research and Therapy, 35*(5), 559–564.

Marshall, W.L., & Hall, G.C. (1995). The value of the MMPI in deciding forensic issues in accused sexual offenders. *Sexual Abuse: A Journal of Research and Treatment, 7*(3), 205–220.

McCarthy, C. (1994). In denial, addicted to violence, America may be losing its soul. *National Catholic Reporter, 30*(25), 13.

Merriam Webster's collegiate dictionary (10th ed.). (1996). Springfield, MA: Merriam-Webster.

Moon, R.S., Platt, F.W., Keller, V., Wiseman, E.J., Ness, D.E., & Ende, J. (1995). Denial in the medical interview. *Journal of the American Medical Association, 273*(22), 1734.

O'Donohue, W., & Letourneau, E. (1993). A brief group treatment for the modification of denial in child sexual abusers: Outcome and follow-up. *Child Abuse and Neglect, 17,* 299–304.

Perkins, R.E., & Moddley, P. (1993). Perception of problems in psychiatric inpatients: Denial, race and service usage. *Social Psychiatry and Epidemiology, 28*(4), 189–193.

Pithers, W.D. (1989). Relapse prevention with sexual aggressors: A method for maintaining therapeutic gain and enhancing external supervision. In D.R. Laws (Ed.), *Relapse prevention with sex offenders* (pp. 343–360). New York: Guilford Press.

Pithers, W.D., Beal, L.S., Armstrong, J., & Petty, J. (1989). Identification of risk factors through clinical interviews and analysis of records. In D.R. Laws (Ed.), *Relapse prevention with sex offenders* (pp. 83–85). London: Guilford Press.

Salter, A.C. (1988). *Treating child sex offenders and victims.* Beverly Hills, CA: Sage.

Simkins, L., Ward, W., Bowman, S., & Rinck, C.M. (1989). The Multiphasic Sex Inventory: Diagnosis and prediction of treatment response. *Annals of Sex Research, 2,* 205–226.

Snell, W.J., Belk, S.S., Papini, D.R., & Clark, S. (1989). Development and validation of the Sexual Self-Disclosure Scale. *Annals of Sex Research, 2,* 307–334.

Strate, D.C., Jones, L., Pullen, S., & English, K. (1996). Criminal justice policies and sex offender denial. In K. English, S. Pullen, & L. Jones (Eds.), *Managing adult sex offenders: A containment approach* (pp. 4-11–4-15). Lexington, KY: American Probation and Parole Association.

We are a nation in denial. (1995 March 13). *Newsweek, 125*(11), 22.

Wormith, J.S. (1983). A survey of incarcerated sexual offenders. *Canadian Journal of Criminology, 25,* 379–390.

4 Cognitive Distortions and Restructuring in Sexual Abuser Treatment

William D. Murphy
Mark S. Carich

Contemporary approaches to the treatment of sexual offenders have given increased attention to cognitive and attitudinal factors that are hypothesized to have potential etiological significance or, at a minimum, may maintain deviant sexual behavior (Murphy, 1990; Segal & Stermac, 1990; Stermac, Segal, & Gillis, 1990). The investigation of cognitive and attitudinal factors in sex offender treatment developed from a number of sources (Murphy, 1990). Cognitive-behavioral approaches described the concept of cognitive distortions (minimizations, excuses, justifications) as one factor that may maintain offender behavior. The women's movement stressed the role of male socialization and attitudes toward women and aggression (sexual stereotyping, rape myths, acceptance of interpersonal violence) as shaping males' sexual aggression (Burt, 1980). Also integrated into cognitive approaches is the more general concept of thinking errors as a precursor to general criminal behavior derived from the criminological literature (Yochelson & Samenow, 1977).

These cognitive and attitudinal factors may also be closely related to other important aspects of offender functioning. For example, denial may be viewed as an extreme cognitive distortion (Barbaree, 1991; Pollock & Hashmill, 1991). In addition, victim empathy is precluded if offenders can tell themselves it was "only sex education" or can maintain the belief that "women mean yes when they say no," as well as holding the generalized criminal thinking of "me first." It can also be hypothesized that offenders would have more difficulty maintaining deviant sexual arousal if they were unable to use cognitive processes to minimize the harm they caused or to convince themselves that "most women enjoy rape."

This chapter reviews assessment approaches, including the empirical literature on cognitive distortions and rape-supportive attitudes, and summarizes the current treatment outcome literature. The final portion of the chapter focuses more specifically on direct treatment approaches to modifying offenders' cognitions and attitudinal structure.

ASSESSMENT APPROACHES AND EMPIRICAL LITERATURE

Because our empirical knowledge regarding cognitions in sex offenders is tied to assessment instruments, this section presents the current empirical literature within a review of each of the primarily used assessment instruments and concludes with a brief outline of empirical literature on changes in cognitive distortions and attitudes during offender treatment.

Clinical treatment programs basically use three instruments to assess cognitive distortions: the Abel-Becker Cognition Scale, the Justifications and Cognitive Distortions subscales of the Multiphasic Sex Inventory, and the series of attitudinal scales developed by Martha Burt (1980). Two other promising scales, the Rape and Molest Scales (Bumby, 1996), are also available.

ABEL-BECKER COGNITION SCALE

One of the original scales developed for assessing cognitive distortions, specifically in offenders against children, was the Abel-Becker Cognition Scale (Abel et al., 1984). The original scale was composed of 29 items rated on a 1-to-5 Likert scale. Items include such statements as "Sex between an adult and a child causes the child no emotional problems" and "A child will never have sex with an adult unless the child really wants to." Although enjoying widespread usage, the scale has limited data, as do many of the assessment instruments in the field. In addition, the scale has been criticized because of the transparent nature of the questions (Horley & Quinsey, 1994). Basic reliability and validity data are provided in an extensive dissertation (Gore, 1988) and summarized in a publication (Abel et al., 1989). Abel et al. (1989) suggest deletions of items 28 and 29, as they measure attitudes toward treatment rather than cognitions supporting molestation, and the deletion of item 19 of the original scale because of its failure to load on any of the factor–analytically derived subscales.

The overall scale has good test-retest reliability ($r = .76$), and the six-factor analytically derived subscales have good internal consistency (Cronbach alphas ranging from .59 to .84) and good test-retest reliability ranging from .64 to .77 (Abel et al., 1989; Gore, 1988). Gore (1988) also found significant differences between a sample of 240 offenders against children and 86 nonoffender controls; however, no differences were found between the child molesters and a group of 48 mixed pedophilic subjects. Stermac and Segal (1989) did find that the Abel-Becker Cognition Scale significantly discriminated child molesters from a number of control groups that included rapists, clinicians, law enforcement officers, and lawyers. Similarly, Hayashino, Wurtele, and Klebe (1995) found that extrafamilial molesters had higher scores than rapists, incarcerated nonsex offenders, laypersons, and incestuous child molesters. However, incestuous child molesters did not differ from other groups. In terms of social desirability, Stermac and Segal (1987) found a small ($r = .25$) but nonsignificant relationship between scores on the Abel-Becker Cognition Scale and scores on the Marlowe-Crowne Social Desirability Scale (Crowne & Marlowe, 1960).

Abel et al. (1989) and Gore (1988) also provide some evidence that the six factors of the cognition scale account for approximately 24 percent of the variance in terms of duration of child molestation and 11 percent of the variance for a number of different categories of molestation (male/female, incest/nonincest, child/adolescent). However, they account for little of the variance in terms of amount of aggression or number of attempted or completed acts of molestation.

In summary, the Abel-Becker Cognition Scale appears to have good test-retest reliability, and the factor-derived scores appear to have good internal consistency. There are some basic validity data; three studies have shown the ability to separate offenders from nonoffenders, and two studies have separated child molesters from rapists. However, there is still mixed evidence on whether incestuous offenders show similar distortions to extrafamilial offenders. The relationship of the Abel-Becker Cognition Scale to social desirability is basically unknown. Although Stermac and Segal (1987) did find a nonsignificant correlation, their sample size was relatively small. Until further data are available, one should assume, as with most instruments in the sex offender field, that responses can be minimized.

COGNITIVE DISTORTIONS AND IMMATURITY (CDI) SCALE AND JUSTIFICATIONS SCALE

The CDI and Justifications Scales are two subscales from the Multiphasic Sex Inventory (MSI) (Nichols & Molinder, 1984), a specialized instrument developed to assess a variety of issues relevant to sex offenders. The Justifications Scale is a 29-item scale measuring the degree to which the offender justifies his or her behavior, including psychological justifications, such as "My offense occurred as a result of my wife's lack of understanding of my needs," and items related to blaming the victim: "My sex offense would not have occurred if the victim had not been sexually loose." The CDI scale is described by Nichols and Molinder as assessing self-accountability and early childhood cognitions. It is specifically designed to measure the concept of victim stance and in some ways parallels the more general thinking errors as described by Yochelson and Samenow (1977); it appears to measure a more characterological trait. Although some items seem to clearly measure the concept of victim stance, such as "I feel like a victim as a result of the accusations against me," other items appear to fit under more traditional concepts of cognitive distortions ("My problem is not sexual, it is that I really love children"), and others appear to be related to denial of sexual feelings ("I became interested in sex after high school"). In the original MSI test manual (Nichols & Molinder, 1984), both of these scales are described as experimental, and the standardization samples for both were relatively small ($n = 31$). The original test manual provides little psychometric data, although other studies are now beginning to provide some support for the reliability and validity of this scale.

Simkins, Ward, Bowman, and Rinck (1989) report relatively good test-retest reliability for an outpatient sample of child molesters. Test-retest reliability for the CDI Scale was .71 and for the Justifications Scale .78. Kalichman, Henderson, Shealy, and Dwyer (1992) also present basic psychometric data related to this scale using a number of offender samples that included both incarcerated and nonincarcerated samples and child molester and rapist samples. They found that the Justifications Scale had good internal consistency (alpha = .82); however, as might be expected given the nature of the questions described above, the internal consistency of the CDI Scale was much lower (alpha = .53). The complexity of this scale is further supported by data from Simkins et al., who factor-analyzed subscales of the MSI. The Justifications Scale basically loaded on one factor, termed the dysfunction/justification factor, and the CDI Scale showed moderate loadings on three different factors: a sexual fantasy factor, the dysfunction/justification factor, and a negative load on what they termed a "normal" factor.

Kalichman et al. (1992) also found that the CDI Scale tended to correlate significantly with other measures of general emotional distress and psychopathology such as trait anger, trait anxiety, and a number of scales of the Minnesota Multiphasic Personality Inventory (MMPI) and was negatively correlated with self-esteem. The Justifications Scale, although showing some significant correlations with the other scales, generally had lower correlations with measures of emotional distress and psychopathology. In general, the results from Kalichman et al. also suggest that the CDI Scale had higher correlations with general psychopathology and appeared to be more influenced by social desirability than the Justifications Scale.

In terms of group differences, Simkins et al. (1989) found no differences on the Justifications Scale among extrafamilial abusers, intrafamilial abusers, and those who abused both intra- and extrafamilial victims. However, there were significant differences among these groups on the CDI Scale, where the intrafamilial group tended to score lower than the extrafamilial group or the mixed group. They also reported data regarding the sex of the victim, comparing subjects who molested males with those who molested females and with those who molested both males and females. Again, there were no differences among these groups on the Justifications Scale but significant differences on the CDI Scale; those with female victims scored lower, and those with male victims or both scored higher. However, it should be noted that this analysis is somewhat confounded with the extrafamilial-intrafamilial distinction, since the majority of those who victimized females were intrafamilial offenders. Simkins (1993) also found higher scores on the CDI Scale for a group of child molesters classified as sexually repressed versus those who were nonsexually repressed. This result is not surprising, given that some of the CDI items appear to be related to a denial of sexual feelings.

Finally, Simkins et al. (1989) found significant differences between deniers and nondeniers on the Justifications Scale: Those not denying and those partially denying scored higher than those in complete denial. No such differences were found on the CDI Scale. This raises one of the significant problems with the Justifications Scale of the MSI. The nature of the questions, which are usually in the framework of "my sex offense occurred because . . . ," requires an admission of having offended. Offenders in denial tend not to endorse any of the distortions because to endorse them is to admit that they have offended. Therefore, the scale's usefulness in deniers is limited.

Further support for the relationship of the CDI Scale to general psychopathology and emotional distress comes from two studies that used cluster analyses of MMPI profiles (Kalichman, 1990; Kalichman, Szymanowski, McKee, Taylor, & Craig, 1989). In both of these studies, the cluster-derived MMPI profile groups that tended to reflect the most severe psychopathology also produced the highest scores on the CDI Scale.

In general, the CDI and Justifications Scales are in widespread use, and some psychometric data are beginning to emerge. Both appear to have good test-retest reliability, at least in outpatient samples, and the Justifications Scale appears to have good internal consistency. The CDI Scale is more complex and tends to relate to general personality disturbance and emotional distress, which is not inconsistent with Nichols and Molinder's (1984) description of this scale as measuring more characterological functioning. The CDI Scale appears to be more influenced by social desirability than the Justifications Scale, but it also seems to be somewhat more sensitive to different subtypes of child molesters, at least in the one sample presented. However, in interpreting elevations on the CDI Scale, the user should remember the complex nature of the scale: In some offenders, it might be measuring general emotional distress rather than what are typically considered distortions. The primary advantage of the CDI and the Justifications Scales over the Abel-Becker Cognition Scale is that they are applicable to both rapists and child molesters. However, the Abel-Becker Cognition Scale probably covers a wider range of distortions used by child molesters than the Justifications and CDI Scales (Murphy, 1990).

BURT SCALES

The Burt scales (Burt, 1980) are six scales (Rape Myth Acceptance, Adversarial Sexual Beliefs, Sexual Conservatism, Sex Role Stereotyping, Sex Role Satisfaction, and Acceptance of Interpersonal Violence) that are subsumed under the category of attitudes supportive of rape. These scales have good internal consistency and Cronbach alphas above .78, except for the Acceptance of Interpersonal Violence Scale, which has a Cronbach alpha of .59. The majority of research has been with college student populations or general community samples involved in sexually coercive behavior in dating situations. Numerous studies have found significant correlations between these scales and self-reported sexually aggressive behavior (Koss & Dinero, 1987; Koss, Leonard, Beezley, & Oros, 1985; Malamuth, 1986; Malamuth, Sockloskie, Koss,

& Tanaka, 1991; Murphy, Coleman, & Haynes, 1986; Rapaport & Burkhart, 1984).

In general, the most widely used of the Burt scales (Rape Myth Acceptance, Sex Role Stereotyping, Adversarial Sexual Beliefs, and Acceptance of Interpersonal Violence) have considerable support as predictors of coercive behavior in nonforensic populations. However, there is a dearth of information on these scales in legally identified offenders. In addition, clinicians should realize that these scales are not factorially pure and are fairly highly intercorrelated (Briere, Malamuth, & Check, 1985).

RAPE AND MOLEST SCALES

Two scales (Bumby, 1996) have been developed to assess distortions of child molesters (Molest Scale) and rapists (Rape Scale). Although relatively new, the initial validation study by Bumby suggests that the scales have strong psychometric properties and appear promising for clinical and research use. The Molest Scale is a 38-item scale with strong internal consistency (alpha = .97) and a two-week test-retest reliability of .84. It shows moderate correlation with the Abel-Becker Cognition Scale (−.54) and the CDI Scale (.43), although a nonsignificant correlation with the Justifications Scale of the MSI. In an initial evaluation sample, the Molest Scale appeared to be relatively free of social desirability effects, and its correlation with the Marlowe-Crowne Social Desirability Scale was near zero and nonsignificant. The scale also discriminated child molesters from rapists and nonsexually offending inmates.

The Rape Scale is a 40-item scale that also has excellent internal consistency (alpha = .96) and test-retest reliability (r = .96). It is unrelated to social desirability and has small but significant correlations with the CDI Scale (.33) and the Justifications Scale (.34). However, it was not correlated with the Burt Rape Myth Scale. It significantly discriminated rapists from noninmate offenders, and although rapists' scores were higher on the Rape Scale than those of child molesters, this difference was not significant.

In further validation studies, the Molest Scale was found to correlate significantly with number of victims (r = .22) and years of offending (r = .33). The Rape Scale was also correlated with number of years of offending (r = .30) but not with number of victims. The two scales are moderately correlated with each other (r = .61).

At this point, the data related to the scales are limited to one study conducted with an incarcerated population. Further data are needed from other populations, including outpatient samples. In addition, the original sample consisted of individuals who had volunteered for treatment; therefore, they may have been a group who responded in a more open manner. The scales' use with more defensive offenders is unknown. However, the scales appear to have a number of positive features, including strong internal consistency and test-retest reliability and freedom from social desirability effects.

RELATIONSHIP OF DISTORTIONS TO TREATMENT OUTCOME

A number of studies have specifically measured cognitive distortions during treatment and/or looked at the relationship of various distortions to treatment outcome. Simkins et al. (1989) described the relationship of the CDI and Justifications Scales to therapists' rated treatment outcome (number of goals achieved, attitudes and behaviors, and likelihood of reoffending). The CDI Scale showed a small but significant (−.22) relationship with therapists' rated treatment outcome, suggesting that subjects with high scores on the CDI Scale had the poorest treatment outcome. The Justifications Scale showed a small but positive relationship to outcome (r = .15). In this study, neither scale showed a decrease over nine months of treatment. However, this program appeared to have a large dropout rate over the nine months and was said to be modeled after Giaretto's (1991) approach; therefore, it was not typical of cognitive-behavioral programs.

Abel et al. (1989) and Gore (1988) basically found no relationship between recidivism and scores on the Abel-Becker Cognition Scale.

Marques, Nelson, West, and Day (1994) also failed to find any relationship between the CDI and Justifications Scales and sexual recidivism. However, the CDI Scale was related to nonsexual violent offenses. This finding may not be surprising, given that the CDI Scale is considered an assessment of characterological functioning and may be related to more general criminal behavior rather than just sex offender behavior.

Although Simkins et al. (1989) did not find decreases in distortions and justifications, the majority of other studies have found decreases in denial and distortions in cognitive-behavioral programs. Miner, Marques, Day, and Nelson (1990) and Marques et al. (1994) found decreases on the CDI and Justifications Scales of the MSI among participants in their extensive relapse prevention program. Barbaree (1991) also found a significant decrease in denial and minimization in the group treatment program, including a decrease in scores on the Justifications Scale but no change in the CDI Scale. These findings might suggest that brief treatments focused on specific distortions may not address the more characterological types of thinking patterns assessed by the CDI Scale. Similarly, Marshall (1994), also describing a group treatment format, showed significant decreases in therapists' ratings of offender denial and minimization. In the original validation study of the Rape and Molest Scales, Bumby (1996) also showed significant decreases in scores on these two scales among subjects participating in an overall cognitive-behavioral program.

There are indications that other cognitive-behavioral treatments may also lead to decreases in subjects' self-reported ratings of distortions. Gore (1988) found decreases on the Abel-Becker Cognition Scale not only in subjects participating in a specific module designed to decrease cognitive distortions but also in subjects participating in treatments to reduce deviant arousal and in those participating in a treatment specifically designed to improve social skills and assertiveness. Similarly, Pithers (1994) described a specific group treatment module for increasing victim empathy and found that participants showed significant decreases on the Abel-Becker Cognition Scale and on the Burt Rape Myth Scale.

In general, the vast majority of data support the conclusion that cognitive-behavioral approaches do lead to decreases in denial, minimization, and distortion measured in a variety of ways. What is not clear at this point is whether such decreases actually relate to long-term outcome. It also appears, given the limited studies, that other types of cognitive-behavioral treatments may lead to reductions in distortions even when such beliefs are not the primary target for intervention.

TREATMENT APPROACHES

Clinical approaches to modify or restructure cognitive distortions and rape-supportive attitudes are generally based on traditional rational emotive therapy (RET) and cognitive-behavioral therapies adapted for use with sex offenders (Beck, 1976; Ellis; 1989; Ellis & Grieger, 1977; Lange, 1986; McMullin, 1986). Lange's (1986) integration of RET into contemporary sex offender treatment involves teaching the offender that the activating event (A) does not cause behavioral/emotional consequences (C). Offenders are further taught that their irrational beliefs (B) and cognitive distortions cause dysfunctional consequences. In essence, offenders learn to identify distorted beliefs by monitoring self-talk contents and logically or scientifically disputing (D) them (Ellis, 1989; Ellis & Grieger, 1977; McMullin, 1986). Key words and types of thoughts indicating distorted thinking include should, must, how awful, ought, unwarranted entitlements, absolutes, blaming, extremist thinking, self-pity, and so forth. These traditional approaches are based on teaching offenders to identify, analyze, challenge, and change specific distortions (i.e., justifications), irrational beliefs, and thinking errors to rational and realistic ones. These approaches have been successfully integrated into relapse prevention approaches (Jenkins-Hall, 1989; Lange, 1986).

As outlined by Murphy (1990), these approaches have four common themes: (1) education of patients about the role cognitions play in the development and maintenance of abusive sexual behavior, (2) interventions to assist patients in identifying distortions, (3) interventions geared to challenging and disputing offenders' distortions and replacing them with more rational and realistic thoughts, and (4) the development of an understanding of victim impact and victim empathy. It is not the purpose of this chapter to focus on issues related to victim empathy (see chapter 8), but clinicians need to be aware that accurate understanding of victim impact and development of victim empathy are integral parts of the treatment of cognitive distortions and minimizations. Offenders who truly understand victim impact and have truly developed victim empathy are unlikely to engage in distortions to justify or minimize their behavior.

GENERAL ORIENTATION AND APPROACH TO PATIENTS

Although specific techniques are important in restructuring offenders' distortions and beliefs, clinical experience suggests that it is important for patients to have an understanding of the role cognitions play in the maintenance and/or development of deviant behavior. Murphy's (1990) clinical example includes educating patients that (1) therapists recognize that offenders are not all bad and that they know right from wrong; (2) offenders develop methods of avoiding the negative feelings associated with their abusive behavior; (3) these methods are the things they tell themselves to try to convince themselves that what they are doing is not "too bad"; (4) challenging these beliefs is going to be difficult and painful, because they are going to have to take a realistic look at what they have done; and (5) their willingness to engage in this aspect of treatment is a good sign of their willingness to change.

In orienting patients to this form of treatment, a clinician is attempting to acknowledge that although the person's behavior is unacceptable, he or she will receive acceptance as a human being, that distortions are an expected part of the offending behavior, and that it is recognized that challenging them will be difficult. In addition to general orientation, the *style* of challenging distortions may also be important. If cognitive restructuring approaches are successful, offenders will be faced with recognizing the harm they have caused. For all but the most antisocial offenders, this is and probably should be emotionally painful. The clinician needs to be sensitive to this effect but to guard against the offender using his or her emotional pain to "wallow in self-pity" rather than using this recognition as a motivation to actually avoid future abusive behavior.

Disputing and challenging distortions will naturally be somewhat confrontational. However, therapists engaged in this endeavor need not become abusive (Marshall, 1994; Murphy, 1990); confrontations can be done in a matter-of-fact, nonangry way. Many clinicians have read the victim and police statements about an offense, and while listening to the offender's extreme distortions of the event, they feel angry about the degree of discrepancy. Although these feelings are normal, cognitive restructuring activities are not opportunities for clinicians to vent anger.

GENERAL GROUP INTERVENTIONS

Marshall (1994) and Barbaree (1991) described a group intervention, summarized here, that is similar to those used in many treatment programs. The intervention begins with the patients providing written and oral histories of their offenses to their group and therapist. The history might provide details about events preceding the offense; the thoughts and feelings during and after the offense; the methods used to manipulate, coerce, or force the victims; the specific sexual behaviors engaged in; and the offenders' perception of the victims' reactions.

Following this disclosure, group members are encouraged to challenge the minimizations and distortions noted, and the therapist may read a summary of the official statements by the victim and the police. The group members again challenge each offender regarding the discrepancies in this history; the process is repeated until the offender can provide a history free of minimizations and distortions.

Within this process, we have found it helpful to begin the process of educating offenders about why their distortions are "distortions." For example, if one of the offender's distortions was, "The child did not say no," we would educate the offender about the difficulties victims have saying no to authorities, especially to parent figures. We might also discuss the grooming process prior to the offense that basically set the child up not to say no. If an offender made a statement that the sexual activity did not seem to harm the victims, we would begin providing basic education regarding what we know about long-term victim impact. Although the assumption may be that offenders know that their distortions are distortions, this may not always be true. Because offenders spend many years convincing themselves that what they are doing is not causing harm, we need to counter those thoughts with accurate information.

Abel et al. (1984) described another variance of this approach using a role-reversal procedure. In this procedure, the therapist plays the offender and uses the offender's distortions; the offender plays a family member of the victim or a police or probation officer whose job is to challenge these distortions. Such role playing requires that the offender not only have the ability to recognize the distortions but also be able to dispute and challenge them in another person.

Another approach to assist offenders in recognizing distortions is to have the members of the group name all the distortions they have either used or heard others use. They are written on a board. Most offender groups can produce a list of 50 to 100 specific distortions and minimizations in a relatively short time. Over the years, we have compiled lists of these offender-generated

distortions. Following the group exercise, the list is presented to the offenders, who are asked to check all the distortions they have applied. If they check a large number of distortions, they are asked to rank in order the 5 or 10 distortions they use most frequently. Then they are instructed to explain in writing why each statement is a distortion and to write an appropriate counterstatement. The counterstatements are brought back to the group for further discussion and refinement. The aim is for the offenders to (1) recognize their distortions; (2) clearly understand why they are distortions, including explanatory factual information; and (3) to be able to replace them with more realistic and rational thoughts.

These examples are fairly similar to approaches used in most programs. Most programs also use various listing procedures and homework formats that require offenders to list their distortions along with counters or challenges. An example of a "reprogramming format" is displayed in the appendix. In this format, the offender selects a distortion, defines it, and provides a list of the different ways it is used in his or her cycle and throughout the offender's lifestyle. The offender indicates on a numerical scale the magnitude of the problem. The offender then lists a variety of counters to defuse the distortion.

It is also important for the clinician to realize that in addition to these specific techniques, the challenging of distortions and minimizations is an ongoing process throughout offender treatment. Regardless of what component of treatment is being engaged, the clinician must be alert to offenders' use of distortions and minimizations. As time passes, offenders will use blatant and obvious distortions less often, turning to more subtle ones. In addition, the clinician needs to recognize how offenders are generalizing their understanding of distortions to the rest of the environment. When an offender is verbally stating an understanding of distortions and showing an ability to challenge them but is still engaging in manipulative behaviors outside the therapy situation, it is fairly obvious that the offender has not made the necessary changes of belief and thought.

JOURNALING TECHNIQUES

Journaling techniques, which are forms of self-monitoring, allow ongoing monitoring of distortions. Journals or diaries are written logs in which offenders record significant and insignificant experiences. The types of experiences recorded include triggers or high-risk situations, seemingly unimportant or insignificant decisions and events, stressors, interpersonal conflicts, reflections on past developmental or historical experiences, interpersonal relationships, past offenses, boredom, deviant fantasies, deviant thinking and behaviors, and urges and reactions to them (thoughts, feelings, behaviors, and physiological responses). Journal formats may include daily entries with the date, day, time, event, and reaction. Once the reaction is recorded, the offender can reflect on daily entries and highlight the distortions. In a new entry, the distortion can be written out with counterstatements.

AUTOBIOGRAPHIES OR LIFE HISTORIES

Many programs require offenders to write lengthy autobiographies. These autobiographies include the significant events in offenders' lives and their perceptions of and reactions to them. These autobiographies generally include histories of abuse, deviant fantasies, offenses, and significant positive and negative experiences. In providing such histories, offenders may reveal numerous distortions and a number of criminal thinking errors in their perceptions and descriptions of events. These thinking errors may include their difficulties with delaying gratification, their me-first attitude, or their general bullying style. The therapist can review these autobiographies and use them to assist the offenders to identify specific distortions and thinking errors that have occurred throughout their lives.

USE OF DEVIANT FANTASIES TO CONFRONT DISTORTIONS

Murphy (1990) described the use of specific behavioral techniques, such as verbal satiation or masturbatory satiation, to challenge distortions as well as to reduce sexual arousal. In this application of the technique, the offender is required to verbalize his or her deviant fantasies in detail and repeatedly into a tape recorder. Initially, these fantasies include multiple distortions and minimizations. These tapes are reviewed with the offender, either in individual therapy or within the group, with the therapist stopping the tape each time a minimization or distortion is heard. The therapist then challenges the distortion (generally through the use of Socratic questions), provides specific information to dispute the distortion, and helps the offender identify a more rational, realistic appraisal of the situation. As treatment progresses, the offender is required to signal the therapist whenever he or she notes a minimization or distortion on the tape and to specify to the therapist why it is a distortion and what a more realistic self-statement would be.

Another variation on this technique is having offenders rewrite their deviant fantasies. A simple procedure consists of having the patients write out their deviant fantasies, highlight the distorted thoughts, and rewrite the deviant fantasies without distorted beliefs and deviant behaviors, with the goal being to create a normal fantasy. Again, there is an opportunity to educate clients about the impact their behavior has on victims.

SUMMARY

This chapter reviewed current theoretical models of the role cognitions play in sex offending and outlined the empirical data. We also outlined some specific treatment approaches drawn primarily from the literature or from the authors' own practices. In 1990, Murphy wrote a chapter on cognitive distortions. At that time, limited data were available. In the last five years, the empirical literature has increased, providing more reliability and validity data on the scales used to measure distortions; some basic data on the nature of these distortions are also appearing. Evidence is being presented that cognitive-behavioral approaches do lead to changes in distortions, although whether this is a general or a specific treatment effect is not known. We are still lacking proof that changing these distortions actually relates to long-term outcome; the outcome data are mixed at this point. As is often the case in the offender treatment field, more data are needed. However, there have been some significant advances in our knowledge, a number of clinical procedures are available that appear to be effective, and we have at least the beginning of an empirical base to demonstrate the effects of these treatment components. Further work on whether cognitions have etiological significance or play a role in maintaining abusive behavior is still needed, as are studies looking at the role of cognitive distortions in long-term treatment.

REFERENCES

Abel, G.G., Becker, J.V., Cunningham-Rathner, J., Rouleau, J.L., Kaplan, M., & Reich, J. (1984). *Treatment manual: The treatment of child molesters.* Atlanta: Emory University.

Abel, G.G., Gore, D.K., Holland, C.L., Camp, N., Becker, J.V., & Rathner, J. (1989). The measurement of the cognitive distortions of child molesters. *Annals of Sex Research,* 2, 135–152.

Barbaree, H.E. (1991). Denial and minimization among sex offenders: Assessment and treatment outcome. *Forum on Corrections Research,* 3, 30–33.

Beck, A.T. (1976). Cognitive therapy and the emotional disorders. New York: International Universities Press.

Briere, J., Malamuth, N., & Check, J.V.P. (1985). Sexuality and rape-supportive beliefs. *International Journal of Women's Studies,* 8, 398–403.

Bumby, K.M. (1996). Assessing the cognitive distortions of child molesters and rapists: Development and validation of the Molest and Rape Scales. *Sexual Abuse: A Journal of Research and Treatment,* 8, 37–54.

Burt, M.R. (1980). Cultural myths and supports for rape. *Journal of Personality and Social Psychology,* 38, 217–230.

Crowne, D., & Marlowe, D. (1960). A new scale of social desirability independent of psychopathology. *Journal of Consulting Psychology,* 24, 349–354.

Ellis, A. (1989). Rational emotional therapy. In A. Corsini & D. Wedding (Eds.), *Current psychotherapies* (pp. 197–238). Itasca, IL: F.E. Peacock.

Ellis, A., & Grieger, R. (1977). *Handbook of rational-emotive therapy.* New York: Springer.

Giaretto, H. (1991). A comprehensive child sexual abuse treatment program. *Child Abuse and Neglect,* 6, 263–278.

Gore, D.K. (1988). *Cognitive distortions of child molesters and the cognition scale: Reliability, validity, treatment effects, and prediction of recidivism.* Unpublished doctoral dissertation, Georgia State University, Atlanta.

Hayashino, D.S., Wurtele, S.K., & Klebe, K.J. (1995). Child molesters: An examination of cognitive factors. *Journal of Interpersonal Violence,* 10, 106–116.

Horley, J., & Quinsey, V.L. (1994). Assessing the cognitions of child molesters: Use of the semantic differential with incarcerated offenders. *Journal of Sex Research,* 31, 171–178.

Jenkins-Hall, K. (1989). Cognitive restructuring. In D.R. Laws (Ed.), *Relapse prevention with sex offenders* (pp. 207–215). New York: Guilford Press.

Kalichman, S.C. (1990). Affective and personality characteristics of MMPI profile subgroups of incarcerated rapists. *Archives of Sexual Behavior,* 19, 443–459.

Kalichman, S.C., Henderson, M.C., Shealy, L.S., & Dwyer, M. (1992). Psychometric properties of the Multiphasic Sex Inventory in assessing sex offenders. *Criminal Justice and Behavior,* 19, 384–396.

Kalichman, S.C., Szymanowski, D., McKee, J., Taylor, J., & Craig, M. (1989). Cluster analytically derived MMPI profile subgroups of incarcerated adult rapists. *Journal of Clinical Psychology,* 45, 149–155.

Koss, M.P., & Dinero, T.E. (1987, January). *Predictors of sexual aggression among a national sample of male college students.* Paper presented at the New York Academy of Sciences Conference on Human Sexual Aggression: Current Perspectives, New York.

Koss, M.P., Leonard, K.E., Beezley, D.A., & Oros, C.J. (1985). Nonstranger sexual aggression: A discriminant analysis of the psychological characteristics of undetected offenders. *Sex Roles,* 12, 981–992.

Lange, A. (1986). *Rational-emotive therapy: A treatment manual.* Tampa, FL: Florida Mental Health Institute.

Malamuth, N.M. (1986). Predictors of naturalistic sexual aggression. *Journal of Personality and Social Psychology,* 50, 953–962.

Malamuth, N.M., Sockloskie, R.J., Koss, M.P., & Tanaka, J.S. (1991). Characteristics of aggressors against women: Testing a model using a national sample of college students. *Journal of Consulting and Clinical Psychology,* 59, 670–681.

Marques, J.K., Nelson, C., West, M.A., & Day, D.M. (1994). The relationship between treatment goals and recidivism among child molesters. *Behaviour Research and Therapy,* 32, 577–588.

Marshall, W.L. (1994). Treatment effects on denial and minimization in incarcerated sex offenders. *Behaviour Research and Therapy,* 32, 559–564.

McMullin, R.E. (1986). *Handbook of cognitive therapy techniques.* New York: W.W. Norton.

Miner, M.H., Marques, J.K., Day, D.M., & Nelson, C. (1990). Impact of relapse prevention in treating sex offenders: Preliminary findings. *Annals of Sex Research,* 3, 165–185.

Murphy, W.D. (1990). Assessment and modification of cognitive distortions in sex offenders. In W.L. Marshall, D.R. Laws, & H.E. Barbaree (Eds.), *Handbook of sexual assault: Issues, theories, and treatment of the offender* (pp. 331–342). New York: Plenum Press.

Murphy, W.D., Coleman, E.M., & Haynes, M.R. (1986). Factors related to coercive sexual behavior in a nonclinical sample of males. *Violence and Victims,* 1, 255–278.

Nichols, H.R., & Molinder, I. (1984). *Multiphasic Sex Inventory manual.* Tacoma, WA: Authors.

Pithers, W.D. (1994). Process evaluation of a group therapy component designed to enhance sex offenders' empathy for sexual abuse survivors. *Behaviour Research and Therapy,* 32, 565–570.

Pollock, N.L., & Hashmill, J.M. (1991). The excuses of child molesters. *Behavioral Sciences and the Law,* 9, 53–59.

Rapaport, K., & Burkhart, B.R. (1984). Personality and attitudinal characteristics of sexually coercive college males. *Journal of Abnormal Psychology,* 93, 216–221.

Segal, Z.V., & Stermac, L.E. (1990). The role of cognition in sexual assault. In W.L. Marshall, D.R. Laws, & H.E. Barbaree (Eds.), *Handbook of sexual assault: Issues, theories, and treatment of the offender* (pp. 161–174). New York: Plenum Press.

Simkins, L. (1993). Characteristics of sexually repressed child molesters. *Journal of Interpersonal Violence,* 8, 3–17.

Simkins, L., Ward, W., Bowman, S., & Rinck, C.M. (1989). The Multiphasic Sex Inventory: Diagnosis and prediction of treatment response in child sexual abusers. *Annals of Sex Research,* 2, 205–226.

Stermac, L.E., & Segal, Z.V. (1987, November). *Cognitive assessment of child molesters.* Paper presented at the 21st annual convention of the Association for the Advancement of Behavior Therapy, Boston.

Stermac, L.E. & Segal, Z.V. (1989). Adult sexual contact with children: An examination of cognitive factors. *Behavior Therapy,* 20, 573–584.

Stermac, L.E., Segal, Z.V., & Gillis, R. (1990). Social and cultural factors in sexual assault. In W.L. Marshall, D.R. Laws, & H.E. Barbaree (Eds.), *Handbook of sexual assault: Issues, theories, and treatment of the offender* (pp. 143–159). New York: Plenum Press.

Yochelson, S., & Samenow, S.E. (1977). *The criminal personality: Vol. 2. The change process.* New York: Jason Aronson.

APPENDIX
COUNTERING COGNITIVE DISTORTIONS, THINKING ERRORS, AND DEFENSES

Date: _____

Name: _____

Number: _____

Select one cognitive distortion, thinking error, or defense and complete A, B, C, and D.

Some common cognitive distortions and defenses include: denial, lying, justifying (making excuses), blaming, minimizing, entitlement, power, depersonalization, pride, vagueness, poor me/self-pity, avoidance, dumping, trashing, unrealistic expectations, walling or blocking, extreme magnification, ownership, negative thinking, phoniness, apathy.

A. Definition of _____:

_____

_____

_____

B. How do I use _____
in my offending and/or offending cycle?

1. _____
2. _____
3. _____
4. _____
5. _____
6. _____
7. _____
8. _____
9. _____
10. _____

Scale:
(small problem) 1 2 3 4 5 6 (big problem)

C. How do I use _____
in my lifestyle or in general everyday life?

1. _____
2. _____
3. _____
4. _____
5. _____
6. _____
7. _____
8. _____
9. _____
10. _____

Scale:
current problem—
(small problem) 1 2 3 4 5 6 (big problem)

past problem—
(small problem) 1 2 3 4 5 6 (big problem)

Select one cognitive distortion, thinking error, or defense and develop counters to defuse it.

D. List of counters to _____:

1. _____
2. _____
3. _____
4. _____
5. _____
6. _____
7. _____
8. _____
9. _____
10. _____

5 Relapse Prevention and the Sexual Assault Cycle

Mark S. Carich
Alison Gray
Sacha Rombouts
Mark Stone
William D. Pithers

Relapse prevention and the sexual assault cycle are theoretical models purporting to describe the cognitions and behaviors of sex offenders before, during, and after their abusive acts. The relapse process and the assault cycle delineate a series of internal and external landmarks experienced as a sex offender nears the commission of another abusive behavior. Both models propose that the progression toward abuse can be disrupted if offenders are aware of their abuse precursors, successful in detecting them, able to employ relevant coping strategies, and motivated to do so. Each model articulates a structured approach to treatment, enhancing both the integrity of service delivery by healthcare professionals and the clients' comprehension of the treatment model.

In learning that relapse is a process occurring over time, offenders discover that they have many opportunities to control their behaviors to avoid abusing again. Offenders report experiencing greater hopefulness about their potential to change as they begin to unearth the patterns of behaviors that preceded their abuses, with each precursor to past offenses now viewed as an opportunity to avoid reoffending.

The process of relapse is comparable to a "local" train, making frequent stops. The frequent stops give passengers the opportunity to repeatedly check to avoid missing their stops. Should a traveler on a local train become inattentive and miss the intended stop, the passenger can quickly correct the error by getting off at the next stop and doubling back. Although it may be embarrassing to admit that one has committed such a simple mistake, the error is minor and often easily reversed. Sex offenders can learn that their abusive pattern is like a local train, with many opportunities to get off the relapse train and reverse their course. Although most sex offenders seem to ride local trains, some (e.g., sociopaths, career criminals) ride express trains toward recidivism that, once boarded, irrevocably carry them to the end of the line. However, most sex offenders can learn that there are many potential stops before they reach relapse.

Relapse prevention and the abuse cycle propose that sexual abusers can develop detailed maps containing a number of landmarks that allow them to estimate where they are on the train toward relapse. The prevention map shows where the exits are located. During treatment, offenders are given practice in identifying these exits and using them quickly.

This chapter summarizes the evolution of relapse prevention and the sexual assault cycle, compares the two theoretical models, presents a revision of a prior effort to integrate the two models, and describes the application of relapse prevention in clinical settings.

HISTORY OF ADAPTING RELAPSE PREVENTION FOR SEX OFFENDERS

Relapse prevention was originally developed by Alan Marlatt as a method of maintaining change in substance abusers who had participated in other forms of treatment. As originated by Marlatt, relapse prevention remained exclusively a method of avoiding risky situations and rehearsing coping strategies to mitigate the influence of high-risk situations that could not be avoided.

In the late 1970s, William Pithers and Janice Marques discussed adapting Marlatt's traditional relapse prevention approaches to sex offender treatment. In 1982, the Vermont Treatment Program for Sexual Aggressors, created by Pithers, was the first to employ relapse prevention with sex offenders. The initial publication introducing the concept appeared in 1983 (Pithers, Marques, Gibat, & Marlatt, 1983). In 1984, the state of California funded the Sex Offender Treatment Evaluation Project, directed by Marques, which was intended to assess the efficacy of relapse prevention with sex offenders. Thus, as recently as 1983, only two sex offender treatment programs were using relapse prevention. Each of these programs employed a straightforward modification of Marlatt's self-management model.

Pithers and his colleagues in Vermont grew dissatisfied with their initial adaptation of Mar-

latt's self-management model of relapse prevention. Their experience suggested that Marlatt's original model assisted sex offenders' self-management only if the offenders' lives remained free of notable distress. As the everyday challenges of life accumulated, some abusers elected to deviate from their self-control strategies, occasionally lapsing in relatively minor ways and sometimes reoffending. Many abusers reported that their initial indulgences, or lapses in self-management, were intended to relieve distress. Lapse behaviors (e.g., masturbating to a deviant fantasy) were being used in maladaptive attempts to alleviate perceived distress. Although such behaviors permitted a temporary reduction in stress, the final outcome of maladaptive coping responses was a heightened level of distress, since the abuser was one step closer to relapsing. The original relapse prevention model bolstered self-management when offenders were already functioning effectively but decayed in the face of distress.

Marlatt (1993) recently reported that the self-management dimension of relapse prevention, when used with substance abusers, demonstrates no greater long-term efficacy than other interventions. Stitzer and Cox (1996) observed, "it appears likely that a single distinct cause of relapse will not be discovered. Rather, there appear to be a multiplicity of intra- and extra-organismic factors associated with relapses" (p. 3). Thus, the determinants of relapse are not only multiple in nature but sometimes extrinsic to the offender. Given this premise, the limited effect of a relapse prevention model based entirely on enhanced self-management is quite notable.

Frustrated by the limitations of the self-management dimension of relapse prevention, Pithers and colleagues instituted several modifications (Pithers, 1986; Pithers, Cumming, Beal, Young, & Turner, 1989; Pithers, Kashima, Cumming, Beal, & Buell, 1988). First, they developed a process for selectively informing community members about the offenders' risk factors and coping strategies. This modification was motivated by two beliefs: People attempting to control compulsive behaviors will benefit from supportive confrontation by those who know them well; and community members will, at critical moments, be more reliable informants about offenders' behaviors than the offenders. Pithers initially referred to this new element of relapse prevention as the "external supervisory dimension" but more recently has called it the "prevention team" (Gray & Pithers, 1993).

A second modification, although not specific to relapse prevention, was devised to amplify offenders' motivation to use the knowledge they gained about how to interrupt the relapse process. Pithers recommended that, under optimal circumstances, interventions designed to enhance empathy for sexual abuse survivors should be introduced prior to relapse prevention groups. Instead of approaching relapse prevention simply as an interesting intellectual exercise promoting greater self-knowledge, sex offenders began to demonstrate recognition of the importance of *employing* their knowledge, even during those moments when they would rather not.

The prevention team is central to the efficacy of relapse prevention with sex offenders and may prove important with other populations as well. It is critical to note that relapse prevention–based treatment programs reporting less favorable outcome data than others have tended to neglect the importance of external supervision and of *training* members of the external network on the relapse prevention model, or they have had such a low density of offenders distributed throughout a wide geographic area that highly specialized supervision was impractical. Given the conclusion of Stitzer and Cox (1996) that relapses are attributable to internal and external factors, treatment programs employing only the self-management aspect of relapse prevention are not likely to attain the most favorable outcomes.

Since the mid-1980s, interest in relapse prevention has grown explosively. In 1989, Laws edited a highly regarded book, *Relapse Prevention with Sex Offenders*, which contained information from programs in Vermont, California, and Florida. As Laws stated in that text, relapse prevention has become a significant part of con-

temporary sex offender treatment, expanding from utilization at only two sites in 1985 to nearly 90 percent of all the practitioners in North America working with sex offenders in 1994 (Freeman-Longo, Bird, Stevenson, & Fiske, 1995). In addition to its widespread use in North America, relapse prevention serves as the foundation for adult sex offender treatment programs in Australia, New Zealand, and the United Kingdom.

Relapse prevention has been adapted for juveniles (Steen, 1993) and for children with sexual behavior problems (Gray & Pithers, 1993; Pithers & Gray, 1990). Gray, Busconi, Houchens, and Pithers (1996) found that their modification of relapse prevention for children with sexual behavior problems and their families resulted in statistically significant change in objective behavioral rating instruments (e.g., the Child Sexual Behavior Inventory, the Child Behavior Checklist) after only 16 weeks of treatment and that this treatment method appeared to be most effective with specific subtypes of children.

One manifestation of the surging interest in relapse prevention is the emergence of a virtual cottage industry that has produced a variety of excellent workbooks and treatment manuals for use with offenders (Bays & Freeman-Longo, 1989; Bays, Freeman-Longo, & Hildebran, 1990; Eldridge, 1995; Freeman-Longo & Bays, 1988), audiotapes for therapist training (Freeman-Longo & Pithers, 1992), and videotapes for use with offenders in treatment programs (Freeman-Longo & Pithers, 1992).

GOALS OF RELAPSE PREVENTION

Nearly all variations of relapse prevention intend to accomplish the same general and specific goals. General goals of relapse prevention include:

1. Teaching each offender skills that are central to avoiding another offense, including

an enhanced ability to detect the earliest signs of risk and reliable coping responses that may be used to lessen risk.

2. Developing external sources of supervision, involving people who are explicitly aware of the offender's crime, risk factors, and coping strategies and who have been trained in the relapse prevention model.

Specific goals of relapse prevention include assisting the offender to:

1. Gain a thorough comprehension of the key concepts of the relapse prevention model, since the model can be used only to the extent that the offender understands it.

2. Learn effective methods of self-monitoring, such as journaling, since these skills are essential to the detection of risk factors.

3. Identify specific risk factors, triggering events, and other precursors to abuse.

4. Learn specific indicators (i.e., cues) that signify when risk factors are imminent or present.

5. Employ specific interventions to disrupt the relapse process.

6. Inform individuals involved in the offender's day-to-day environment about the relapse process so that they can assist his or her self-management through confrontation and support.

In essence, relapse prevention focuses on creating multiple sources of informed and effective supervision, fostering the offender's skills in identifying risk factors that promote the potential to reoffend, and enhancing the offender's ability to avoid or cope with risk factors. The ultimate goal, of course, is the prevention of additional victimizations.

DETERMINANTS OF RELAPSE AND THE COGNITIVE-BEHAVIORAL MODEL OF RELAPSE: Traditional Relapse Prevention

As originally outlined by Marlatt and modified by Pithers and colleagues (Gray & Pithers, 1993; Pithers, 1990; Pithers, Marques, Gibat, & Marlatt, 1983), the relapse process was a linear, staged model. Figure 5.1 reflects the sequence of specific relapse determinants that sex offenders may experience as they progress closer to the point of reoffending. The figure depicts the "cognitive-behavioral model of relapse," which was the initial attempt to explain the chain of cognitive and behavioral events experienced as sex offenders move from being in adequate behavioral control to abusing again. In reviewing these processes and models, readers are cautioned not to conclude that *all* offenders necessarily pass through *all* the stages of each diagram exactly as they are depicted. Although these diagrams present a common pathway toward offenses, the essence of relapse prevention is that it must be applied uniquely to each offender. Treatment effects will be greatest when interventions are adapted to each offender's treatment and supervision needs.

Pithers et al. (1988) analyzed the precursors to relapse in 136 pedophiles and 64 rapists. They identified multiple determinants of sexual aggression. A common sequence of changes in the behavior of the offender appeared to precede a sexual offense: a change in affect ⇒ fantasy ⇒ justification ⇒ passive planning ⇒ disinhibition ⇒ acting out.

The first determinant of relapse observed in many offenders was a change in predominant affect. This affect often seemed to be responsive to a disruption in the offender's homeostasis, reflecting an underlying event such as a lifestyle imbalance, a critical interpersonal event, or simply boredom. Negative emotions (e.g., anger, depression, anxiety) were the predominant affective determinants, but positive emotions preceded relapses in some offenders.

FIGURE 5.1   A COGNITIVE-BEHAVIORAL MODEL OF THE RELAPSE PROCESS

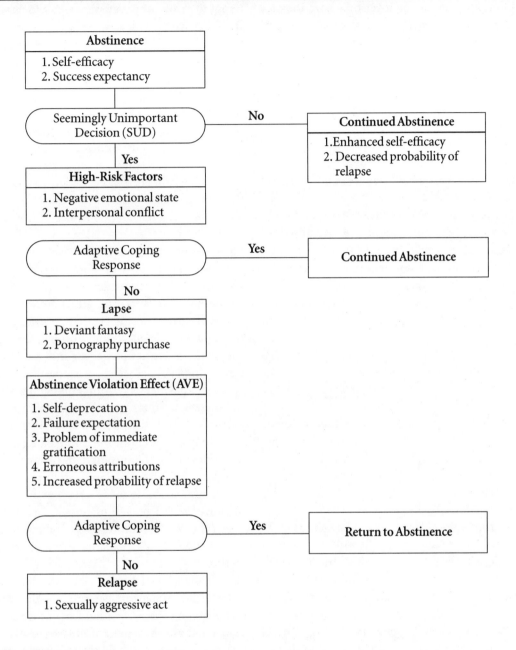

This change in affect required the offender to do something to return to homeostasis. If the affect was used to mobilize a constructive activity (e.g., exercising, asserting concerns), the abuser's likelihood of a significant lapse or a complete relapse was diminished. If the offender responded maladaptively to the affective arousal (e.g., masturbating as an escape from oppressive loneliness), the likelihood of a serious lapse increased, which created greater opportunity for relapse. In Pithers's model, the determinant of relapse that most commonly followed a maladaptive effort to deal with affective arousal was an abusive fantasy.

These abusive fantasies often entailed both sexual and nonsexual content. Offenders imagined themselves screaming a vitriolic stream of obscenities at an employer by whom they felt belittled or battering a spouse whom they perceived as challenging their authority. Some offenders masturbated to their fantasies about sexual abuse. Since the offender's fantasy either was congruent with the affective state (e.g., thoughts of yelling at an employer when angry) or offered relief from the affective state (e.g., a lonely pedophile's thoughts about being sexual with a child), the abusive fantasy was reinforced, becoming increasingly frequent and appearing across time.

Passive planning involved seemingly undirected ruminations about the circumstances that might enable an abusive act to be performed. Although not consciously directed, this process actually represented an opportunity for the abuser to refine conditions that might foster an offense and minimize chances of discovery. An equivalent process is used by nonabusers when, for example, they are generally dissatisfied with their life circumstances and idly think of all the places they'd rather live, even while watching television.

"Cognitive distortions" were used to create excuses about why the desired and abusive behavior was rational (e.g., "If she didn't really want to have sex with me, she wouldn't have touched my arm *like that* and looked at me *that way*").

Disinhibition involved indulgence in some activity that reduced the offender's own prohibitions against abusive acts (e.g., imbibing alcohol); that sexualized a situation with an intended victim (e.g., showing adult erotica to children); or that might enable the abuser to explain his or her behavior as the result of unusual circumstances, often using a cognitive distortion in the process (e.g., "I took ecstasy that night and I *never* do drugs"). The sexually abusive act typically occurred shortly afterward.

In practice, disinhibitors had similarities to, and differences from, cognitive distortions. Cognitive distortions enabled offenders to justify why it was acceptable to *think about* acting out an abusive behavior or a potential victim. In

contrast, offenders used disinhibitors in an attempt to justify why they were about to *engage* in the behavior.

Pithers's model of relapse prevention proposes that these specific determinants of relapse are embedded in the distinct relapse process depicted in Figure 5.1—the cognitive-behavioral model of relapse. First, we assume that the individual experiences a sense of perceived control while maintaining abstinence, and that this perception of self-control grows until the person encounters a high-risk situation. A high-risk situation is one that threatens an individual's sense of control and thus increases the risk of relapse. If an individual in a high-risk situation enacts a coping response (e.g., resisting an urge to purchase pornography), the probability of relapse decreases. But if an individual fails to cope successfully with a high-risk situation, a decreased sense of control and associated feelings of helplessness ensue. If these reactions occur in a situation containing cues associated with past sexually abusive behaviors (e.g., a hitchhiking female), the stage is set for a probable relapse. This is particularly true if the person also holds positive expectancies about the immediate effects of performing the prohibited behavior. A rapist might focus on the immediate effects of performing a sexual assault, such as a feeling of power and a release of hostile emotions, rather than being mindful of the full ramifications of the act, particularly to the intended victim.

In the sequence of determinants preceding sexual aggression, the first determinant that discriminates most sex offenders from other individuals is the *predominance* of fantasies involving sexual aggression. Specific changes in affective state provide the abuser with the earliest possible information relevant to self-management, but affective states may not reliably differentiate abusers and nonabusers. Therefore, the first occurrence of fantasy about performing a sexually aggressive act may be considered the first significant *lapse*. Recurrence of sexually aggressive *behaviors* is defined as a *relapse*.

Whether a lapse becomes a relapse depends on a number of factors, one of which is called the abstinence violation effect (AVE). A major source of the AVE is a conflict between the individual's previous self-image as an abstainer and his or her recent experience of a prohibited behavior (e.g., deviant sexual fantasy). To the extent that the person views a lapse as a personal failure, the expectancy for continued failure increases, and the chances of a full-blown relapse also grow.

Ward, Hudson, and Marshall (1994) also suggest that the AVE, in which the offender engages in self-recrimination, occurs only after abuse has occurred. We agree that this may be true in at least three circumstances: with offenders who have yet to derive significant gains from treatment, with career criminals who engage in sexually abusive acts as part of an entirely indiscriminate pattern of antisocial acts, and with highly sociopathic offenders. With sex offenders who have had prolonged exposure to treatment, if a sense of remorse is not present after the abuser experiences a significant lapse (e.g., finding an abusive fantasy appealing), one might have reason to be concerned about the quality of treatment. An argument can be made that as offenders make therapeutic gains (e.g., increased recognition of the harmfulness of their abusive acts), they may begin to experience some semblance of the AVE at earlier and earlier points in the cognitive-behavioral model of relapse (Hanson, 1996). Career criminals may not experience the AVE at all, since they have made the lifestyle choice to violate others' rights (Pithers, 1993). Similarly, sociopathic individuals are, by definition, not likely to be concerned about the effects of their conduct on others.

Thus far, the relapse process has been depicted from the point at which a person encounters a high-risk situation. Relapse prevention also examines events that precede a high-risk situation. Although some sex offenders relapse in situations that would have been difficult to anticipate, the majority (in our experience) appear to set the scene for relapse by placing themselves in high-risk situations. One can covertly set up a relapse by making a series of seemingly unimportant decisions (SUDs) or seemingly insignificant decisions (SIDs), each of which represents a step toward a high-risk situation.

MODIFICATIONS OF OFFENSE PRECURSORS: RISK FACTORS AND RELAPSE CUES

There are different ways to look at offense precursors that occur within the offending process. As discussed earlier, in traditional relapse prevention, Pithers and colleagues initially viewed SUDs as leading to high-risk situations or factors, both precursors to an offense. Offense precursors are overt or covert events that occur prior to the offense.

Risk factors are any overt or covert event that brings or places the offender closer to offending (Carich, 1996, 1997; Cumming & Buell, 1997; Freeman-Longo & Pithers, 1992). By definition, risk factors could be both offense precursors and cursors. In this chapter, as well as in the relapse prevention literature, the term *risk factors* is often used interchangeably with *triggering events* (Freeman-Longo & Pithers, 1992; Laws, 1989, 1995a). In this context, a triggering event is any internal or external event or situation that initiates, stimulates, or "triggers" an offending-related response (i.e., cycle behavior, lapse, or relapse) or any part of the offense chain.

Risk factors and/or triggering events have been categorized several different ways, besides the previous distinctions between SUDs and risk factors. Pithers and colleagues modified the concept of risk factors by subdividing them into three categories: predisposing (historical and developmental risk factors), perpetuating (ongoing situations), and precipitating (occurring immediately prior to the offense). Each category was subdivided by thoughts, feelings, and behaviors (Freeman-Longo & Pithers, 1992; Gray & Pithers, 1993; Laws, 1995a). In general, risk factors can also be categorized by content (substance), intensity, and temporality or time of occurrence. The above categories consist of both time and content. Types of content categories include cognition, affect, behavior, situations, interpersonal relationships, and context (Carich & Stone, 1992b). Categories of intensity range from low risk (i.e., seemingly unimportant, insignificant decisions or events that can lead to high risk, lapse, or actually relapse) to high risk (i.e., a high potential to trigger and lapse and/or relapse) (Carich & Stone, 1992b). It is important that offenders understand the concepts of SUDs and low and high risk factors, that they identify their own low- and high-risk factors, and that they have well-developed interventions in place.

Another major type of offense precursor is relapse cues. Relapse cues are any type of event that serves as a warning of a potential or actual risk factor or situation, lapse, or relapse. Cues are warnings, signals, or red flags to the offender concerning potential problems and problematic situations. Like triggers, cues can be categorized by content, process, and temporality or time of occurrence. Content cues include cognitive, affective, behavioral, social, physiological, contextual, or situational (Bays, Freeman-Longo, & Hildebran, 1990; Carich & Stone, 1992a, 1993, 1996; Freeman-Longo & Pithers, 1992). Temporal cues (first outlined by Bays, Freeman-Longo, & Hildebran, 1990; and Freeman-Longo & Pithers, 1992) include early warnings, middle and late occurring cues, and the destructive warning line or last-minute cues prior to relapse. It is important for offenders to identify their earliest cues and last-minute warnings. Although offenders can interrupt the offending process or cycle at any point, the earlier the better.

Although sex offenders can deter relapse once they are in extremely high-risk situations, it is more difficult. They must accept responsibility for initiating the chain of events that got them there in the first place. They can learn to recognize the conditions that precede relapse and be prepared to intervene before it's too late. A major goal of relapse prevention entails helping abusers identify the relapse process, disrupt it at the earliest possible moment, and analyze be-

haviors so that they might learn from their experiences.

In the early to mid-1980s, Marques and colleagues developed a view of the relapse process as a chain of cognitive distortions and behaviors (Laws, 1995a; Nelson & Jackson, 1989, Nelson, Minor, Marques, Russell, & Achterkirchen, 1988). Nelson and Jackson (1989, p. 172) best describe the behavioral chain as "a fairly complete map of the antecedents and precipitants of the offense. It explains how the offender arrived at the point of molesting." Offenders are instructed to identify specific events that led up to the offense. Each event or risk factor is then interpreted by the offender. Thus, a full picture of the offense emerges. At various points in the chain, offenders can develop specific interventions.

MODIFICATIONS TO TRADITIONAL MODELS OF RELAPSE PREVENTION

Recent contributions to the development of relapse prevention can be grouped into two broad areas. First, in addition to Pithers's (1993) suggestion that enhancement of empathy should be a prerequisite to treatment designed to inform abusers about their relapse process, other investigators have emphasized the importance of motivating and preparing offenders for treatment (Beech & Fordham, 1997; Kear-Colwell & Pollock, 1997; Mann & Rollnick, 1996). Second, several theorists have proposed modifications in the goals or proposed modifications of the cognitive-behavioral model of the relapse process (Laws, 1999; Ward & Hudson, 1998; Ward, Hudson, & Marshall, 1995; Ward, Louden, Hudson, & Marshall, 1995).

LOWE'S MODIFICATION

Lowe (1993) altered the original linear model by adding two stages (social situation and celebration), proposing "masturbation" as a distinct stage (which had been included in the original model as part of the "fantasy" stage), and changing the sequence of stages. Thus Lowe's model consists of these stages: (1) social situation, (2) feeling (adverse), (3) fantasy, (4) masturbating, (5) disinhibitors, (6) cognitive distortions, (7) plan, (8) offense, (9) celebration.

Lowe's model asserts that the offender's change in affect occurs as a result of an event occurring in a social context (i.e., problems in relation to another person). This stage appears to imply that changes in affect must necessarily result from an unpleasant social situation. However, change in affect can occur as a result of internal stimuli, endogenous factors, and, at times, a social violation rather than social interaction.

Lowe's suggestion of "celebration" is a particularly noteworthy addition to the original model, suggesting that offenders may experience enduring fantasies about abuse they have performed, which may generate an increased drive to engage in further abusive behavior.

LAWS'S RECOMMENDATIONS

Other suggestions to advance relapse prevention appear more questionable. In a recent review, Laws (1999) made a number of recommendations regarding present and future developments of relapse prevention. First, he proposed that the major goal should be relapse *minimization*, not relapse *prevention*, as all relapses to sexual offending cannot be prevented.

First, Laws's suggestion seems similar to a comment by Pithers and Cumming (1989), who suggested that relapse prevention was a misnomer and that it could more accurately be considered *relapse reduction*. However, in reviewing the potential implications of that term, Pithers and Cumming rejected it as an unacceptable goal. A philosophy of "harm reduction" or "relapse minimization" may offer confirmatory support for cognitive distortions that maintain offending behavior (e.g., rationalizations) or equip offenders with a ready justification for reoffenses that are not as "serious" as their prior acts.

Laws also recommended a "stepped care" approach whereby offenders are exposed to a grad-

uated series of interventions so that treatment strategies with the highest probability of success will be utilized for particular offenders in order to increase cost-effectiveness. In actual practice, this suggestion amounts to a good clinical practice that has existed for more than a decade (Pithers, 1987). One drawback of a stepped care approach, however, is that it hampers treatment evaluation research, as standardized treatment protocols may be eliminated in the process.

Finally, Laws emphasized the need for motivational interviewing (MI) (Miller, 1983) to minimize resistance to treatment. This suggestion was first advanced simultaneously by Beech and Fordham (1997) and Kear-Colwell and Pollock (1997) and further emphasized by other researchers (Ward & Hudson, 1998). Ward and Hudson (1998), in particular, were the first authors to highlight the usefulness of MI in preparing the offender for specific aspects of the relapse process.

A SELF-REGULATION MODEL OF THE RELAPSE PROCESS

In a culmination of their earlier studies (Ward, Fon, Hudson, & McCormack, 1998; Ward, Hudson, & Marshall, 1995; Ward, Louden, Hudson, & Marshall, 1995), Ward and Hudson (1998) proposed a revision of the cognitive-behavioral model of relapse. Their aim was to provide a model of the relapse process that would (1) incorporate various pathways to relapse involving different types of goals and planning, and different affective states throughout the offense cycle; (2) provide an integration of cognitive, affective, and behavioral factors; (3) account for the dynamic, temporal nature and the various phases of the offense process; and (4) provide a description of the mechanisms inhibiting or encouraging relapse.

This model involves nine distinct phases incorporating differences in offenders goals, offense planning, and levels of affect (attached either to preoffense, high-risk situations or to postoffense behavior). In the first phase, a life event (which may be either a minor hassle or a major stressor) activates knowledge structures related to the offender's goals and needs, which in turn trigger patterns of thoughts, emotions, and intentions. A desire for deviant sex or inappropriate activity is then activated, which includes sexual and aggressive fantasies. In the third phase, the abuser establishes offense-related goals (either avoidance or approach). Goals and strategies are then selected either consciously or automatically. Four offense pathways to relapse are proposed:

1. Avoidant-passive: desire to avoid offending plus failure to actively prevent this from occurring (the traditional cognitive-behavioral model of relapse).

2. Avoidant-active: desire to avoid offending plus direct attempt at mental control, which itself is inappropriate and, in fact, enhances the likelihood of reoffending (maladaptive coping responses).

3. Approach-automatic: desire to reoffend plus underregulation (planned impulsiveness).

4. Approach-explicit: conscious planning (intact self-regulation) toward inappropriate goals.

The offender then enters a high-risk situation (e.g., contact with a victim). This could be the result of earlier planning by the offender (either implicit or explicit), or it may occur unexpectedly. The sixth phase, a lapse, includes the immediate precursors to sexual offense. All offenders experience positive affectivity during this phase due to a combination of high levels of arousal and cognitive deconstruction. The sex offense constitutes the seventh phase and may be self-focused, victim-focused, or a mutually focused activity.

The eighth phase involves postoffense evaluations whereby avoidant offenders evaluate their actions negatively and feel guilt and shame (a classic abstinence violation effect), whereas approach offenders experience positive self-evalu-

ations (a response less well accounted for by the traditional cognitive-behavioral model of relapse). The last phase, attitude toward reoffending, incorporates the notion that offenders learn from each offense and may either continue on an avoidant path (resolving not to persist offending) or move to an approach or acquisitory path (resolving to offend again in the future).

Ward and Hudson's (1998) modification of relapse prevention also suggests that therapists should assess the types of goals their clients possess and evaluate whether they are acquisitory or inhibitory. Furthermore, depending on the specific self-regulatory deficits that offenders possess, different types of interventions may be associated with maximal efficacy (Ward & Keenan, 1999). For example, offenders with intact self-regulatory styles may be most meaningfully treated with interventions intended to enhance victim empathy and to reduce dysfunctional cognitions (i.e., core schema). In contrast, misregulated or undercontrolled offenders might need interventions targeting impulsivity, emotional modulation, and coping skills to deal with unexpected high-risk situations.

Ward and Hudson (1998) proposed different treatment strategies according to the types of goals offenders may possess. The avoidant-passive pathway approximates the traditional relapse prevention process and therefore requires the acquisition of relationship skills, problem solving, and mood management. To reduce passivity, it may also be necessary to target offenders' core schema regarding their personal efficacy. These offenders may need to develop greater meta-cognitive control to more effectively monitor and remediate various components of their offense cycles. The avoidant-active pathway also requires skill acquisition, especially with respect to meta-cognitive control, as well as interventions aimed at increasing the offender's awareness of the effects of current coping strategies and developing adaptive coping styles.

According to Ward and Hudson (1998), offenders following the approach-automatic pathway demand a strengthening of meta-cognitive control and need to be taught not to rely on overlearned behavioral scripts. Perspective taking and cognitive restructuring also play an important role in changing these offenders' goals. The primary treatment targets for the approach-explicit pathway are the offender's goals and, as such, core schemata (e.g., self, intimacy, sexuality). Ward and Hudson (1998) suggest that these offenders may require reconditioning of urges and cravings. Additionally, due to the possibility of offenders shifting from approach to avoidance goals and vice versa, reoffending may not take the same form as the initial offense, and changes in goals and knowledge structures may expose further deficits in skills and self-regulation.

Hudson and Ward (1996a) note that "the existence of multiple offense pathways overcomes the problem of incompatible mechanisms; different pathways are mediated by different mechanisms at different points" (p. 254). This allows for the incorporation of new offense pathways as they arise. Their model involves other components of the cognitive-behavioral model of relapse (Pithers et al., 1983), such as the abstinence violation effect and the problem of immediate gratification. The modifications suggested by Ward, Hudson, and colleagues appear worthwhile and beg for replication in further research.

These recent advances in the theoretical and practical aspects of the relapse process provide exciting weapons for the clinician's arsenal. There is obviously a need to incorporate motivational interviewing procedures as part of the first phase of relapse prevention, bridging the gap from assessment to treatment. This can be used to motivate offenders to (1) enter treatment, (2) recognize the need to change either their current self-regulatory processes or their goals, (3) develop an awareness of cognitive distortions and their underlying implicit theories, and, most importantly, (4) take personal responsibility and make a choice to "own" the treatment process.

As we have recommended in other publications, sex offenders should be treated in the least restrictive conditions consistent with community safety. Pithers and Gray (1998) reported that only one in five adult offenders could not be effectively treated as outpatients, as long as treatment was mandated through special conditions of probation and coordinated with specialized probation supervision. Individuals with approach goals may constitute those who are traditionally the hardest to treat as outpatients, as they express no desire to change their offending behavior. These offenders are likely to require a more intensive form of treatment focusing more exclusively on goals and core schemata underlying their offending lifestyles.

It must be noted that although the relapse prevention model has seen a number of suggested modifications, the fundamental approach taken by these researchers remains consistent with the original approach suggested by Pithers nearly 20 years ago (Pithers et al., 1983). The revisions represent efforts to broaden the basic relapse prevention model to encapsulate a greater range of offense styles. The inclusion of offenders goals, self-regulatory strategies, and different offense pathways provides a more complete picture of the relapse process and offers exciting new areas for individualized assessment and treatment of this diverse clientele. However, before these modifications are accepted as practice parameters, further research is needed to confirm these promising findings.

A CYBERNETIC-CIRCULAR VIEW OF THE OFFENDING PROCESS: THE ASSAULT CYCLE

A second way of conceptualizing the process an offender undergoes is the assault cycle. This chapter discusses three models of assault cycles: the original three-stage model developed by Lane and Zamora (1978, 1984), the classic four-stage model (Bays & Freeman-Longo, 1990), and a six-stage model (Carich & Stone, 1994a).

Carich (1994b, 1996, 1999) observes that, regardless of the number of stages proposed, all variations of the sexual assault cycle share some common concepts, including:

- The duration of offense cycles varies greatly; some cycles take minutes, others years.

- Offenders can skip phases or experience several phases simultaneously.

- Offenders can have several distinct cycles.

- Offenders can have subcycles (i.e., small cycles of emotion, thought, and behavior that exist within a larger cycle).

- The cycle consists of thoughts, feelings, and behaviors that are related to abuse.

- The cycle is both progressive and regressive in nature.

- The cycle can be defused at any point.

- The cycle applies to all offenders; however, the exact content of the cycle is specific to each offender.

- The cycle applies to all sex offenders regardless of their choice of abusive behavior or preferred victim.

- Offenders do not have to be in cycle.

THREE-PHASE CYCLE. The first sexual assault cycle was referred to as a "rape cycle" and was devised by Lane and Zamora (1978) at the Closed Adolescent Treatment Center (CATC) in Colorado. Their model was used internally at the CATC and was first formally published in 1984 (Lane & Zamora, 1984). The rape cycle was later modified into a more general sexual assault cycle (Isaac & Lane, 1990; Lane, 1991).

The assault cycle resulted from the astute observations of clinicians working with very high risk juvenile offenders.

While each juvenile had unique perceptions concerning the offense or the victim involved, as well as unique motivations and justification for engaging in the behavior, there seemed to be a general pattern common to each of their sexual abuse incidents. . . . Despite each incident of sexual abuse being unique relative to the style of the offense, the type of behaviors involved, and the manner of selecting a victim or obtaining victim compliance, there were common processes for each. Moreover, there appeared to be an identifiable antecedent pattern among these juveniles that was interrelated and somewhat predictable. (Lane & Zamora, 1984, p.103)

They described a rape cycle as an identifiable and predictable sequence that included:

an event or perceived event ⇒ an emotional response ⇒ stimulation of an emotional response which is, for that youth, an intolerable set of feelings or reactions ⇒ attempts to compensate with substitute feelings (thoughts, power behaviors, soliciting certain types of reactions from others, etc.) that give the youth a feeling of having or being in control ⇒ feelings of anger, even rage ⇒ decision to rape ⇒ refinement of rape plan (during this part of the cycle thoughts, fantasies and rape walks are anxiety reducing) ⇒ selection of victim ⇒ selection of when and where to rape ⇒ rape or sexual assault ⇒ internal feelings or reactions compensating for the original event. (Lane & Zamora, 1984, pp.354–355)

Subsequently, Lane (1991) made several modifications in the rape cycle to create the sexual assault cycle. This included three phases: precipitating, compensatory, and integration. The precipitating phase involves the exposure to an event, the subsequent interpretation of the event as having a negative meaning about oneself, and the individual's initial efforts to cope with the situation by avoidance. Next, in the compensatory response phase, the potential offender attempts to increase his or her sense of self-esteem and reduce anxiety through power-based or compensatory thoughts and behaviors, which eventually culminate in the offense behavior. Finally, in the integration phase, the individual attempts to rationalize or support the offense behavior in an effort to accept it without self-deprecation (Lane, 1991, pp.115–116).

Within each of these three broad phases, different subevents might occur that propel the cycle forward. In this model, cognitive distortions provide the linkage across the subevents within each phase and across phases.

In the precipitating phase, three types of subevents were discerned: events that evoked feelings of helplessness, accompanied by a diminution in self-image; negative anticipations that entailed the expectation that others were going to reject them; and avoidance, which resulted in withdrawal and isolation. The compensatory phase has three subevents: power and control seeking via passive-aggressive behaviors, at which time the abuser begins to manifest a greater level of anger and uses this emotion to dominate others or retaliate against them; fantasy, which, in addition to sexual or masturbatory thoughts, might include actual planning of offenses or mental rehearsal of the plan; and the actual performance of an inappropriate sexual behavior. In the integration phase, two subevents were observed: transitory guilt, largely associated with fear of getting caught, and reframing.

FOUR-STAGE CYCLE. One of the most widely used cycle models is the four-stage cycle, which has been attributed to various authors (Bays & Freeman-Longo, 1989; Isaac & Lane, 1990). The four stages, depicted in Table 5.1, are (1) buildup, (2) acting out, (3) justification, and (4) pretend-normal.

Once an individual has engaged in a sex offense, the offense cycle begins in the pretend-normal stage. In this stage, the abuser may attempt to portray himself as someone who has never had a problem with sexual abuse. He may attempt to "build a new life" in which he distances himself from everyone who is aware of his past acts, including those people who have lived pro-social lives and could be important sources of support.

In the buildup stage, the offender begins to re-experience the internal and external stimuli that foster his interest in abusing (e.g., mismanaged emotions, disordered cognitions, accessible children). This process creates a momentum that culminates in another sexually abusive act.

In the justification stage, the offender attempts to cognitively redefine the victimization. An assumption appears to be made that the offender inevitably endeavors to excuse his act or, even more powerfully, to create a "rational" explanation for his conduct. If the offender's efforts are successful, he may continue to engage in abuse. If the attempt to rationalize the abuse does not succeed, or if outside influences (e.g., the court, family members) exert pressure for the offender to stop, he may enter the pretend-normal stage. The justification stage is similar to stages 7 and 8 of the Ward modification of the cognitive-behavioral model of relapse. However, in contrast to the justification stage of the offense cycle, Ward et al. permit the possibility that an abuser may recognize the traumagenic aspects of the victimization and, rather than attempting to justify the harm he has inflicted, make an enduring commitment to adopt an abuse-avoidant lifestyle.

SIX-STAGE CYCLE. Carich and Stone (Carich, 1991b, 1994b; Carich & Stone, 1994a) mapped out a six-stage cycle along with specific strategies to identify the cycle. Their cycle represents a

TABLE 5.1   FOUR-STAGE CYCLE

PHASE 1: BUILDUP
Fantasy about pleasure/excitement
Building sexual interest (often with pornography)
Planning the sexual assault
Commitment to do the assault

PHASE 2: ACTING OUT
The sexual assault

PHASE 3: JUSTIFICATION
Fear and guilt
Rationalization (or other defense mechanisms used to deny the problem)
Vowing never to do it again

PHASE 4: PRETEND-NORMAL
Working hard to make up for the deviant behavior
Return to daily routine
Boredom

refinement of earlier cycle models and was based on clinical observations of a wide range of offenders, from exhibitionists to serial killers. They proposed a six-stage cycle in order to permit more precise specification of an abuser's behaviors, processes, and motivational dynamics to offend. Of course, the increased precision of this model makes it more complex and, at times, difficult for lower-functioning offenders to comprehend. The specific stages are displayed in Table 5.2.

COMPOSITE CYCLE. The simplicity of three stages enhances offenders' ability to learn the cycle. All cycles can be conceptualized in terms of three stages: (1) preassault phase, (2) assault phase and (3) postassault phase (Carich, 1996). The preassault phase consists of all different types of behaviors, events, precursors, and risk factors found in the buildup to the offense. The assault phase is any type of offending. The last phase consists of the aftermath of the assault. The offender does not necessarily have to be in cycle.

IDENTIFYING CYCLES

A variety of ways to help offenders identify their cycles has been suggested (Carich 1996, 1997; Carich & Stone, 1994a, 1994b). Some of the basic techniques include writing autobiographies, highlighting significant experiences or perceptions, including offenses; maintaining journals by recording all daily significant events, along with reactions and coping responses; and preparing detailed summaries of each assault. These tasks highlight the offender's cognitive distortions; the efficacy of various attempts to manage emotions and behaviors; and the way in which the offender hoped the victim would respond to the assault, which may provide some indication of the offender's motivations. This information can then be distributed into various stages of the offense cycle. A generic five-step strategy for identifying cycles is: (1) write out offenses, in detail, including all the precursors; (2) analyze each offense by listing the events; (3) list all reactions (thoughts, feelings, behaviors) to each event; (4) select a cycle form

and insert the information in step 3; and (5) develop a composite or summary cycle for each victim type (Carich, 1997). For more detailed information about specific techniques that can be used to gain information relevant to offense cycles, a number of excellent resources can be consulted (see Bays & Freeman-Longo, 1989; Carich, 1994c, 1996; Carich & Stone 1994a, 1994b).

INTEGRATION OF RELAPSE PREVENTION AND ASSAULT CYCLE MODELS

Freeman-Longo and Pithers (1992) proposed an integration of the cognitive-behavioral model of relapse and the four-stage sexual abuse cycle. In their initial effort, all the events associated with the cognitive-behavioral model of relapse (i.e., SUDs, high-risk factors, lapses, AVE, relapse; see Figure 5.2) were placed within the buildup phase of the four-stage model. This integration was attempted in an effort to coalesce the two theoretical models and the treatment providers who used them.

With the benefit of hindsight, the initial effort to integrate the two theoretical models contained several errors. A revision of this integration contains elements of the cognitive-behavioral model of relapse (Pithers et al., 1983; Ward, Louden, et al., 1995) and the abuse cycle. First, we introduce the concept of "normality" into the abuse cycle. We believe that with sufficient treatment and considerable support, some offenders can go beyond the point of pretending to be normal. This does not mean that the offender is cured but signifies that he or she has successfully managed life for a prolonged period without engaging in any high-risk behaviors or lapses. This stage is referred to by some authors as "dormancy." To define the optimal outcome of treatment for all offenders as pretend-normal discounts the positive potential of treatment and of all human beings, regardless of their past behaviors.

Second, for those offenders who resume the

TABLE 5.2   SIX-STAGE DEVIANT CYCLE

1. **TRIGGERING EVENT**
   a. Type of triggering events that set off the cycle
   b. Subjective processing of event (at conscious and unconscious levels)
   c. Needs evoked by triggering event (e.g., questions worth, needs reassurance)
   d. Initial attempts to cope — reactions to triggers may involve adaptive or mal-adaptive attempts to cope
   e. Trigger defused or lapse ensues

2. **PRESEARCH STAGE**
   a. Abuse-predisposing ideation/feelings
   b. Problem/issues reemerge (motivating purposes or needs, loneliness)
   c. Coping/disowning/enablers (e.g., rationalization, denial, isolation, secrecy, blame, avoidance)
   d. Urges/cravings
   e. Deviant fantasy
   f. Buildup
   g. Depersonalization/repersonalization initiated
   h. Planning
   i. Pattern enablers/enhancers (e.g., pornography, masturbation, drugs or alcohol)
   j. Sexually "turned on"
   k. Dissociation/detachment
   l. Lowering of inhibitions
   m. Defused/lapse

3. **SEARCH STAGE**
   a. Type of preferred/ideal victim
   b. Type of victim available/victim selection process
   c. Further depersonalization and repersonalization (distortion)
   d. Further planning the setup to fit or fix needs, problems, or issues at conscious/unconscious levels
   e. Implementation of plans: "the hunt"
   f. Look for opportunity to offend
   g. Location of victim
   h. Defused/lapse

4. **SETUP STAGE**
   a. Conscious/unconscious planning of the setup
   b. Manipulation of victim to the point of offending
   c. Engaging in the setup
   d. Grooming behavior (e.g., developing false love, threats)
   e. Stalking
   f. Isolating victim(s)
   g. Commitment to offend
   h. Gaining access to victim(s)
   i. Defused/lapse

5. **RELAPSE—OFFENDING BEHAVIOR STAGE**
   a. Engaging in actual offending behavior
   b. Some offenses may be precursors to others (e.g., preparing to rape, rape to murder); one may have subcycles or multiple cycles.
   c. Dissociated and detached
   d. Defused/relapse

6. **POSTOFFENDING EXPERIENTIAL STAGE**
   a. Aftermath
   b. Victim's response
   c. Distortion of victim's response (i.e., justification)
   d. Temporary solutions to needs
   e. Subjective processing (conscious/unconscious levels)
   f. Disowning/coping
   g. Pretend all is okay (and back to normal)
   h. False remorse (self-pity)
   i. False apology
   j. Daily routine
   k. Good-guy role
   l. Possible compensation (making up for offenses)
   m. Possible celebration/trophies
   n. Defused/lapse

FIGURE 5.2   SEXUAL ABUSE CYCLE

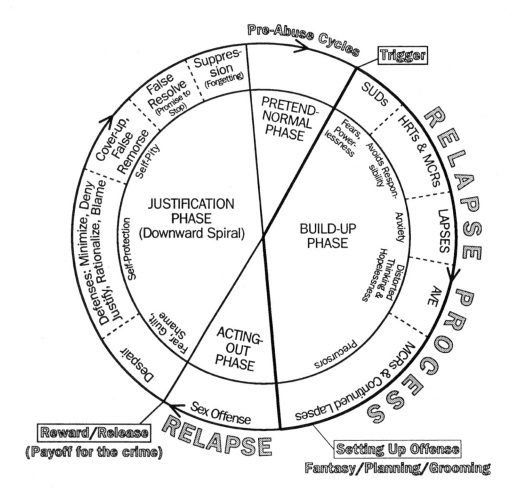

Note: This sexual abuse cycle diagram represents an "average" offender's cycle and its various phases. The particular parts and their order within each phase may vary among offenders and some offenders may not experience all parts shown. (Reproduced from Freeman-Longo & Pithers [1992, p. 4], *A Structured Approach to Preventing Relapse.*)

relapse process, we believe that SUDs usually take place during the pretend-normal phase of the abuse cycle, rather than during the buildup phase. The offender basically is making decisions that, at least early in the stages of acting abusively, appear unrelated to sexual abuse. Some of these decisions may even appear to have noble intent in others' eyes (e.g., a rapist who seeks to work with a fire department rescue squad). However, the SUDs allow the abuser to gain greater access to situations in which people are vulnerable and victimization is possible (e.g., a

woman who has been traumatized and feels indebted to compassionate rescue workers).

Third, high-risk situations and lapses are placed in the buildup phase of the abuse cycle. Most offenders experience a number of different risk situations and lapses in the buildup phase. Offenders may remain in the buildup phase, testing their self-management skills or savoring their lapse, with maladaptive coping responses and cognitive distortions linking several risk factors and lapses. If the offender is discomforted by a lapse or risk factor and escapes from it but does nothing to address the influences that may have permitted the lapse, he or she may return to the pretend-normal phase, but is unlikely to regain "normal" functioning. If an offender actively discloses a lapse and addresses it in treatment and with the prevention team, he or she may be able to resume "normality."

For offenders who are not highly sociopathic, have not manifested criminality as their career choice, and have gained empathy for sexual abuse victims, at least some elements of the AVE are experienced during the buildup stage. Among these elements are the sense of personal disappointment and guilt at having been unable to maintain the promise they made to themselves to avoid lapsing. For offenders who are career criminals or who have not made substantial treatment gains, the AVE does not occur until after a relapse, if at all.

Of course, the relapse or reoffense takes place during the acting-out phase of the cycle. During this phase, many abusers experience, at least momentarily, some semblance of the "positive" outcome that was anticipated during fantasies (e.g., sense of power and domination, relief from loneliness, orgasm). Other offenders find that at least some of their assaults do not result in an even momentarily rewarding outcome. No one knows how many people have acted abusively but, after recognizing that the victim's response did not match their expectation (e.g., the victim fights with the perpetrator and cries rather than regarding it as good but forceful sex), never repeat the abusive behavior. However, failure to attain the positive expectancy does not necessarily result in a reduced likelihood of subsequent offenses for all abusers. Some offenders blame their victims for failing to respond in the way they had desired and become more determined to ensure that their next victim does not "deprive them of their goal."

Acting out is generally followed by the offender's appraisal of the abuse and a reframing of himself or herself. In some cases, the offender may find the abuse to be intensely rewarding and soon begins planning the next abusive act. Enjoyment of the abuse becomes part of his or

her identity. In other cases, the offender may experience transitory guilt. This could occur because the offender broke the promise not to reoffend and therefore is a manifestation of the AVE. It could also take place because the victim's distress penetrated the offender's defenses. In such cases, the offender initially may resolve not to abuse again but later reframes the event as the victim's fault or decides that even though the victim cried, she or he probably was not permanently harmed. Either reframing would increase the possibility of the offender abusing again. In still other cases, the abuser may decide that he or she was repulsed by the abusive conduct and elect never to repeat it.

Based on their appraisal and reframing of the assault, abusers may follow any of several courses. An abuser who relishes the memory of the assault may return immediately to the buildup phase, eagerly seeking high-risk situations and potential victims. An abuser who experiences transitory guilt may enter the pretend-normal stage and work to convince others that nothing is wrong until, after reframing the assault as the victim's fault, the offender resumes making SUDs. Finally, an offender who realizes that he or she has acted wrongfully may self-correct or receive treatment. Likely, most offenders enter treatment in the pretend-normal phase.

CLINICAL APPLICATION OF RELAPSE PREVENTION AND OFFENSE CYCLES

Clinical applications are discussed in this section. First, specific types of interventions or skills are reviewed. Then a 17-stage relapse prevention group process is discussed.

RELAPSE INTERVENTIONS

Relapse interventions are any methods one uses to defuse or interrupt any relapse (deviant responses, lapses, or relapse). They are adaptive coping strategies (Bays, Freeman-Longo, &

Hildebran, 1990; Carich & Stone, 1993, 1996; Gray & Pithers, 1993; Laws, 1989; Pithers, 1990). For convenience, interventions have been categorized into cognitive, social, behavioral, cognitive-behavioral, and imagery and futuristic interventions.

More recently, Carich (1995) developed a four-step cognitive process for problem solving and interrupting cycles called STOP. STOP is an acronym for stop, think, options (plans or interventions), and practice (or implementation). This generic procedure can be used with any intervention.

COGNITIVE INTERVENTIONS. Numerous studies have examined the role of cognitions in the process of sexual offending. To enrich our understanding of cognitive distortions and affective deficits in sex offenders, Ward, Hudson, and Marshall (1995) apply Baumeister's (1991) theory of cognitive deconstruction to explain factors involved in the initiation, maintenance, and treatment of sex offenders. When sex offenders enter the state of cognitive deconstruction, they suspend their normal self-regulatory processes and instead think in a more concrete, lower-order mode in order to escape from the negative implications of self-awareness. Ward and colleagues used this paradigm to explain a number of components of the relapse process, including denial, minimization, passivity, covert planning, the problem of immediate gratification, empathy deficits, intimacy deficits, social competency deficits, and alcohol and drug problems.

Viewing cognitive deconstruction as a loss of mental control, Johnston, Ward, and Hudson (1997) propose that effective cognitive control is vital to developing self-management skills. They support inclusion of thought suppression techniques in relapse prevention to reduce the occurrence of inappropriate sexual thoughts and to lessen the chance that such thoughts might result in offenses. This approach can be differentiated from cognitive restructuring, because the treatment target becomes cognitive processes rather than fixed beliefs (Ward, Hudson, & Marshall, 1995).

Johnston et al. (1997) provide practical guidelines for instituting thought suppression techniques. First, therapists need to help offenders acknowledge that their deviant thoughts and behaviors are unwanted. Consistent with relapse prevention, the goal is sexual adjustment rather than the total banishment of unwanted thoughts. It is important that the offender feels in control of his or her mental state yet is still willing to change that state during therapy. The authors recommend motivational interviewing as a tool to help instill this sense of responsibility and control.

Johnston et al. (1997) suggest that abusers practice identifying unwanted sexual thoughts and replacing them with more appropriate distractor thoughts (which may themselves be sex related). Ward, Hudson, and Marshall (1995) propose that the identification of unwanted cognitions may be enhanced through the use of a group format as group members can more accurately perceive other abusers' distortions than their own. The use of role-plays was recommended to make mental control more automatic. In addition to thought suppression, Johnston et al. recommend that therapists need to prepare offenders for lapses in mental control and the feelings of uncontrollability and helplessness that may accompany these lapses. In essence, Johnston et al. emphasize the importance of adhering to the fundamental philosophy of relapse prevention when exploring the characteristics of high-risk situations to identify factors hampering the use of thought suppression.

Cognitions and implicit theories in child molesters. To classify sex offenders' cognitions about their offending, Ward, Fon, Hudson, and Mc-Cormack (1998) analyzed the offense descriptions of 20 child molesters to develop a Model of Dysfunctional Cognitions (MDC). This model provides clinicians with a greater awareness of the cognitive processes operating during assessment and treatment. The offense chain constituted the core of the model and has since led to several adaptations of the relapse process. The three other core dimensions of the MDC were cognitive operations, cognitive content, and cognitive meta-variables. A total of seven categories of cognitive operations were derived to account for the ways offenders presented information regarding their offenses: describing, explaining (i.e., providing reasons for certain aspects of the offense), interpreting (e.g., attaching meaning to victims' behavior), evaluating (i.e., a positive or negative appraisal of some aspect of the offense), denying, minimizing, and planning. Interpretations, explanations, and planning tended to occur early in the offense process. Evaluations, denial, and minimization were used more frequently after the offense.

Cognitive content reflects offenders' attitudes, beliefs, and perceptions (Ward et al., 1998). These are arranged into three main areas: self-related internal (the offenders' mental, affective, cognitive, or behavioral state), self-related external (external factors influencing offenders' internal states), and victim related (offenders' attitudes, beliefs, and perceptions of the victim).

The last major category, meta-variables, concerns the overall way in which the offender presents himself or herself during assessment and, consistent with the notion of cognitive deconstruction, varies on a continuum from lower-level to higher-level processing. These are grouped into four domains: (1) detail — the amount of information provided; (2) euphemisms — use of slang "abbreviations" to disguise aspects of the offense; (3) concreteness — the depth of the offender's cognitive processing, which ranges from concrete to abstract; and 4) passivity — the offender's representation that he or she played a passive role in the offense.

An analysis of these meta-variables for any given offender may provide the clinician with important information concerning the complexity of the offender's cognitive style and may thereby aid in treatment planning. For example, offenders possessing a self-related external orientation may be less likely to accept responsibility and, therefore, could require more intensive motivational interviewing (Ward et al., 1998).

Ward and Keenan (1999) propose that cognitive distortions may be driven by offenders' underlying schemata regarding themselves, their

victims, and the world. They identify five major implicit theories commonly held by child molesters. Two implicit theories related to the offender, *entitlement* and *uncontrollability*, were used by offenders to suggest that they were authorized to abuse as a result of a self-perceived special status or because humans are driven by external, uncontrollable factors. Implicit theories concerning the victim are *children as sexual objects* (i.e., believing that children are capable of enjoying and wanting sexual activity) and *nature of harm* (i.e., there are degrees of harm, and sexual activity alone is unlikely to harm others). Last, the *dangerous world* implicit theory relates to the abuser's belief that others wish to hurt or dominate the offender, so it is therefore necessary to dominate and control others and to perceive oneself as capable of retaliation (Ward & Keenan, 1999).

In clinical application, Ward and Keenan (1999) recommend that treatment focus on the identification of the implicit theories associated with each offender's relapses rather than the analysis of individual statements reflecting these core schemata. They further propose that just as cognitive restructuring is utilized to challenge offenders' thoughts, treatment is necessary to challenge offenders' implicit theories and replace these with more adaptive ways of thinking about themselves, their victims, and the world.

Theory of mind in sex offenders. Ward, Keenan, and Hudson (2000) propose that deficits in cognition, intimacy, and empathy may all be encapsulated by the developmental construct of theory of mind, that is, an awareness of others' beliefs, desires, perspectives, and needs. The capacity for this awareness develops in a particular order: feelings, perceptions, desires, intentions, and beliefs (for a comprehensive description, see Ward et al., 2000). The authors further outline four ways in which a dysfunctional theory of mind might develop: a failure to acquire a theory of mind (either a general or a specific deficit); a delay in the acquisition of a theory of mind; a pervasive affective (empathy) deficit that fails to trigger mental ability; and a self-regulatory failure, whereby an offender may possess a theory of mind but its application is influenced by state variables (e.g., affect). At present, the theory-of-mind interpretation is based mainly on child molesters and is still at a conceptual stage. Yet this framework provides a good example of "theory knitting" in order to unify related etiological variables within a rich, logical, developmental picture.

Ward et al. (2000) point out that most treatment approaches assume that offenders choose not to utilize their perspective-taking abilities, whereas the theory-of-mind perspective suggests that offenders may find it extremely difficult to infer others' mental states. They believe that different theory-of-mind deficits require different types of interventions. For example, offenders with more pervasive deficits may require a focus on developing abilities to infer mental states and take the perspective of others. Conversely, offenders whose theory of mind is strongly influenced by state variables (such as positive or negative affect) may require more intensive work in the area of affect regulation.

SOCIAL INTERVENTIONS. Social interventions consist of a variety of techniques involving interpersonal skills and types of interpersonal relationships. Interpersonal skills are specific communication and social skills, including empathy, victim empathy, active listening, paraphrasing, eye contact, "I" messages, respect, appropriate confrontation skills, assertiveness, listening skills, emotional recognition, appropriate expression of affect, and so on. Basic conversational skills are also important. Conversational skills include initiating, maintaining, and terminating conversations. Another aspect is the development of positive peer networks and support groups. It is very difficult for offenders to survive without peer group support networks. These networks must consist of peers who do not enable deviant behaviors but can be supportive.

BEHAVIORAL INTERVENTIONS. Behavioral interventions involve using the principles of conditioning and overt activities. Covert (internally oriented) interventions are considered behavioral, based on the conditioning procedures of instrumental or operant conditioning, classical conditioning, and their variations (e.g., modeling). Operant conditioning procedures involve learning through reinforcement or the consequences of behavior. Offenders can learn to set up behavior modification schedules, thus reinforcing positive behaviors while reducing negative behaviors. Classical conditioning involves learning through the pairing of two or more stimuli and/or the pairing of stimuli with responses. Thus, deviant responses are reduced and appropriate behaviors are enhanced by learning through association. Some of the variations include self-aversive conditioning techniques, covert sensitization, stimulus control, escape, and avoidance.

Self-induced aversive conditioning techniques involve using an aversive overt event following any targeted deviant response (e.g., urges, cravings, deviant fantasies). Aversive events may include "popping" rubber bands around the wrist, using noxious odors, pinching, and so on. Staff monitor the process to ensure that the offenders are not selecting aversive events that stimulate deviant behavior.

Covert sensitization is the pairing of a negative internal covert stimulus with deviant responses. The offender imagines a noxious negative or "turn-off" type of image (e.g., an event or a specific person). Covert images need to be strongly aversive and follow the deviant response immediately. Initially, the deviant response is interrupted; over time, the deviant behavior is reduced.

Stimulus control techniques center around controlling the risk factor and/or the situation. This involves the offender controlling the environment to reduce the risk of reoffense. There are two related tactics: avoidance and escape. In relapse prevention, avoidance refers to the offender avoiding specific high- and low-risk situations or factors such as baby-sitting, frequenting bars, viewing pornography, going out at night, aimless driving, and so on. Escape refers to getting out of or leaving high- and low-risk situations such as dating women with children, grocery shopping during after-school hours, walking at the mall, and so on. Escape is generally a last-resort intervention before committing an offense.

COGNITIVE-BEHAVIORAL INTERVENTIONS. Cognitive-behavioral interventions encompass a variety of techniques that involve primarily thinking and behavioral (activity) domains. There are several tactics that offenders can use as relapse interventions, including writing techniques such as journals or logs, tracking systems, lists, letters, repetitive listing, reminder cards, and notes; "crashing" fantasies; lapse contracts; and reprogramming formats.

Writing techniques include any form of writing. Journals, logs, and any type of tracking system are methods of self-monitoring. More specifically, offenders track significant events, triggers, and/or risk factors throughout the day and record their reactions. Their reactions consist of thoughts, feelings, social behaviors, or any overt activities and physiological responses. Offenders can also monitor risk factors, coping skills, and distorted thinking. Specific relapse prevention journals can be designed to enable offenders to analyze triggers and reactions, as well as keeping an ongoing list of risk factors, cues, distortions, interventions, and so on.

Listing techniques are also helpful. Offenders can make single lists of separate elements such as triggers, risk factors, interventions, cues (early, late, last-minute, and destructive warning line), consequences of decisions, and common distortions, as well as dichotomy lists. Letter lists can be comparative or can list likes and dislikes related to situations, decisions, people, events, things, self, and so forth. This process helps offenders analyze decisions, events, relationships, and intervention outcomes.

Writing and using letters can be a very effective way to interrupt or defuse a cycle. Letters or notes consisting of victim impact statements are carried in a pocket or wallet by the offender. Letters written by the victims of the offender's own abusive behavior or those of others are powerful ways to remind the offender about the consequences.

Repetitive listing is the rewriting of specific statements. Statements usually begin with "I choose to . . ." and are completed with something meaningful (e.g., to avoid certain situations, learn new coping behaviors). Typically, offenders are instructed to write four or five pages front and back. The goal of this intervention is the unconscious reprogramming of the offender.

Reminder notes and cards are written statements, messages, goals, risk factors, and interventions placed on index cards or notes. Offenders can write out specific key messages on notes and hang them up in their living quarters. Likewise, key messages can be written on index cards and carried with the offender. Messages may consist of risk factors with interventions, key risk factors and cues, positive affirmations, key support group numbers, key interventions, and the like.

Reprogramming formats are specific formats designed to reprogram the offender's thinking and behavior. Typical formats include appropriate self-statements and new consequences.

Lapse contracts are specific agreements with built-in plans. Offenders agree to follow certain plans and sign the agreement. The plans usually consist of goals, options, plans, or interventions and a commitment to follow through.

IMAGERY AND FUTURISTIC INTERVENTIONS. Much of the offender's deviant fantasy process involves some form of imagery. Imagery is also a powerful intervention. Imagery and futuristic interventions refer to the specific internal visualizations and representations of behaviors, thoughts, feelings, behavioral sequences with themes, events, situations, objects, animals, scenarios, and so forth. Imagery involves using all five sensory modes (visual, auditory, kinesthetic, olfactory, taste) and can take the form of single images or actual scenarios. For example, specific images of animals that provide the offender with strength (confidence, competence, and esteem) are paired with images of places that can be associated with relaxation (pleasant places, mountains, and beaches). Through imagery, specific interventions can be reviewed and rehearsed. Similarly, futuristic risk situations or scenarios with appropriate coping strategies and plans are rehearsed through imagery. Thus, offenders project themselves into the future by rehearsing specific scenarios.

RELAPSE PREVENTION GROUP PROCESS

Relapse prevention is optimally introduced as a unique treatment group or as a specific focus within community-based treatment. This group provides a structured process through which abusers become increasingly aware of their SUDs, high-risk factors, lapses, AVE, and coping strategies. The following treatment sequence (a modification of one delineated by Gray & Pithers, 1993) is appropriate for adolescents and adults but would not be useful with children. A treatment manual describing the use of relapse prevention with families of children with sexual behavior problems is being prepared for publication (Gray, Busconi, Houchens, & Pithers, in press). It is the result of six years of research demonstrating that this form of treatment can be effective within 16 weeks.

STAGE 1: EXPLANATION OF THE RELAPSE PREVENTION MODEL. The first group session educates clients about core relapse prevention concepts including offense precursors, planned impulsiveness, SUDs, high-risk situations, risk factors, the problem of immediate gratification, coping strategies, lapses, the AVE, and relapse. In order to benefit maximally from this treatment component, it is critical for clients to understand the basic concepts of relapse prevention and the cognitive-behavioral model of relapse. Therefore, clients must demonstrate knowledge of these concepts before the group moves forward.

STAGE 2: IDENTIFYING RISK FACTORS. Once knowledge of relapse prevention concepts has been demonstrated, group members complete a homework assignment by preparing a list of their own risk factors (predisposing, precipitating, and perpetuating) for sex offenses and the thoughts, feelings, and behaviors that accompany them. We recommend introducing the relapse prevention group after empathy-building

exercises have been completed, so that clients are prepared to disclose their offense risk factors.

Although this approach to delineating risk factors can be useful with adult clients with adequate intellectual functioning, it can be confusing to less gifted clients and to younger adolescents. When this is a concern, the critical matter is to help clients appreciate that some risk factors tend to occur early during the relapse process and some are encountered later. A goal for clients is to identify the earliest known risk factors as quickly as possible.

STAGE 3: REPORTING RISK FACTORS. Once each client has prepared his or her own list of risk factors, all the clients' risk factors are shared in the group. Each group member reads aloud one of his or her risk factors. A group leader writes each risk factor on a flipchart. This process continues until all clients' risk factors have been exhausted. Therapists are free to introduce risk factors that group members may have neglected to mention.

STAGE 4: INDIVIDUAL REVIEW OF RISK FACTORS. As a homework assignment, each client reviews the complete list of risk factors. Abusers look at the risk factors generated by the entire group, since other members may have noted risk factors they had not listed but that apply to them. Each client identifies his or her five most problematic risk factors, rating them along two dimensions: how frequently the risk factor occurs, and how strongly it influences their affect (or mood), thoughts, fantasies, or behaviors. Even relatively weak risk factors can exert powerful influences on behavior if they are encountered frequently over a prolonged time. Other risk factors may affect the client's fantasies with an almost mystical power.

Some clients have difficulty listing only five risk factors, for a multitude of reasons. Some clients prepare an overly exhaustive list of risk factors to demonstrate their dedication to treatment or their openness to examining their own behaviors. Other clients may attempt to make extremely fine but unnecessary distinctions between risk factors. Sometimes clients list as risk factors events that are really cues to other risk factors. Although it is not a recognized category in the *Guinness Book of World Records*, the longest list that any of us has witnessed exceeded 50 risk factors.

Given that several of the authors have difficulty remembering their nine-digit social security numbers, we believe that our clients may have trouble differentiating an excessive number of risk factors. Therefore, we initially require our clients to limit themselves to working on their five highest risk factors. Ultimately, the number of risk factors may increase beyond five, but we recommend that clients seldom exceed a final list of 10 risk factors.

STAGE 5: IDENTIFICATION OF MOST COMMON RISK FACTOR. In the group, each abuser describes his or her highest risk factor. As each factor is written on a flipchart, all clients with that risk factor as one of their top five raise their hands and a frequency count is taken. The exercise continues until every group member has listed his or her five highest risk factors. This process identifies the risk factor most common to the entire group. The structure of this exercise requires all group members to participate in the process, minimizing any tendency toward secrecy and self-protection.

STAGE 6: CUE IDENTIFICATION. As homework, clients identify cues enabling them to detect the presence, or imminence, of the group's most common risk factor. At least one of the cues must be externally observable. This requirement ensures that cues identifiable by the prevention team will be listed, fostering its ability to assist clients in discerning the presence of risk factors.

STAGE 7: ANALYSIS OF CUES. Group members sequentially list their cues to the most common risk factor. Group discussion fosters understanding of the meaning of each cue, differentiation among cues, and disclosure of secrets. Cues to risk factors can come from a wide variety of sources: affect, thoughts, situational stimuli, behaviors, and so on.

STAGE 8: IDENTIFICATION OF COPING RESPONSES. As homework, group members identify potential coping strategies for the group's

most common risk factor. Coping strategies are methods that the client might use to disrupt the progression toward a sexual offense. The assignment calls for the abusers to create as many potential coping strategies as possible.

STAGE 9: BRAINSTORMING OF COPING STRATEGIES. Clients brainstorm potential coping strategies for the group's most common risk factor, using the list from their homework assignment as a starting point. During this process, therapists interrupt any attempts to evaluate the adequacy of any suggested coping response, since one goal is to increase the cognitive flexibility of clients who see very few options when confronted with challenging circumstances. The process continues until all suggestions are exhausted.

STAGE 10: ANALYSIS OF COPING STRATEGIES. As homework, each client analyzes the potential coping responses identified by the group. Coping responses are rated on a seven-point scale along two dimensions: the likelihood that the coping response will effectively deal with the risk factor, and the client's ability to perform the coping strategy. Each client selects his or her five optimal coping strategies for presentation to the group.

STAGE 11: REVIEW OF OPTIMAL COPING STRATEGIES. Each group member presents his or her five optimal coping strategies to the group. The client's own ratings of the likely success and his or her ability to use each strategy are discussed. Group members challenge unrealistic ratings and suggest alternative coping strategies.

STAGE 12: PREPARATION OF REMINDER CARD. As homework, each client is requested to prepare a reminder card for the group's most common risk factor. The name of the risk factor is written on one side of a 3-by-5 index card. The five most reliable cues and the five optimal coping strategies are written in two columns on the reverse side. Clients prepare two sets of reminder cards, keeping one and giving the other to the therapists. Clients are instructed to review the cards several times every day.

STAGE 13: PROCESSING OTHER RISK FACTORS. Clients repeat the processing of other risk factors common to group members (identification of cues, potential coping strategies, rating of potential coping strategies, and preparation of reminder cards). Throughout this period, clients may be quizzed about risk factors, cues, and coping strategies by the therapists or other group members.

STAGE 14: TESTING PREPAREDNESS. Without warning, clients may be requested to engage in a relapse fantasy. At any point in the relapse fantasy, a therapist may interrupt and ask the client to state how he or she would cope with the imagined high-risk situation. Clients are pressured to respond as quickly as possible. Proposed coping responses that are unrealistic are confronted. At unexpected moments, therapists use reminder cards to quiz group members about the cues and coping strategies for their risk factors.

STAGE 15: PREPARATION OF RESPONSE CHAINS. Group members are asked to develop specific response chains. Response chains are realistic coping behaviors connected by the offender to effectively cope with specific risk factors. Response chains typically consist of cognitive-behavioral coping strategies.

STAGE 16: ANALYSIS OF EFFECTIVENESS. Group members are asked to report any risk factors they have encountered and to discuss how they identified the risk factor and how well they were able to cope. If group members are reluctant to self-report risk factors or lapses, they are asked to confront other group members whom they have observed in lapses or risk behaviors. The group analyzes the risk factor, cues, and coping strategies and makes suggestions about how the offender might deal with precursors to the risk factor more effectively in the future.

STAGE 17: INFORMING THE PREVENTION TEAM. The last stage of the relapse prevention group is also the first step in establishing the external supervisory dimension of relapse prevention. Clients are required to meet with their therapists, probation supervisors, spouses, and adult family members and fully disclose their relapse process. Abusers present their reminder cards to the prevention team and ask for its assistance in identifying cues and risk factors.

Abusers are expected to state their clear understanding that others may assist their monitoring of cues and risk factors but that they alone are responsible for decisions and behaviors. The prevention team and abusers then discuss who else needs to be informed about the offense history and relapse process. By following this group therapy format, sex offenders become acutely aware of their relapse process and the steps they can take to interrupt that process.

EVOLUTION OF RELAPSE PREVENTION

Although relapse prevention and the assault cycle are similar, they are not historically identical. We believe that the two theoretical models have become more similar over time. An integration of the models is not only feasible but necessary.

Laws (1996) noted that relapse prevention introduced hope into the field of sex offender treatment. It provided a road map for therapists and offenders about how sex offenses typically occur and delineated a process enabling change.

It is remarkable that relapse prevention and the abuse cycle could have existed as the foundation of sex offender treatment, without significant modification, for almost two decades. Perhaps the durability of this model can be attributed to its generality. The relapse prevention model describes a change process applicable to anyone struggling to manage problematic behaviors.

We hope that theorists will continue to refine the relapse prevention model and the assault cycle. Extension of these models to other populations is already under way. Our greatest hope is that implementation of this model with sex offenders and people engaging in other forms of abusive behavior will contribute to the creation of a safer society.

Relapse prevention is not the sole component of treatment. Thus, program sequencing plays an important role when planning to use relapse prevention and the assault cycle. The assault cycle can be introduced early in treatment and used throughout treatment. It can be the backbone of a program. The relapse prevention component is recommended to follow victim empathy. It is commonly viewed as an intellectual exercise, whereas victim empathy involves both cognitive and emotional elements. While developing empathy, the offender is highly motivated, is aware of the impact of his or her actions on the victim, and is more likely to recognize the importance of internalizing relapse prevention skills. The offender is less likely to use intellectual exercises to further evade and avoid emotional processes of treatment.

REFERENCES

Baumeister, R.F. (1991). The self against itself: Escape or defeat? In R.C. Curtis & G. Stricker (Eds.), *How people change: Inside and outside therapy*. New York: Plenum.

Bays, L., & Freeman-Longo, R. (1989). *Why did I do it again? Understanding my cycle of problem behaviors*. Orwell, VT: Safer Society Press.

Bays, L., Freeman-Longo, R., & Hildebran, D.A. (1990). *How can I stop? Breaking my deviant cycle*. Orwell, VT: Safer Society Press.

Beech, A. & Fordham, A.S. (1997). Therapeutic climate of sexual offender treatment programs. *Sexual Abuse: A Journal of Research and Treatment, 9*(3), 219–237.

Carich, M.S. (1991a). The basic stages of offending and relapse processes: A theoretical proposal of the deviant cycle. *INMAS Newsletter, 4*(3), 3–7.

Carich, M.S. (1991b). A progressive relapse intervention model: A brief review. *INMAS Newsletter, 4*(2), 3–9.

Carich, M.S. (1991c). Relapse interventions: A brief review. *INMAS Newsletter, 4*(3), 7–11.

Carich, M.S. (1993). A list of disowning behaviors. *INMAS Newsletter, 6*(1), 9–11.

Carich, M.S. (1994a). Basic types of distorted thinking and behavior. *INMAS Newsletter, 7*(3), 10–11.

Carich, M.S. (1994b). 6 stage deviant cycle. *INMAS Newsletter, 7*(3), 5–7.

Carich, M.S. (1994c). The use of RP/RI part IV: Basic 5 step cognitive-behavioral strategy to identify assault cycles. *The Post, 2*(1), 3–7.

Carich, M.S. (1995a). Utilizing relapse interventions — Part I. *The Post, 2*(2), 7–8.

Carich, M.S. (1995b). The use of RI/RP in sex offender treatment — Part VI: Overview of the RI model. *The Post, 2*(3), 3–9.

Carich, M.S. (Ed.). (1996). *Identifying risk behaviors of sex offenders*. Springfield, IL: Illinois Dept. of Corrections.

Carich, M.S. (Ed.). (1997). *Sex offender treatment and overview*. Springfield, IL: Illinois Department of Corrections.

Carich, M.S. (1999). In defense of the assault cycle: A commentary. *Sexual Abuse: A Journal of Research and Treatment, 11*(3), 249–251.

Carich, M.S., Michael, D., & Stone, M. (1992). Categories of disowning behaviors. *INMAS Newsletter, 5*(4), 2–13.

Carich, M.S., & Stone, M. (1992a). Basic categories of relapse warning cues or signals. *INMAS Newsletter, 5*(2), 21–22.

Carich, M.S., & Stone, M. (1992b). Basic categories of triggering events. *INMAS Newsletter, 5*(2), 20–21.

Carich, M.S., & Stone, M. (Eds.). (1993). *Offender relapse prevention*. Chicago: Adler School of Professional Psychology.

Carich, M.S., & Stone, M. (1994a). *Developing an assault cycle profile*. Unpublished manuscript.

Carich, M.S., & Stone, M. (1994b). *Relapse interventions and prevention for sex offenders: A monograph*. Unpublished manuscript.

Carich, M.S., & Stone, M. (1996). *The sex offender relapse intervention workbook*. Chicago: Adler School of Professional Psychology.

Cumming, G.F., & Buell, M. (1996). Relapse prevention as a supervision strategy for sex offenders. *Sexual Abuse: A Journal of Research and Treatment, 3*, 231–242.

Cumming, G.F., & Buell, M. (1997). *Supervision of the sex offender*. Brandon, VT: Safer Society Press.

Drieschner, K., & Lange, A. (1999). A review of cognitive factors in the etiology of rape: Theories, empirical studies, and implications. *Clinical Psychology Review, 19*, 57–77.

D'Zurilla, T. J. (1988). Problem solving therapies. In E.S. Dobson (Ed.), *Handbook of cognitive-behavioral therapies* (pp. 85–135). New York: Guilford Press.

Eldridge, H. (1995). *Maintaining change: A relapse prevention manual for adult male perpetrators of child sexual abuse*. Birmingham, England: Faithful Foundation.

Freeman-Longo, R., & Bays, L. (1988). *Who am I and why am I in treatment*. Orwell, VT: Safer Society Press.

Freeman-Longo, R., Bird, S., Stevenson, W.F., & Fiske, J.A. (1995). *Nationwide Survey of Treatment Programs & Models*. Brandon, VT: Safer Society Press.

Freeman-Longo, R., & Pithers, W.D. (1992). *A structured approach to preventing relapse: A guide for sex offenders*. Orwell, VT: Safer Society Press.

Geer, J.H., Estupinan, L.A., & Manguno-Mire, G.M. (2000). Empathy, social skills, and other relevant cognitive processes in rapists and child molesters. *Aggression and Violent Behavior, 5*, 99–126.

Gray, A.S., Busconi, A., Houchens, P., & Pithers, W.D. (in press). *The effectiveness of treatment for families of children with sexual behavior problems*.

Gray, A.S., & Pithers, W. D. (1993). Relapse prevention with sexually aggressive adolescents and children: Expanding treatment and supervision. In H.E. Barbaree, W.L. Marshall, & S.M. Hudson (Eds.), *The juvenile sex offender* (pp. 289–319). New York: Guilford Press.

Hanson, R.K. (1996). Evaluating the contribution of relapse prevention theory to the treatment of sexual offenders. *Sexual Abuse: A Journal of Research and Treatment, 8,* 201–208.

Hudson, S.M., & Ward, T. (1996a). Relapse prevention: Future directions. *Sexual Abuse: A Journal of Research and Treatment, 8,* 249–256.

Hudson, S.M., & Ward, T. (Eds.). (1996b). Special issue: Relapse prevention. *Sexual Abuse: A Journal of Research and Treatment, 8*(3), 171–256.

Isaac, C., & Lane, S. (1990). *The sexual abuse cycle in the treatment of adolescent sexual abusers* [Video]. Orwell, VT: Safer Society Press.

Jenkins-Hall, K. (1989). Cognitive restructuring. In D.R. Laws (Ed.), *Relapse prevention with sex offenders* (pp. 207–215). New York: Guilford Press.

Johnston, L., Ward, T., & Hudson, S.M. (1997). Deviant sexual thoughts: Mental control and the treatment of sexual offenders. *Journal of Sex Research, 34,* 121–131.

Kear-Colwell, J., & Pollock, P. (1997). Motivation or confrontation: Which approach to the child sex offender? *Criminal Justice and Behavior, 24,* 20–33.

Knopp, F.H., Freeman-Longo, R., & Stevenson, W. (1994). *Nationwide survey of juvenile and adult sex-offender treatment programs.* Orwell, VT: Safer Society Press.

Lane, S. (1991). The sexual abuse cycle. In G.D. Ryan & S.L. Lane (Eds.), *Juvenile sexual offending: Causes, consequences and correction* (pp. 103–141). Lexington, MA: Lexington Books.

Lane, S. (1994, June). The cycle. *Interchange,* 1–18.

Lane, S., & Zamora, P. (1978). Syllabus materials from inservice training on adolescent sex offenders at the Closed Adolescent Treatment Center, Division of Youth Services, Denver, CO.

Lane, S., & Zamora, P. (1984). A method for treating the adolescent sex offender. In R. Mathias, P. Demuro, & R. Allinson (Eds.), *Violent juvenile offenders.* San Francisco: National Council on Crime and Delinquency.

Laws, D.R. (Ed.). (1989). *Relapse prevention with sex offenders.* New York: Guilford Press.

Laws, D.R. (1995a). Central elements in relapse prevention procedures with sex offenders. *Psychology, Crime and Law, 2,* 41–53.

Laws, D.R. (1995b). A theory of relapse prevention. In W. O'Donohue & L. Krasner (Eds.), *Theories in behavior therapy* (pp. 446–473). Washington, DC: American Psychological Association.

Laws, D.R. (1996). Relapse prevention or harm reduction? *Sexual Abuse: A Journal of Research and Treatment, 8,* 243–248.

Laws, D.R. (1999). Relapse prevention: The state of the art. *Journal of Interpersonal Violence, 14,* 285–302.

Lowe, G. (June 1993). Introduction to sex offender treatment. Presentation to Illinois Department of Corrections, Big Muddy River Correctional Center, Ina, IL.

Mann, R.E., & Rollnick, S. (1996). Motivational interviewing with a sex offender who believed he was innocent. *Behavioural and Cognitive Psychotherapy, 24,* 127–134.

Marlatt, G.A. (1993). *Relapse prevention: Origins and adaptations.* Paper presented at the annual research and treatment conference of the Association for the Treatment of Sexual Abusers, Boston, MA.

Marlatt, A., & Gordon, J. (Eds.). (1985). *Relapse prevention.* New York: Guilford Press.

Marques, J., Day, M., Nelson, C., & Miner, M. (1989). The sex offender treatment and evaluation project: California's relapse prevention programs. In D.R. Laws (Ed.), *Relapse prevention with sex offenders* (pp. 247–267). New York: Guilford Press.

Marshall, W.L., & Anderson, D. (1996). An evaluation of the benefits of relapse prevention programs with sexual offenders. *Sexual Abuse: A Journal of Research and Treatment, 8,* 209–222.

Miller, W.R. (1983). Motivational interviewing with problem drinkers. *Behavioural Psychotherapy, 11,* 147–172.

Nelson, C., & Jackson, P. (1989). High-risk recognition: The cognitive-behavioral chain. In D.R. Laws (Ed.), *Relapse prevention with sex offenders* (pp. 167–178). New York: Guilford Press.

Nelson, C., Minor, M., Marques, J. Russell, K., & Achterkirchen, J. (1988). Relapse prevention: A cognitive-behavioral model for treatment of the rapist and child molester. *Journal of Social and Human Sexuality, 7,* 125–143.

Pithers, W.D. (1986, February). *Recent developments in relapse prevention with sex offenders.* Invited presentation at a meeting sponsored by the National Institute of Mental Health, Tampa, FL.

Pithers, W.D. (1987, January). Relapse Prevention of Sexual Aggression. Paper presented to the New York Academy of Sciences. New York, NY.

Pithers, W.D. (1990). Relapse prevention with sexual aggressors: A method for maintaining therapeutic gain and enhancing external supervision. In W.L. Marshall, D.R. Laws & H.E. Barbaree (Eds.), *Handbook of sexual assault: Issues, theories, and treatment of the offender* (pp. 343–361). New York: Plenum Press.

Pithers, W.D. (1993, October). Relapse prevention: Origins and adaptations. Paper presented at the annual research and treatment conference of the Association for the Treatment of Sexual Abusers, Boston, MA.

Pithers, W.D., & Cumming, G. F. (1989). Can relapses be prevented? Initial outcome data from the Vermont Treatment Program for Sexual Offenders. In D.R. Laws (Ed.), *Relapse prevention for sex offenders* (pp. 313–325). New York: Guilford Press.

Pithers, W.D., Cumming, G.F., Beal, L.S., Young, W., & Turner, R. (1989). Relapse prevention. In B. Schwartz (Ed.), *Sex offenders: Issues in treatment.* Washington, DC: National Institute of Corrections.

Pithers, W.D., & Gray, A.S. (1990). *The pre-adolescent sexual abuse research project.* Grant proposal submitted to the National Center on Child Abuse and Neglect, Washington, DC.

Pithers, W.D., & Gray, A.S. (1996). Utility of relapse prevention in treatment of sexual abusers. *Sexual Abuse: A Journal of Research and Treatment, 8*(3), 223–230.

Pithers, W.D., & Gray, A.S. (1998). The other half of the story: Children with sexual behavior problems. *Psychology, Public Policy and Law, 4,* 1–18.

Pithers, W.D., Kashima, K., Cumming, G., Beal, L., & Buell, M. (1988). Relapse prevention of sexual aggression. In R.A. Prentky & V.L. Quinsey (Eds.), *Human sexual aggression: Current perspectives.* Annals of the New York Academy of Sciences (Vol. 528). New York: New York Academy of Sciences.

Pithers, W.D., Marques, J.K., Gibat, C.C., & Marlatt, G.A. (1983). Relapse prevention: A self-control model of treatment and maintenance of change for sexual aggressives. In J. Greer & I.R. Stuart (Eds.), *The sexual aggressor: Current perspectives on treatment.* New York: Van Nostrand Reinhold.

Steen, C. (1993). *The relapse prevention workbook for youth in treatment.* Brandon, VT: Safer Society Press.

Stitzer, M.L., & Cox, W.M. (1996). Relapse to substance abuse: Recent findings from basic and clinical research. *Experimental and Clinical Psychopharmacology, 4,* 3–4.

Ward, T., Fon, C., Hudson, S.M., & McCormack, J. (1998). A descriptive model of dysfunctional cognitions in child molesters. *Journal of Interpersonal Violence, 13,* 129–155.

Ward, T., & Hudson, S.M. (1996). Relapse prevention: A critical analysis. *Sexual Abuse: A Journal of Research and Treatment, 8,* 177–200.

Ward, T., & Hudson, S.M. (1998). A self-regulation model of the relapse process in sexual offenders. *Journal of Interpersonal Violence, 13,* 700–725.

Ward, T., Hudson, S.M., & Marshall, W. L. (1994). The abstinence violation effect in child molesters. *Behavior Research and Therapy, 32,* 431–437.

Ward, T., Hudson, S.M., & Marshall, W.L. (1995). Cognitive distortions and affective deficits in sex offenders: A cognitive deconstructionist interpretation. *Sexual Abuse: A Journal of Research and Treatment, 7,* 67–83.

Ward, T., & Keenan, T. (1999). Child molesters' implicit theories. *Journal of Interpersonal Violence, 14,* 821–838.

Ward, T., Keenan, T., & Hudson, S.M. (2000). Understanding cognitive, affective, and intimacy deficits in sexual offenders: A developmental perspective. *Aggression and Violent Behavior, 5,* 41–62.

Ward, T., Louden, K., Hudson, S.M., & Marshall, W.L. (1995). A descriptive model of the offense chain for child molesters. *Journal of Interpersonal Violence, 10,* 342–472.

6 Using Behavioral Techniques to Control Sexual Arousal

Robert J. McGrath

Modifying disordered sexual arousal patterns is an essential element in the effective treatment of sex offenders. The importance of intervention in this area has been recognized for quite some time. Abusive sexual fantasy has been linked with abusive sexual behavior in the psychoanalytic literature since Freud's (1953) initial formulations of infant sexuality over 40 years ago. During the past 30 years, clinicians who are more behaviorally oriented have also identified this association (Abel & Blanchard, 1974; Association for the Treatment of Sexual Abusers, 1993; McGuire, Carlie, & Young, 1965). Practitioners from both of these divergent theoretical schools have consistently reported that sex offenders frequently describe ruminating about and masturbating to sexual fantasies involving the types of abusive sexual behavior in which they engage.

These clinical observations have also gained empirical support. The factor that most consistently distinguishes male sex offenders from other males is disordered sexual arousal profiles as measured by phallometric assessment (Murphy & Barbaree, 1994). In addition, sex offend-

ers whose sexual arousal to abusive themes is greater than their arousal to nonabusive themes have higher rates of recidivism (McGrath, 1991).

This chapter reviews practical strategies for treating sexual arousal disorders among sex offenders. The primary focus is on the use of four behavioral techniques; orgasmic reconditioning, covert sensitization, assisted covert sensitization, and verbal satiation. Other interventions that can complement these behavioral techniques are briefly highlighted. Because there has been minimal application of these techniques with females, the focus of this chapter is on male sex offenders.

DEVELOPING A TREATMENT PLAN

A thorough initial assessment of an offender's sexual arousal pattern is an essential first step in developing an appropriate treatment plan. Follow-up assessments during the course of treatment are also important for evaluating a client's progress and, if necessary, modifying the treatment plan.

A sexual arousal assessment should determine the age, gender, and sexual behavior preferences of the offender. The primary data sources for obtaining this information are client self-report, collateral reports, and, if possible, phallometric testing. The reader can consult several resources for information on conducting such arousal assessments (e.g., Laws & Osborn, 1983; Quinsey & Earls, 1990; Roys & Roys, 1994).

The evaluator can develop an appropriate treatment plan after he or she has conducted the assessment. Treatment plans for arousal disorders are designed to achieve two goals. The first goal is to help offenders control, reduce, or eliminate their abusive sexual arousal and interests. The second goal is to help offenders develop, maintain, or strengthen their appropriate sexual arousal and interests.

Treatment professionals can select several types of interventions to help sex offenders achieve these goals. The four behavioral treatments selected for the focus of this chapter are summarized and compared in Table 6.1.

These procedures have been selected because each meets several important criteria. Each of these procedures has the confidence of a large number of clinical practitioners (Knopp, Freeman-Longo, & Stevenson, 1992). Each has at least some empirical support (Kelly, 1982; Kilman, Sabilis, Gearing, Bukstel, & Scovern, 1982; Lanyon, 1986; Laws & Marshall, 1991; Maletsky, 1991). These procedures generally "make sense" to offenders, and they are easy to learn and use; they can be self-administered; they require minimal or no equipment; and each of these procedures requires limited staff time.

A decision concerning when to introduce these procedures in the treatment process depends on the needs of each particular client. In general, if a client enters treatment complaining that he does not feel in control of his sexual arousal to abusive themes, sexual arousal control should be one of the first therapy tasks. Helping an offender control his abusive arousal leads to recognition that treatment can be beneficial. Once an offender is not distracted by troubling sexual fantasies, he can better focus his attention on other aspects of treatment.

Often, arousal control procedures are introduced later in therapy. Understandably, many offenders are initially reluctant to honestly report their sexual arousal control problems. In addition, some offenders genuinely experience a diminution or elimination of their abusive sexual fantasies as a result of the naturally aversive process of arrest. Unfortunately, the effects of "arrest therapy" are generally short-lived. In these cases, treatment must initially educate offenders about the likelihood their sexual arousal to abusive or inappropriate themes will return and the need to develop strategies to control it when it does.

Sexual arousal control treatments often logically follow empathy training. Offenders who have successfully completed victim empathy treatment have increased motivation to control their abusive arousal so as to prevent further victims.

CONDUCTING TREATMENT

The following general protocols describe how to use each of the behavioral methods selected for review. Each method can be tailored to fit the clinician's own treatment approach and to meet special clinical challenges posed by individual offenders.

ORGASMIC RECONDITIONING

Orgasmic reconditioning (Marquis, 1970) is an overt, positive conditioning procedure in which the client pairs appropriate sexual fantasies with masturbation and orgasm. Because almost all sex offenders fantasize while masturbating or engaging in sexual relations with a partner, conditioning principles should be taught to all clients.

Orgasmic reconditioning is probably most successful with individuals who already have at least some arousal to appropriate themes. The goal is to help them increase their appropriate

TABLE 6.1   SELECTED BEHAVIORAL PROCEDURES TO ALTER SEXUAL AROUSAL

Name of Procedure	Type of Procedure	Goal of Procedure	Mechanism	Special Issues
Orgasmic Reconditioning	Overt Positive Conditioning	Increase appropriate arousal	Pair appropriate fantasy with mastur-bation and orgasm	Requires offender to masturbate
Covert Sensiti-zation	Covert Aversive Conditioning	Decrease deviant arousal	Pair deviant fantasy with aversive imagery	Use of audio tape recorder encouraged
Assisted Covert Sensitization	Overt Aversive Conditioning	Decrease deviant arousal	Pair deviant fantasy with foul odor	☐ Requires use of foul odor ☐ Clients with certain health problems excluded ☐ Use of audio tape recorder encouraged
Verbal Satiation	Extinction and Overt Positive Conditioning	Increase appro-priate arousal and decrease deviant arousal	Pair appropriate fantasy with mastur-bation and orgasm and satiate deviant fantasy through boredom	☐ Generally requires offender to masturbate ☐ Use of audio tape recorder encouraged

arousal, which may concurrently result in a de-crease of abusive arousal. Sample instructions to individuals in this group are as follows:

You have told me that when you were molesting children you would think about your victims and potential victims when you masturbated and often when you were having sex with your wife. What you were really doing was some-thing that is very interesting; it's called condi-tioning. Let me explain. Sexual feelings and orgasm feel good. When you paired—put to-gether—these thoughts about children with the pleasurable feelings of orgasm, you were ac-tually conditioning—strengthening—your in-terest in children. In fact, the more you did this, the stronger your desire for children became. Of course, it is probably difficult to remember how this all started, and you may not have been consciously thinking about what you were doing. That's understandable. What's impor-tant now is that you know how you have been conditioning yourself to be sexually interested in children and how you can use this same strategy to become more sexually aroused to

adults. From now on, it is very important for you to use appropriate fantasies—fantasies about consensual adult sex—when you are masturbating or having sex with your wife.

Some offenders have never been aroused to appropriate sexual themes and are therefore un-able to masturbate to orgasm using an appro-priate fantasy. An example of such an offender would be a pedophile whose sexual arousal has been exclusively toward children. Obviously, helping such an individual "condition" himself to sexual themes he has never been aroused to is exceedingly difficult. These individuals are often destined to be plagued by persistent abusive fan-tasies for the rest of their lives. A masturbatory fantasy change strategy is one of the few positive conditioning strategies that can be used with such an offender. In this strategy, the offender begins masturbating to his abusive fantasy of choice but changes to and uses an appropriate fantasy just prior to and during orgasm. Over time, the offender is encouraged to introduce an appropriate fantasy earlier and earlier into each treatment session. Although empirical support for this procedure is slight (Laws & Marshall, 1991), its use seems justified, given the lack of alternative treatments that can help such an offender develop appropriate arousal. Aversive procedures may improve the efficacy of fantasy change strategies, and pharmacological interventions are often appropriate for these individuals. Sample instructions are as follows:

I know that when you were young you "discovered" your sexual interest in children and that you have been aroused to them ever since. I know that you didn't choose to be this way and that your sexual interest in and behavior with children has caused you and your victims a lot of pain. There is a treatment that may be helpful. It's called masturbatory fantasy change. This procedure can help you condition yourself to become sexually aroused to fantasies and behavior with adults.

This is what I want you to do. Each time you masturbate, begin the way you usually do, thinking about young boys [or young girls]. But when you get the feeling that you are about to have an orgasm, about two to four seconds before it is going to happen, switch to an appropriate fantasy of an adult. After you are able to do that for a few weeks, you can start to fantasize about adults earlier and earlier during masturbation until you can masturbate from start to finish using adult fantasies.

Some clients need help constructing appropriate fantasies. Clients are instructed that an appropriate fantasy should generally include the following elements: (1) an adult partner; (2) care and concern for your partner; (3) a detailed description of your partner, your relationship, and your ages; (4) nonsexual activity and conversation; (5) your partner's permission for sexual activity; (6) foreplay such as kissing, hugging, and touching; (7) climax for both you and your partner; and (8) afterplay such as hugging and talking.

Clients are instructed to secure a private location where they will not be disturbed to complete their masturbatory reconditioning assign-

ments. They are also told that they should employ appropriate sexual fantasies whenever they masturbate or have sex. Having a client tape-record his masturbatory reconditioning sessions while verbalizing his fantasies allows the therapist to monitor whether a client completes his masturbatory reconditioning assignments correctly. Such monitoring can initially enhance compliance. Ultimately, however, success is dependent on the client's internal motivation.

COVERT SENSITIZATION

Covert sensitization (Abel et al., 1984; Cautela & Wisocki, 1971; Maletsky, 1991) is a covert and aversive counterconditioning technique in which the client imagines performing the chain of behaviors that led to his sexual offending; prior to imagining actually committing an offense, the client interrupts that chain by imagining an aversive consequence. This technique was originally designed to reduce an individual's deviant sexual arousal. It is also an effective method of helping offenders cognitively rehearse effective strategies to escape from high-risk situations. For this reason, it can be used with offenders regardless of whether they demonstrate arousal to deviant stimuli. Clients are typically introduced to this procedure with the following instructions:

Before committing your offenses, you may have thought about the negative consequences of what you were about to do. You may have thought about your family finding out, going to jail, or harming your victim. But clearly, when you committed your offenses, your desire to have illegal sex was stronger than your fear about getting caught or harming your victim. Reality tapes, sometimes called covert sensitization, can help you with this problem. Reality tapes are a way for you to interrupt your offending patterns by imagining upsetting scenes as soon as you start to have deviant sexual fantasies. Reality tapes help you put thoughts about the trouble you will get into and the harm you will cause your victim in the front of your mind. Reality tapes help you push thoughts about having a victim to the back of your mind.

The instructions should be broken down into as many small steps as necessary for the offender to understand and carry out the procedure following this introduction. A three-stage process is recommended. First, the offender is asked to make a list of approximately 10 abusive and 10 aversive scenes. The abusive scenes should be about offenses the offender has committed or thought about committing. They can also include high-risk situations that the offender thinks might lead to an offense in the future. The aversive scenes should describe something terrible happening to the offender or the victim as a result of reoffending. For example, logical negative consequences of reoffending, such as going to jail, losing one's family, and harming a victim, are fitting aversive scenes. Some practitioners use aversive scenes that are not logical consequences of a reoffense but elicit strong negative emotions, such as imagining the pain of a dentist's drill on a nonanesthetized tooth.

The second step is for the offender to write out sample abusive and aversive scenes. Each abusive scene should include all the elements of the offender's offense chain. For example, the scene might include the following elements: negative emotional state, thoughts about offending, sexually arousing deviant fantasies, cognitive distortions, planning, and grooming a victim. The offender should stop the abusive scene just before he would have committed an offense. The offender should describe his feelings, thoughts, and behaviors in detail and write the scenes in the first person, present tense. Each scene should take between one and two minutes to speak aloud. Aversive scenes should also be written in the first person, present tense. They should be emotionally powerful enough to cause an unpleasant autonomic reaction and generally should be longer than the abusive scenes. Treatment staff and the offender can critique these written scenes in either individual or group treatment. Once the offender demonstrates that he understands how to construct

these scenarios, he can move on to the next step in the process.

The third step is for the offender to begin pairing his abusive fantasies with the aversive scenes he has developed. He is told to obtain a tape recorder and several blank cassette tapes. He is also told to find a private place where he will not be disturbed. His homework task is to record one of his abusive scenes, to say "Stop!" out loud just before he fantasizes committing an offense, and to immediately record one of his aversive scenes. This tape is reviewed the following week in treatment. If he has had any problems, he is given supportive instruction for the next effort. If he demonstrates that he can carry out the procedure successfully, he is instructed to complete the remainder of the assignment.

Clients complete a minimum of two covert sensitization tapes per week for five weeks. Each tape includes five abusive scenes paired with five aversive scenes. More tapes or pairings per tape are added if either the treatment staff or the client thinks that this would be beneficial or is necessary. Preferably, the offender will not need to rely on written scenarios to complete this treatment. An example follows:

It's Saturday morning. It's been a long week, and what have I got to show for it? Nothing. I don't have any money. I don't have any friends. Where's my wife? She's off visiting her mother again. It's my day off. She should be with me. At least it's a nice day for fishing. I'm walking down by the river. I can see some of the neighbor boys down a ways. Jimmy is over there by himself. He always looks so lonely too. I'm saying hi to him and he seems happy to see me. He is so pretty. He looks so good in shorts. His skin's so soft. I wonder if I can get him to take his shirt off and see more of his body. I'm taking my shirt off and telling him how much I like to get a tan in the summer. I'm telling him he should try it. He's taking off his shirt. He's so beautiful, so soft. I'm getting turned on, getting hard. Wonder how it would be to touch his skin. Bet I could get him hard. No one would know. At least I would be showing him some attention. I care about him, his parents certainly don't. I don't want him to get sunburned. I'll see if he wants to use some of my tanning lotion. He's rubbing it on his legs. I'm so horny. He's putting it on his belly. I'm offering to do his back. Yes, he said OK! I'm reaching out to touch him. STOP! I'm sitting in court. They're going to sentence me today. I can't stop my hands from shaking and I'm sweating and I feel like I'm going to throw up. Oh no! Jimmy's here, and his parents, and a bunch of his relatives. I'm all alone. My wife and kids didn't show up. I knew they wouldn't. They don't want anything to do with me anymore. I can't blame them. I'm a two-time loser. I don't think my lawyer really cares either. He got my money but hasn't done much. It doesn't make any difference, I know I'm going to do time. I don't know if I can handle it. The judge's door is opening. Oh no! It's Judge Martin. He's looking right at me. He looks mad. He told me before if he ever saw me again in his court I'd be sorry. They are calling Jimmy's dad to the stand. He's screaming at me. He's telling everyone how Jimmy can't sleep, about his nightmares, about being afraid to go out of the house. He's saying I'm a monster, a danger to society, an evil person. I never wanted to hurt Jimmy. What have I done to him? What have I done to myself? The judge is looking down at me. I know he's angry. My mind is blank. It's just a garble of sounds. Then I hear it. Twenty years. There's a gasp in the courtroom. Everyone is happy. They're hugging each other. They're saying I got what I deserved. The sheriff has the handcuffs on tight now. I'm all alone. He's leading me out the side door. Oh my God! What have I done?

Although clinicians who use covert sensitization follow the same basic principles, variations exist (Picard & Sutker, 1994). For example, some practitioners advocate employing a backward chaining paradigm. In this paradigm, the offender introduces the aversive scene earlier and earlier in the abusive cognitive-behavioral chain in each successive treatment session. Thus, each element of the offense chain is directly paired with an aversive consequence.

A variation that this author advocates is for offenders to audiotape treatment sessions at home and have them reviewed by the therapist, generally in group therapy. This strategy is very cost-effective and allows staff to verify treatment compliance. Some programs, rather than using audiotapes, have offenders write their abusive and aversive scenes on note cards and read them several times a day. Other programs advocate conducting the entire procedure in the therapist's office.

Another variation is for the client to use an escape scene instead of or following the aversive scene. An escape scene entails imagining oneself successfully escaping from a high-risk situation. It is a way for offenders to cognitively rehearse strategies for escaping from potential real-life situations. An example of an escape scene used by an exhibitionist who has stopped himself in his deviant covert scene before committing an offense follows:

STOP! What am I doing? I don't want to reoffend. I'm not going to take my penis out of my pants. I'm not going to hurt that woman. I'm walking out from behind these bushes, away from her (the potential victim), back onto the sidewalk, out under the streetlights so everyone can see me. I'm shouting over to say hi to a guy I know across the street. He knows I'm here now, that will make me think twice about exposing myself now. I'm walking back to the parking lot to get my car. I'm driving home now, directly home. I stopped myself. I didn't reoffend. I didn't harm that woman. I can control myself. I won't let myself get into my offense pattern again. I'll need to figure out how I got myself into my offending pattern. I'll talk with my therapist and group as soon as I can. I'm making progress. I'm getting better. I didn't hurt anyone. I'm proud of myself.

Covert sensitization protocols using escape scenes tend to enhance an offender's feelings of self-efficacy.

Some clients find covert sensitization protocols that use aversive scenes upsetting; the use of a positive covert conditioning strategy can sometimes ameliorate this side effect. At the end of each treatment session, the client can include a positive scene in which he imagines himself as being successful and competent in some area of his life unrelated to sexual issues. Hence, what has been an aversive and difficult treatment experience can end on an affirming note.

ASSISTED COVERT SENSITIZATION

Assisted covert sensitization (Maletsky, 1974, 1991) is an overt aversive counterconditioning procedure in which the client pairs abusive sexual fantasies with the smelling of a foul odor. This procedure is essentially the same as covert sensitization except for the use of a foul odor as an aversive stimulus as opposed to aversive imagery. A foul odor is probably a more powerful and effective aversive stimulus and is certainly a more invasive one. It should be used with individuals for whom aversive imagery is not powerful enough or as an additional arousal control tool.

Directions and procedures are similar to those used in covert sensitization. The client is instructed to make a list of abusive scenes and write out a sample of those scenes for the therapist's review. The therapist then meets with the client in one or more individual meetings and instructs the client how to use the foul odor. As in covert sensitization, the client should introduce the aversive stimulus just before he imagines committing a sexual offense. In a variation developed by Jensen (1994), called minimal arousal conditioning, the offender administers the foul odor as soon as he becomes minimally sexually aroused during the scenario. After administering the foul odor, the client imagines an escape scene in which he extricates himself from the abusive scene.

Several foul odors may be used. Maletsky (1991) argues that a nauseating odor, such as putrefying tissue, is a more effective aversive stimulus than one that simply causes physical irritation, such as irritation of the nasal mucosa by ammonia. The National Adolescent Perpetrator Network (1993) recommends ammonia as the most commonly used overt aversive stimulus used with adolescents. Whatever foul odor is used, the client should be taught how to self-administer it. Ammonia capsules may be used or an ammonia-soaked cotton ball may be placed in a plastic 35mm film container or other appropriate container. Olfactory conditioning should be avoided if an offender has or develops respiratory problems or has other serious medical problems.

Once the client has appropriately employed this procedure under the supervision of his therapist, he can continue using it alone in a private setting. He should tape-record his self-administered treatment sessions so that his therapist and treatment group can verify his compliance and critique his therapy. If done conscientiously, the client's coughing or sounds of other physical reactions to the foul odor can be heard on the audiotapes he submits for review.

Clients complete a minimum of two assisted covert sensitization tapes per week for five weeks. Each tape includes five abusive scenes, each paired with the administration of a foul odor followed by an escape scene. More tapes or pairings per tape can be added if either the treatment staff or the client thinks that this would be beneficial or is necessary. Offenders can also use this technique in real-life situations by carrying a small vial of ammonia with them at all times.

VERBAL SATIATION

Verbal satiation (Hunter & Goodwin, 1992; Laws & Osborn, 1983) is an extinction procedure in which the client repeatedly verbalizes his abusive sexual fantasies until their sexually arousing properties have been extinguished through boredom. Clients refer to this procedure as "boredom therapy." For optimal effectiveness, immediately prior to beginning the satiation procedure, the client is instructed to masturbate to orgasm using appropriate fantasies. In doing so, the client begins the satiation procedure when his sexual arousal is already low. As such, this technique is really a combination of orgasmic reconditioning (previously reviewed) and a satiation procedure. Sample client instructions follow:

Let me explain by giving you a strange example. Make believe for a minute that pizza is against the law. How could you make yourself so sick and tired of pizza that you would never want to look at—much less taste—it again? Let me tell you. If you ate pizza for breakfast, lunch, dinner, and all your snacks and nothing else, you would get sick and tired of it. Now, if you were to do this, you might never want pizza again for the rest of your life, or you might gradually begin thinking about pizza in a few years or maybe even in a few months. What I can tell you, though, is that doing this strategy would eliminate any craving you have for pizza "right now."

You can use the exact same strategy to control your impulses to rape women. You can actually use this strategy to lower or eliminate your interest in raping women by repeating your rape fantasies over and over and over again until they become so boring that you have no interest in them anymore. Also, because you will be masturbating to an appropriate fantasy just before you begin repeating your abusive fantasies over and over, you will be doing two things that will make this technique more effective. First, you will be strengthening your arousal to appropriate fantasies. And second, you will be repeating your abusive fantasies after you have already had an orgasm to appropriate fantasies, so your sexual arousal will already be low and the technique will work faster.

As with other treatment interventions, the verbal satiation procedure is broken down into as many small steps as necessary for the offender to understand and complete the procedure. First, the client is asked to list five or more appropriate sexual fantasies and five or more of his most arousing abusive sexual fantasies. Second, he is asked to write out one or two appropriate fantasies and one or two abusive fantasies. The client should write them in the first person, present tense and should include his own thoughts, feelings, and behaviors, as well as those of the person with whom he is having sex. The criteria for constructing appropriate fantasies were detailed in the section on orgasmic reconditioning. For constructing abusive fantasies, the offender is told to include the following: his age and the victim's age (if the age difference is significant); his sexual arousal; the force, tricks, bribes, or coercion used on his victim; and his abusive sexual behavior.

Although the client may begin by writing out one of his complete abusive fantasies, the goal is for him to isolate the most arousing segments of this fantasy so that each of these can be targeted for satiation. When the client's written scenarios demonstrate an understanding of the procedure, he can begin the next step. An example of a abusive fantasy segment that would be repeated over and over is as follows:

I'm 35 and he's 11. I'm making him suck on my penis. It feels so good. He's real scared. He thinks I'll hit him if he stops doing it. It feels so good.

The client is instructed to obtain a tape recorder and several 90-minute audiotapes (45 minutes each side) and find a private place where he will not be disturbed. He then masturbates to orgasm to an appropriate fantasy as quickly as possible, all the while verbalizing his appropriate fantasy into the tape recorder. The client turns the tape over and rewinds it to the beginning as soon as any one of three conditions has been met: (1) he has had an orgasm, (2) 10 minutes have elapsed and he has not had an orgasm, or (3) masturbating to the appropriate fantasy is not arousing. The rationale for the last two criteria is to prevent the appropriate sexual fantasy from becoming aversive. On the second side of the audiotape, the client immediately begins verbalizing his abusive fantasies and continues for the remainder of the 45-minute tape without interruption. He should repeat each arousing element of each selected abusive fantasy for at least five minutes after the point of complete boredom. He should continue this process until he has satiated all his abusive fantasies.

To ensure a powerful satiation effect, clients should complete at least as many tapes per week as their usual number of orgasms per week; three to five tapes is typical. After 20 tapes have been completed, the therapist and client can assess whether treatment has been successful or should be continued.

There are some variations of verbal satiation. Masturbatory satiation is a variation in which the client masturbates to orgasm to an appropriate fantasy and then continues masturbating while repeatedly verbalizing his abusive fantasies (Abel et al., 1984; Maletsky, 1991; Marshall & Lippens, 1977). Obviously, masturbatory satiation is a more arduous technique. Treatment acceptance and compliance are sometimes a concern, especially with adolescents (Becker & Kaplan, 1993). Because of these issues, verbal satiation may be the preferred approach.

Another variation addresses the unwillingness or inability of some men to masturbate. In these cases, the clients can be instructed to eliminate the orgasmic reconditioning portion of the procedure and use verbal satiation alone. An increased number of treatment sessions is often required in such instances, because these men will not have lowered their sexual arousal prior to beginning the satiation component of treatment.

INTEGRATING OTHER TYPES OF TREATMENTS

Several other types of treatment interventions can complement the behavioral arousal control procedures reviewed in the preceding section (Carey & McGrath, 1989).

PHARMACOLOGICAL INTERVENTIONS. The use of pharmacological interventions with sexually aggressive and compulsive men is increasing. Antiandrogen medications have been employed with some success for over two decades (e.g., Bradford, 1990). More recently, some antidepressant medications have shown promise in helping men control aberrant sex drives (e.g., Kafka, 1994; Kafka & Prentky, 1992). Pharmacological interventions are particularly appropriate for men whose aggressive sexual behavior does not respond to any other type of intervention or when the severity of the problem requires a swift-acting intervention. These medications are often used in combination with behavioral procedures; although they may reduce an offender's sex drive, they do not necessarily change the types of stimuli to which he is aroused.

ENVIRONMENTAL CONTROLS. Reducing an offender's access to potential victims and other potentially high-risk situations through court conditions and treatment agreements enhances his ability to control his deviant sexual urges and cravings, albeit temporarily. Regardless of how effective behavioral treatments might be, offenders still need to avoid stimuli that trigger deviant sexual urges and cravings.

INDIRECT METHODS. It is important to note that interventions that do not directly target the altering of sexual arousal patterns can have a positive effect on an offender's sexual arousal. For example, child molesters who undergo victim empathy training may experience a decrease in arousal toward children because they recognize the harm they have caused their victims. Rapists whose aggressive sexual fantasies are triggered by feelings of anger will probably not benefit from sexual arousal control procedures unless they also learn to manage their anger. As a final example, social and dating skills training is critical for offenders who were too socially inadequate to initiate and maintain sexual relationships with adults, even though they may have been aroused to adults.

ADDRESSING SPECIAL PROBLEMS AND ISSUES

The behavioral treatments reviewed in this chapter are some of the more demanding and controversial interventions employed in sex offender programs. Treatment staff must consider these challenges when developing programs and carrying out these therapies. Several strategies can address these special problems and issues.

INFORMED CONSENT. Clients should be informed prior to entering treatment of any arousal control procedures they may be asked to undergo and whether failure to participate may result in termination from the program. This information allows offenders to make informed decisions about entering treatment before they have invested a considerable amount of time and resources.

SIDE EFFECTS. Arousal control procedures are quite safe but not totally benign. For example, a small group of clients may experience reactions such as excessive stress, anxiety, depression, guilt, or anger when confronting the wrongfulness of their acts during these treatments. Clinicians need to monitor their clients' responses carefully and intervene as necessary.

NETWORK EDUCATION. Successful sex offender programs depend on the backing of referral sources, facility administrators, and other interested parties. Program staff should obtain support from these individuals through educational and other efforts. Referral sources and other key individuals should be educated about arousal control procedures from program staff first, rather than from dissatisfied offenders who may present an inaccurate portrait of these techniques.

PARTNER EDUCATION. The sexual partners of clients also need education. For example, an anticipated side effect of verbal satiation is a temporary decrease in sex drive. The sexual partners of offenders should be informed of this effect so that they do not conclude that their husbands or boyfriends are no longer sexually interested in them. A partner's understanding and support of treatment can be very beneficial.

CLIENT MOTIVATION. The most powerful motivation for clients to complete arousal control procedures is for them to understand and value the goals of treatment. Clients also are more likely to become and stay motivated if they are treated with respect and dignity. Other factors that may help client motivation include

breaking assignments down into component parts based on the offender's comprehension level to avoid overwhelming clients with limited intellectual resources; helping clients develop a schedule for completing assignments; aiding clients in finding private locations to make tapes; and providing consequences for not completing assignments.

VERIFICATION. Therapists should verify treatment compliance and be alert to certain types of client faking. This chapter has advocated that offenders audiotape homework sessions, allowing the therapist to critique the client's work and offer suggestions for improvement. This also enables the therapist to verify that the client is doing his prescribed homework. Such a verification procedure can enhance client compliance. Because listening to clients' tapes is time consuming, emotionally draining, and often clinically unfruitful, spot-checking tapes by listening to several 30-second sections is generally adequate. Erasing portions of the client tapes after review prevents clients from turning in the same tape on different occasions. Offenders who go to great lengths to fake behavioral assignments may not have the motivation required to benefit from this or other types of treatment.

IMAGERY PROBLEMS. Almost all the arousal control procedures presented in this chapter require the client to fantasize, a task that may pose some difficulty for some clients. An offender's ability to fantasize may be enhanced by teaching him to use relaxation strategies at the beginning of treatment sessions. Also, clients often find that recalling images of past events or real people is generally easier than constructing imagined fantasies. Clients who are still unable to fantasize can write out their entire sexual offense scenes and read them during treatment sessions.

BOOSTER SESSIONS. Arousal control procedures are generally effective in the short run but may "wear off" over time. Each offender needs to be educated about this possibility or even its likelihood. A return of arousal control problems does not necessarily signal a treatment failure;

rather, it is an indication that the client needs to reapply strategies that have been effective in the past. Treatment staff should encourage offenders to periodically undergo booster sessions to help them maintain treatment changes.

CONCLUSION

Although not universally effective with all offenders, the behavioral arousal control procedures reviewed in this chapter play a central role in the comprehensive treatment of sex offenders. An ongoing challenge for the therapist is identifying which of these treatments is most appropriate for which clients. This is a process whereby offenders frequently test the efficacy of a variety of arousal control strategies. Ideally, each offender can find several strategies that help him reduce or eliminate his abusive sexual urges and develop or maintain appropriate sexual interests. The ultimate reward of successful treatment in this area is an important one. Sex offenders who learn to control their sexual arousal reduce their risk of reoffending.

REFERENCES

Abel, G.G., Becker, J.V., Cunningham-Rathner, J., Rouleau, J., Kaplan, M., & Reich, J. (1984). *The treatment of child molesters: A manual.* Unpublished manuscript, Columbia University.

Abel, G.G., & Blanchard, E.B. (1974). The role of fantasy in the treatment of sexual deviation. *Archives of General Psychiatry, 30,* 467–475.

Association for the Treatment of Sexual Abusers. (1993). *The ATSA practitioner's handbook.* Lake Oswego, OR: Author.

Becker, J.V., & Kaplan, M.S. (1993). Cognitive-behavioral treatment of the juvenile sex offender. In H.E. Barbaree, W.L. Marshall, & S.E. Hudson (Eds.), *The juvenile sex offender* (pp. 264–277). New York: Guilford Press.

Bradford, J.M.W. (1990). The antiandrogen and hormonal treatment of sex offenders. In W.L. Marshall, D.R. Laws, & H.E. Barbaree (Eds.), *Handbook of sexual assault: Issues, theories, and treatment of the offender* (pp. 297–310). New York: Plenum Press.

Carey, C.H., & McGrath, R.J. (1989). Coping with urges and cravings. In D.R. Laws (Ed.), *Relapse prevention with sex offenders.* New York: Guilford Press.

Cautela, J.R., & Wisocki, P.A. (1971). Covert sensitization for the treatment of the sexual deviations. *The Psychological Record, 21,* 37–48.

Freud, S. (1953). Three essays on the theory of sexuality. In *Standard Edition, 7* (pp. 172–201). London: Hogarth Press.

Howes, R.J. (1995). A survey of plethysmographic assessment in North America. *Sexual Abuse: A Journal of Research and Treatment, 7,* 9–24.

Hunter, J.A., & Goodwin, D.W. (1992). The clinical utility of satiation therapy with juvenile sexual offenders: Variations and efficacy. *Annals of Sex Research, 5,* 71–80.

Jensen, S.H. (1994). *Minimal arousal conditioning.* Unpublished manuscript.

Kafka, M.P. (1994). Sertraline pharmacotherapy for paraphilias and paraphilia-related disorders: An open trial. *Annals of Clinical Psychiatry, 6,* 189–195.

Kafka, M.P., & Prentky, R. (1992). Fluoxetine treatment of nonparaphilic sexual addictions and paraphilias in men. *Journal of Clinical Psychiatry, 53,* 351-358.

Kelly, R.J. (1982). Behavioral reorientation of pedophiliacs: Can it be done? *Clinical Psychology Review, 2,* 387–408.

Kilman, P.R., Sabalis, R.F., Gearing, M.L., Bukstel, L.H., & Scovern, A.W. (1982). The treatment of paraphilias: A review of the outcome research. *Journal of Sex Research, 18,* 193–252.

Knopp, F.H., Freeman-Longo, R., & Stevenson, W.F. (1992). *Nationwide survey of juvenile and adult sex-offender treatment programs and models: 1992.* Orwell, VT: Safer Society Press.

Lanyon, R.I. (1986). Theory and treatment in child molestation. *Journal of Consulting and Clinical Psychology, 54,* 176–182.

Laws, D.R., & Marshall, W.L. (1991). Masturbatory reconditioning with sexual deviates: An evaluative review. *Advances in Behavior Research and Therapy, 13,* 13–25.

Laws, D.R., & Osborn, C.A. (1983). How to build and operate a behavioral laboratory to evaluate and treat sexual deviance. In J.B. Stuart & I.R. Greer (Eds.), *The sexual aggressor: Current perspectives on treatment* (pp. 267–289). New York: Van Nostrand Reinhold.

Maletsky, B.M. (1974). "Assisted" covert sensitization in the treatment of exhibitionism. *Journal of Consulting and Clinical Psychology, 42,* 34–40.

Maletsky, B.M. (1991). *Treating the sexual offender.* Newbury Park, CA: Sage.

Marquis, J. (1970). Orgasmic reconditioning: Changing sexual object choice through controlling masturbation fantasies. *Journal of Behavior Therapy and Experimental Psychiatry, 1,* 263–271.

Marshall, W.L., & Lippens, K. (1977). The clinical value of boredom: A procedure for reducing inappropriate sexual interests. *Journal of Nervous and Mental Diseases, 165,* 283–287.

McGrath, R.J. (1991). Sex-offender risk assessment and disposition planning: A review of empirical and clinical findings. *International Journal of Offender Therapy and Comparative Criminology, 35,* 328–350.

McGuire, R.J., Carlisle, J.M., & Young, B.G. (1965). Sexual deviation as a conditioned behavior: A hypothesis. *Behavior Research and Therapy, 2,* 185–190.

Murphy, W.D., & Barbaree, H.E. (1994). *Assessments of sex offenders by measures of erectile response: Psychometric properties and decision making.* Brandon, VT: Safer Society Press.

National Adolescent Perpetrator Network. (1993). The revised report from the national task force on juvenile sexual offending, of the National Adolescent Perpetrator Network. *Juvenile and Family Court Journal, 44,* 1–121.

Picard, A., & Sutker, L.W. (1994, November). The value of covert sensitization as a treatment technique with offenders in the British Columbia forensic system. Paper presented at the 13th annual Association for the Treatment of Sexual Abusers conference, San Francisco.

Quinsey, V.L., & Earls, C.M. (1990). The modification of sexual preferences. In W.L. Marshall, D.R. Laws, & H.E. Barbaree (Eds.), *Handbook of sexual assault: Issues, theories, and treatment of the offender* (pp. 279–295). New York: Plenum Press.

Roys, D.T., & Roys, P. (1994). *Protocol for phallometric assessment: A clinician's guide.* Brandon, VT: Safer Society Press.

7 The Sex Abuser Treatment Group Process

Peter Loss

The ongoing sex offender treatment group is the core element of specialized intervention with this difficult and challenging population. Although programs vary in the design of the various corollary interventions such as family work and educational programs, the long-term treatment group is the mainstay of the sex offender treatment program (Schwartz, 1995). The ongoing treatment group is the intensive and personal focus of the program, centralizing and integrating the skills, issues, and information from other aspects of the program. The format of the group process described in this chapter is applicable to both juvenile and adult sex offenders who receive offense-specific treatment in a wide range of settings, from community programs to correctional facilities. Before commencing any treatment procedures, all offenders must be screened and accepted for ongoing treatment following a specialized sex offender risk assessment, such as that outlined by Loss and Ross (1988).

The basic assumptions and components of treatment described herein are based, in part, on 10 years of specialized juvenile and adult sex offender treatment, training, consultation, and publication (from 1978 to 1988) with my longtime partner and colleague Jonathan E. Ross. The treatment philosophy and procedures in this chapter have been developed from providing direct treatment and program development services in a variety of community-based, residential, and correctional programs.

Due to staffing and budgetary limits, many programs are unable to initially provide a full range of services, including formal psychoeducational classes, family programs, or follow-up community treatment. The components discussed in this chapter can be viewed as a framework to be gradually adopted as program development proceeds, with one important exception. The basic ongoing sex offender treatment group described in this chapter must be employed throughout treatment. Corollary treatment such as psychoeducational classes or family intervention are extremely important, but they cannot be substituted for ongoing treatment groups. The regularly scheduled, personally intensive treatment group is the focus of each offender's identification of contributing factors to sexual assault and ongoing integration of positive change resulting from such a learning process.

If the ongoing treatment group is absent, the provider will be less able to verify that internalization is taking place. Offenders are generally able to parrot classroom material and demonstrate surface-level participation or progress. However, in a recapitulation of previous offending patterns, some offenders fail to emotionally, behaviorally, and substantively incorporate what they have heard. Unfortunately, this usually results in a contrived flurry of jargon and buzzwords that providers have legitimately embraced, such as control, recovery, cycles, and triggers. Conversely, providers should be aware that most offenders begin legitimate change with superficial examination of these same concepts. Presentation of material about power abuse and cycles should be integrated experientially and behaviorally over time. This important change is more likely to be observable and verifiable in an ongoing intensive treatment group than in a class.

Psychoeducational material may be presented to pretrial offenders in some cases as an attempt to encourage honesty and participation in treatment. It is common for offenders to misrepresent participation in psychoeducational programming as treatment in order to gain a positive outcome in courts, in parole and classification board hearings, and with other decision-making bodies. Consequently, all programs should emphasize the limits of psychoeducational material to offenders and their families and especially, in writing, to clients' attorneys and the courts. Psychoeducational intervention is not a substitute for ongoing sex offender treatment. It cannot provide risk assessment information or a parole or classification evaluation, and it should not be represented as such to anyone.

TREATMENT PHILOSOPHY AND GOALS

To maximize offender accountability and safety, providers should strongly consider the following basic philosophy and goals used in treatment programming by the author:

- Sexual assault is a crime that violates the rights, safety, and dignity of others.

- Individuals victimized by offenders should be identified to the proper authorities. They need an opportunity to obtain treatment, recover from victimization, and live with physical and psychological safety.

- Offenders should be arrested, prosecuted, and held accountable for their crimes, regardless of their juvenile or adult status, and regardless of the availability of treatment. They require legal and personal accountability for their destructive actions in order to recover effectively.

- Offenders require physical and psychological separation from their victims. Resumption of contact may eventually take place when sexual assault involves family members, using specific safety guidelines.

- Offenders should have available, and be mandated to receive, a sex offender–specific risk assessment and ongoing specialized structured treatment by an individual or program with demonstrated experience, training, and/or licensure in treating sex offenders in a wide range of settings.

- All offenders must sign waivers of confidentiality prior to the assessment interview, to allow the provider to report risk information and unreported crimes against persons and generally to safeguard the community from potential harm.

- The treatment provider's ultimate goal is public safety, consistent with the safety of a sex offender who is genuinely committed to recovery.

- Sex offender treatment is long-term, recovery-based group treatment that involves specific safeguards, family intervention, treatment contracting, identification and control of contributing personal and interpersonal factors to crimes, the building of alternative means of meeting personal needs, and the prevention of future reoffending.

- The success and safety of sex offender treatment are determined by the degree of direct coordination with victim treatment, residential/secure line staff, criminal justice, corrections, law enforcement, child protection, judicial, and other agencies in an interagency, interdisciplinary, and collaborative approach to sexual aggression.

The principal goal of sex offender treatment is to use the interpersonal power of the sex offender group process to identify and control destructive thinking and behavior patterns and to replace dysfunctional patterns with positive and healthy patterns. Sex offenders are individuals with multiple deficits in many personal and interpersonal areas. They typically are capable of developing honesty, self-awareness, personal responsibility, self-esteem, decision-making and problem-solving skills, a range of positive emotions, and communication skills, as well as organizing their recovery into goals, safeguards, rules, and other practices that prevent reoffending.

THE PSYCHOEDUCATIONAL GROUP PROCESS

Psychoeducation is an extremely important corollary to sex offender treatment. Some form of this intervention is employed formally and informally throughout the treatment process. The specialized sex offender treatment process begins with a formal emphasis on educating offenders and their families or spouses. Offenders entering a weekly treatment group after participating in the psychoeducational process have a basic understanding of the various issues involved in sexual aggression and the expectations of a specialized treatment program. Their later work on their offending and living patterns will be analyzed using the information provided during this psychoeducational phase of treatment.

The initial psychoeducational group is a classroom-style intervention with material that is didactically presented by one or more staff members. The material and discussion are general and include overall patterns of sexually aggressive behavior, motives, profiles, and consequences to the victim. Offenders are advised that treatment groups, which are the most important aspect of the program, will occur at the conclusion of the psychoeducational phase and will be explained in detail during the last sessions of the psychoeducational process. Offenders are notified that as a general rule they will be postponing in-depth personal discussions and detailed crime analysis until they are in the ongoing treatment group. Discussions containing personal information are appropriate as long as the primary goals of educating and orienting the entire group are met. Since offenders commonly tend to disclose specific personal information, they may be instructed to record the items in a journal, along with written assignments given to offenders at this stage.

All offenders are required to follow safety conditions outlined during assessment, such as no contact with their victims and, for child sexual abusers, a requirement that they not be alone with minors. Offenders are required to report any information involving safety violations or any potential risk to others or themselves at any time during the treatment process. Under these circumstances, it may be necessary to file a statutory child abuse and neglect report, notify law enforcement or other authorities, or impose program sanctions.

The basic outline for the initial psychoeducational group should include the following topics: offenderology (or the psychology and profile of the offender); victimology, both short- and long-term effects; and the expectations of a sex offender treatment program (for more detail on these topics, see Loss, Ross, & Richardson, 1988). Offenders commonly retain only a fraction of the material presented due to their anxiety levels and the presence of continuing offender characteristics, such as denial and minimization. Thus providers should maintain a narrow focus for the topics in the beginning of intervention in order to maximize offender retention, and the issues mentioned are best repeated throughout treatment by providing ongoing educational groups to supplement the sex offender treatment groups described in this chapter. Although one can present broader initial information than is suggested by this outline, experience has shown that additional and more specific topics will be better received after ongoing treatment has had an impact on the offender.

The psychoeducational information is presented in an informative and matter-of-fact manner, similar to that used in the initial assessment interview. All information should be provided with the explicit rationale that educational material can be directly incorporated into each offender's understanding of the onset of sexual aggression, factors that contribute to sexual assault, and safe management of the offending cycle. Educational material should include:

- specific case-based information about myths and misconceptions about sexual assault, sex offenders, and victims

- typical past histories of sex offenders, including past offenses and sexually aggressive fantasizing

- other related crimes, such as animal abuse, fire setting, and burglary

- the role of pornography in offending patterns

- related behavior patterns such as denial, minimization, manipulation, power abuse, violence, substance abuse, and avoidance

- childhood and developmental patterns and family issues

- a listing of short- and long-term personal, interpersonal, and developmental effects of sexual aggression on the victim

Parents, spouses, significant others, or in some cases residential care staff are expected to attend psychoeducational classes, depending on geographic location, practicality, and an initial family assessment that screens out disruptive or high-risk parents and spouses. The participation of parents and significant others fosters their ability to understand and comanage the various issues involved in treatment. If geographic circumstances make regular attendance impractical, parents can be invited to a single lengthier, condensed session to receive the information. Material can be sent in written form or provided through agencies working with the family in the home community.

Offenders with educational deficits are expected to address their limitations through school, GED programs, Literacy Volunteers, or other available services. To assist their reading in sex offender treatment, they can work with another recovering offender or a staff member in residential/secure settings identified by the treatment provider. If necessary, reading and writing assignments can be replaced by behavioral assignments, such as a personal or phone interview of individuals or professionals assigned by the program, or by watching videotapes with a diligent and responsible oral report to the class.

All offenders are provided a copy of *Who Am I and Why Am I in Treatment?* (Freeman-Longo & Bays, 1988), a workbook specifically designed for sex offenders. Workbooks designed specifically for juvenile sex offenders are also available. The workbook provides an opportunity to begin documenting past experiences, offending cycles, and other material germane to ongoing sex offender treatment. Workbook-oriented publications focusing on self-reflection and responsibility facilitate the initial personal work on contributing factors to offending and goal setting and can include documents developed internally by various programs. Workbooks and other readings are especially important, because the offender can generalize the work and issues of the program outside the class, particularly in residential and correctional environments. The writing generated by assignments in a workbook should be reviewed as it is completed during the psychoeducational class, with written comments and questions for the offender.

As with the psychoeducational material presented during assessment, offenders should be reminded about the waiver of confidentiality and the policy of reporting unreported sexual assault crime. The removal of secrecy from sex offender treatment is essential to offender accountability and victim recovery and significantly conflicts with the nondisclosure recommendations by Freeman-Longo and Bays (1988) and some other treatment programs.

During the psychoeducational class, as well as throughout treatment, participants are given reading assignments. Offenders are expected to provide brief reports on the basic points of the reading and its impact on their understanding of their offending. A variety of publications about sexual assault and the impact on the victim by noted authors in the field are available. Examples of publications used for reading assignments are *Men Who Rape* by A. Nicholas Groth (1979), *Child Sexual Abuse* by David Finkelhor (1984), and any publications by Suzanne Sgroi or Ann Burgess. Providers should also consider publications about related topics such as substance abuse, family dysfunction, domestic violence, self-esteem, or relationships, which encourage a view of sexual assault beyond the crime itself. John Bradshaw's publications on family issues, including *Healing the Shame that Binds You* (1988), and Thomas Gordon's *Parent Effectiveness Training* (1975) have been informative and helpful to offenders. Other written information from victim organizations or rape crisis centers or generated by the sex offender program itself can also be used.

Videotaped material is also presented to offenders, generally containing interviews with survivors of sexual assault and offenders discussing various aspects of their crime or treatment. These videotapes have been recorded by the author during many years of treating offenders and survivors of abuse. Also, since numerous television productions contain themes about sexual aggression, offenders are assigned to watch movies, news presentations, or documentaries, followed by reports and discussion. Media or news shows containing inaccurate or misleading accounts of sexual assault are a helpful source of material for this class, provided that the material and presentation are directly challenged by the treatment provider. Providers may choose to videotape their own material, seek material from local agencies, or purchase commercially produced interviews and programs from organizations such as the Safer Society Foundation or Forensic Mental Health Associates.

It can be helpful for recovering sex offenders to function as facilitators. Facilitators are offenders who have successfully completed a minimum of two to three years of long-term treatment (higher-risk offenders require longer periods of treatment or may not be appropriate as facilitators). Facilitators who have accepted full responsibility for their crimes, have been honest and self-disclosing, and are safely managing their cycles to prevent reoffending are in a unique position to offer credible participant information to offenders who are new to treatment. Recovering offenders also provide an example of responsible recovery, as well as a tangible and reachable goal for offenders who may be discouraged or pessimistic in the early stages of treatment.

In residential settings, such facilitators may be available to consult with new offenders or to answer questions, provided that facilitators are monitored and that all information and interactions are funneled through the providers and their group. With full disclosure to new offenders, facilitators in secure and residential environments are also requested to provide feedback on offenders in class, including any observations about offenders' commitment to treatment and observations of risky or cooperative behavior during their secure treatment.

Extreme caution must be used in selecting offenders for the facilitator role, and only after programs have had long-term experience with the treatment of sex offenders. First, the role of facilitator implicitly involves power, and premature assignment to this role may reinforce abusive power attitudes and thinking. Second, a common form of avoidance involves covering present unresolved personal conflicts with a convincing display of legitimate education and confrontation of other offenders. Premature assignment to the facilitator role strengthens this superficiality and may indirectly encourage offending patterns to reemerge. Third, offender facilitators who are unclear about their role or who are unable to handle the responsibility may create destructive subgroups.

All offenders, including facilitators, must be reminded that facilitators are not treatment providers. They are limited to an advisory role only, and no secrets are to be kept during any interactions. Although facilitators offer significant and effective feedback, final clinical decision making lies exclusively with the treatment provider. Such clear delineation of responsibilities is important for the facilitator as well as for the offenders receiving treatment. Offenders should be given concrete statements about the roles of providers and facilitators in order to minimize role confusion and discourage potential manipulation by offenders in treatment.

The psychoeducational class is concluded with a detailed presentation of the specific expectations, policies, and procedures of the specialized sex offender program. At this time, offenders are provided with copies of an offender treatment contract (described later) and a list of written assignments. Each offender is required to read the contract and, at the next session, to review, ask questions, and in some cases add special conditions. Offenders must then sign the contract. Depending on the setting and the level of parental involvement in the treatment of juvenile offenders, parents read and sign a parental supplement to the contract acknowledging that they have read and understand the agreement, as well as an agreement to additional supervisory and safety measures. Facilitators or guest offender speakers are especially helpful at this time to provide the participant perspective concerning treatment.

Written assignments include completion of a reoffense risk list. The list is similar to material contained in the workbook (Freeman-Longo & Bays, 1988) but is done as a single assignment.

Each offender is asked to list attitudinal, behavioral, and emotional information that appears to coincide with the onset or timing of past and present offending. This information, along with workbook material and class discussion, represents the early analysis of contributing factors for the offender and will ultimately be used to identify warning signs so that the offender can choose safe behavior and avoid future reoffending.

Offenders must also complete an assignment entitled the reoffense scenario. Similar in intent to the reoffense risk list, this assignment requires offenders to specifically recite a plan to reoffend, including how they would gain access to victims, and, on a personal level, the factors that may lead to offending. The purpose of this assignment is to anticipate and avoid future unsafe patterns, locations, and behaviors or any contributing factor to offending. Offenders regularly express confusion about this assignment, since they view their goal as to avoid reoffending, and writing a plan appears to encourage additional crimes. On the contrary, participants must be advised that the more personal and specific the information about the dynamics of their destructive problem, the greater their ability to recognize and prevent future aggression.

Lastly, each offender is required to formulate specific, detailed, and, if possible, verifiable treatment goals. Goals should be directed toward the general issues identified during assessment that might contribute to the sexual assault cycle. Examples of these issues include isolation, poor communication, anger, low self-esteem, and manipulation. Having the offenders write and meet specific goals avoids the limits of conventional insight-oriented treatment work and encourages practical, reachable change. The more specific the goal, generally the greater the emphasis on skill building and the greater the feeling of success on the part of the offender, whose experience with positive gains is usually limited. Legitimate and lasting improvement in self-worth usually begins to deter the tendency toward dehumanizing the self and others inherent in sexual assault and translates positively into curbing destructive and aggressive crime patterns. Offenders tend to initially identify legitimate but broad areas they perceive as needing change. Providers should assist offenders in specifying concrete means to reach their goals.

THE ONGOING SEX OFFENDER TREATMENT GROUP

GROUP COMPOSITION AND ASSIGNMENT

At the conclusion of the psychoeducational class, offenders are assigned to an ongoing sex offender treatment group. Other than age considerations and experience with specialized treatment, treatment providers can group offenders in a way that will generally provide a homogeneous fit in terms of levels of maturity, risk, general functioning, learning and personal limitations, and interpersonal skills, as well as type of offense. Group assignments should be flexible enough so that reassignment is possible if ongoing observation indicates that an offender should be reclassified. Sex offenders should not be assigned based solely on classification status, legal crime status, or length of sentence unless the assignment is based on a sex offense–specific risk assessment. In terms of functioning and risk levels, offenders are frequently housed heterogeneously within secure facility privilege levels, within correctional classification or security levels and facilities, or in the community. Despite these external or legal groupings, group assignment should optimally be based on differences in functioning, risk, and limitation levels.

Juveniles and adults should be treated separately, although some overlap should be allowable so that more habituated juvenile offenders can be assigned to younger adult groups in some cases. Immature adult offenders or those with interpersonal deficits should not be assigned to juvenile treatment groups. This precaution is important in order to avoid direct or symbolic recapitulation of the age and sophistication dif-

ferential present in sexual assault, as well as minimizing the reenactment of the "victim role" for any younger offender.

Other age considerations involve grouping juvenile sex offenders into younger and older adolescent groups. Again, depending on age, maturity level, and seriousness of offending, juvenile offenders can be divided into a younger group ranging in age from approximately 12 to 14 and an older group ranging in age from approximately 15 to 18. This categorization scheme takes into account developmental and experiential differences between early and later adolescence. Such a division also minimizes the potential for older and more serious offenders to gain controlling access to younger and more vulnerable adolescent offenders. Providers should keep in mind that, regardless of the categories being used, reenactment of offending relationships can occur in any group and should be monitored by observation and open discussion.

Group assignment based solely on offense type, such as child sexual abuse and rape assault, is not necessary. If the characteristics of the particular pool of offenders are such that categorization by offense would provide the most sensible and cohesive work on recovery, then such an assignment can be therapeutically useful. However, groups combining offense categories can be conducted, provided that the offender-perceived differences in crime categories are openly addressed during the group process. Rape offenders often initially view themselves as having committed a more "socially acceptable" crime compared to child sexual abuse offenders, especially in correctional environments. Such "pecking-order" distortions usually dissipate with the group process and with direct challenge by group leaders.

Sadistic assaults, homicide or attempted homicide, abduction, habitual and/or commercial exploitation of others, and institutional sexual assaults are a few examples of behaviors committed by offenders who should be classified as higher risk. This group includes offenders classified at a high risk level by a specialized assessment, even though they may not have committed or been charged with the specific high-risk offenses outlined here. High-risk offenders are generally not initially treatable in community settings. Some high-risk offenders may require indefinite treatment in a secure setting, with a much higher degree of supervision and electronic monitoring if release is legally imminent. Treatment of higher-risk offenders requires much longer-term intervention, more provider preparation, and a higher degree of both skill and caution in measuring *genuine* progress. Mixing risk categories may allow a more habituated offender's deeper dysfunction and misbehavior to contaminate the progress of positive skill development by an offender with a lower risk level.

Offenders can also be assigned to specific groups based on general functioning level, which may contribute to their risk level. Functionally and intellectually impaired offenders require separate group sessions so that the entire group process can be scaled to match their limitations. Offenders functioning at lower intellectual levels, those with specific learning disabilities or social skills deficits, significantly isolated offenders, and some selected psychotic offenders in secure environments may best be treated if they are assigned to a lower-functioning group. Conversely, offenders possessing the ability to participate in a group process that requires social skills and abstract thinking can be assigned to a higher-functioning group session. The emphasis on social skills is only for the purpose of general placement in a group setting and should not be confused with genuine emotional attachment to others that develops with ongoing treatment.

One assignment variable that departs from the others is that of experience in specialized treatment. Treatment providers should strive to attain a heterogeneous mixture of experienced and inexperienced offenders in order to allow "veteran" offenders to act as positive role models to offenders who are new to treatment. First, experienced group members can help new group members in addressing sexual assault, safety issues, group expectations, and support for honesty and compliance. Experienced members are in an ideal position to confront new members who exhibit uncooperative or risky behavior. Second, experienced members personify a goal to strive for and provide practical demonstration of positive or constructive behavior. Providers should simultaneously ensure that the needs of the more experienced members are met by assignment to a group with varied experience.

Providers with too small a group of offenders to divide them using these guidelines can provide group treatment to offenders with heterogeneous functioning levels as their program and client base increase. However, the provider should prepare for and discuss the inevitable imbalances that will be evident to the offenders. Functionally limited offenders will require time to address basic social skills deficits and cognitive concepts and may be less able to participate in an abstract examination of contributing factors than a higher-functioning offender. This dynamic can slow the group's development as a cohesive support system, but it can also encourage the identification and toleration of differences.

GROUP STRUCTURE

The ongoing sex offender treatment group is a long-term, open-ended group. New offenders are continually entering the treatment group after completing the psychoeducational class. Group members may have graduated to an advanced type of treatment or transferred to another correctional facility; on occasion, members are terminated from the group due to uncooperativeness or failure to address risk problems. Rather than using narrow time or classification limits, the treatment process is defined by the tasks and changes each offender faces in ongoing recovery and treatment.

It is recommended that an ongoing sex offender treatment group contain a maximum of six to seven members. A group session may be conducted with as few as two members. The author has found that convening a treatment group with more than seven members significantly reduces the number and depth of issues that can be personally addressed in the session and in the program. Given that many offenders avoid responsibility by behaving in a superficially compliant manner, larger groups often decrease the treatment provider's ability to distinguish between genuine and feigned progress. Larger groups can also diminish the offender's ability to achieve intimacy and trust and to report and address contract violations.

The treatment group should meet at least once a week for approximately 90 to 120 minutes, with meetings held at a regularly scheduled time. Shorter meetings, even in aftercare arrangements following intensive residential treatment, do not allow sufficient opportunity to provide effective support and monitoring. Upon release from a secure treatment setting, an offender's issues that need to be addressed may change, but the need to have ample time to implement learned changes does not. The frequency of the group meetings may change once treatment providers elect to move a recovering offender to a more advanced recovery group. Programs that charge a fee should collect fees upon the participants' arrival at each group session. Fiscal responsibility is another personal responsibility that should be incorporated into group discussions and the treatment contract.

Ideally, regardless of the setting, programs should attempt to provide one to three weekly ongoing sex offender treatment groups, supplemented by a variety of related psychoeducational groups, skill-building sessions, and task groups whenever possible. In some settings, especially residential and secure settings, such educational information may be available in the form of job interview training, parenting classes, daily management skills, and sex education. If staffing or funding limits the ability to provide separate group sessions, providers may elect to schedule ongoing treatment groups and convert the content of those groups to an educational or skill-building format. Residential or correctional sex offender programs can be conducted either at a central location where offenders living in various areas assemble for their group ses-

sions or, optimally, in a facility expressly designed for the separate housing of sex offenders in ongoing specialized treatment.

Ongoing psychoeducational sessions can be conducted by one staff member and may be made available to all program participants rather than one particular group. Classes can be offered on a variety of topics and also may be conducted by guest speakers or facilitators from outside the program. Topics can include analysis of offending history and sexual assault motives; the sexual assault cycle and emotional, familial, and environmental contributing factors or triggers; victimology and empathy; ongoing recovery issues and characteristics; relationships with women; dating and human sexuality; sex education; authority issues; parole preparation and community planning; assertiveness training; and family issues. Psychoeducational sessions include new topics as well as repeated and more in-depth examination of issues previously discussed.

The correctional program conducted by the author provides a weekly ongoing psychoeducational forum that includes information about healthy versus unhealthy childhood development and relationship characteristics, self-worth issues, family communication patterns and couples issues, and parenting skills. Offenders are asked for their input and to suggest topics so that the classes target the specific issues they face. Subgroups of offenders with specific needs, such as those who require basic social skills training, attend separate and smaller sessions.

All participants are also expected to attend a weekly series of classes provided by individuals such as prosecutors, corrections officers, police officers, parole officers, and representatives from other agencies. Such classes focus on the effects of sexual assault on the victim; safeguards and supervision for sex offenders; substance abuse; sex education; identification of available aftercare resources; assistance with various personal management issues upon release; male victimization and men's issues; and coping with authority issues.

TASK GROUPS

A portion of the psychoeducational forum can be devoted to developing task groups. A task group is a group of offenders who focus their attention on relevant legislative, correctional, or educational issues. Offenders are selected on the basis of their having demonstrated a commitment to ongoing long-term recovery. Participants are asked to provide written information that may benefit the legislative or policy-making process by explaining the dynamics of sexual assault and the nature of specialized treatment. This information should be screened and edited by program staff.

Two current examples of task group issues are laws requiring community notification when sex offenders are released from correctional institutions and measures providing for civil commitment of sex offenders to correctional facilities. These issues have generated considerable attention in the news media and discussion among offenders in ongoing treatment. A task group can generate valuable offender-based written information about risk factors and recovery, which could aid in the promotion of public safety. This information can be offered to a legislative body drafting or considering public safety laws. Task groups can also provide information about sexual assault, public safety, and treatment to the judiciary, parole and classification authorities, correctional staff, juvenile correctional facilities, police departments, and the media.

Task groups not only foster interpersonal growth and collaborative skills but also allow offenders an opportunity to educate, provide information, and otherwise constructively address broader social and systemic problems. As an additional contribution to the field of sex offender treatment, offenders who have committed themselves to recovery are asked to videotape interviews about their offending and treatment for the ongoing training of other professionals and agencies.

GROUP STAFFING PATTERNS

Each ongoing treatment group requires two providers to share responsibilities. Co-therapists must obviously work well together and embrace the program philosophy equally. Using two group leaders allows one provider to function as a clinical observer while the second provider directly addresses group issues. Also, offenders entering treatment tend to exhibit traits such as avoidance or disruption, or they try to control and manipulate others. Maintaining an appropriate level of control often requires two leaders to effectively manage the group process and facilitate adherence to treatment contract rules. In addition, two therapists can provide each other with moral support in this difficult work, as well as the opportunity to critique each other's group facilitation.

Group leaders prepare, plan, and maintain a record of each group's activities, assignments, and attendance. Documented attendance may be reported to probation or parole and other authorities; explicit recording of assignments and issues promotes continuity. During preparation time, the co-providers can pool information gathered from collaborating agencies and classes (see chapter 2). If issues or conflicts have been identified, the providers decide during this preparatory time which one of them will address the conflict with the offender and what approach will be necessary to manage the problem.

On some occasions, it is helpful to choose one provider to confront the offender, while the second provider generally offers support to the offender. In the case of serious misbehavior or risk, both providers need to confront the offender, set limits, and outline expectations for a change in behavior. When an offender discloses his or her own victimization or another traumatic event, both providers may assume a supportive role.

Programs should equally divide the authority and ally roles between male and female providers to avoid stereotypical sex roles, despite the fact that the providers may have an employer-employee relationship outside the group. Unequal group leader relationships encourage attempts to split and manipulate the treatment providers by group participants. During the group session, documentation in the file may be added, and at the conclusion of the session, both providers should review the dynamics of the group, provide constructive criticism to each other, and plan for the next scheduled session.

Co-therapists should be able to deal with offender histories and behaviors that include sexually explicit and aggressive material. Such information can evoke normal feelings of outrage in the provider and can create a dilemma, since the provider needs to respond professionally to the offender. A balance can be struck by clearly confronting the offender in a matter-of-fact manner with the serious nature of sexual assault crimes, together with the hope and basic ingredients for change. All confrontations should be based on the necessity that the offender hear, learn, and accept the association between an outrageous, hurtful crime and the damage caused by such a crime. Offenders must understand that such an association is a normal and empathic appraisal of sexual assault that may assist them in avoiding such behavior in the future. Providers who are recovering from their own victimization need to have attained a balanced perspective on their experience through treatment or another mode of healthy integration. Providers with unrecovered sexual victimization might replicate destructive and hurtful experiences for themselves and may negatively affect sex offender treatment due to their unmanaged anger or their need to intimidate the offenders with whom they are working.

Extragroup team members should be notified of or notify the group treatment providers about pertinent offender behavior or risk issues, and offenders should be made aware of their roles and boundaries. The type of information provided must generally be limited to issues of risk and cooperativeness. Personal issues not involving potential risk to others are kept private. Information covered by the previously mentioned waiver of confidentiality is defined as that involving potential risk to others or unreported recent sexual assaults or violent crimes and is *not* to be kept private. Such information should be reported directly and immediately to authorities, including reports made under the mandatory child abuse reporting laws.

Most offenders have abused secrecy, and treatment secrecy or confidentiality reinforces the power-abuse position offenders have held over others. Confidentiality about sexual assaults, deviant sexual behavior, or current risk situations also prevents offender accountability for crimes. Such secrecy places victimized people in a nameless and faceless position, akin to the objectification imposed by the offender during his or her crimes. Sexual assault victims should be identified and aided in recovery, and legitimate concerns about additional sentencing and court response should be addressed with the criminal justice system.

TREATMENT CONTRACTS

Treatment can be structured by using a treatment contract specifically designed for sex offenders, such as the Adult Offender Treatment Contract, the Adolescent Offender Treatment Contract (Loss & Ross, 1987a), or the Correctional Sex Offender Treatment Agreement (Loss 1994). Such agreements outline the safety and behavioral rules for offenders who participate in the program. The contract is first discussed in the latter parts of the psychoeducational phase of the program and is generally used throughout treatment.

Contract conditions are specific and detailed. The wording of the contract must be clear so that offenders can understand it, and there should be no room for offenders to manipulate or distort program rules. For example, offenders typically distort the rule forbidding contact with victims to mean that they cannot have body contact but may call, write, or have visual contact with the persons they victimized. Such an interpretation is based on the offender's self-serving desire to retain destructive power and shows a total lack of appreciation for the potentially destructive psychological consequences for the victim. An explicitly worded no-contact rule is necessary to make it clear to offenders the various types of contact they are required to avoid.

Contract rules include specific safeguards regardless of setting, such as not being alone with children or no child-oriented activity or employment for child sexual abuse offenders, no driving or walking without a specific destination for rape offenders, and any other special condition necessary for offender and community safety. Any other conditions found to be necessary by the assessment or ongoing observation are added under "special conditions," such as mandatory attendance at an alcohol or drug rehabilitation program. Some examples of contract rules are:

- "I will attend all treatment sessions required by staff and I will attend on time. I understand that 'on time' means not being late at all, not even a few minutes."

- "I agree to be completely honest during all treatment sessions and assume full responsibility for my offenses and my behavior. I understand that being honest includes not giving false information as well as not leaving out important information."

- "I will not have in my possession or view any pornographic material at any time. I understand that staff may require me to dispose of or restrict my viewing of any other material deemed to be sexually aggressive or destructive to my treatment."

- "I will have absolutely no contact with any victims of my sexually aggressive behavior unless directly approved by program staff. I understand that this includes visits, writing letters, and telephone contact. I will not directly or indirectly encourage anyone else to have such contact with any of my victims on my behalf. I will not initiate, continue, or be party to any legal actions, or threat of legal actions, intimidation, or manipulation against my victims. I will cooperate with and, if I am requested to do so, provide information to any legitimate professional who is involved in counseling any of my victims, but only through a program staff member."

- "I will notify my partner, spouse, girlfriend, or significant other person with whom I am seriously or consistently involved that I am a sex offender, and I will review my history and safeguards for avoiding future reoffending within a time period agreed upon with program staff."

- "I will not commit any type of criminal offense, including any sex offense, or violate correctional regulations. I will not engage in any sexually aggressive behavior. I will not engage in any sexual activity with any person while I am incarcerated, nor will I engage in sexually or nonsexually exploitive relationships with other inmates or other parties. If I violate this condition, I will notify both the sex offender treatment program and correctional authorities immediately. I will be prosecuted for any behavior considered criminal and will be restricted from relationships with any of the individuals involved."

- For offenders who have sexually abused children: "I will not be alone with any minor child unless another adult is present who is aware of my history of sexual aggression and has been approved as a supervisor by sex offender treatment program staff. I will also not be anywhere that I know minors to frequent. If I have any accidental situation where I am alone with a minor, I will remove myself from the situation immediately."

In a correctional setting, offenders are expected to notify program staff if they witness another group member or program participant violate the contract. The participant violating the contract is expected to disclose the violation at the next scheduled group session. If he or she does not, the witnessing offender is under equal obligation to report the violation. This rule must be emphasized and positively reframed as sexual abuse control in a prison setting, where such behavior is negatively viewed as informing or "ratting." Similarly, contract rules strictly prohibit inmate disclosure of the identity of and any personal information about anyone attending the program, past or present. This is a cardinal rule in a correctional or residential setting, where the disclosure of personal or group information can have direct negative and destructive results, including the possible compromise of personal safety.

THE GROUP PROCESS

It is important to begin the group on time and move immediately to issues and problems in an efficient and organized manner, as outlined by the treatment contract. Offenders require providers to demonstrate that treatment is serious business and that such a process will be rewarding but hard work. Providers should maintain a no-nonsense and nontraditional posture, consistent with the dual role of treatment provider and social control agent.

Assigning each ongoing treatment group a secretary on a rotating basis, usually monthly, facilitates the continuity of the group process from session to session. The secretary is a group member who conducts the basic format of each group session. The purpose of having a secretary is to allow each offender to assume responsibility and a leadership role under the supervision of the treatment providers. The group secretary can record attendance and pertinent notes in a group notebook, including significant group developments, assignments, and contract additions and deletions. The notebook is returned to the treatment providers at the conclusion of each session and is kept in a locked area, especially in a correctional environment, where such information could be used against participants.

Personal introductions and offense disclosures are an important component of ongoing treatment. All group members introduce themselves to new members or observers by standing and stating their names, the type of offense committed (without legal discussion), the first name of the person victimized (e.g., "I raped Susan"), their sentences or legal status, and the length of time they have been attending specialized treatment. In their introductions, group members may briefly discuss what they have learned in treatment or what issues they are now facing. This ritual reinforces ownership of their problem and personalizes the individuals they victimized.

The group process is most time-efficient when divided into segments. The first segment of the meeting has come to be known as "the week's exercise." During this time, offenders review any pertinent contract violations, potential crises, difficult issues, family visits, or school problems that have arisen between sessions. This initial period allows sex offenders, who usually have difficulty prioritizing, to identify the most important problems to address first. Group participants submit any written assignments that are due or provide notification that they have completed behavioral assignments. Offenders must have medical excuses for any missed appointments, and all excuses for missed sessions, lateness, or incomplete assignments should be verified. Group participants are not held responsible for external conditions affecting their contract compliance. For example, a prison inmate may be late to a group session due to circumstances having to do with institutional security or routine. However, sex offenders may contribute to such conditions; for example, inmates may not have acted responsibly enough to be allowed release from their cellblock to the group location.

At this time, group participants hand in their daily journals to the therapist. Daily journals help orient offenders toward self-reflection and analysis. Offenders typically do not internalize, recognize emotion, or realistically evaluate personal issues and processes. Journals provide an organized means to promote emotional development and increase self-awareness, similar to workbooks and written assignments in the psychoeducational phase of treatment.

Recommended format and content for daily journals include detailing of any sexually aggressive thinking or fantasizing between sessions, along with a self-reported strength rating. Tracking sexually aggressive thinking is an additional tool toward the goal of relapse prevention. Journal material reports any thinking about nonconsensual sexual interactions, including peeping, exposing oneself, obscene phone calling, physical and verbal sexual harassment, and other more subtle forms of sexual intimidation and control. Offenders appear to disclose more fantasy material if they understand that recording aggressive fantasizing is an expected component of managing their sexual assault problem. Otherwise, offenders may view themselves as treatment failures if such thinking occurs. During the treatment process, offenders become accustomed to reporting their sexually aggressive fantasizing. With time and treatment, their fantasies usually decrease in strength and/or frequency as they learn to replace past sexually aggressive actions with constructive healthy behaviors.

A deviant fantasy management tool that has proved particularly helpful is "thought stopping" or imaging techniques. Offenders using this technique verbalize one or more cognitive images that they learn to associate with sexually aggressive thinking. For example, when offenders experience fantasies about rape or child sexual abuse, they are asked to provide content-appropriate deterrent images to be associated with the aggressive fantasy. Examples of deterrent images are the sound of handcuffs being snapped on as the offender is arrested, the doors of the prison slamming closed, or the judge reading the sentence. With imaging, offenders develop specific self-employable strategies to interrupt deviant thinking as a means of improving their overall self-management skills and, consequently, self-confidence.

Offenders are generally not encouraged to use images regarding the victim, such as the crying child who was victimized, since in the beginning stages of treatment, this may inadvertently reinforce the sexual aggression problem and the pursuit of destructive power. In the author's experience, treatment should take place for at least one to two years before victim images can be safely used. This procedure involves the manipulation of cognitive imagery only and should not include actual props such as handcuffs, firearms, or restraints. Prop use is an inappropriate strategy that can be intimidating to the offender and may constitute a criminal offense as well (as in the case of firearms). Overtly aggressive actions may also activate victim-like experiences, if not direct victimization, and should be ruled out.

An additional feature of fantasy management and reporting is that it provides an opportunity to understand some of the motives of sexual assault. Fantasies may contain information about unmet emotional needs or may indicate what the offender hoped to achieve during the fantasized assault but did not actually carry out. Since fantasizing usually precedes offending, offenders are asked to determine the strength of the fantasy. Usually this rating is accomplished by self-report on a one-to-ten scale; stronger fantasies contain a plan to offend, including how to target the victim and get him or her alone. In addition to understanding the emotional factors or warning signs that tend to trigger sexual aggression, offenders should be expected to recite a plan of action to deter taking sexually aggressive action following the abusive fantasy. In secure environments, such a plan can include talking to a line staff member or counselor if the treatment provider is not present, discussing the fantasy with a carefully selected and approved peer counselor, or calling a previously arranged pager number. With continued treatment and recovery progress, offenders can understand that although it is protective for them to call if they are fantasizing, the ultimate prevention lies in calling before the fantasy, when they experience triggers or contributing issues.

In the initial stages of treatment, journals include any events, thoughts, problems, or conflicts that were disturbing or difficult to manage for the offender. These items may need discussion during the group session. Issues specific to each offender that require tracking may be included in the journal later. For example, an offender who demonstrates a particular problem with self-image, need to control, or isolation or who tends to play the victim role or displays other offender characteristics can track that specific issue in the journal for ongoing discussion and monitoring. Likewise, special conditions can be added to the treatment contract throughout the group treatment process.

When priority issues are identified, either during the first segment of the group process or through the group members' journals, the group secretary writes these issues in the group notebook and reviews any other issues remaining from the previous session that require attention or completion. The second segment of the group process, the "business" portion, begins after the week's exercise. Offenders identifying priority issues discuss them and any sexually aggressive fantasy episodes that require examination. At this time, offenders also discuss any priority issues identified between sessions by the treatment providers. Since many offenders have demonstrated poor prioritizing and personal management in the past, it is useful to set a positive precedent by addressing the most important problems early in the group session.

At first glance, some of the between-session issues identified as priorities by offenders may appear to be trivial management issues. However, sex offenders tend to offend as an end point of a long-standing pattern of mismanagement of day-to-day personal and interpersonal problems. Discussing the issues as they emerge presents an opportunity to meet personal goals, attempt positive changes, and generalize and internalize recovery principles outside group sessions. Therefore, each negative event offers the offenders a chance to improve their skills and attitudes when facing conflict. Using such a procedure in treatment also encourages the anticipation of problems and potential solutions, once again building positive personal power and self-image.

TREATMENT PHASES

The events and tasks involved in the second segment of each group session are not determined by a specific time limit but are best defined by the phase of treatment the particular group members are engaged in. Due to a wide variation in risk level, setting, degree of progress, and program characteristics, offenders move through these phases at different paces. The time frames described are rough, overlap to accommodate differences among offenders, and exist only to estimate and organize the various issues. A lower-risk offender in a community setting may accomplish treatment tasks and responsibilities relatively quickly, whereas a high-risk habituated offender in a correctional program may take several years to accomplish basic treatment goals.

PHASE 1. During the first phase of treatment, the business portion of the sex offender group is defined largely by analysis of members' offending patterns and ongoing discussion and implementation of personal goals. This phase generally lasts approximately six months to one year.

It is important that all participants review in detail their past and present sexual aggression, as they did during the assessment phase. Group members are encouraged to ask questions, probe, confront, and examine one another's offenses in detail. Intent, fantasizing, weapons, exact nature of the assault, choice of victim, verbalizations made during the offense, reaction of the victim, how the offender ensured the victim's compliance, and how the assault stopped are all potential areas of inquiry. In time, all past sexual and sexually related offending, including offenses without actual visual victim contact, should be openly discussed. As with assessment, law enforcement–oriented investigative interviewing is effective when employed by treatment providers, especially in community settings, to obtain details about the exact locations of crimes, the typical profile of offending, the type of victim commonly sought, and other specific items beyond the scope of the traditional clinical assessment. Crimes and details related to the group member's sexually aggressive history can then be recorded by the treatment provider in a group file.

Target behaviors should include rape; child sexual abuse; exhibitionism; obscene phone calling; verbal and personal sexual harassment;

sexual involvement with any "partner" when, despite age similarity, there are significant power differentials in functioning and vulnerability; voyeurism; theft of underwear or other items of clothing or footwear for use as masturbatory objects; animal cruelty or animal sexual involvement; any nonsexual offense with sexual themes, especially breaking and entering when destruction of personal items such as clothes, underwear, or mattresses is an element; fire setting and arson; and generalized violence. Treatment providers should remind offenders about the reporting obligation during this phase, as offenders may disclose crimes against persons that must be reported to law enforcement under mandatory child abuse reporting statutes or the waiver of confidentiality. If necessary, treatment providers may elect to repeat the waiver of confidentiality and reporting policy at the onset of the offense analysis.

Since sex offender treatment groups are open-ended, with new members entering the group at various times, participants will be undergoing the initial offense analysis at different times. The treatment providers structure the bulk of the group time and perform the majority of the questioning responsibilities during this treatment phase for each offender. In an ongoing, cohesive group with more treatment-experienced offenders, the group members would be expected to do most of the questioning. Also, in-group analysis of offending patterns evolves over time and requires repetition, as do most other issues of importance in group treatment. An offender's review of his or her abuse history is never provided the same way twice. During subsequent reviews, offenders frequently add information they previously avoided or offer what they have come to recognize as important, subtle aspects of their offending, including grooming, power abuse, role changes, physical and emotional abuse, and sexual harassment. Treatment providers usually require group members to undergo several sessions of offense analysis before they can develop a clear clinical picture of the motives and dynamics of each offender's crimes.

Offenders begin writing their autobiographies in the first few months of treatment. They can be instructed to complete this lengthy assignment in installments while informing the providers about their progress. Autobiographies should be in the offenders' own words and from their own recollections and perceptions rather than those of other family members. The writing is most readable and examinable when recorded in a rough age time frame and usually includes details on personal development, family environment, role structures, discipline, school issues, relationships and dating, alcohol and substance abuse issues, violence, self-esteem, sexuality, emotional development, intimacy, communication, victimization, negative and positive experiences, and generally any events they can recall.

Offenders should be encouraged to free-associate and to provide all information rather than screening for "important" information, since their screening and perception mechanisms are often open for question and analysis. Offenders may elect to recall their workbook assignments from the psychoeducational phase of treatment, which provides a framework. Offenders give their completed autobiographies to the treatment provider to read, and the offenders summarize the information for the group. Autobiographies can reveal contributory information similar to that found in the analysis of offending patterns and may help illuminate the onset of sexual aggression and basic deficits in development.

During the early stages of treatment, the treatment providers should warn the group that offenders will experience treatment as a tumultuous process that will change their perceptions of themselves and their environment. Because many offenders have developed long-standing patterns of minimization and rationalization, they tend to diminish the reality and the gravity of their offending as well as their past victimizations, conflicts, problems, and emotions. Further, some offenders are unable to fully empathize with the victims of their crimes until they allow themselves to fully recognize and recover from their own histories of sexual victimization and other negative experiences.

Offenders should be advised to anticipate an increase in anxiety, depression, and perceived conflicts as they progress through treatment. Many offenders have used avoidance, control, and superficiality as coping strategies. Since treatment gradually removes such defense mechanisms, it follows that long-standing basic emotions and raw conflicts will be uncovered. Offenders can be helped to reframe a newly uncovered sense of depression following a past victimization as a normal response to a traumatizing event. Offenders can be instructed to identify normal and healthy strategies as a new response to past issues, such as discussing feelings with other group members and family members. Conversely, offenders can reduce minimization and begin to recognize outrage as a normal response to the fact that sexual assault against another person is a hurtful crime that violates the safety of others. Therefore, the offenders should begin to approximate a normal response to their own crimes with appropriate guilt.

Providers can use this opportunity to educate offenders about healthy emotional and behavioral patterns in their continuing role as symbolic parental figures. Offenders can be taught to recognize the practical value of their emotional transformation in treatment. When faced in the future with some of the identified emotional factors or experiences that were contributory to their crimes, their increased normal responses to destructive behavior will likely provide confidence and deter previous sexual aggression patterns.

Providers can help offenders understand that effective treatment, especially in the early stages, must be intrusive and is frequently emotionally painful. Only through rigorous self-disclosure and commitment to honesty will they be able to understand and control sexual aggression, to genuinely and positively improve self-respect, accountability, and the quality of recovery. Offenders have used statements such as "This is a dues-paying club" to illustrate the emotional turmoil involved in early phases of treatment, as well as to acknowledge the group support received.

In this phase, and throughout treatment, the treatment providers rely on a number of techniques to facilitate the ongoing group process. First, respectful confrontation and support are key skills employed by both the providers and more experienced group members. Offenders who engage in avoidant or disruptive behaviors, who minimize offenses, or who manipulate and control others, whether inside or outside the group, must be directly and respectfully confronted about their negative behavior. Direct confrontation is defined as a clear and concise identification of specific behavior as inappropriate, harmful, and unacceptable; it is not character assassination of the individual. The behavior itself is inappropriate and must be stopped, not the individual who is attempting to change. When confronted in this fashion, offenders have a face-saving means of changing their negative behaviors and avoid the risk of lowering self-esteem. The treatment of individuals who have patterns of power abuse requires a responsible but clear sense of personal and professional power. Offenders will not abandon their power abuse unless the providers directly remove such a pattern and replace it with continued demonstrations of the appropriate use and development of personal power. Upon direct confrontation, providers should suggest or allow discussion on what appropriate behavior should replace destructive, unacceptable behavior.

Confrontation about various misbehaviors and contract violations should be performed directly during the group process, in order to model the behavior that the providers want the group members to witness and adopt. New groups require frequent modeling of this response to misbehavior, whereas ongoing groups with experienced members can be directed to address misbehavior using peer confrontation under provider supervision. Some group leaders handle offender disruption and risk issues outside the group meeting or after the group session. Such a strategy fails to take advantage of the positive power of the group process. Focusing on such issues within the group gives members an opportunity to learn to control the components of aggression and to learn a skill in handling conflict. Other group members also need to witness and understand the typical consequences of negative behavior as a deterrent, as well as the consequences of positive behavior as an incentive.

The treatment provider's response to an offender's contract violations and misbehavior depends on the nature and seriousness of the problem behavior. The final decision about which strategy to employ must be evaluated on a case-by-case basis. Factors to consider include the specific characteristics of the offender, risk assessment, and the exact nature of the misbehavior. An offender who is generally cooperative and accountable but misses a group session in a community treatment setting warrants a far different response than an offender who has more consistently avoided responsibility or has shown a pattern of contract violations. The former situation may be an isolated incident requiring a relatively low-key response, whereas the latter may be an indication of hidden power abuse, a deeper failure to assume responsibility for recovery, or reoffending, in which case both the situation and the offender represent a higher risk to public safety. Provider response also depends on the characteristics of the setting in which the treatment occurs. An offender who is treated in a prison setting can be suspended from participation in the treatment program, in part because it does not directly affect public safety. Suspension of an offender in a community-based treatment setting may pose an unacceptable risk due to the potential compromise of public safety.

Relatively minor violations not indicative of an ongoing disruptive or avoidant pattern can be addressed by group and/or provider confrontation through a written assignment, verbal warning, or report to the probation or parole officer. Minor violations include a single instance of lateness to a group session, one or two sessions of nonparticipation in the group process, or innocuous group disruption in the initial stages of treatment as an offender adopts a more serious attitude about his or her offending. Conversely, support and praise should be employed when each offender is legitimately demonstrating honesty, genuine group participation, assumption of responsibility, and affective involvement in discussing offending or past victimizations and is generally embracing the issues involved in true recovery.

Role-play and written and behavioral assignments are helpful in educating offenders, building skills, and punishing minor instances of misbehavior. Role-play is extremely effective in helping offenders meet specific goals. Offenders in role-plays get a concrete opportunity to practice their new skills with the assistance of group members. They can experience immediate success with positive feedback from co-participants, unlike their previous negative experiences with failure and impaired self-image. Role-play, because it is observable, allows verification by the group leaders that treatment goals have been reached. Common themes of role-plays and assignments are control issues, anger management, social skills development, relationship and dating skills, and coping with authority, as well as various offender-specific issues that contribute to sexual aggression.

PHASE 2. The second phase of sex offender treatment, lasting approximately nine months to two years, focuses on the contributing factors to sexual aggression. After the details of the current offense and past sexual aggression history are reviewed, offenders are expected to discuss their crimes with an emphasis on personal, social, familial, environmental, and psychological factors that may pertain to the onset and continuation of the aggressive pattern. This phase also includes the completion and review of the offenders' autobiographies, which provide additional information about the possible contributing factors to sexual aggression.

During this treatment phase, offenders discuss their perceptions of their lives, problems, conflicts, and other issues that may assist in understanding the motives for their aggression. Such discussion may cover current observations of the offenders' behavior and attitudes that appear to be representative of past contributing factors unrecognized by the offenders. Investigative interviewing is again pivotal in outlining the details of behaviors, time frames, and family members. Examples of issues include:

- self-esteem
- communication skills
- isolation
- personal intimacy
- feelings of depression
- trust
- sexuality and dating
- control and power issues
- anger management
- perceptions of women
- authority issues
- family communication patterns, secrecy, roles, and boundaries
- marital issues
- physical, sexual, and verbal abuse and neglect
- substance abuse
- violence
- mental and medical illness
- school performance
- history of treatment

The group members' summaries of their autobiographies during group sessions can be analyzed using this same format. In the case of juvenile sex offenders, their previous offending histories and autobiographical material will likely overlap.

Offenders are expected to revise their treatment goals to directly and specifically address personal traits and motivations that have led to sexual aggression as they become more aware of such issues. Group participants are also witnessing an emerging picture of their offending cycles and can therefore better identify the emotional and interpersonal triggers that can lead to reoffending. Offenders are required to continually discuss and integrate the reoffense risk list, the

personal list of triggers and warning signs used to avoid future aggression. This list includes specifics from a review of contributing factors, as well as detailed strategies offenders expect to employ when such triggers are experienced. Offenders' families and spouses also need to become familiar with this list to enhance recognition and prevention efforts.

As offenders complete the various tasks in this phase, it will become evident that their risk factors and attitudes and the types of interventions needed to bring about change vary widely. Providers should use a basic, structured treatment contract and a public safety–oriented approach to sex offender treatment that holds offenders accountable for their crimes and teaches them to recognize contributing factors to their offending in order to avoid reoffending. The literature contains a mulitiude of interventions for sex offenders, including relapse prevention, cognitive restructuring, social skills development, behavioral approaches, and family-oriented treatments (Freeman-Longo, Bird, Stevenson, & Fiske, 1995). Many programs employ common elements such as cognitive restructuring and behavioral interventions without adopting the specific label of a behavioral or cognitive restructuring approach. Components of all these approaches can be helpful in sex offender treatment. When deciding which specific treatment strategies to use with each offender during the group process, the provider should be familiar with all these interventions. An eclectic approach is most effective—selecting various components from some or all approaches based on an individualized offender risk assessment and ongoing treatment planning.

PHASE 3. The third treatment phase, beginning after approximately 18 months to 2 years and beyond, focuses primarily on the effects of offenders' sexual assaults on their victims and on empathy development, both specifically with the victim and generally with others. A treatment group with offenders in this phase assumes the characteristics of a higher-functioning, ongoing psychotherapy group committed to ongoing safety, accountability, and recovery.

Group participants are expected to have made a continuing and in-depth commitment to honestly address all areas identified in their treatment goals and to their overall participation in the group process. Offenders are expected to be self-aware and self-reporting, and they expect the same from fellow group members. They confront and support others as well as themselves, and the group self-enforces honesty, timeliness, and the forthright addressing of ongoing recovery issues. Offenders may be more heavily involved in making contributions to the program through working with other treatment groups, providing information to psychoeducational classes, recording videotapes for training purposes, planning the treatment program, or participating in the training of professionals working with sex offenders.

Offenders are advised, during this period, that they are now to review their offending patterns, from the standpoint of the experience of the persons victimized. Offenders can be guided through a step-by-step recitation of the events of past and present aggression, through the experience of the victim. In addition, offenders are required to write assignments about specific effects of sexual abuse or assault on their victims, either known or anticipated. It is recommended that offenders be given an assignment to write letters to their victims. These letters are not mailed but are intended to elicit an empathic emotional reaction and to foster emotional development. Any actual contact between offender and victim, if appropriate, should be negotiated separately from this exercise. The providers may, at this point, be able to illustrate the parallels between the effects of the offenders' own childhood victimization and the damaging experience of the people they victimized.

Sex offender treatment is, in most cases, an indefinite commitment to recovery and public safety. Programs should consider offering ongoing group treatment services after sufficient time in weekly and more intensive community-based sex offender treatment, including that offered after release from secure environments. Advanced treatment group seessions may be held less often, sometimes outside the umbrella of the treatment program, but with provider supervision or facilitation. The advanced treatment group allows continued monitoring of offense cycles and prevention of reoffending, as well as ongoing resolution of personal and interpersonal issues in perpetuity. The advanced group involves a less rigid structure; for example, treatment contracts are removed, since they are assumed to have been internalized. Most offenders are no longer probationers or parolees, which may be one of the entrance criteria to the group. In addition, offenders are expected to participate with families or spouses, to have demonstrated a sufficiently long-term change, to be offense free, and to be maintaining a lifelong quest for recovery and safety.

SUSPENSION AND TERMINATION

The behaviors of offenders committing serious contract violations require more drastic response measures, especially if the disruptive or risk behavior begins to fit into an overall pattern of resistance, dishonesty, manipulativeness, disruption, or compromise of public safety. More drastic responses include more intensive confrontation, restrictions or privilege loss in residential settings, loss of favorable classification rating or parole assessment in correctional settings, and/or program suspension or termination. Serious violations include:

- sexual aggression, harassment, sexually aggressive "grooming" behavior, and other forms of victimization

- violence or threats of violence toward other offenders or staff

- significant patterns of manipulativeness, including misrepresentation of facts, "splitting" of staff members or community agencies

- exploitation of others, including personal ridicule, humiliation, or intimidating other inmates into, or targeting vulnerable inmates for, subservient roles

- contacting the victim without authorization

- compromise of safety rules, such as reports of an offender who sexually abuses children being alone with a child

- blatant refusal to attend group sessions, to attend in a timely manner, or to complete assignments

- interruption of basic group process expectations and exercises by persistent argumentativeness and monopolization of the group process

All crimes should be reported to the police or child protective services, and offenders should be held accountable for their actions, regardless of the fact that they are participating in a treatment program or are already incarcerated.

Emerging patterns of disruption, failure to follow the program rules and treatment contract, approximating any offending pattern, or a single instance of victimizing or risky behavior can lead to suspension or termination from the program. Except in the case of direct compromise of safety, suspension or termination should be employed only when other measures have been tried and have failed during the course of the normal group process. Offenders should be given a clear message, during the group process, about their misbehavior and be required to present a plan of correction to the group regarding how they will change the problem behavior. If offenders have consistently failed to address the identified problems, they should usually be suspended for a limited period and given written assignments or behavioral activities to complete during this time; the appropriate authorities are notified about such a status change. The length of suspension varies from one session to several months, depending on the particular misbehaviors.

Program termination is necessary when offenders have committed the most serious violations or when they have established clear patterns of disruption, despite treatment efforts or suspension. In such cases, the offender has al-ready been suspended or has been advised that termination is possible or likely. When the decision is made to terminate an offender's participation in the treatment program, both providers need to advise the offender directly in a group session, discuss the problem behaviors that led to termination, and require the offender involved to leave the group immediately without further discussion. Depending on the setting, remaining offenders should be made aware that they cannot have contact with this offender because he or she may attempt to manipulate group members and undermine treatment.

Treatment providers should consider revisiting a termination decision only after a substantial and observable change is made in the offender's overall behavior or attitude over a period of time. In addition, offenders should not be reconsidered unless they have been held legally accountable for any criminal offense. Offenders typically make last-minute superficial changes and promises at this point. It is rarely helpful to accept "eleventh-hour" changes or promises as a reason to defer termination.

In a community setting, if an offender was incarcerated as a result of his or her failure to participate and the offender's attitude has changed after the period of incarceration, reconsidering his or her program involvement may be appropriate. In a residential setting, if an offender was placed in a detention facility and likewise demonstrates an attitude change, he or she can be reconsidered. In a correctional environment, if an offender spends a period of time (depending on misbehavior and risk assessment) in terminated status or segregation and then requests reinstatement with corresponding positive changes in attitude, that offender can similarly be reconsidered. The decision to rescind termination depends wholly on the seriousness of the violation or misbehavior, the overall risk assessment of the offender, and the judgment of the treatment provider. Obviously, the less restrictive the treatment environment, the more important the public safety concerns become.

FAMILY INTERVENTION

Couples and family treatment for adult offenders or family treatment for juveniles is strongly recommended whenever it is not ruled out during assessment due to potential risk to or disruption of the treatment process. Family intervention is critical to understanding and addressing the various emotional and environmental issues that may have contributed to the offender's state of mind and facilitated the offending. Families who participate in treatment are in a unique position to augment treatment efforts by providing supervision, strengthening treatment messages and philosophy, and supplying positive and negative consequences when appropriate. Each offender's spouse and/or family participates in family treatment sessions in addition to group sessions, depending on the setting. However, the dynamics and procedures of family intervention and offender-victim contact are beyond the scope of this chapter and are not detailed here.

It should be made clear to all families that, with the exception of direct participation by the family in the offending, the family is not responsible for the offender's choice to offend. Although the family or the parents are accountable for numerous other environmental and developmental issues that may be critical, the offender alone is responsible for his or her abusive actions and their effects. The family should be made aware that the offender is not responsible for all the family's problems, as many families inappropriately blame their anxiety, poor communication, secrecy, and other forms of dysfunction on the offender.

Parental attendance at ongoing juvenile sex offender treatment groups on a regular basis, once every three to four sessions, is an important group requirement. This session is usually reserved to discuss family issues that require attention and have been identified during the group sessions. Some offenders may be given specific assignments that require them to initiate discussion on a particular family issue, with the group's assistance. The parents are provided the opportunity to understand sexually aggressive thinking and to openly hear and participate in the various issues in their son's or daughter's present and future recovery. Similarly, providers may elect to schedule a spouses group during a regularly scheduled adult sex offender treatment group to discuss marital and sexual assault management issues.

THE IMPORTANCE OF LONG-TERM GROUP TREATMENT

The field of sexual assault treatment has generated healthy debate over the past 10 years about the variety of strategies useful in treating sex offenders, including relapse prevention, psycho-education, cognitive restructuring, behavioral approaches, social learning, and family approaches. A point that bears repeating, however, is that the long-term weekly sex offender treatment group plays a pivotal role in the client's abandonment of destructive behavior patterns, the development of new positive patterns, and the direct and personal verification that such changes are taking place. The ongoing group is most valuable when it focuses on sexual assault as a crime, offender accountability, and the identification and change of contributing factors to sexual aggression. The basic treatment group is an important foundation to any intervention, regardless of the provider's specific etiological or treatment orientation.

REFERENCES

Bradshaw, J. (1988). *Healing the shame that binds you.* Deerfield, FL: Health Communications.

Finkelhor, D. (1984). *Child sexual abuse: New theory and research.* New York: Free Press.

Freeman-Longo, R.E., & Bays, L. (1988). *Who am I and why am I in treatment?* Brandon, VT: Safer Society Press.

Freeman-Longo, R.E., Bird, S., Stevenson, W.F., & Fiske, J. (1995). *1994 nationwide survey of treatment programs and models.* Brandon, VT: Safer Society Program and Press.

Gordon, T. (1975). *Parent effectiveness training.* New York: Penguin Putnam.

Groth, A.N. (1979). *Men Who Rape.* New York: Plenum Press.

Loss, P. (1994). *Correctional sex offender treatment agreement.* Unpublished document.

Loss, P., & Ross, J. (1987a). *Adult offender treatment contract, adolescent offender treatment contract.* Unpublished document.

Loss, P., & Ross, J. (1987b). Reoffense risk list and the reoffense scenario, from *Sex Offender Treatment Assignments.* Unpublished document.

Loss, P., & Ross, J. (1988). *Risk assessment/interviewing protocol for adolescent sex offenders.* Unpublished document.

Loss, P., Ross, J., & Richardson, J. (1988). P*sycho-educational curriculum for adolescent sex offenders.* Unpublished document.

Schwartz, B.K. (1995). Group therapy. In B.K. Schwartz & H.R. Cellini (Eds.), *The sex offender: Corrections, treatment, and legal practice* (14-1–14-15). Kingston, NJ: Civic Research Institute.

8   Empathy Training

William Marshall
Y. M. Fernandez

There is an apparent consensus among clinicians that empathy training is a vital component of any sexual offender treatment program. In fact, Knopp, Freeman-Longo, and Stevenson (1992) found that 94 percent of North American treatment programs make some attempt at enhancing empathy in their participants. Unfortunately, few of these programs provide descriptions that indicate the nature of the empathy deficits being addressed, nor do they describe how they deal with this issue in treatment. This is not surprising, in view of the fact that in the more general psychological literature, empathy has proved to be an elusive concept.

Notions about the importance of empathy in human social functioning have been expressed since at least the 18th century. There now exists a considerable body of literature addressing the nature of empathy and suggesting its role in diverse human behaviors. Most important, for our purposes, is the inhibiting effect of empathy on the expression of aggression. It has consistently been found that children who score high on measures of empathy characteristically terminate aggressive displays when the target of their aggression becomes upset, whereas children scoring low on empathy continue to aggress, regardless of the response of the victim. These findings have obvious implications for the treatment of sexual offenders.

Despite the wealth of research on empathy and the various theoretical articles written about it, there remains little agreement on exactly what constitutes empathy. As a consequence, there are numerous measures of empathy that bear little empirical relationship to one another, arising from each particular researcher's conceptualization of the issues. Some theorists see empathy as the recognition of emotion in others and have developed cognitive measures of empathy (e.g., Hogan's [1969] Empathy Scale); others consider empathy to be the vicarious replication of another person's emotional state and have developed emotional measures of empathy (e.g., Mehrabian and Epstein's [1972] Emotional Empathy Scale). Davis (1983) sees empathy as a multicomponent response, and his measure (the Interpersonal Reactivity Index) reflects this view.

All the measures presently available, whether they consider empathy to be a single or a multi-component response, construe empathy as a trait manifest toward all people across all situations. What limited research is available on the empathy capacity of sexual offenders has employed one or another of these trait measures, although it appears that most therapists attempt to enhance empathy in their clients either toward the offender's own victims or toward all victims (and potential victims) of sexual abuse. Nevertheless, the first published report of treatment changes resulting from empathy training evaluated these changes using a trait measure (Pithers, 1994).

In our theoretical analysis of empathy among sexual offenders (Marshall, Hudson, Jones, & Fernandez, 1995) we concluded that empathy was a multistaged process and was likely to be most markedly deficient in sexual offenders only toward their own victims. Our recent research has supported this view (Fernandez, Marshall, Lightbody, & O'Sullivan, 1999).

We construed empathy as having four states. A person must (1) be able to recognize another's emotional state; (2) demonstrate the ability to see the world as the other person does; (3) experience, without effort, the same emotional state as the observed person; and (4) feel impelled to act accordingly (i.e., either stop the action, if it is distressing the other person, or offer comfort). We have found that sexual offenders are indeed deficient at emotional recognition (Hudson et al., 1993), and they are unskilled at seeing things from the perspective of sexual abuse victims and at replicating the emotional distress of victims (Fernandez et al., 1999).

As a consequence of our conceptualization of empathy deficits in sexual offenders and the support for this view provided by our research, we developed a treatment component aimed at enhancing empathy in our clients. This treatment component, which is described in more detail below, targets the stages of empathy we have outlined and focuses primarily on the of-

fender's own victims, although we do encourage generalization to all potential victims.

TREATMENT COMPONENTS

It must be kept in mind that our attempt to enhance empathy is only one aspect of our comprehensive cognitive-behavioral program for sexual offenders (for a fuller description, see Marshall & Eccles, 1995; Marshall & Fernandez, 1997). One important feature of our overall program is respect for the dignity of our participants. We believe that behavioral, attitudinal, and emotional changes are facilitated by enhancing each participant's self-esteem. Accordingly, we constantly draw attention to the positive features of our clients' functioning and strengths, while at the same time challenging their current beliefs, thinking, perceptions, and behaviors. Since we require all participants to challenge one another, we model for them a challenging style that is firm but not confrontational. We encourage participants to be mutually supportive, but also to question one another's views of their behaviors and the consequences of their actions to themselves and others. We require group members to expressively participate rather than await their possible response to the ongoing processes. This participation is initially somewhat threatening to some clients, but persistent encouragement facilitates their involvement, and this involvement also serves to enhance their self-confidence. In fact, we have evidence that pretreatment self-esteem and improvement in self-esteem with treatment are highly correlated with initial scores on various other measures of dysfunctional features of sexual offenders, as well as with positive changes in these other important indices of treatment benefits, including enhanced empathy (Marshall, Champagne, Brown, & Miller, 1997; Marshall, Sturgeon, & Bryce, 1995).

Empathy training is preceded by a component that addresses issues of denial and minimization to overcome these initial obstacles to treatment (Marshall, 1994). The denial/minimization component involves, among other things, challenges to the offenders' rationalizations, including their belief that the victims were not harmed by their abuse. Effectively nullifying these and other rationalizations facilitates offenders' responsiveness to the empathy component.

All components of our program are presented within a group context involving 10 to 12 patients and 2 therapists (a male and a female). Treatment sessions focusing on empathy last three hours each and occur twice weekly over a period of approximately six to eight weeks, depending on the rate of progress of the individuals. We do not terminate this empathy component until we are satisfied that all participants have made satisfactory gains.

EMOTIONAL EXPRESSION AND RECOGNITION

The first of the three segments of our empathy component attempts to train the offenders to be emotionally expressive, since we believe that the ability to recognize emotions in others is proportional to the degree to which one is in touch with one's own feeling states. This segment is meant to encourage the offenders to identify and express their own feelings and to recognize feelings expressed by other group members. Most therapists observe that when sexual offenders are asked to describe what they were feeling at the time of their offense, many draw a blank and simply claim that they were not feeling anything or that they have no idea what they were feeling. Our impression is that this lack of capacity to identify feeling occurs generally in offenders' lives, not just in abuse situations. If offenders cannot recognize their own feelings, then even if they somehow miraculously recognize their victims' distress, they will not respond empathically because they have limited or no emotional responsivity.

Offenders describe events from their past (other than being arrested) that they remember as emotionally distressing. They are encouraged

to relive the experience as vividly as possible to allow their feelings to be expressed. An experience that generates an expression of sadness or fear is preferable, but initially it may be necessary to accept an experience involving anger. Some offenders describe the loss of an important family member, the end of a significant relationship, or being physically abused or emotionally neglected as a child. Often one of the group members describes his or her own sexual abuse as a child. This typically has a notable impact on the entire group and generates many emotions in the speaker as well as in the listeners. We believe that this is the best place in our treatment program for offenders to describe their own abuse, because the focus is on developing compassion toward others, decreasing the possibility that speaking of their own experience of being abused will encourage them to adopt a victim stance. If we had a prior or separate component dealing with the offenders' own abuse (sexual, physical, or emotional), it might be far more difficult to shift them away from seeing this abuse as a justification for their offending. We certainly believe that it is necessary to help offenders resolve the emotional problems resulting from their own abuse, but we think that this is best accomplished within the context of the empathy training component.

Other participants are required to identify the emotions displayed by the speaker and rate the depth of these emotions. The other participants are also asked to indicate the feelings they had when listening to the description. If their emotional responses matched the speaker's expression of feelings, the therapist indicates that what they have described is empathy. At this point, the therapist takes the opportunity to fully define empathy for the group. This process of describing a distressing event and having this description appraised by the other participants is repeated until everyone has offered a description.

If offenders have trouble identifying a distressing experience, or if they have trouble expressing their emotions during the description, they are given a homework assignment to write an essay on distressing emotional experiences from the past. In particularly difficult cases, this process may need to be repeated several times. Throughout this segment, all participants are encouraged to discuss their emotional responses with one another between sessions. These discussions appear to be helpful, particularly for those who are having difficulties.

An advantage to this approach is that group members benefit from repeated practice in identifying and expressing emotions, as they are required not only to describe their own emotionally distressing experiences but also to appraise other members' accounts. Having the therapist provide feedback to the participants in terms of the degree to which each member's response reflects empathy tends to reinforce their expressions of emotions and their developing capacity to experience empathy.

Practice at these within-group and between-session exercises continues until each participant is able to identify his or her own feelings and those of others and has become more emotionally expressive. For extreme intellectualizers, challenges and appraisals from other group members frequently provide the most effective mechanism of change.

VICTIM HARM

The next treatment segment is meant to sensitize group members to the harm (actual and potential) that victims experience as a result of sexual abuse and to reduce their objectification of their victims. Bandura (1973) has shown in laboratory studies that the more subjects are able to objectify, or see as different from themselves, another person, the easier it is for them to inflict pain on that person. To continue to sexually abuse others, offenders must either believe that they are not harming their victims or construe their victims as so different from themselves that the issue of harm is not relevant or is perhaps even justified. Humanizing victims and identifying the inevitability of harm break down these barriers to victim empathy. Fortunately, one or more of the participants are likely to describe their own sexual victimization as

their most emotionally distressing experience. Since by this time, group members know one another quite well, the impact of this revelation, and its relevance for their own victims, characteristically occurs with little prompting from the therapist, although it is important for the therapist to make the connection explicit.

We begin this segment by attempting to personalize, or make human, the victims. We have participants describe the differences and similarities between themselves and their victims. After each offender has indicated these features of his or her victims, the group discusses the accuracy of the descriptions. Challenges to the accounts are directed at helping offenders see that in terms of wants, needs, rights, and feelings, their victims are far more like than unlike them. As this process proceeds with each group member, the participants typically come to recognize that their victims are indeed humans just like themselves. This is meant to reduce their capacity to objectify their victims.

Next, offenders describe one of their offenses from the victim's perspective. The group member portrays the victim in a role-play and expresses the thoughts and feelings the victim might have been having during and immediately after the abusive act. As the offender describes the event and the victim's responses, other members of the group challenge the offender when, as is usually the case, he or she reports the process in ways that excuse his or her own offending behaviors.

Because offenders characteristically base their challenges on their own personal experience, this approach has the advantage of revealing how well each group member understands the distortions shown in the role-playing offender's account. In addition, this process provides the therapist with further information about each offender's distorted thinking. When the other participants challenge them, group members are forced to consider their offenses from a new perspective and at a greater depth.

In response to these challenges, the role-playing offender is required to modify the description until the group is satisfied that it is an appropriate account of the victim's experience. It is sometimes necessary to repeat this process for offenders to fully appreciate how the victim reacted to the assault.

Offenders are then required to describe what victims of sexual abuse might suffer as a consequence of the abuse. They describe the experiences such victims might have during the offense, in the few months following the offense (or for the period during which offending occurs, if the victim is repeatedly abused), and the long-term consequences of molestation. The description given by each offender of these harmful effects is listed on a flipchart. We ensure that participants offer their own original ideas rather than simply agreeing with what has already been said; each participant must add something to the list. These harmful effects include behavioral changes, emotional distress, social changes, and problems arising in relationships and in sexual functioning. When each offender has contributed to the list, the therapist adds any important known consequences that have been omitted.

The group then discusses the more general meaning of these harmful effects for the lives of victims and for victims' families. Participants identify the consequences that their own victims might have experienced and might continue to be experiencing. The remarks of each offender are evaluated by all the other group members, who are encouraged to challenge the views expressed. The therapist points out that as a result of their distorted thinking at the time, the offenders may have been oblivious to the harm they were causing, or they may have attributed harmful effects to factors outside of themselves. Of course, in the case of rapists, or child molesters who seek out victims previously unknown to them, the offenders may not have had a chance to observe any postmolestation effects. In those cases, they are required to imagine what harm might have befallen their victims.

In the final facet of this segment, we require each participant to write two hypothetical letters: one supposedly from the victim, and the other as the offender's response to the victim's letter. Although offenders are encouraged to discuss the content of their letters with other group members between treatment sessions, it is important to make it clear that the letters must express their own views. In the case of illiterate offenders, they tell their chosen letter-writers what they want to say. Illiteracy is not an obstacle to treatment, although it does present its own special—but not insurmountable—problems.

The victim's letter must identify the anger, hurt, confusion, loss of trust, and guilt the victim likely feels, as well as any other distress and behavioral problems the victim might be experiencing. Each letter is read to the group by the therapist and challenged by every participant. We have the therapist read the letter rather than the offender for two reasons: The therapist can typically be more emotively expressive than the offender, and it facilitates greater recognition of harm for the offender to hear the victim's account from someone else.

If the offender's initial letter as victim unsatisfactorily reveals the victim's likely distress, the offender is required to rewrite it according to the feedback provided. The rewritten version is again read to the group by the therapist and again challenged and, if necessary, rewritten once more. This process is repeated until the letter is deemed satisfactory.

Once the letter from the victim is acceptable, the offender writes a hypothetical response that is never sent to the victim. This response is meant to indicate to the victim that the offense was entirely the offender's responsibility, that the victim's feelings are legitimate, and that the victim should not blame himself or herself. This letter should also point out that not all people act as the offender did, so that trust in others might be reestablished. The offender is to apologize for the harm done but not to ask for forgiveness. Finally, the offender is to express hope the victim can overcome the harm the offender has done and live a reasonably comfortable life. Again, this letter is read out loud to the group by the therapist, and each participant appraises it, provides feedback about what is missing, or comments favorably on what has been included. The letters are refined by the offenders according to this feedback and reread with further feedback until they are acceptable to the group.

VICTIM EMPATHY

Although this whole treatment component is aimed at enhancing empathy, the final segment uses the changes gained in the two prior segments to directly increase empathy. The focus here is on accounts by actual victim-survivors of sexual abuse so that the participants can use their emotional recognition skills and their ability to recognize victim harm within a relevant practical context. At times, we have had a victim-survivor volunteer visit the group to describe his or her distress resulting from the abuse. Although this strategy can be useful, the risks inherent in such interactions are unpredictable. Occasionally, even with our best attempts at preparing the victim-survivor volunteer and the group, the encounter has collapsed into a hostile confrontation. On some occasions, the victim-survivors have become unexpectedly distressed while talking about their experiences and feelings.

If any offenders still seem to have problems effectively empathizing, they are required to consider how they would feel if someone they loved (but had not abused) was sexually assaulted. They are told to describe this hypothetical assault in sufficient detail to make it clear that it was against the victim's will and would cause significant distress. They are asked to describe the victim's suffering and their own feelings about this hypothetical assault. The therapist and the rest of the group then help the offenders see that this is how their own victims must have felt.

With some offenders, even this process may not be sufficient, and it may be necessary for them to go through the whole empathy component again. However, these problematic offenders continue with the rest of the program, and we emphasize for them throughout each subsequent component the relevance and nature of empathy. The components that follow empathy training include attempts to modify attitudes toward women and children and to enhance social competency. In both these goals, empathy plays an important role. It is therefore rather easy to extend, for all participants, a focus on empathy throughout treatment. In fact, we have rarely found it necessary to have offenders repeat the empathy component after the full treatment program. Even if they have not made sufficient gains during the empathy component itself, by the end of the complete program, most offenders display satisfactory victim empathy (see Marshall, O'Sullivan, & Fernandez [1996] for an appraisal of the effectiveness of our empathy training).

Between sessions, in this final segment, a number of readings are assigned to participants to help them come to a better understanding of the effects of sexual abuse on their victims and to facilitate emotional sensitivity. For example, *Voices, a Collection of Writings by Survivors of Sexual Abuse* (Woods, 1985), and *No Safe Place: Violence against Women and Children* (Guberman & Wolf, 1985) are written by sexual abuse survivors and vividly describe their suffering during and after sexual abuse. Repeatedly, throughout this final segment, we ask all participants to offer their comments on these readings, and one final session is devoted to discussing the meaning of these articles for the empathy training component.

REFERENCES

Bandura, A. (1973). *Aggression: A social learning analysis.* Englewood Cliffs, NJ: Prentice-Hall.

Davis, M.H. (1983). Measuring individual differences in empathy: Evidence for a multidimensional approach. *Journal of Personality and Social Psychology, 44,* 113–126.

Fernandez, Y.M., Marshall, W.L., Lightbody, S., & O'Sullivan, C. (1999). The child molester empathy measure: Description and examination of its reliability and validity. *Sexual Abuse: A Journal of Research and Treatment, 11*(1), 17–32.

Guberman, C., & Wolf, M. (Eds). (1985). *No safe place: Violence against women and children.* Toronto: Women's Press.

Hogan, R. (1969). Development of an empathy scale. *Journal of Consulting and Clinical Psychology, 33,* 307–316.

Hudson, S.M., Marshall, W.L., Wales, D., McDonald, E., Bakker, L., & MacLean, A. (1993). Emotional recognition in sex offenders. *Annals of Sex Research, 6,* 199–211.

Knopp, F.H., Freeman-Longo, R.E., & Stevenson, W. (1992). *Nationwide survey of juvenile and adult sex offender treatment programs.* Orwell, VT: Safer Society Press.

Marshall, W.L. (1994). Treatment effects on denial and minimization in incarcerated sex offenders. *Behavior Research and Therapy, 32,* 449–564.

Marshall, W.L., Champagne, F., Brown, C., & Miller, S. (1997). Empathy, intimacy, loneliness, and self-esteem in nonfamilial child molesters. *Journal of Child Sexual Abuse, 6,* 87–97.

Marshall, W.L., & Eccles, A. (1995). Cognitive-behavioral treatment of sex offenders. In V.M.B. Van Hasselt & M. Hersen (Eds.), *Sourcebook of psychological treatment manuals for adult disorders* (pp. 295–332). New York: Plenum Press.

Marshall, W.L., & Fernandez, Y. M. (1997). Cognitive/behavioral approaches to the treatment of paraphilias. In V.E. Caballo (Ed.), *International handbook of cognitive/behavioral treatment for psychological disorders.* Oxford: Elsevier Science.

Marshall, W.L., Hudson, S.M., Jones, R., & Fernandez, Y.M. (1995). Empathy in sex offenders. *Clinical Psychology Review, 15*(2), 99–113.

Marshall, W.L., O'Sullivan, C., & Fernandez, Y.M. (1996). The enhancement of victim empathy among incarcerated child molesters. *Legal and Criminological Psychology, 1,* 95–102.

Marshall, W.L., Sturgeon, C., & Bryce, P. (1995). Increasing self-esteem of child molesters. *Sexual Abuse: A Journal of Research and Treatment, 9*(4), 321–334.

Mehrabian, A., & Epstein, N. (1972). A measure of emotional empathy. *Journal of Personality, 40,* 525–543.

Pithers, W.D. (1994). Process evaluation of a group therapy component designed to enhance sex offenders' empathy for sexual abuse survivors. *Behavior Research and Therapy, 32,* 565–570.

Woods, G. (Ed.). (1985). *Voices, a collection of writings by survivors of sexual abuse.* Ontario, Canada: The Community Mental Health Program of Hastings and Prince Edward Counties.

9 Enhancing Social and Relationship Skills

William Marshall

It has long been assumed that sexual offenders are typically deficient in various social skills. However, the evidence relevant to this assumption is not particularly extensive and is certainly not always supportive (for a review of this evidence, see Marshall, 1996). Despite this lack of substantial support from research findings, most sexual offender therapists evaluate and then attempt to enhance social skills in these clients.

The notion of social skills deficits covers a broad range of problems. Sexual offenders may be deficient in their ability to enact appropriate behaviors because they are either unskilled or too anxious or both. They may not know how to start and maintain conversations, or they may be so anxious that they avoid conversations. They may be deficient in the ability to read social cues emitted by other people, and they may lack the necessary skills to establish and maintain intimacy in relationships or may be anxious about doing so. Sexual offenders may also lack other skills (e.g., communication, problem solving) involved in relationships. When individuals are unskilled in, inexperienced at, or apprehensive about intimacy, they may nevertheless attempt to establish relationships; however, they will likely not gain satisfaction in the relationship or may simply opt to avoid closeness.

Most treatment programs for sexual offenders assume that these clients suffer from some or all of these deficits. In fact, most programs are rather vague about the types of social skills problems sexual offenders have, even though they have a component that explicitly addresses these issues. When therapists do not clearly specify the deficits they are targeting, their programs are hard to replicate, and it is difficult to know what aspects of functioning have been changed. Well-defined treatment flows from clearly stated goals and operationalized assessments. Nowhere in the field of sexual offender treatment are these aspects (goals of treatment and assessment) less clearly defined than they are in the area of social skills.

Theoretical work of the type exemplified by McFall (1990) and empirical analyses of social skills are urgently needed. Almost three decades have passed since Marshall (1971) first suggested that treatment for sexual offenders should include social skills training, yet we know precious little more now than we did then. This is a relatively straightforward area that lends itself to research and theory. I urge readers to take up the issue and attempt to provide some clear answers. What we need to know from research is not simply whether, as a group, sexual offenders are relatively deficient in social skills (although this is valuable information). We also need to know the range of deficits or skills among sexual offenders. Even if sexual offenders, as a group, are shown to be competent in one or another aspect of social functioning, it may still be the case that individual offenders have problems that are functionally related to their offending and, therefore, in need of treatment and/or remediation.

According to the empirical literature available, sexual offenders may hold templates of what they believe to be socially appropriate behavior that differ from the templates of other people. We (Marshall, Barbaree, & Fernandez, 1995) found that child molesters and rapists held quite inappropriate models of social behavior; when our training efforts contradicted their models, the conflict generated resistance to treatment. Child molesters and rapists have been found by some researchers to be unassertive (Segal & Marshall, 1985), whereas others have found them to be appropriately assertive (Stermac & Quinsey, 1985). We found that child molesters were good at recognizing problems but generated poor-quality solutions (Barbaree, Marshall, & Conner, 1988).

The findings are most consistent in the area of intimacy, attachments, and loneliness. Most of the evidence comes from our group, and essentially, we found that sexual offenders of all types (rapists, nonfamilial child molesters, incest offenders, and exhibitionists) score low on measures of intimacy (Seidman, Marshall, Hudson, & Robertson, 1994), score high on measures of loneliness (Seidman et al., 1994), and have poor-quality attachments (Ward, Hudson, & Marshall, 1996).

Our treatment component for social skills deficits has two parts: general social skills training, and intimacy training. Each of these elements is done in groups for efficiency and effectiveness. Indeed, we believe that individual therapy with sexual offenders is both difficult and far less productive than group therapy. Groups are composed of 8 to 12 offenders (depending on the therapist's experience and skill) and one or two therapists, depending on available resources. Group sessions last 2.5 to 3 hours, with a 10-minute break in the middle. We run no more than three sessions each week in order to avoid emotional overload for both therapists and participants. All our clients participate in the intimacy component, as we have consistently found some degree of difficulty in this area in all the offenders we treat. Only those who display deficits in other aspects of social functioning at initial evaluation are placed in the more general social skills training component. I describe both components here, although we only have evidence supporting the value of our intimacy training package (Marshall, Bryce, Hudson, Ward, & Moth, 1996).

GENERAL SOCIAL SKILLS COMPONENT

The first step in this process involves helping participants identify the areas in which they have problems. We indicate that group members may have problems in initiating, maintaining, and terminating conversations; may have difficulty understanding the feelings of others; may be socially anxious; may lack self-confidence in social situations; may be unassertive; may not know how to solve interpersonal problems; or may get angry very easily, which interferes with their relationships.

Generating these lists can take several sessions. The process is facilitated by having participants do most of the work between sessions in discussions with one another. Once the lists have been completed, we begin the training proper, although it is important to note that these lists are constantly revised throughout training.

CONVERSATIONAL SKILLS

The typical problems here include starting a conversation; identifying when to talk, when to stop, and when to be silent; proper listening; recognizing cues from the other person; emitting cues; maintaining eye contact; maintaining appropriate interpersonal space; using gestures and body movement; and modulating behavior according to context. We begin this component by asking each client to indicate which skills typify an effective conversational style and the behaviors and problems that interfere with adequate functioning. The therapist lists these suggestions on a flipchart and adds any features that have been missed. This is followed by a discussion in which group members identify the limits to their skills and define their treatment needs, if any.

The best way to instill these skills is through directed practice. Initially, we use role-play in the group to identify problems and use these experiences to point to both the positive and the negative features of the client's performance. Simple corrective instructions are followed by role-played modeling of appropriate behaviors by the therapist. This, along with subsequent repeated role-play practice by offenders, is typically sufficient to produce more appropriate behavior in the therapy group. However, a client's anxiety and/or lack of self-worth may be so inhibiting that behavioral rehearsal alone will not lead to satisfactory performance within the group or outside it. In those cases, we initiate procedures for anxiety reduction and self-esteem enhancement.

Anxiety management techniques involve teaching the clients muscle relaxation exercises and then having them practice engaging in self-instructional cues to relax (see Cautela & Kearney, 1990, for a description of these procedures). They practice these anxiety-inhibiting procedures in the group so that we are certain they know what to do. Most importantly, they are re-quired to practice self-instructed relaxation in various situations in their everyday lives. This daily practice is monitored in group sessions. Once clients have mastered these skills to a sufficient degree, we have them return to role-plays. In fact, we have shown, in most cases, that behavioral rehearsal alone is sufficient to both overcome social anxiety and develop appropriate skills (Gordon, Weisman, & Marshall, 1980; Hayes & Marshall, 1984; Marshall, Gauthier, & Gordon, 1979). When it is necessary to first acquire counteranxiety skills, it is still essential to employ repeated role-plays to develop the skilled enactment of conversational interactions.

Self-esteem–enhancing procedures begin with having the client list 8 or 10 personal features that are positive. Typically, this suggestion is met by a denial of any positive features. However, with prompting by other group members (particularly between treatment sessions), it is typically easy to generate a satisfactory list. In fact, this process has the effect of facilitating group coherence and support. The positive features we usually look for tend to be quite general (e.g., "I am a good worker" or "I am a generous person"), although we always try to include one or two specific skills (e.g., "I am a skilled carpenter" or "I am a good hockey player"). Once the list is produced, the client is instructed to rehearse, in as convincing a manner as possible, each of the positive self-statements at least three times each day. The client is also told to do this whenever he or she has engaged in a pleasurable activity or whenever he or she is feeling in a positive mood. However, even on bad days, the client must rehearse the statements. Again, we check on this practice at each group session. This repeated practice, mechanical though it may seem, does produce changes in self-esteem (Marshall & Christie, 1982). We continue working on role-played conversational skills while the client continues these practices. We point to positive features of the clients' enactments and compliment them on any signs of improvement throughout the role-plays.

After some degree of progress is evident, clients are required to begin to expand the range and frequency of their social contacts. They are to put into daily practice the skills they have acquired in the role-plays. This daily practice is, to some extent, determined by group discussions aimed at identifying situations in which the possibility of positive experiences and feedback is maximized. However, we prepare our clients for failure and rejection. We have shown that expanding the range of social interactions not only improves social skills but also enhances self-confidence (Khanna & Marshall, 1978).

Within group therapy, the enhancement of self-esteem is facilitated by always approaching issues in a supportive way, even when it is necessary to firmly challenge a client. Therapists should respond to clients in a way that respects their dignity and integrity. This requires an ability to shun a confrontational approach while, at the same time, refraining from collusion with a client who is avoiding issues.

In vivo practice provides a basis for identifying specific problems, such as lack of appropriately assertive behavior; dealing with unsatisfactory reactions from others; and coping with rejection. We also provide assertiveness training, assisting clients in defining appropriately assertive responses and distinguishing them from compliance, obsequiousness, or aggression. The problem is defined, the group brainstorms various alternative responses, these responses are practiced in role-plays and then evaluated, and the most effective response is chosen and practiced in the real-life problem situation. This social problem-solving approach typifies our approach to all problems as they arise in treatment, so that by the end of therapy, our clients have learned to deal with various problems in this analytic way.

Throughout these processes, each client is required to engage in extensive between-session homework. Most of this homework involves actual practice of acquired skills. It also serves to identify unanticipated problems for further analysis and training in the group. Each client keeps a diary of social interactions and rates them for effectiveness. The client also notes the duration and quality of these interactions and

any problems that arise. This feedback assists the group in further enhancing each client's skills.

ANGER MANAGEMENT

Many sex offenders, although emotionally inhibited in other ways, have no trouble expressing anger, except that they have difficulty doing so appropriately. This poorly controlled anger seems to reduce their inhibitions toward offending and often serves (sometimes inadvertently) to threaten victims into compliance. In fact, Pithers, Beal, Armstrong, and Petty (1989) reported that anger (either global anger or anger specifically toward women) was an important immediate precursor to sexual offending in both rapists (88 percent of whom were angry prior to offending) and child molesters (32 percent of whom were angry at the time of their offense).

One of the problems that we have discerned concerning aggression and anger in sexual offenders is also relevant to dealing with their assertiveness (Marshall et al., 1995). We found that the model of appropriate behavior held by male sexual offenders differed from that held by other males. Firmly but politely standing up for one's rights was deemed to be appropriately assertive behavior by nonoffenders. Child molesters, however, considered an acquiescent response, in which the person forgoes his or her own needs (i.e., what most people would deem to be an unassertive response), to be the most appropriate response. Rapists thought that an aggressive response was most appropriate. Clearly, if sexual offenders hold inappropriate models of behavior, it will be difficult to instill appropriate responses unless these models are also changed.

Accordingly, our first focus involves a discussion of appropriate and inappropriate behavior and the likely costs and benefits of adopting one or another style. To this end, we ask clients to identify a recent instance when they became angry and, as a result, either reacted aggressively or withheld their anger and acted compliantly. We then have group members generate alternative responses to the problem situation and ask them to indicate what they think the likely outcome will be in terms of the effects on them and on the other person. Each client is required to role-play at least two or three of the suggested responses; discussion then follows concerning which response was most appropriate and why. Once an appropriate response is selected, the client is required to practice this with the person who is causing distress.

In addition, we discuss the nature of anger and search with clients for the possible common threads in the various situations that trigger their anger. Anger, we tell them, is a perfectly reasonable response to many situations, and in any event, feelings, to some extent, just are. They are neither right nor wrong, although what one does in reaction to these feelings may be beneficial or not.

Each client describes various situations that have led to the feeling of disruptive anger, allowing the group and therapists to analyze various aspects of the problems. We assist clients to recognize just what makes them angry and challenge their perceptions of the situation or other person involved. Often clients have formed a belief prior to any encounter that other people will be nasty to them, so their perceptions of what the other person says or does is distorted in a negative way. These descriptions of problematic situations also allow clients to evaluate whether the intensity of their anger is appropriate and to identify why it is so strong. We point out that repeatedly experiencing intense anger is harmful to their health and well-being. It may lead them to behave inappropriately (by striking out at the other person, destroying property, or sexually offending), or it may cause them to bottle up their anger, inevitably leading to displaced aggression, possibly including sexual offending.

From their descriptions, we help clients identify their perceptions and consequent thoughts and feelings, the self-statements they make, and the likely actions they will take. We challenge each aspect of these responses and offer alternative formulations and responses. The therapist models appropriate responses, and role-plays provide the opportunity for offenders to try out various alternative interpretations and behav-

iors. Clients select from these responses the ones they believe will have the most advantageous consequences, and the group discusses the likely value of the choices. Next, clients are required to practice the alternative positive responses they rehearsed and identified in the group in everyday life. These practices (role-plays and in vivo practice) not only instill skills but also desensitize clients to the aversive quality of feedback they may get from others, so that the intensity of the angry response diminishes. This, of course, makes it easier for clients to engage appropriate responses and allows them to begin to feel in control without expressing anger.

RELATIONSHIP SKILLS COMPONENT

In the relationship skills component of treatment, the focus is primarily on developing the desire for intimacy and the skills necessary to attain it. Our research has shown that sexual offenders lack intimacy and experience loneliness (Bumby & Marshall, 1994; Garlick, Marshall, & Thornton, 1996; Seidman et al., 1994), and our theoretical work has linked these deficits both to a general disposition to sexually offend (Marshall, 1989) and, depending on the nature of their attachment styles, to a tendency to offend in specific ways with particular partners (Ward, Hudson, Marshall, & Seigert, 1995). The predictions concerning the relationship between dysfunctional attachment styles and specific offense patterns were confirmed in our most recent research (Ward, Hudson, & Marshall, 1996). These observations suggest quite clearly that enhancing intimacy skills and thereby changing attachment styles to more secure and functionally appropriate ways of relating should reduce the risk of reoffending in child molesters. Our recent evaluation of this component demonstrated that it reduced loneliness and enhanced intimacy in a group of nonfamilial child molesters (Marshall et al., 1996).

INTIMACY TRAINING

Available evidence indicates that the most effective way to enhance intimacy in men is to work with them in groups (Sternbach, 1990). Presumably this is true because group therapy provides an opportunity for vicarious learning and allows each group member to challenge other participants' thinking and attitudes by illustrating the issues with his own experiences. These seem to be the essential virtues of group treatment, in addition to its obvious efficiency in allowing us to deal with more clients than is possible with individual therapy.

Our earlier treatment components, such as overcoming denial and minimization, changing attitudes, and training in empathy, and the conversational skills and anger management segments of the present component, prepare clients for the intimacy component. The preparation is accomplished by providing practice in self-disclosure, promoting self-confidence, encouraging recognition of and responsiveness to emotions in others, enhancing the awareness and expression of the client's own emotions, and changing attitudes in the direction of more gender-egalitarian views. Many of our clients are also involved in one or more additional programs, such as substance abuse, cognitive skills, and life skills, that also facilitate the processes involved in the intimacy component.

Although we focus primarily on the development of enduring romantic sexual relationships, we strongly encourage our clients to employ many of the skills to extend their current range of friendships or to deepen some of their current friendships. Intimacy is best seen as dimensional in nature, so that some relationships may be deeply intimate and others may be less so. People who are able to meet their intimacy needs satisfactorily typically have close friends with whom they are not sexually involved. We suggest to our clients that these other close friendships may be particularly helpful during the breakup of a romantic relationship or when such a relationship is stressed.

PREPARATION

We provide information meant to persuade our clients that enhancing their intimacy skills will lead to increased enjoyment of relationships, in the hope that this knowledge will motivate them to effectively participate in this treatment component.

Research has indicated that individuals who score high on measures of intimacy are more resilient to stress, suffer less physical and psychological problems, and are seen by others as more egalitarian, cooperative, warm, and friendly and as less aggressive compared with low-scoring individuals. Intimate relationships provide opportunities to be nurturing, give a sense of belonging, offer support during adversity, and give participants a sense of meaning to their lives. Low-intimacy individuals experience few or none of these features and are inclined to be self-centered, lacking in empathy, and aggressive, as well as decidedly unfulfilled and unhappy.

We point out that the quality of their childhood attachment bonds with their parents are critical to acquiring the skills and confidence to be intimate. We have clients identify the nature of their relationships with their parents and of their adult experiences in relationships (with both males and females). We outline Bartholomew's (1993) analysis of adult attachment styles (secure, anxious-ambivalent, avoidant-fearful, or avoidant-dismissive) and the views of self and others that are associated with these various attachment styles. Table 9.1 outlines these relationships. We then assist clients in identifying their adult attachment styles and the personal costs associated with these styles. At this point, clients are reminded of the benefits to be derived from more adequate relationships. For some clients, identifying attachment problems with their parents raises unresolved emotional issues. If so, it is necessary to spend time resolving these difficulties.

Although many of our clients seem to assume that happiness in a relationship is a matter of good luck, we point out that this is not so. How happy a couple is depends on many factors, in-

TABLE 9.1   ATTACHMENT STYLES IN ADULTS

Attachment Style	View of Self and Others	Interpersonal Style	Intimacy Level
Secure	Positive self Positive other	Appropriate disclosure Seeks mutual support	High
Anxious/ambivalent	Negative self Positive others	Seeks approval Controlling Preoccupied with relationships	Fluctuating but never satisfactory
Avoidant 1 (fearful)	Negative self Negative others	Avoids social contact Afraid of closeness Afraid of rejection	Superficial
Avoidant 2 (dismissive)	Positive self Negative others	Aloof Sees no value in closeness	Almost zero

Adapted from both Bartholomew (1993) and Ward, Hudson, Marshall, and Seigert (1995).

cluding how partners are chosen, how the couple relates to each other, and how respectful they are of each other's needs. Equitable relationships, in which the couple participates in joint pleasurable activities such as sports, hobbies, social events, and other leisure activities, maximize the possibility of having an enjoyable relationship. In equitable relationships, couples have sex more frequently and derive greater satisfaction from their sexual relationships than do people whose relationships are less equitable. To maximize pleasurable mutual activities, we ask clients to identify a range of leisure activities they would enjoy and might share with a partner. We encourage them to pursue these activities with their partners as soon as they have the opportunity, but in the meantime, we suggest they attempt to share activities with friends. In fact, we advise them that practicing all the skills they learn in this component of treatment with friends is a first step toward extending the intimate nature of their relationship with romantic partners.

Finally, in this introductory section, we consider what facilitates intimacy and what inhibits the development of closeness in a relationship. A "distancing" style, for example, is destructive of intimacy. This style typically involves inhibition of emotional expression and a restricted range of self-disclosures. In addition, intimacy is hampered by jealousy, by dysfunctional expectations about relationships (e.g., disagreements are destructive, partners should always remain the same), by terminal hypotheses (e.g., "My partner is mean and unchangeable" or "I am inadequate and always will be"), and by an inadequate way of sexually relating. The subsequent elements of the intimacy training, we advise our clients, will address these difficulties.

SEXUAL RELATIONS

The therapist must be knowledgeable about and comfortable with discussing sexual matters. Any awkwardness on the part of the therapist will be counterproductive. Such awkwardness or feelings of discomfort about sex have led many therapists to focus on sex education, which typically describes the physical aspects of sex and omits from consideration the behavioral and relationship features. In fact, no more than minimal knowledge of the physical basics of sex is needed to attain mutual sexual satisfaction. It is the beliefs and practices of sexual *relations* that are crucial to effective functioning.

Many male sexual offenders express the belief that men and women are so radically different in sexual matters that their desires are mutually incompatible and that women are, accordingly, incomprehensible. Certainly there are differences, and it is important to understand them, but they are few and not impossible to accommodate or resolve. For example, males are more visually oriented and body oriented toward sex, whereas females are more person oriented and are concerned with the social and romantic context in which sex occurs. The primary motive driving males to engage in sex is more likely to be physical pleasure, whereas females report emotions and commitment to be primary. In all aspects of their intimate relationships, including sex, women see love as more important than males do. These differences, of course, do not typify all males and females, and, most importantly, they disappear over time. Once men are over age 45, they consider physical gratification to be no more important than do women of the same age, and love is seen as equally salient in the lives of both males and females over age 35 years. These issues are discussed in detail in the group. As a homework assignment, clients write down their beliefs about the feelings of men and women concerning sex. These written beliefs are read out to the group, and their accuracy and value are discussed.

We remind the group that satisfaction in sexual relations is a function of the equitable nature of the relationship. Satisfaction is also facilitated by effective communication about sexual desires and needs. But first, it is necessary to examine various desires and their origins and to examine beliefs and expectations about sex. Some men wish to engage in particular sexual behaviors because they want to humiliate their partners. Common among these desires is a wish to engage in anal sex (which the majority of clients view as disgusting, even though many of them have enacted this behavior with their victims and thus presumably find it appealing on some level). We encourage the discussion of this and other behaviors that may be construed as repulsive but desirable, and we point out that as long as both partners desire to engage in a behavior, it should not be seen as wrong.

Frequency of sexual relations is often a point of conflict between sexual partners. When men report dissatisfaction with sex, they request an increase in the frequency of orgasmic sex, whereas women ask for increased displays of affection. The literature on sexual practices reveals that there is no standard for frequency. Some people desire sex once or more each day; for others, once a month is satisfactory. Differences in acceptable frequency of sex are not so much age related but are related to the duration of the relationship; differences in frequency expectations or a decline in frequency is not necessarily a sign of a decline of the relationship. Accordingly, setting standards for frequency is self-defeating. Likewise, types of preferred sexual activities vary among individuals, although a greater variety of practices and an avoidance of routine appear to be functionally related to greater satisfaction.

On these two points (frequency and types of activities), we emphasize the need for communication aimed at maximizing the attainment of the wishes of both partners. Our clients are instructed to commence practicing effective communication with their partners and with close friends, beginning with issues that are nonsexual and nonthreatening, and gradually moving toward more problematic areas (e.g., finances, discipline of children) or emotionally loaded topics. Finally, with their sexual partners they can begin to broach sexual issues.

Next we consider with the group any anxieties, fears, aversions, or sexual dysfunctions they may have. As clients identify relevant issues, we ask them to examine where and when these problems may have arisen. If the problems are extreme, clients are referred to specialized services, but in most cases, an open discussion and advice to use the skills learned in the earlier components for dealing with anxieties are sufficient to allow them to begin to practice more effective interactions with their partners.

We point out that sexual satisfaction is largely related to levels of satisfaction in the rest of the relationship. If couples frequently quarrel or are emotionally unexpressive toward each other, the chances are slim that they will mutually enjoy sex. Effectively communicating honestly in a way that maximizes the equitable nature of their relationship will enhance sexual relations. Even in these circumstances, however, an acceptance of various myths about sex can be destructive. These myths include the idea that orgasm is the primary source of pleasure and is the goal of sex, that simultaneous orgasm must occur if mutual satisfaction is to be secured, that physical stimulation sufficient for a woman's orgasm occurs as a result of penile penetration of the vagina, that sex is dirty, and that sex should be only for procreation. We have the group discuss these and any other idiosyncratic beliefs, with the goal of examining the rational basis of these myths and diminishing their importance.

These are, of course, not the only issues relevant to having a satisfactory sexual relationship, but they are among the most important. We encourage clients to do outside reading, although we ask that they show us any books they read to ensure that they do not contain misinformation, as do so many popular books on sex.

JEALOUSY

Jealousy is a common and destructive response in our clients and is frequently a feature of their relationship histories. Discussion of jealousy is intended to make it clear that these feelings arise as a result of, among other things, a lack of self-confidence, their own practice of unfaithfulness, perceptions (accurate or distorted) of their partners' motives and behavior, and a perceived external threat to the relationship. We indicate to clients that jealousy is such a common human experience that it should not necessarily be judged as always unproductive. Problems arise only when the degree of jealousy is pronounced and perhaps disproportionate to the actual threat, and when the underlying perceptions (of self and others) are inaccurate. Unfortunately,

many of our clients believe that jealousy is a sign of "true love." No doubt jealousy is a sign of an intense attachment. It also reflects a desire to control the relationship, and from this perspective, jealousy can be seen as reflecting selfish desires rather than love. This self-centered aspect of jealousy and the attempts at control that it generates are made clear; clients are shown that these dispositions destroy any possibility of achieving equitability in their relationships.

Some degree of suspicion about a partner's motives may be warranted by the partner's past behavior, but even then, jealousy often becomes exaggerated or persistent, despite obvious and positive changes in the partner. A disproportionate response to a partner's possible infidelity is called "suspicious jealousy" and is strongly related to the client's low sense of self-worth and (all too often) his own unfaithfulness. We try to get our clients to understand that it is inconsistent to condemn others for behavior one enacts oneself and that unfaithfulness fuels suspicion of others. We assist our clients to understand these issues more fully and to develop more appropriate perspectives. "Reactive jealousy" occurs when there is clear evidence of infidelity, but again, the degree of jealousy needs to be proportional to the degree of betrayal. Factors that influence the degree of jealousy are the frequency of the partner's unfaithfulness (greater frequency produces greater jealousy), the degree of emotional involvement of the partner and the lover (the longer and more emotional the involvement, the greater the jealousy), how the client judges the qualities of the partner (a more attractive person is usually seen as more likely to stray), and the degree of faithfulness of the client (typically, unfaithful men feel more threatened by their partners' infidelity). Of course, if the client's partner has consistently been involved in extramarital affairs, we ask the client to consider the wisdom of continuing the relationship.

For men who lack self-confidence, the independence of their partners typically represents a threat that manifests as persistent but inappropriate jealousy. However, in order to attain equality in a relationship, some degree of independence is essential. Thus, clients must learn to both tolerate independence and define a reasonably tolerable level of independence in their partners. The capacity to tolerate independence in a partner is strongly related to self-esteem; the more self-confidence clients have, the more partner independence they can tolerate and the less likely they are to doubt the sincerity of their partners' affection. Obviously, then, enhancing the self-esteem of our clients is essential to reducing their destructive jealousy and to providing the confidence necessary for them to enact the behaviors—and take the risks—required to effect a fully intimate relationship. Since confidence is also crucial to making changes in all other aspects of the functioning of sexual offenders, it is a target throughout our program and is not specifically addressed here. We remind clients of the importance of self-esteem and point out why it is particularly relevant to developing intimacy.

Although most people consider unfaithfulness by their partners to indicate that the partners are bad people and that they themselves are unworthy or inadequate, we point out to the group that these are not necessarily rational conclusions. We encourage clients, in all aspects of our treatment, not to look for blame but rather to analyze problems in a way that leads to changes that are likely to result in increased happiness. We point out that when they assign blame to their partners or to themselves, they are more likely to act in destructive rather than constructive ways. Of course, a rational reaction does not reduce suffering. Indeed, suffering may be worse when we reduce the degree to which we blame others. However, a rational response is more likely to produce benefits and reduce long-term distress.

One rational solution may be to terminate the relationship if trust cannot be reestablished or if the partner has been persistently unfaithful and shows no signs of changing. Reacting rationally, however, is not a denial of the emotional turmoil generated by betrayal. Self-reliant strategies that involve making an effort not to give up and not allowing oneself to be overwhelmed are

the most effective responses. Therefore, we have clients outline how they might deal with future feelings of jealousy. These lists of self-reliant responses are read to the group and discussed in terms of the group's understanding of the individual's relationship history and present capacities. When necessary, responses can be rehearsed in role-plays within the group.

DEVELOPMENT OF RELATIONSHIP SKILLS

Prior training in general social skills, particularly conversational skills, is often essential as a preparation for this element of our program. It is necessary to have conversational skills so that effective communication and appropriate self-disclosures can be achieved. There is no point in encouraging this behavior if the skill required to enact the behavior is not yet present. Similarly, prior empathy training is necessary if our clients are to engage in effective relationship skills.

Establishing a relationship is the first step in developing intimacy, and it is essential that our clients determine what sort of features they might look for in a possible partner. We have clients list the features they consider important, and the group discusses the relevance of each feature. Physical attractiveness is frequently given top priority, with little regard for the potential partner's personal qualities and interests. Discussion is aimed at assisting clients to appreciate the importance of compatible features rather than features that might impress others. Typically, we have them revise their initial lists to identify possible compatible features of potential partners. Associated with the tendency to look for superficial features in a partner is our clients' typical history of rushing into relationships without first finding out how compatible the potential partners are. We have clients describe their past relationships in these terms, and we consider the adequacy of their behaviors. Related to this rushing into relationships is the notion of "love at first sight." Although this concept is an enduring romantic notion in Western society, acceptance of this belief may doom clients to either rush into relationships with incompatible partners or endlessly delay initiating relationships while waiting for the one "special person."

In our discussions of these issues, we note that not every relationship has to lead to a long-term commitment in order to be valuable. We remind clients that we learn about relationships and practice our skills by engaging in various levels of involvement with various people. We foster the understanding that good sense may lead to friendships even if they do not lead to continued intimate sexual relationships. We also discuss the difference between initial infatuation (which is a quite appropriate and enjoyable experience and may be the initial stage of an enduring relationship) and the gradual development of love that is not exclusively sexually passionate. Our aim here is to have our clients understand that the affection involved in a long-term relationship is no less valuable or pleasurable than the fleeting infatuation of the early stages of a sexual relationship.

Many of our clients complain that after the first year or so of their relationships the excitement disappears; unfortunately, they take this to mean that their love has subsided. Also, for many clients, the infatuation stage of love is so attractive that they wish to repeatedly reexperience it at the expense of developing enduring relationships. The group discusses the long-term value of this practice, and we raise the possibility that it is a tactic for avoiding intimacy.

Once a relationship is established, the client must learn the skills necessary for developing and nurturing intimacy. Nurturing relationships, in order to enhance and maintain the level of intimacy, requires understanding the relevant issues, developing the appropriate skills, and changing dysfunctional attitudes, beliefs, and response styles.

Good communication skills are, of course, essential to effecting intimacy. However, to be adequately communicative, clients must first learn trust. Unless clients have the capacity to trust another person, they will not be able to communicate honestly and they will not be able to develop intimacy. We remind group members that the greater their self-confidence and the more faithful they are to their partners, the greater their capacity to trust others and to communicate their thoughts and feelings. Discussion focuses on having clients identify how they came to be distrustful of others, and we ensure that they include their own behavior as part of the basis for their distrustfulness. The distrustfulness of most of our clients represents an overgeneralization from a few experiences or even a single incident. Sometimes it arises from their observations of their parents' behavior, sometimes from their experiences as victims of abuse, and sometimes from unfortunate adult relationships. Often, in these latter cases, it is not so much the partners' behavior that is to blame but rather the clients' perceptions of their partners. Discussion focuses on how reasonable their perceptions and generalizations about trustworthiness are. We challenge the bases of their distrust and help them restructure the way they construe the relevance of past experiences for their current or prospective relationships.

Communication involves both verbal and nonverbal behaviors, and the only reasonable way to determine the quality of these features is to have each client describe in detail some past illustrative interchanges and also role-play them. Many of our clients say the right thing in the appropriate way, but their physical posture, tone of voice, and facial expressions convey quite the opposite information. Role-play practice provides an opportunity to give clients feedback about their nonverbal messages, which assists them in making these responses congruent with what they are saying. By reversing roles in these role-plays, clients can get a clearer picture of how they appear to others. Once again, clients are reminded to initially practice communication by talking to friends and partners about less problematic issues, and then moving gradually to more difficult areas. We also encourage clients to practice self-disclosure in these role-plays by revealing things about themselves that they usually keep private or reveal only to someone in whom they have confidence. Barriers to self-disclosure are identified by each client and then challenged by the group. We ask them to consider the possibility that excessive personal self-disclosure early in a relationship might frighten the other person away. This outcome, of course, is particularly likely if they reveal their history of offending too early. As with all other aspects of developing a relationship, a slow pace is best.

Conflict resolution skills are also essential to attaining and maintaining intimacy. Conflict resolution becomes easier when self-esteem is enhanced, trust is established, and communication skills are present. When communication skills are good and adequate self-disclosure (based on trust and self-esteem) is part of a relationship, conflicts tend to be rare. We point out to the group that when conflicts do arise (as is inevitable in all relationships), they need to be addressed promptly, as delaying things only worsens the problem. Conflicts, we note, are not necessarily unresolvable or destructive. It is only when they are either ignored or addressed in a hostile manner that conflicts erode relationships. Group discussion focuses on not only the content of conflict and the processes of resolution but also on the timing of the attempt at resolution. For example, there is no point in raising problematic issues unless there is time for both partners to address them. Similarly, it is not opportune to raise problems when the other person is tired or ill. Nevertheless, time must be made as early as possible to deal with conflicts as they arise.

As outlined in our program, the steps in conflict resolution are much the same as in problem solving. The client is required to identify the problem; determine the degree of agreement about the nature and magnitude of the problem; generate solutions that are, as far as possible, in the interests of both partners; agree on a course of action; and then enact it and evaluate its usefulness. A negotiating style that is not demanding or threatening, that involves listening to and acknowledging what the other person is saying, and that progresses toward a solution satisfactory to both partners is what constitutes effective conflict resolution.

We find it important to repeatedly stress to our clients that some conflict is to be expected as relationships develop, and they should learn to tolerate some of the less important aspects of their partners' behavior that might otherwise be seen as irritating. Adjustments are necessary in relationships. Conflict resolution is not predicated solely on how the client wants the relationship to be but should be seen as a process of negotiating during which both partners adjust and change. Interpersonal warmth, so critical to effective negotiating, is shown when clients listen to their partners, display caring behaviors, and accept what their partners are saying. All these features of conflict resolution are raised and discussed by the group, with the focus shifting from client to client until all group members have analyzed and reviewed their approaches. They are reminded of the value of earlier training components (e.g., the development of empathy and control over anger) in achieving an adequate style of conflict resolution.

Many of our offender clients have inappropriate and dysfunctional expectations about relationships. Some of these ideas include that partners should not change ("I want you to always be the same person that I married"); that both partners should always be in a good mood; that disagreements are destructive; that sex must be perfect; that men and women are so different that common ground is unattainable; and that men should be in charge of, and responsible for, all the important aspects of family life. We ask clients to indicate their expectations about relationships and where they are dysfunctional. They are challenged, and alternatives are offered. Associated with these inappropriate expectations are what have been called "terminal hypotheses." These hypotheses suggest, for example, that nothing can be done to change the problematic aspects of a relationship, that the partner will be unresponsive to a discussion of problems, or that the client is inadequate and incapable of dealing with the issues. When these notions are expressed to the group, they are challenged, and more useful perspectives are offered. We encourage clients to specifically generate hypotheses that link current problems to factors that are changeable. These hypotheses are called "instrumental" and reflect optimistic views of both partners and of the possibility of change.

Finally, an often neglected aspect of intimacy concerns the fact that it is significantly enhanced by engaging in enjoyable activities involving both partners. This concept does not mean that independent leisure activities should be denied—they are essential to encouraging some degree of independence. It is, however, essential to also pursue *mutually* enjoyable activities. Clients are assisted in generating a list of possible activities that they and their partners (or potential partners) might enjoy. We are careful here to ensure that clients are not simply listing activities that only they enjoy; they must consider how likely it is that their partners will enjoy these things, and they are required to list activities that might be suggested by their partners. The group assists each client in evaluating the appropriateness of these activities and how feasible they are.

DEALING WITH LONELINESS

In keeping with the general literature on loneliness, we distinguish social from emotional loneliness. Social loneliness refers to feelings that arise when we are cut off from our friends, for example, as a result of moving to a new city to seek employment. These feelings are usually transitory, because we typically develop new friends. Social loneliness does not seem to produce other problems. Emotional loneliness occurs when we are separated for a prolonged period from our loved ones or when a love relationship is terminated. Emotional loneliness is more difficult to endure and frequently causes a person to act inappropriately. Many of our clients behave as though they are terrified of not being involved in a sexual or romantic relationship. Lonely people are often afraid of spending time alone, and for this reason, they often rush into relationships without considering the compatibility of their partners.

Clients need to learn to tolerate being alone and to understand that not being involved in a relationship does not necessarily mean that they have to feel lonely. We indicate to the group that loneliness is often experienced when we are with others and can occur within a relationship. We have clients evaluate their present or past relationships in terms of the effort they put into them and whether the return for that effort was satisfactory. Discussion of this issue should result in clients recognizing the need to reduce the experience of loneliness by changing the nature of their relationships or terminating them. Termination of a relationship, however, can occur only when clients are confident that they can handle being alone.

When they are not in relationships many of our clients experience anxiety and depression. We challenge these feelings and assist clients in restructuring the way they think about the prospect of being alone. They often think that being without a current partner means that they are unlovable and that other people will judge them to be worthless. Sexual offenders typically believe that they must be in a relationship and that if they are not, it is disastrous and their fault. These beliefs about the consequences of being without a partner are commonly observed in people who report feeling desperate about relationships; for sex offenders to remain reoffense-free, these beliefs obviously need to be changed.

As the research on intimacy indicates, some men have learned to avoid any disappointment that may result from relationships by adopting a "proud loner" style. Such a style is hard to move because it is seen as safe. Our challenges of these men are directed at what they are missing and what the long-term consequences are likely to be. Having group members describe their feelings about being alone reveals their attitudes and provides the opportunity to challenge these beliefs and attributions. Through these challenges, we attempt to have our clients restructure their attitudes toward being alone.

Perhaps the best approach to dealing with loneliness is to have clients identify positive features of being without a partner. For example, being on one's own provides the opportunity to do many things that may be difficult or impossible in a relationship: The client does not have to share his income; he can travel, go to expensive shows, and indulge himself in various other (nonoffending) ways. Solitude offers the chance to acquire self-knowledge, explore various hobbies or sports, develop a greater range of friends, and, most importantly, learn self-reliance. These possibilities can make life without a partner enjoyable, and they can also result in the self-confidence needed to be carefully selective about potential partners. Having a sense of self-reliance can enhance clients' belief that they are worthwhile enough for someone else to love.

REFERENCES

Barbaree, H.E., Marshall, W.L., & Connor, J. (1988). *The social problem-solving of child molesters*. Unpublished manuscript, Queen's University, Kingston, Ontario, Canada.

Bartholomew, K. (1993). From childhood to adult relationships: Attachment theory and research. In S. Duck (Ed.), *Learning about relationships* (pp. 30–62). Newbury Park, CA: Sage.

Bumby, K., & Marshall, W.L. (1994, November). *Loneliness and intimacy dysfunction among incarcerated rapists and child molesters*. Paper presented at the 13th annual research and treatment conference of the Association for the Treatment of Sexual Abusers, San Francisco.

Cautela, J.R., & Kearney, A.J. (1990). Overview of behavioral treatment. In M.E. Thase, B.A. Edelstein, & M. Hersen (Eds.), *Handbook of outpatient treatment of adults: Nonpsychotic mental disorders* (pp. 71–88). New York: Plenum Press.

Garlick, Y., Marshall, W.L., & Thornton, D. (1996). Intimacy deficits and attribution of blame among sexual offenders. *Legal and Criminological Psychology, 1,* 251–258.

Gordon, A., Weisman, R. G., & Marshall, W.L. (1980, November). *The effects of flooding with response freedom on social anxiety*. Paper presented at the 14th annual convention of the Association for the Advancement of Behavior Therapy, New York.

Hayes, B.J., & Marshall, W.L. (1984). Generalization of treatment effects in training public speakers. *Behaviour Research and Therapy, 22,* 519–533.

Khanna, A., & Marshall, W.L. (1978, November). *A comparison of cognitive and behavioral approaches for the treatment of low self-esteem*. Paper presented at the 12th annual convention of the Association for the Advancement of Behavior Therapy, Chicago.

Marshall, W.L. (1971). A combined treatment method for certain sexual deviations. *Behaviour Research and Therapy, 9,* 292–294.

Marshall, W.L. (1989). Invited essay: Intimacy, loneliness and sexual offenders. *Behaviour Research and Therapy, 27,* 491–503.

Marshall, W.L. (1996). Assessment, treatment, and theorizing about sex offenders: Developments over the past 20 years and future directions. *Criminal Justice and Behavior, 23*(1), 162–199.

Marshall, W.L., Barbaree, H.E., & Fernandez, Y.M. (1995). Some aspects of social competence in sexual offenders. *Sexual Abuse: A Journal of Research and Treatment, 7,* 113–127.

Marshall, W.L., Bryce, P., Hudson, S.M., Ward, T., & Moth, B. (1996). The enhancement of intimacy and the reduction of loneliness among child molesters. *Journal of Family Violence, 11,* 219, 225.

Marshall, W.L., & Christie, M.M. (1982). The enhancement of social self-esteem. *Canadian Counselor, 16,* 82–89.

Marshall, W.L., Gauthier, J., & Gordon, A. (1979). The current status of flooding therapy. In M. Hersen, R. Eisler, & P. Miller (Eds.), *Progress in behavior modification: Vol. 7* (pp. 205–275). New York: Academic Press.

McFall, R.M. (1990). The enhancement of social skills: An information processing analysis. In W.L. Marshall, D.R. Laws, & H.E. Barbaree (Eds.), *Handbook of sexual assault: Issues, theories, and treatment of the offender* (pp. 311–330). New York: Plenum Press.

Pithers, W.D., Beal, L.S., Armstrong, J., & Petty, J. (1989). Identification of risk factors through clinical interviews and analysis of records. In D.R. Laws (Ed.), *Relapse prevention with sex offenders* (pp. 77–87). New York: Guilford Press.

Segal, Z.V., & Marshall, W.L. (1985). Heterosexual social skills in a population of rapists and child molesters. *Journal of Consulting and Clinical Psychology, 53,* 55–63.

Seidman, B.T., Marshall, W.L., Hudson, S.M., & Robertson, P.J. (1994). An examination of intimacy and loneliness in sex offenders. *Journal of Interpersonal Violence, 9,* 518–534.

Stermac, L.E., & Quinsey, V.L. (1985). Social competence among rapists. *Behavioral Assessment, 8,* 171–185.

Sternbach, J. (1990). The men's seminar: An educational and support group for men. *Social Work with Groups, 13,* 23–29.

Ward, T., Hudson, S.M., & Marshall, W.L. (1996). Attachment style in sex offenders: A preliminary study. *Journal of Sex Research, 33,* 17–26.

Ward, T., Hudson, S.M., Marshall, W.L., & Seigert, R. (1995). Attachment style and intimacy deficits in sex offenders: A theoretical framework. *Sexual Abuse: A Journal of Research and Treatment, 7*(4), 317–336.

10 Family Treatment of Adult Sexual Abusers

Jerry Thomas
C. Wilson Viar III

The focus of this chapter is the clinical importance of including family therapy in adult male sexual offender treatment program design. This approach benefits not only the offender but the members of his family as well. The offender needs support in treatment and relapse prevention, the members of his family need clarification and healing, and the family as a whole needs reconciliation, reunification, or closure. In particular, if the goal is family reunification, it is crucial that all members of the family learn to implement and live in an abuse-free environment.

One of the primary treatment goals for sexual offenders is to reach a clear and empathetic understanding of the full impact of their behavior on others and to accept full responsibility for their behavior and its impact. Because adult sex offenders live and abuse within a social context, others besides their victims are likely to experience these effects and harmful consequences. Those who suffer the greatest impact and are at continued risk of harm are members of offenders' immediate social environment, particularly their fami-

lies. This dynamic is true for both intrafamilial and extrafamilial offenders.

In fact, recent studies suggest that the range of those who are sexually at risk from offenders may be greater than previously believed. This information has important implications for the families of extrafamilial offenders as well as some intrafamilial offenders. One study showed that as many as one-third of adult sexual offenders display multiple paraphilias, rather than the single paraphilia traditionally attributed to all but a small fraction of offenders (Laws, 1994). These findings suggest that family members' sexual risk from offenders should not be evaluated solely on the basis of offenders' initially identified victimization patterns.

Intrafamilial abuse, the abuse that occurs directly within the context of a family system, involves victims, offenders, nonoffending spouses, nonvictimized siblings, and even extended family members. All these individuals share a highly important social system, and all are affected by the breakdown of that system. Approaching the intrafamilial offender's abuse in its family context allows everyone to adequately address both individual and family treatment issues (Giaretto & Einfield-Giaretto, 1990; Maddock & Larson, 1995; Mayer, 1983; Pitsch, 1992; Thomas, 1991). The authors believe that important treatment processes such as clarification, reconciliation, and reunification are impossible without intensive family intervention and treatment.

Extrafamilial sexual offenders also operate within a social context that can, and often does, involve their families. Whether the offender is living in his childhood family, independently, or with his nuclear family, family members are often devastated by the disclosure of the sexually abusive behavior and the fact that they have a sexual offender in their midst. However, in these instances, involving the family in treatment is important not only to help the family deal with this disclosure but also to provide support for the offender in the treatment and relapse prevention process. Even though the sexual abuse takes place outside the nuclear family setting, the need for clarification, healing, and reconciliation is still important.

Indeed, the impact of the disclosure of a sexually abusing family member must never be minimized. The discovery that a family member is a sexual offender is extremely traumatic and damaging for all family members, particularly if the initial discovery places the burden of disclosure on the family members. Disclosure to social authorities and the passing of the secret into common knowledge can cause shame and humiliation, the loss of social support systems and resources, hostility directed at the family, and economic distress (Childress, 1992; Lamb & Edgar-Smith, 1994; Roesler & Wind, 1994; Thomas, 1991). Any one of these effects is stressful and painful, and many families suffer from all of them.

In fact, there are many risk factors to consider for the families of adult sexual offenders. These risk factors arise not only from the adult offenders' underlying psychological and interpersonal problems but also from the powerful roles adults play in families. Sexual offenders typically have problems with power and control, gender roles, sexual expression, and communication, to name a few salient issues. These problems can even predispose a family member toward abusing behavior, and their resolution or remediation is central to healthy family functioning. These issues are likely to be unhealthy and risky contributors to the family system, even when an extrafamilial sexual offender does not also engage in sexual, physical, or verbal abuse of family members.

A final advantage of the family treatment orientation proposed here is its facilitation of victim identification and healing, as well as the therapeutic safety for the family in general. The treatment of child sexual abuse in a family context provides an opportunity for the development of resources within the family to promote trauma resolution and safety barriers. These benefits are valuable whether or not the family and offender are ultimately reunited.

Certainly these areas are not typically included in an adult sexual offender treatment provider's formal job description, which is complex enough already. Yet here, victim advocacy becomes a natural by-product of the family assessment and involvement. Moreover, the facilitation of victim treatment and/or family healing is of therapeutic benefit not only to the victim and other family members but to the offender as well.

It is important to assess the health of the offender's family and facilitate its optimal functioning because of the tremendous treatment benefit and relapse prevention potential of family support and participation in offender treatment. Mussack (1994) documents the importance of family support and involvement in sex offenders' engagement with and continuation of treatment. In a sample of 76 offenders studied over a 20-month period, Mussak found that 86 percent of offenders with family involvement remained in treatment, whereas only 35 percent of offenders without family support and involvement remained in treatment.

A basic point to keep in mind, however, is that just as an offender may have had a variety of negative impacts on his social environment, his social environment may have had a variety of negative impacts on him (Allen & Lee, 1992; Ballard, Blair, Devereaux, Horton, & Johnson, 1990; Bear

& Dimock, 1988; Elliot, 1993; Kapp, Schwartz, & Epstein, 1994; Kobayashi, Sales, Becker, Figueredo, & Kaplan, 1995; Thomas, 1991).

To summarize, including family-oriented components and/or perspectives in adult sexual offender treatment facilitates:

- full accountability and development of victim empathy

- identification, protection, and treatment of all those harmed or at risk from the offender

- healthy family support of the offender in treatment and relapse prevention

- understanding of the conditions that influenced, supported, and/or allowed the offender's sexually abusive behavior, and the therapeutic interventions necessary to change those conditions

THERAPIST ISSUES

Serving as the therapist for a family that includes a sexual offender is a formidable undertaking. Working with a family affected by sexual abuse compounds professional responsibilities and personal challenges. It means blending mental health, social service, and criminal justice aspects in your work. It means accepting the fact that the work will be difficult and emotionally draining, that you will be working with complex relationships over long periods of time, that this work will involve dealing with sexually deviant behavior, and that you may not even have the reinforcement of being liked or having grateful clients. It is also necessary to be skilled in a variety of therapeutic techniques, to have a knowledge of the field of child sexual abuse, and to understand the interwoven dynamics of treatment that include the offender, the victim, nonoffending spouses, and nonvictimized children. In addition to the requisite understanding of child sexual abuse, you must also know how to be a family therapist, be famil-

iar with the techniques of family therapy, and be comfortable discussing openly and honestly all aspects of human sexuality. These requirements are crucial, regardless of the relation of the victim to the offender. This may seem like an overwhelming number of requirements and skills for one therapist to achieve. Yet many programs and therapists regularly provide all these skills and more, both in solo therapist facilitation and in co-therapist teams.

The therapist's role from this perspective is expanded and nontraditional. The therapist becomes director, crisis manager, systems organizer, teacher, guide, advocate, resource person, compassionate but accountable family therapist, and sex offender specialist. In addition, while keeping the welfare of the victim foremost, the therapist must respond to the needs of family members and consider the offender a worthwhile human being who is capable of change through treatment.

The therapist's numerous tasks when working with a family include:

- performing family assessment and evaluation

- making appropriate referrals for all family members who haven't already had an individual assessment, or gathering this information if it has been done

- engaging the family as part of a collaborative team

- developing a treatment plan that outlines step by step the process of clarification and then reunification as appropriate

- involving the family in treatment plan development, and sharing the finished plan with them

- monitoring and updating the treatment plan

- working with other therapists, community agencies, and members of a treatment team to provide case management if that is called for

- providing single-family therapy and working with subsystems

- participating in multifamily therapy and multifamily education if that mode is utilized

- developing reunification and discharge criteria

- developing a family relapse prevention plan when appropriate

- setting up and monitoring visitation and home visits

- assessing readiness for reunification

- preparing the family for transition

- providing and monitoring aftercare

Sometimes, when we look realistically at what is expected from family therapists, we wonder what kind of superbeings can accomplish all this. Just look at what is expected. These therapists must have a very specialized, yet broad base of knowledge and skills; engage a family that is likely to be resistant, if not hostile; make sure that everyone who needs it is referred for individual or group treatment; and coordinate and cooperate with all the systems involved. In the process, therapists deal with transference and countertransference issues; ensure their own emotional and sexual health; provide assessment, treatment planning, and treatment interventions that are calculated to heal a very dysfunctional family; look pain and anger and despair in the face all day long on a daily basis; and sleep at night. Remarkably, clinicians have consistently demonstrated that those who wholeheartedly commit themselves to the challenges of working with sexual offenders are capable of meeting these requirements.

Many therapists prefer to work solely with abusers or just with victims or only with non-abusing spouses rather than with families as a whole. When this is the case, coordination with a family therapist specialist is an acceptable method of obtaining the necessary comprehensive coordination. Whatever the design of the treatment plan, however, the key to its success will be those who are responsible for considering the system as a whole and for integrating the different therapists' interventions in an overall treatment plan.

All therapists should be aware of the advantages of having a working knowledge of all segments of the family in an abuse case. As a therapist, the more perspectives you gain, the more effective your work will be with any of those involved. The act of learning to simultaneously view the facts of a case of sexual abuse objectively and to establish an empathetic understanding of the individuals involved is one of the greatest professional challenges and professional development opportunities available to any therapist.

THERAPIST MODELING

Modeling refers to the ways therapists demonstrate—or fail to demonstrate—the concepts, coping skills, and benefits of the treatment program through their daily behavior in the treatment environment. In addition to conscious attempts to display treatment-appropriate behaviors, modeling is also concerned with the subtleties of behavior. Style, mannerisms, mood patterns, and all other nonverbal cues are also relevant. Although active modeling is a treatment technique that therapists may or may not employ, it is important that they be aware that clients will perceive and treat them as models regardless of their decision.

Although a great deal of emphasis is placed on didactic and experiential learning in treatment, people also learn observationally, particularly with regard to social and life-coping skills. The more significant a person is in the observer's life or immediate environment, the more likely he or she is to be observed. Teachers are especially significant. For these reasons, therapists and other staff members of a treatment program are extremely significant people in the lives of their clients (aside from their role in imposing legal penalties on offenders who do not satisfy the terms of treatment).

Clients observe therapists and staff in three primary ways. First, they observe treatment providers to assess and evaluate their qualifications as program representatives and, through them, the fitness of the treatment program itself. All of us not only resist "do as I say, not as I do" authority but also tend to judge what is said by how the speaker actually behaves.

Second, sexual abusers as a group rely on highly developed observational skills to manipulate people and situations to their benefit. They actively attempt to learn not only the rules and procedures of treatment but also the relationships between staff and their personal strengths, weaknesses, and sore spots for potential leverage or exploitation.

Finally, once clients have accepted the therapists' competence and trustworthiness, they observe them as "role models." Therapists who successfully engage their clients are naturally seen as people whose professional standing and representation of the treatment program verify their achievement of a level of personal functioning and social respect that the clients would like to achieve.

Each of these types of observation presents both opportunities to enhance the effectiveness and safety of the treatment program and challenges for professional growth to the individual therapist. The dangers of ignoring modeling issues and the benefits of capitalizing on them are vital considerations for all treatment providers. In general, by constantly modeling the philosophical tenets of the treatment program, therapists encourage client engagement with treatment, enlarge the number of therapeutic opportunities, enrich the overall treatment environment, and protect themselves and the program as a whole by increasing the cohesion of the program. If all staff model the program, then all are operating from the same script, and every moment clients spend in treatment becomes an opportunity for them to learn treatment information and skills (Blanchard, 1995; Minuchin, 1974; Thomas & Viar, 1995).

CO-THERAPIST TEAMS

The use of co-therapist teams, particularly mixed-gender teams, is strongly recommended in group work involving sex offenders (Garner, 1988; Krueger & Drees, 1995; Schwartz & Schultz, 1991; Thomas, 1991). The same reasoning recommends the use of co-therapists in family therapy. The pragmatic rationale is that there are unusually high demands of work and time on therapists. Co-therapists can share and co-process the burdens of treatment and support each other's efforts. A single therapist cannot both interact directly with an individual client and observe that interaction and the reactions of the other family members.

The clinical rationale for using co-therapy teams is based on the irreplaceable and vital role that modeling by therapists plays in the therapeutic process, particularly when there is a male and female co-therapist team who model healthy gender roles, interactions, and relationships. The demonstration of cooperative decision making and problem solving, as well as respect between the co-therapists, is a valuable teaching tool for developing relationships based on equality instead of on power and control. It can be a nonthreatening and effective way of forcing clients to consider many of the basic, day-to-day terms of healthy gender interaction and is a healthy and constructive way of challenging sexual offender family systems.

The most common objection to the use of co-therapist teams is based on money. Sometimes financial realities make it difficult to provide adequate single-therapist coverage, much less two therapists. However, with the use of creativity and imagination, both financial and therapeutic needs can often be met. The potential benefits more than justify the effort. If the lead therapist has trouble engaging another therapist as a partner, properly prepared and experienced staff, interns, or qualified therapists from other fields can serve as the second member of the co-therapy team.

This emphasis on imagination to overcome

organizational difficulties does not imply any relaxation in professional standards. Every therapist involved in the treatment of sexual offenders and/or their families must be prepared to assume a very high standard of personal and professional responsibility, despite the constraints on time and money. The results of professional irresponsibility are measured in client pain and suffering.

In short, although a mixed-gender pair of family therapists is the ideal, as long as basic professional standards can be met, two minds are better than one.

ENGAGING THE FAMILY

The first step in working with this complicated and painful family situation is to get the family to want to cooperate. A common mistake of family therapists is to try to institute change before the family is properly engaged in the process of treatment.

First, the therapist must identify and overcome the barriers to engagement. Family members often come into treatment involuntarily; even when they are motivated to get help, they may be suspicious of the therapist's motives or ability. Disclosure is likely to have left family members shocked, humiliated, and afraid of what will happen to them as a result of the necessary invasion of privacy by numerous governmental and social agencies. Many victims, families, and offenders experience hostile and treatment-disparaging responses from legal and social services professionals (Giaretto & Einfield-Giaretto, 1990). The treatment professional is often perceived as just another authority figure. Overcoming this image is one of the first tasks in working with the family.

Family members are also likely to project their own feelings of shame and failure onto the therapist and expect to be judged harshly. This view can pose a significant barrier to the family's willingness to work in the treatment program. An attitude that is empathic, respectful, and non-judgmental on the part of the therapist can help dispel these negative expectations.

The next likely barrier to engagement in treatment is the fear that participation will result in the loss or isolation of family members; sometimes this fear is connected to an unwillingness to fully accept the facts of the abuser's behavior. Accepting the necessary changes that this confrontation with reality requires is painful at best, and family members understandably wish to avoid it. Here it is essential for the therapist to convince the family that the object is to help rather than to punish the family.

Once family members feel understood and respected by those who intervene, they will be more likely to want to cooperate. It is the therapist's responsibility to provide a professional and humane atmosphere that encourages families to trust the therapist and his or her judgment by being competent, nonjudgmental, and caring. It is this attitude, coupled with respect for them as individuals, that makes engagement a possibility.

The next step, after a therapist establishes trust, is to build family members' belief in the positive changes they can make through treatment and identify the resources they already possess that can assist them in reaching their goals. Building a family's confidence in their abilities is as important as building their confidence in the treatment program. It is the therapist's responsibility to discover and to reflect those strengths to the family that will help them face the abusive behavior, the problems it has caused, and the challenges of successfully completing treatment. A focus on the strengths and resources that family members already possess will help them see that life can actually be much better for everyone as a result of the disclosure of the abusive behavior and their own efforts to heal and restructure the family.

In addition to reassuring family members about the normalcy of their current feelings, frustrations, and confusions, the therapist needs to prepare them for the many reactions and emotions they are likely to have in the future. This preparation is important, because these families have generally acted out their feelings in the past instead of sharing them. Encouraging them to share their thoughts and feelings is therefore an important treatment goal necessary for the development of alternative strategies to prevent such outcomes in the future.

It is perfectly natural for families to resist change. Resistance is one of the dynamics that should be expected and addressed in treatment planning. Such resistance is a self-protective response the therapist should accept and respect, using it constructively in the treatment process.

Sometimes it is easier to start out by providing the family with an intellectual understanding of what has taken place. The therapist also needs to become established as a professional with each particular family, acting to gain the family's confidence in his or her competence. The easiest route to both goals is to empower family members with information and preliminary game plans that include their participation, providing a measure of control over their own lives. The therapist should demonstrate empathy for their feelings of helplessness and loss of control, collectively as well as individually. It is often the case that families have little or no skill in expressing empathy. When the therapist demonstrates a willingness to share their pain, he or she is modeling this behavior for them.

A therapist who does not understand human diversity—physiological, mental, cultural, racial, and ethnic—will have another barrier to overcome and will have difficulty establishing trust and competence with a family that differs greatly from the therapist's own life experience. Ethnic and cultural diversity is another important dynamic that must be respected and considered when engaging a family in the treatment process (Bowden, 1994; Heras, 1992; Thrasher, 1994). Some lifestyle and child-rearing methods may be drastically different from the therapist's, but they must be accepted if they are not objectively damaging to the people involved. It is not enough to just conceptually believe that "diversity is good." The therapist must be sensitive to it, understand it, and become culturally competent. The less a client's fundamental socializa-

tion is altered to effect a healthy behavioral outcome, the more likely it is that the client will be able to maintain the change over the long term.

Ironically, one thing that may prove helpful in forming a therapeutic relationship with family members is the tremendous personal crisis they are experiencing when they first enter treatment. One or all of the crises of intrafamily disclosure, public disclosure, or entering family therapy itself can create a charged atmosphere in which the family's image of itself has been challenged. During a crisis, the family will probably be most open to help.

However, we are interested not only in engaging the family with the treatment program emotionally but also in getting them to join in a collaborative effort with the therapist to work for positive change as part of a team. When a therapist operates from an absolute power or authority base, clients are apt to be resistant and disempowered. The therapist is placed in the role of passing judgments and providing "magic bullet" solutions. Our goal is family empowerment, and if we fail to help the family become empowered, it will be almost impossible for the members to acquire the behavioral skills and confidence necessary to prepare them to reconcile or reunify or even to be as healthy as possible.

The facilitation of a collaborative team does not mean that the therapist gives up therapeutic leadership. Collaborative teamwork need not divest the therapist of any therapeutic control. On every team there are different hierarchies of roles and responsibilities. The role of the therapist is to lead, to mold behavior, and to assemble an ever-changing, comprehensive picture of a family's problems and needs, the goals that must be reached to graduate from treatment, and the treatment interventions necessary to meet those goals. Effective therapeutic leadership empowers families to identify and solve their own problems.

A good framework for eliciting this collaboration is one that invites the family to work with the therapist to answer the question, What happened to us? The therapist must prepare the family for the difficulties it has faced and will face in dealing with such a painful problem and then execute a plan to prevent the recurrence of such a tragic and painful event. When clients are feeling hopeless and helpless, that is the time for the therapist to give them hope for the future based on their work in treatment. Increased self-respect begins with a demonstration of respect by the therapist.

By encouraging family members' involvement in a therapist-guided team approach, and by lending them a means to retake control of their lives, the therapist ensures that treatment objectives are being realized from the very beginning.

ASSESSMENT AND EVALUATION

Assessment and evaluation are the most important components of any family therapy program, because the information compiled provides the basis for a valid and useful treatment plan. The major goal of assessment has always been to develop the fullest possible understanding of the circumstances surrounding the problem so that the therapist can adequately plan necessary interventions. If the assessment and evaluation are not accurate, the plan for treatment will be based on erroneous information and will be worthless.

Besides the obvious function of providing information for treatment planning, assessment, and evaluation are actually much more. The process of assessment is also an initial intervention that furnishes an important opportunity to meet with each family member and with the family as a whole and to establish the therapist professionally as someone who is trustworthy and competent.

The following definitions (Maddock & Larson, 1995, pp. 85–117) are helpful in clarifying the terminology of assessment and evaluation: "Assessment is the process of gathering information and applying expert knowledge in order to judge the status of a client's problem and to

understand the context within which the problem is occurring. Evaluation is the application of some criteria and forming of judgments. Data gathering is the obtaining of information about the client system. Observation is looking at patterns of language, nonverbal behavior, and behavior as a whole. A pattern is a process of behavior that is observed over a period of time."

Traditionally, we think of family assessments primarily in terms of the immediate family of an adult intrafamilial offender when the possibility of eventual reunification is being considered. Yet the assessment of families of sexual offenders can include their families of origin and their extended families, as well as their immediate families. It can also include other important social support systems that serve as family for any individual. This procedure is extremely useful for both intrafamilial and extrafamilial offenders. We look to the abuser's families (of origin, foster or adoptive, and current relationships) for information about the abuser, the system within which he or she developed and/or lives, and the support system that will be present during and after treatment. This information can be a vital part of the abuser's relapse prevention program (Allen & Lee, 1992; Ballard et al., 1990; Elliot, 1993; Horton, Johnson, Roundy, & Williams, 1990).

When working with families of sexual abusers, it is particularly important that assessment and evaluation not be treated as discrete, time-limited stages conducted for the purpose of developing an initial diagnosis and treatment recommendation. Assessment typically takes place in a series of stages and interviews and is always an ongoing process throughout treatment. New data will continually emerge over time through new disclosures and discoveries and through the therapist's ongoing observation of family dynamics during treatment. What's more, the accuracy and reliability of any given piece of information are almost always in question. Falsification, distortion, misinterpretation, and incomplete reporting are common. As the family makes progress in treatment, new disclosures and corrections of previous disclosures will occur. It is important to keep in mind, however, that the family members' individual and collective perceptions of facts, regardless of their objective accuracy, are as important to the structure and operation of family dynamics as the facts themselves.

These inherent problems in accurate information gathering from the persons involved make the gathering of collateral information essential. Therapists should attempt to gather as many different perspectives on the family and abuser from professional and nonprofessional sources as possible. In addition to assembling all the documents from the other agencies involved in the investigation, prosecution, and treatment of the family and its members, therapists should consider gathering information from all those with close personal ties to the family.

An assessment is most realistic and useful when "family" is viewed in a larger, more inclusive context. The traditional definition of family isn't always realistic or sufficient anymore. Family may realistically include people with whom we live, people we consider part of our support system, and people who serve as parental figures. Sometimes this more inclusive sense of family consists of extended biological family, foster family, friends, employers, or even neighbors. Some of the functions and processes typically associated with family may be served in a particular offender's life by organizations, professional relationships, or fraternal associations. The key is to make this determination on a case-by-case basis and to explore the specific family system of any sexual offender as fully as possible.

The best person to conduct the family assessment is the family therapist, because this is an optimal time for bonding and engagement. In situations in which the assessment has already been completed, sharing the previously recorded information with the family expedites the development of a mutual base of understanding, gently confronts any discrepancies among the various reports, and pinpoints how distortion and denial have changed the family's statements over time. The sharing of information also demonstrates a climate of openness and begins to confront the patterns of secrecy that may have supported the abuse or other family problems.

STRUCTURE AND TOOLS

Because the etiology, circumstances, and treatment needs of each abuser and his or her family system are unique, the structure and tools used for each assessment will also be different. Listed below, however, are the fundamental areas of concern that need to be evaluated with all families both during the initial assessment and as part of the ongoing assessment and evaluation process. These areas apply to both intrafamilial and extrafamilial offenders.

1. Overinvolvement or enmeshment: The physical, emotional, psychological, and/or sexual boundaries in the family may be blurred or nonexistent.

2. Isolation: The outside world may be seen as hostile, with the family closing itself off to outside influence, leading to family secrecy, loss of objective perception or reality checks, and a lack of support systems within the community.

3. Extreme external and internal stress: A high degree of intra- and extrafamilial problems, including money, illness, legal consequences, and extended family interactions. Constant exposure to stress weakens family resources, and coping mechanisms may be poor or maladaptive.

4. Intergenerational sexual or physical abuse: Offenders and other family members may have been victims of abuse, sometimes dating back generations.

5. Impaired communication styles: Communication patterns tend to be indirect, with feelings and thoughts expressed through behavior or in such obscure ways that family members often misunderstand one another.

6. Conflicting intrafamilial relationship styles: Relations are either too close or too distant. For example, the father may be emo-

tionally distant while the mother is enmeshed. Inadequate control and erratic limit-setting are common.

7. Emotional deprivation: Emotional needs for nurturing and closeness typically are not met, and skills in this area are limited.

8. Abuse of power: Family members, particularly parents, do not know how to use power effectively, often overreacting to external stimuli instead of responding to an internal value system.

In addition to information about the basic functioning and health of the family, it is important to assess the impact of the abuse and its disclosure on the family system as members proceed through treatment. This issue can be broken down into three primary sets of concerns:

1. Family members' perception of the sexual abuse: What happened and how did it happen? What do they think the consequences ought to be, and why? What are the respective and overall levels of denial or minimization? Who knows and who does not know about the sexual offenses? Do the parents insist that uninformed children not be told or be told only minimizing accounts?

2. Reaction of the family to disclosure: Who do family members support, and why? Are they taking adequate steps to support and protect the victim and to get help for the abuser? Are there any new indications that there are other victims or potential victims who need protection?

3. Reaction of extended family or significantly involved others: Who do they support, and why? What are the strengths and the nature of their interactions with the offender and his or her family? What potential treatment resources and/or unhealthy influences do these people bring to the treatment plan?

Because of the variety and amount of information the therapist will be assembling and organizing, assessment model outlines can be extremely useful, and the therapist should be familiar with a variety of available outlines. The following is a psychosexual history outline developed by one of the authors using her own experience as well as a variety of other professional sources.

1. Demographics: Who are the participants? What is their relationship to the abuser? What is their attitude toward the events that led to treatment and toward the treatment process itself, including legal and social services interventions?

2. Family environment: What are the significant processes, intra- and extrafamilial relationships, marked alliances and alienations, discipline patterns, parenting style, socioeconomic environment, and sleeping arrangements?

3. Problem presentation: What does the family perceive as the reason for its inclusion in the treatment? How do the members describe their specific problems, and what are their reactions to the causal events?

4. Historical data: What historical patterns are revealed? What information is available on the criminal, correctional, psychiatric, and medical histories of the offender and significant family members?

5. Abuse history: What prior victimization of the offender and other family members occurred? What other sexual offenses of the offender and other family members took place? What was the extent of prior or ongoing physical and/or emotional violence in the home? What significant lapses of self-control or accountability (e.g., addictive, obsessive, and/or chronically depressive behavior) occurred?

6. Psychological data: Have family members received mental health services in the past? If so, what were the reasons for receiving these services? Did they perceive benefit,

help, or change as a result of these services? Has the family or any subgroup of its members ever been in family therapy or treatment programs before? Corroboration of these reports is important, if possible. Former therapists or service programs can be very useful but may be unpredictably cooperative or uncooperative.

7. Family background: The key elements here are the family history, number of siblings by generation and developmental stage, birth order, character of intrafamilial relationships, religious environment and influences, socioeconomic stability of home(s), perceptions and expressions of sexuality, and disruptions such as single-incident violence, death, divorce, abandonment, financial hardship, long-term or forced separation of family members, and behavior problems.

8. Developmental and medical histories of the abuser: This area should include data concerning the abuser's mother's pregnancy, the abuser's birth, any unusual problems or complications, hospitalizations, developmental patterns and phenomena, physical and psychological trauma, remarkable illnesses, and any suspected or known physical or emotional abuse.

9. Medical and developmental histories of the family: The therapist should collect evidence of physical trauma (treated and untreated), accident proneness, enuresis and encopresis, psychosomatic complaints, venereal disease, addictive or obsessive neuroses, and developmental problems.

10. Educational histories: What are the family members' educational backgrounds and respective levels of cognitive sophistication? Did the offender have any noteworthy problems in school, either educational or disciplinary?

11. Sexuality histories: Exploration here should center on the family's perception of the sexual development of the abuser and the sexual influences and models within the family, instances of sexual acting out within the family, the level of comfort with the subject and specifics of sexuality, the sexual relationship of the parents, sexual dysfunctions of the abuser or family members, and preadult sexual activity of the abuser's siblings and preadult children.

12. Leisure time: How do the abuser and the family spend leisure time? How was leisure time spent in the abuser's family of origin? Look at community activity, social isolation, and "sociability" factors.

13. Legal history of family members: Note any contacts with the legal system.

14. Substance use and abuse, including alcohol, street and prescription drugs, food, and so forth: What are the medical and recreational drugs or foods of choice? Are any negative behaviors due to the effects of the drug or eating disorder? Is the drug use illegal? What effects have these behaviors had on the individuals and the family? How do family members see each other's drug or food behaviors? Has there ever been any drug or eating disorder treatment? Is an additional substance abuse or eating disorder assessment necessary? Should an addiction specialist be consulted?

There are several other good models for structuring assessment in intrafamilial abuse that look at assessment as part of the treatment philosophy. Two that are particularly interesting have been produced by Trepper and Barrett (1988) and by Maddock and Larson (1995).

Trepper and Barrett consider vulnerability to be the key variable in incestuous families. They recommend examining vulnerability in relation to four areas:

1. socioenvironmental factors, including social isolation, chronic family stress, and gender issues

2. family-of-origin factors, including family themes regarding male and female roles

and relationships, generational sexual abuse, and perception of emotional neglect or deprivation

3. family system factors, including structure, communication, and function of incest

4. individual psychological factors, including cognitive distortions, sexual fantasies, and personality disorders

Trepper and Barrett base their assessment philosophy on the assumption that incest most often occurs in families that are highly vulnerable based on the family of origin of parents, personality characteristics of individual family members, family dynamics, and environmental conditions; have experienced a precipitating event; and lack sufficient coping mechanisms to prevent the abuse from taking place.

Maddock and Larson's model is based on their belief that incest occurs as a result of boundary problems. Their model therefore focuses on the assessment of boundaries in four general areas: family-society, intergenerational, interpersonal, and intrapsychic. The initial assessment of boundaries is completed in the following ways:

1. Family-society: The degree to which family members permit the therapist to make a personal connection is a good indication of the status of the family-society boundary. In addition, the therapist's observation of the family's interaction with other agencies can be helpful. Information gathering consists of ascertaining the number and extent of social and support contacts the family members have, both as a family and individually.

2. Intergenerational: Information gathering consists of ascertaining whether the parents and children switch roles or mix roles.

3. Interpersonal: Information gathering is not done directly, as family members are not good sources of information about interpersonal boundaries. The therapist's observations regarding who speaks for the family, which members speak for other members, the tolerance of differences of opinion, and so on shed light on this boundary issue.

4. Intrapsychic: Information gathering here is best done individually and then compared when working with the family as a group. The therapist also needs to compare his or her perceptions of events in the family sessions with those of family members to make sure that no reality distortions are occurring during treatment.

Because of the wide differences between both sexual abusers as a group and sexual abuser treatment facility populations, there is no single, comprehensive, exhaustive model the authors can recommend. Instead, therapists should be aware of a broad range of models, attempt to gather the most extensive body of case-specific information possible, and apply the models (in whole or in part) that best organize and illuminate the immediate case.

Whatever assessment protocol the therapist uses, however, is meant to be only the foundation of a living, constantly developing document that forms the basis for the treatment plan and directs the structure and course of the therapist's interventions.

DEVELOPING A FAMILY TREATMENT PLAN

The data gathered from a comprehensive assessment and evaluation serve as the basis for the treatment plan. The purpose of a treatment plan is to help the therapist develop an organized approach to the treatment process. The components of the treatment plan include diagnoses, identified problems, short- and long-term goals, interventions, an inventory of family strengths and liabilities, the discharge and aftercare plans, and estimated length of treatment. The problems should be observable, measurable, and related to the diagnoses. The goals should be observable, measurable, time-limited, target-dated, realistic, and relevant. The interventions must be specific and should specify treatment modalities, services, activities, frequency of intervention, and the name of the therapist responsible.

It is a working document and is continually refined and updated to allow for ongoing assessment findings and for changes in treatment because of progress or regression. At its very best, it provides an integrated, coordinated approach to treatment and is a guide for both therapist and clients.

GOALS OF FAMILY TREATMENT

Goal setting clarifies what the family must accomplish in order to heal the family pain, clarify the problem behavior, effect either reconciliation or reunification, provide closure for everyone, and support the treatment of the abuser. Goals are set with the understanding that others may be added as needed and indicated. Initially, the complete list of goals will look overwhelming to the family. It is better to start with a complete list, however, than to keep adding to a partial list, a process that inevitably proves discouraging to clients and therapists alike. These goals are not worked on or accomplished simultaneously but are part of a step-by-step process in which the completion of one goal sets the stage for the next goal to be addressed.

One of the basic goals for every family is to learn and experience empowerment. The therapist supports this process by including the family in the establishment of goals and the definition of tasks necessary to reach those goals. Including the family helps clarify and distribute the burden of making long-term decisions, identifies resources available from several family members, and establishes them as contributing resources, thus continuing the process of empowerment.

An English family therapist, Gerrilyn Smith (1994), cites the following comprehensive set of goals for the treatment of families in intrafamilial child sexual abuse cases:

1. Children who are more confident, have higher self-esteem, are more knowledgeable concerning the risks of abuse, and have identified trusted and believing adults whom they can tell.

2. Nonabusing parents who are able to protect children in the future because they have more knowledge regarding the risks both generally and specifically, have a closer relationship to the children, and have outside support.

3. Offenders who take responsibility for abuse, verbalize that to partners and children, take responsibility for maintaining control of their offending behavior, and better understand their appropriate role in relationship to both partners and children.

4. Families who demonstrate changes that have taken place—clear generational boundaries, identified roles, access to outside sources of support, ability to communicate with one another, and ability to raise and discuss sexual abuse issues—and are willing to seek professional help when needed.

SOME TREATMENT ISSUES AND INTERVENTIONS

The family assessment and evaluation conducted in the beginning of the treatment process will alert the therapist to the dynamics that must be addressed and changed in order to establish a family pattern that supports nonabusive behavior. Looking at family dynamics in no way suggests that anyone other than the abuser is responsible for the abuse. There is a difference, however, between being blameless for the abuse and being responsible for developing the safety measures that will protect family members and prevent the abuse from reoccurring.

Many professionals believe that there are high-risk environments for the development of intrafamilial sexual abuse. If this is so, then changing the dynamics of the existing environment will support the development of a nonoffending environment. As noted before, even extrafamilial offenders are likely to have had a variety of unhealthy impacts on their families. Whether the abuse is intrafamilial or extrafamilial, an unhealthy family environment both fails to provide adequate protection to its members and fails to support the abuser's relapse prevention treatment and planning. In worst-case scenarios, the unhealthy family may actually sabotage treatment or actively contribute to the relapse of the sexual abuser.

Some typical treatment issues and interventions include, but are not limited to, those discussed below. They are typical of some of the problem issues and interventions that make up the family treatment plan. We have chosen to discuss as many of the general issues, goals, and dangers as possible, rather than engage in a lengthy discussion of the technical details of coping with a small selection of issues in depth or a comprehensive overview of all possible issues and interventions. Also, although the following issues are discussed specifically in terms of the families of incest offenders, which generally have the most pronounced and easily identified difficulties, these issues are applicable to the families of extrafamilial adult sexual offenders as well.

DENIAL, MINIMIZATION, PROJECTION OF BLAME. These three characteristics of sexual offenders are also often reflected in their families. It is quite common for the first reaction to the news that a spouse has abused a family's child or children to be disbelief. It is difficult for most people to believe that their spouses could be capable of such an act. It is sometimes easier to believe that the child lied, misunderstood, or is playing a payback game. When the denial has been reduced or eliminated, it is quickly followed by a tendency to minimize the harm with such statements as, "She's too young to understand what he did," or to project blame onto the victim, such as, "She could have said no if she didn't want it."

The projection of blame by family members may include the therapist as well, because the therapist has been the bearer of bad tidings and is the safest target of the family's feelings. The therapist is often seen as the person who keeps the problem alive, and therefore is the person to blame for their continued suffering and humiliation.

Defensive denial, minimization, and projection of blame are best confronted by gentle techniques while the therapeutic relationship is still forming. These techniques might include the use of didactic material presented in psychoeducational groups or the use of videos and literature. The chief feature of these materials is that they speak in general terms about denial, minimization, and projection, rather than about the specific behaviors of this family. Once the therapist judges the therapeutic bond to be solid enough to support it, he or she can begin employing stronger, more direct confrontation of these problems.

DIVIDED LOYALTY. When sexual abuse is committed within a family, often both the abuser and the victim are loved and valued by all family members. In this situation, family members often ask themselves questions such as, How can I show my concern, love, and support for everyone in the family? Do I have to reject one in favor of the other? Is this my fault? Wouldn't it be better to just take care of this problem within the family and not let outsiders get involved?

The extent of this reaction often depends on variables such as the age of the children, the type of sexual contact involved, whether force was used, and the consequences for both the victim and the abuser. The offender may also be capitalizing on divided loyalty by expressing remorse, asking for forgiveness, and promising "never again" if the secret is kept in the family. The victim may experience the collective divided loyalty problems of family members and others as well as divided loyalty to herself or himself.

As a fair, impartial authority whose first priority is the safety and health of the family, the therapist can be especially helpful in dealing with loyalty issues. In the process, the therapist can also deepen a family's engagement in treatment and the strength of the therapeutic bond. The therapist's goal is to guide the family into discovering for itself ways to simultaneously meet the needs of the victim, the offender, and all other family members. The therapist provides guidelines and optional ways of perceiving circumstances, such as framing real caring as doing what is best for everyone rather than what is easiest. Often, though, simply getting family members to speak about their loyalty divisions with the others can be a tremendous benefit.

Although sometimes a choice between family members must be made, this kind of decision is by no means inevitable. A therapist should make this decision only after careful assessment of the situation over a period of time.

ABUSE OF POWER, POWERLESSNESS, EMPOWERMENT. In intrafamilial child sexual abuse, abuse of power and powerlessness are displayed by the offender and the victim and, in varying degrees, by other family members. Behind the abuse of power are usually feelings of powerlessness. The therapist must confront the abuse of power, identify the feelings of powerlessness, and provide the necessary education and guidance for family empowerment.

Remember that empowerment must be reality based. Empowerment is the ability to examine one's thinking and correct false assumptions that control subsequent feelings and actions. Empowerment for families is found when they are able to establish clear role boundaries, develop internal controls, and use rational thinking in decision making.

When families feel powerless, they often abdicate responsibility or try to involve the therapist in games of power and control. It is the therapist's responsibility to avoid being manipulated into taking an authoritarian role or some other inappropriate position. The therapist's strategy should be to offer all family members concrete opportunities to gain control, to be empowered. Providing family members with information about their treatment, goals, and expectations is one of the most empowering things a therapist can do for them. The empowerment of all family members is an important deterrent to and barrier against incestuous behavior. It also facilitates effective information gathering and prepares the family to contribute constructively to the treatment process.

FAMILY SECRETS AND HIDDEN AGENDAS. Sometimes, the issues that families do not want to talk about are the most important ones. Family secrets may involve shared information or information withheld to prove loyalty, show power, strengthen boundaries and alliances within the family, or protect members from painful memories or consequences.

The immediate consequences of keeping secrets are distortion of information and loss of communication in relationships. Both are critical elements in intrafamilial child sexual abuse; incest is possible only in secrecy. For this reason, the therapist must be careful never to enter into secrets with either individual family members or the family as a whole. There are usually unpleasant practical and ethical consequences if a therapist makes a commitment to keep a secret, however well-meaning or small the secret may seem. Even the most innocent secret-keeping feeds into and reinforces unhealthy personal and family coping patterns.

A therapist may proactively avoid requests for secret-keeping by being clear with the family from the outset that secrets are damaging and that honesty is expected, by refusing to collude, and by confronting secret-keeping. This emphasis is the natural complement of a strategy of empowerment through open discussion.

INTERGENERATIONAL ABUSE. In families involved in intergenerational abuse, often the dynamics reflect the symptoms of abuse: anger and aggression, inability to trust or bond, depression, and isolation, to name just a few. Sometimes the abuse has been remembered but not disclosed or resolved by either the spouse or the abuser. In other families, intergenerational abuse has been the norm and is not thought of as unusual or damaging. Parents who have never come to terms with their own abuse find it difficult to deal with their children as abused or their trusted spouses (or themselves) as abusers.

The therapist should be aware of the possibility not only of unresolved past intergenerational abuse but also of juvenile sexual abuse within the family of an adult offender. When such disclosures are made in the course of family treatment, the therapist's first priority is to reassess the treatment and referral needs of family members.

SEXUALITY. Confusion about sexuality in general, and positive sexuality in particular, is a common characteristic of families in which intrafamilial abuse has occurred. Sexual issues are difficult for family members to discuss. Their anxiety about approaching sexual topics can be decreased only after the family therapist has established a comfortable relationship with them, and even then it can be difficult. Introducing the family to a sex education class, providing information about healthy sexual values, and talking comfortably with the family about sexual issues are interventions that provide opportunities to teach the family about healthy sexuality.

SOCIAL ISOLATION. There is a tendency toward social isolation in families in which intrafamilial abuse is occurring. The most powerful family members discourage the less powerful from having outside contacts and thereby reduce the number of potential outside allies for family members. The abuser may establish himself or herself as the sole linkage to the outside world. In a family encountered by one author, the abuser was the only one allowed to answer the telephone. Others may go so far as to insist on home schooling. This history of isolation can be a serious cause of treatment avoidance, even among families in which the abuser has been removed from the home.

Although reducing the isolation of family members can be extremely empowering, the therapist should balance each family member's need for reduced isolation with his or her need for greater stability and security. Ultimately, reduced isolation should directly increase the stability of the family system, but some family members may need a more gradual change than others. Obviously, this decision, like many others in family therapy, should be a cooperative effort, made in conjunction with any individual therapist the family member is seeing.

BLURRED BOUNDARIES. Both physical and emotional boundaries are often blurred in these families. The blurring of physical boundaries can include many different types of behavior. In addition to allowing access to the victim's body, boundary blurring may be expressed by demands for access to belongings, sharing of time in the bathroom, inappropriate sharing of beds and bedrooms, and other invasions of personal space. The therapist's responsibility is to identify areas where boundaries are problematic, point them out to the family, and teach the family ways to establish healthy boundaries.

ADJUNCTIVE THERAPY GROUPS

Since family therapists are often confronted with time and resource limitations, it is important to mention that there are several adjunctive therapies that can provide useful support to traditional family therapy and that are time-, energy-, and resource-efficient. These include, but are not limited to, multifamily psychoeducational support and therapy groups, couples groups, parenting groups or classes, survivors groups, siblings groups, and spouses groups. It is assumed that the abuser and any intrafamilial victims are already in primary therapy and in offender-specific and victim-specific treatment programs. In fact, this is a prerequisite for any family work.

MULTIFAMILY GROUPS

Multifamily groups simply bring together families with similar problems in a therapeutic setting to discuss issues of mutual concern. It is an efficient use of the therapist's time, it is cost-effective, and it is beneficial for families.

One of the most immediate benefits for families is relief of their sense of isolation and normalization of their feelings of humiliation and shame. Another benefit arises from the fact that the groups are made up of both new families and families further along in the treatment process. Often, families that have already been through similar experiences and have overcome them have a credibility that the professional therapist does not. Who can confront a family's denial better than another family that has already been through their own and resolved it? This contact can be so valuable that some treatment programs make it a formal part of the treatment process, assigning mentor families to newly admitted families.

Multifamily groups serve three different functions: emotional and social support, education, and therapy. Some programs prefer to provide one group that encompasses all these functions; others prefer to have three distinct and separate groups. Program design, staff time, and financial resources will determine which approach is employed. These three areas are typically addressed as part of individual family therapy, but using multifamily groups can significantly speed up the process.

MULTIFAMILY PSYCHOEDUCATION GROUP. Family education is part of almost every encounter with the family, beginning with the initial interview and family assessment, continuing throughout treatment, and in informal and formal encounters with the family. This education can be delivered in a number of different ways. A simple and easy way is to present families with carefully selected packets of information that will help them understand the treatment program for individual family members and for the family as an entity. The packet can include basic as well as comprehensive information about sexual abuse, both intrafamilial and extrafamilial. The packet should include not only books and articles but audio- and videotapes as well. To supplement this packet of information, a lending library for families can be organized that is user-friendly as well as culturally sensitive.

The psychoeducational group, whether organized as a separate group or as part of the treatment program in family therapy, should cover the following topics at a minimum: human sexuality; basic information about sexual abuse; family problems and ways to address them; direct communication; understanding and sharing feelings; relapse prevention concepts, including abuse cycles, risk factors, and safety barriers; the details of comprehensive sex offender treatment; and cognitive distortions and cognitive restructuring.

PARENT SUPPORT GROUP. Participation in this group is simply an opportunity for families with common experiences to offer support to one another. Although the therapist is available as a facilitator or guide, the families do the work —in a sense, as peer counselors. Usually this is the kind of support received from friends, but because of social isolation and the shame associated with family circumstances, these families often can't or won't rely on their friends for this support.

MULTIFAMILY THERAPY GROUP. The technique of taking families with similar problems and forming a therapeutic group has been used by a variety of disciplines for many years. It is an efficient use of the therapists' time as well as being cost-effective. Another advantage is that it gives therapists an opportunity to see the offenders in the context of their families and to see their families in a social context—the multifamily group setting. Therapists who use this therapeutic mode say that more can be accomplished with eight families together in one hour than with eight families separately in eight hours.

This experience would be good for any family, but it seems to work particularly well with families affected by child sexual abuse because it addresses some of the characteristics of those families, including isolation; rigidity; enmeshment; internal and external stresses; poor coping and problem-solving skills; faulty communication patterns; unmet emotional needs for closeness and nurturing; feelings of hopelessness and helplessness; and feelings of failure, shame, and humiliation. For an isolated family, multifamily therapy decreases the alienation and isolation the members feel by exposing them to other families with similar feelings and problems. This, in turn, decreases the anxiety that often immobilizes them.

For enmeshed families, multifamily therapy provides an opportunity to engage in meaningful encounters with other families—children as well as adults. The opportunity to experience the universality of human needs and emotional ties acts as a catalyst. It promotes genuineness not only within family boundaries between members but also across these boundaries with other families and individuals. Families that are not functioning well individually are generally not functioning well socially either, and the microcosm of the multifamily group gives them an opportunity to work through these issues in a safe and supportive environment.

Not all families can benefit from multifamily therapy; screening is necessary before inviting families to join a group. Each treatment program should develop its own screening criteria based on what is best for the program, the characteristics of the specific population, resources, and so on. In general, heterogeneous groups are better than homogeneous groups, in that they bring more energy and information to the therapeutic interactions.

A basic requisite for entry into multifamily therapy is a recommendation by the family's therapist, who has determined that this milieu would be appropriate and useful. Contraindications for involvement include families with poor reality contact; very chaotic families; families that are keeping secrets from one another and refuse to share those secrets, except with therapists; and parental-incest families in which the perpetrator is in denial and the nonabusing parent is unsupportive. Also, very young children should not be involved in multifamily groups.

Some therapists understandably and realistically feel overwhelmed by the thought of six to eight families in one room together. But this is not a task for a single therapist. Multifamily groups require a co-therapy team at the very least, with more therapists added, depending on the total number of people involved.

The therapist's tasks in multifamily therapy are similar to those in individual family therapy. The first task is to establish a climate of respect and trust. To do so, the therapist consistently models an attitude of fully accepting each person, while simultaneously rejecting any behav-

ior that is hurtful or destructive. Caring for the person while confronting negative behaviors and supporting positive ones, promoting sharing on a feeling level, careful listening, and honest responses are the bread and butter of the methodology.

The goal is for each group to become self-directed, so the therapist's control of the group must be subtle. The therapist should be more of a guide and facilitator than a group leader. Ideally, the therapist will be able to gradually step back and become someone who clarifies the work and goals of the group, serves as a resource person, summarizes and processes group efforts, and, when needed, serves as a catalyst.

Following are the principal processes that make the multifamily learning experience so powerful:

- learning by analogy
- learning by indirect interpretation
- learning from the modeling of the therapists and other families
- learning through identification
- learning through trial and error
- interruption of intrafamilial codes and secrets
- amplification and modulation of signals by the therapist

The results of a successful multifamily therapy session are often awesome to behold. Participants have learned about the sexual abuse cycle and ways to interrupt it. They have learned facts and information that will be helpful in their understanding of the events that have disrupted their lives. They are less isolated and feel more support, and they are able to look at relationships in a more universal sense. Denial and resistance have decreased, and openness and accountability have grown. The group members have been given the opportunity to heal the emotional and behavioral impact of the disclosure. During the process of a multifamily therapy experience, participants move from fear and resistance to increased openness, self-confidence, and self-esteem as they take control and become role models for others in their group.

COUPLES WORK

Couples therapy (whether the participants decide to remain together or to separate) is as important as family work (whether the family will ultimately be dissolved or reunited) to the emotional well-being of the parties involved. Two different treatment modalities are useful for couples: individual marital therapy and couples group therapy. Marital therapy deals with relationship issues, whereas the couples group focuses on skill building. Issues of sexuality and sexual dysfunction can be dealt with in either marital therapy or the couples group. We previously recommended a male-female team for family work, and we believe that it is even more important that such mixed-gender teams be employed for couples work—particularly within the context of a couples group. When making referrals for this kind of group, keep in mind that couples groups work best when they are composed of people who have similar psychological and behavioral concerns.

SPOUSES AND SIGNIFICANT OTHERS GROUP

This group is designed to help spouses and significant others deal with their feelings surrounding the abuser's sexual deviancy, as well as to educate, confront, support, and encourage them. In addition to these goals, this group provides a good opportunity to train spouses as chaperones. The empowerment of spouses is essential to the reunification of the family when intrafamilial abuse has occurred. Spouses attending this group receive education regarding the abuser's rules and restrictions, sexual deviancy, abuse patterns, objective risks for reoffending and warning signs, the effects of sexual abuse, preparation for couples group therapy, assertiveness, communication, stress and anger management, and parenting skills. Participants in the group validate one another's feelings and concerns. They are encouraged to grieve the loss of the relationship they thought they had and to discuss the impact of the disclosure and the multitude of problems stemming from their relationship with a sexual offender, as well as issues of prior victimization and codependency. Problem solving and goal setting aid spouses in deciding what to do now.

SIBLINGS AND CHILDREN'S GROUP

It is easy to minimize the problems of nonabused siblings when there is so much work to be done with the abuser, the victim, and the nonabusing spouse. Families would prefer to believe that these children are not aware of what has happened and that they can protect them from knowing. This is generally a misconception and often results in the children's unspoken fears being much worse than the reality.

Children have thoughts and feelings of guilt, self-blame, anger, and confusion about what has occurred that they need to share with someone. They wonder why they weren't chosen to be abused and what they should or could have done to protect the family member who was. They may feel anger toward the victim for disclosing because of the subsequent disruption of family life, the changes in economic status, the loss of a parent, and so on. They may be angry at the victim even when the victim was not the one who made the disclosure. At least one of their parents, one of the sole sources of stability and security in their lives, has been taken away and accused of horrible things. Their world has been turned upside down, and no one will even talk to them about what has happened.

Everyone is involved in and affected by events that have a significant impact on the family, and therefore everyone should be included in family sessions. During the family assessment, it is important to include the siblings and evaluate their need for individual therapy, as well as their level of involvement in family therapy.

FAMILY REUNIFICATION

Family reunification is a living dynamic based on family members' changing characteristics, needs, and potentialities. It is, in truth, a continuum with levels ranging from full reunification into the family system, to partial reentry, to less extensive structured contact, to no contact at all. The reunification process includes several levels: clarification, reconciliation, and finally reunification. There are times that the reunification process ends with the clarification session or the reconciliation session. It should always be recognized and kept in mind that reunification may not be desirable. Reunification, at whatever level, needs to occur as part of a collaborative process in which all involved parties are in agreement. This means that all the therapists, other agencies, and family members must agree that reunification is in the best interests of everyone. However, the decision not to reunify can be made by any one of these members without the support of the others. For example, the family may desire reunification, but if the decision criteria for reunification have not been met, the therapist must recommend against it.

Family reunification recognizes the importance of family in everyone's life; in particular, it listens to the voice of the child who says, "I didn't want to lose my family, I just wanted the abuse to stop." There is also a recognition of the impact of separation and loss on children and parents. Reunification addresses physical, sexual, and psychological safety issues and the need for environmental and societal supports for the family. While building on the strengths the family already possesses, it facilitates the process of family empowerment.

Reunification is time-consuming, work-intensive, and emotionally and physically draining for all involved. Renewed contact must be gradual and phased, and each step must be completed before the next is attempted. The pace is determined by the simultaneous preparedness of the victim, the offender, the nonabusing parent, and the siblings not overtly abused.

Reunification decisions need to be based on criteria developed through the assessment, evaluation, and therapeutic process. The decision takes into consideration the sexual, physical, and psychological safety of the victim and all other family members. Clearly, sexual safety would most easily be maintained by allowing no contact between the victim and the offender. However, a sole focus on safety by separation precludes any real consideration of the devastating psychological and emotional damage that can occur if separation is the only course considered. This focus also negates the position that a family's resources are a valuable and necessary part of the healing process and prevents any opportunity for the offender to contribute constructively to those he or she has harmed (Carlo, 1991; Childress, 1992; Thomas, 1991). Clearly, focusing solely on the psychological and emotional needs of the family and family members could also result in the therapist and family supporting a reunification that could result in future harm. That is why all decisions must be based on concrete measures of change and realistic safety plans.

Reunification decisions need to be the outcome of an ongoing, stepwise, dynamic process. The therapist and other professionals involved need to take great care to monitor their own countertransference concerning reunification so that family treatment proceeds in the direction that serves the best interests of the client rather than the needs or biases of the therapist (Edwards & Lohman, 1994; Elias, 1994; Erooga, 1994).

It is also important to remember that reconciliation is important to the treatment of the victim and other family members, as well as the abuser. There are risks to everyone if no reconciliation is attempted. The risks to the victim include the continuation of self-blame, continued feelings of helplessness and the inability to face anything fearful, irrational fear of the offender, and continued misattribution of feelings or beliefs to the offender. The victim's pain, anger, and rage need to be directed toward the abuser, where they belong. If the victim does not have the opportunity to see whether the abuser has changed or to validate his or her perception of the abuser, the victim may remain stuck in a loyalty dilemma and in the dynamics of the abusive relationship, which can contribute to future episodes of abuse. The victim needs to see the offender as a human, as a person who can be stopped. This revised perception empowers the victim to make other safe and constructive decisions. True closure is extremely difficult without this opportunity.

There are also risks to the abuser if no reconciliation or reunification is attempted. These significant risks include the probable continuation of the intellectualization of what has taken place, the objectification of the victim, and avoidance of having to face the people harmed and accept responsibility for actions.

Of course, there are risks to both the victim and the offender during the reconciliation or reunification process. The risks to the victim include increased anxiety before, during, and after the encounter; the recall of past experiences; flashbacks; regression; and the opening of old wounds. There are other risks as well, such as experiencing an effort by the offender to manipulate or trigger specific behavior, feeling pressure to forgive or trust when not ready, and having perceptions and memories invalidated. A skilled family therapist, however, can turn these risks into therapeutic moments for the victim.

There are also very real benefits for all involved when an attempt is made at clarification, reconciliation, or reunification. For victims, the process effectively challenges the cognitive distortion that abusers are frightening, powerful individuals by allowing victims to see offenders as they really are; brings empowerment by facing offenders with support and without fear; gives them an opportunity to learn to identify the behaviors that make them vulnerable to victimization; allows victims to get in touch with blocked feelings and to share those feelings of hurt and pain; extends an opportunity to gain understanding of the offenders' responsibility for the abuse; provides reality testing for feelings of guilt about the abuse; and supplies support from therapeutic allies.

The benefits for abusers are also important and include an increased personal awareness of the harmful impact they have had on their victims; a significant decrease of denial, minimization, and projection of blame as they face the facts of victim trauma and the inaccuracy of their cognitive distortions; an opportunity to deal with fear of rejection; a chance to directly accept responsibility for their abusive acts and to make a positive contribution to someone they have harmed; and a reduction in their ability to intellectualize the abuse or objectify the victim.

Some families decide against reunification or are not willing to meet the criteria, which must be very specific. When the abuser has not participated in offender-specific treatment, the victim has not participated in victim-specific treatment, or the family is not willing to make the changes that provide a safe environment or give the victim a feeling of protection—to identify a few issues—reunification is not recommended. Some families are so damaged that reunification would not be in the best interest of all concerned. Sometimes these situations require the therapist to recommend a termination of parental rights. Even in those cases, the individuals in the family need help moving on with their lives and dealing with their feelings of loss and grief.

Participating with a family in a reunification process places a level of responsibility on the therapist that is as great as or greater than any other in the field of psychotherapy. The risks involved in a "wrong" decision in either direction are tremendous. Ongoing consultation and a strong focus on therapist self-care are essential to attain positive clinical outcomes and maintain the emotional and psychological well-being of both the therapist and the clients. This being said, participating as a family therapist with a reuniting family is one of the most gratifying opportunities in the field.

INNOVATIVE PROGRAMS

Treatment programs for adult sexual offenders vary considerably. Some work solely with the offender; some work with the offender and refer the family work to another therapist and another program; some work with the offender and include the offender's family or support system as needed; and still others, primarily child sexual abuse programs, approach the problem comprehensively, treating everyone affected by the same problem within the same agency.

Achieving a comprehensive perspective and approach to the problem of adult sexual abuse is probably the ideal, but resource considerations limit many offender programs' ability to include the other individuals involved in or affected by the offender's abuse, treatment, and relapse prevention planning and training. For these programs, treatment referral and coordination of programs are an excellent strategy for enhancing the level and quality of care beyond the more narrow offender-only focus. However, it is only fair to add that there are treatment providers who believe that sexual abuse has a narrow focus and that the only problem to address lies with the abuser.

The following discussion of three adult sexual offender programs using a family approach will give the reader a basis for understanding some of the different program models. The terminology used is that of each individual program. The examples are drawn from the field of incest treatment. The application of family treatment techniques to incest has progressed faster than in other areas of adult sexual abuse, because the involvement of the family is self-evident to most therapists. The examples were chosen because the authors feel that they balance the need to treat all those involved in terms of the social context of the abuse behavior, while providing the highest standard of protection and sensitivity to family victims and nonoffenders.

INDIVIDUAL PRACTICE

A noteworthy example of a program that provides family treatment for adult incest offenders and their families is that provided by Mary Meinig (Meinig & Bonner, 1990), a clinician in private practice in Seattle, Washington. Meinig provides treatment for the victims and families of adult incest offenders who are already in certified offender-specific programs. She provides no abuser treatment outside of the family context, coordinating instead with offender programs. The result is a comprehensive overall treatment design that allows the agencies involved to cooperatively address the problem of incest in the social context in which it develops and occurs.

There are three entrance criteria for a family to begin treatment under this model: the mother's consistent involvement in appropriate women's groups; the involvement of the victim in individual and/or group treatment; and the expressed willingness of *all* family members to be involved in a treatment process whose goal is reunification.

In order for the offender to begin involvement in family sessions, the family must meet the following criteria: the mother's continued involvement in a women's group; the victim's continued involvement in a victims group; completion of initial face-to-face clarification sessions between the victim and the abuser and between the nonvictimized siblings and the abuser; the presence or development of a protective parent capable of confronting the offender when necessary; the mother's demonstration of self-confidence and the ability to manage her children's behavior; the addressing of mother-victim relationship issues and the identification of positive changes; and identifiable changes made toward the completion of individual treatment programs.

Meinig's model for the reunification of incestuous families is excellent. It is made up of five phases, each built around specific tasks and goals; each phase must be successfully completed before the next can be begun. These five phases are:

Phase I: individual, group, intact family, and marital therapy for victims, siblings, mother, and abuser, leading to family sessions including the abuser

Phase II: visitation with the abuser outside the home and clinic setting

Phase III: visitation in the home

Phase IV: overnight visitation in the home

Phase V: completion of the family reunification process

During each treatment phase, specific criteria must be met prior to moving to the next phase. The decision to continue treatment is reassessed at each treatment phase. By the final phase, the children are able to identify the abuser's warning signs and know the steps they can take to protect themselves from abusive situations.

Prior to the full reunification of the family, the family members enter into a contract that describes in detail what needs to be changed for the abuser to rejoin the family. This might include a rule that the mother make all decisions about the children and that the father not be alone with any child.

The key to the success of a referral service such as that provided by Meinig is the close cooperation among the therapists and programs involved. This approach can work only if the professionals share information and coordinate their activities.

COMPREHENSIVE AGENCY TREATMENT

Because of the importance of comprehensive case management that coordinates all the individual and group assessment and treatment processes, some agencies prefer to provide all the services to the family members involved. Following are descriptions of two programs that utilize a comprehensive treatment model.

CHESAPEAKE INSTITUTE. Chesapeake Institute is a well-known and well-respected private facility serving the Washington, D.C., Virginia, and Maryland area that treats child victims, juvenile and adult offenders, and adult survivors

within the same program. The institute was set up as a response to what the founders perceived as the budgetary vagaries and narrow perspectives of the available public-sector institutions serving these populations. There are two vital aspects of Chesapeake's philosophical orientation: maintaining a comprehensive treatment program that includes all individuals affected by child sexual victimization, and concentrating on the best interests of "the child"—both the specific children involved in a case of sexual abuse and the greater community of children. Chesapeake adopts a victim's-perspective approach that resolves the inherent conflict of interest between offender clients and the community in favor of incarceration whenever the community appears threatened.

Briefly, the clinical program embraces the philosophy that therapy for each of the different groups of clients takes a different path, depending on the characteristics and circumstances of the client, the family, and the offense and/or victimization. Therapy can run from six months to five years, with incest family therapy typically running two to five years. The treatment of adult sex offenders is designed to progress through four stages identified as crisis, narcissism, guilt, and empathy. The treatment of nonoffending spouses is developed to respond individually to their different characteristics, generally ranging along a continuum from complete unawareness to disassociation to active collusion. The individual's place on this continuum and response following disclosure are the first and probably most important keys to the child victim's treatment and recovery and to the children's safety during any level of reunification. Treatment for nonoffending spouses takes into consideration both personal treatment needs and the need to provide support to all other family members, particularly the victim.

The program outlines eight steps of family therapy, including the possibility of reunification.

Step 1. The initial goal of family therapy is to overcome the family's strong drive toward homeostasis and a return to "normal" predisclosure functioning. The family's ability to minimize, ignore, and/or deny dangers and dysfunction, however, is also a useful measure of its dysfunctional dynamics (e.g., enmeshment). The treatment program's first goal, therefore, is to engage the family, gaining both members' acceptance of the desirability and greater possibilities offered by the treatment program and their active participation in the process. Following engagement, the different individual and group issues of the family are addressed, culminating in strictly supervised visits between the abuser and the family. The nature of these sessions and the relevant issues are covered in the requirements that must be met for a family to graduate to step 2 of the treatment program.

Step 2. Family members must demonstrate 10 clinical indicators that they are ready to move beyond the clinically supervised stage. The Chesapeake Institute's 10 indicators (in its terminology, although the authors acknowledge that offenders and victims can be either male or female) are as follows:

1. All parties place appropriate responsibility for sexual abuse on the offender.

2. Siblings of the victim or victims have participated in the therapeutic process to an acceptable degree.

3. The victim's major behavioral symptoms have been totally eliminated in both therapeutic sessions and "real-life" environments.

4. Mother-daughter therapy sessions have demonstrated open communication about the abuse and the child's healing needs, including negative feelings toward the mother.

5. The mother is prepared and able (through her therapy) to respond to her child's questions and issues.

6. Father-daughter sessions have demonstrated open communication, including the child's issues and questions about the abuse.

7. The father is prepared, through his own therapy, to respond to the child's issues, questions, and feelings.

8. The father can discuss the abuse without minimizing responsibility or impact.

9. Family therapy meetings have been held to discuss conditions of mother-supervised visits by the father outside the home.

10. Conjoint parental therapy sessions are initiated.

After these 10 clinical indicators or preconditions are fulfilled, the family is ready to move on to unsupervised visits outside the home and in the community. These visits should involve something that encourages relatively normal family interaction or activity (e.g., not movies, but zoo visits or picnics are okay). Holding these initial unsupervised visits outside the home increases safety and preserves the newly established pro-therapeutic home environment (in particular, the growing mother-child bond).

Step 3. After unsupervised nonhome visits have been satisfactorily completed to the therapist's and the family's satisfaction, the family advances to step 3, which involves in-office planning and preparation for step 4—time-limited, mother-supervised visits in the family home (not overnight). The following criteria must be satisfied:

1. The father can clearly and fully describe his sexual behavior and accepts full responsibility without minimizing responsibility or impact.

2. The father can identify life stressors and unique aspects of his paraphilia that contributed to his abusive behavior and has learned coping skills for stress and inappropriate impulses.

3. The father can articulate the impact of abuse on his daughter. He demonstrates empathy and remorse regarding the total negative effects on the child and family.

4. The mother demonstrates a greater sense of autonomy and independence.

5. The mother demonstrates readiness and availability to protect her daughter and her needs and is unlikely to be influenced by her husband at the expense of her daughter.

6. The daughter's behavior continues to stabilize.

7. The father-daughter relationship continues to show improvement in conjoint sessions.

8. Mother, father, and daughter are able to discuss the abuse in their own therapy, with less negative impact on ego and functioning.

9. The husband and wife begin work on relationship issues, past and present, and discuss the effect of the abuse on their marriage in marital therapy sessions.

10. The daughter indicates approval of and readiness for advancement beyond out-of-home family visits.

11. The mother indicates similar approval and readiness.

12. The father indicates similar approval and readiness.

13. The family is engaged in family therapy sessions in which beginning in-home visits has been fully discussed. The family should be able to present a plan for ensuring that the father will not be alone with the daughter or siblings who may be uncomfortable and should be able to negotiate a contract covering face-to-face contact between father and daughter (only at the daughter's initiation), discipline (the mother is to handle discipline problems), and conflict resolution.

Step 4. This step consists of time-limited weekly visits in the home supervised by the mother (no overnights). Most families want to proceed quickly at this stage, but advancement should be in small, careful increments. The family has been apart for one to two years, and being together in the family home is generally more stressful than anticipated. Time limits provide safety and control and protect against illusory effects, such as the inevitable honeymoon period of family members being on their best behavior.

Step 5. After another period of successful home visits, there is an increase in the frequency of the home visits—generally three per week, but still no overnights. As a result of step 5, the family should demonstrate an ability in individual and family therapy to address issues that arise as a result of more frequent visitation. This ability is an indicator of their level of functioning, since problems can be expected to arise with increased visitation. Likely issues include amplification of the mother's anger and mistrust, children's increased acting out, and problems in cooperative parenting. At this stage, parents should increasingly focus on their own family-of-origin and childhood issues, including their own possible sexual victimization.

Step 6. When step 5 has been successfully completed, the family moves on to one overnight visit per week. The following are criteria for those visits:

1. The victim provides positive and realistic responses to a detailed discussion of risk situations in the home.

2. The mother and father have realistic discussions in marital therapy of the risk situations in the home.

3. The parents can discuss their own sexual expectations.

4. The family discusses fears previously discussed in individual sessions.

5. The family continues to progress in all areas of treatment.

6. The family has been successful at previous stages of reunification. Any stage can precipitate a crisis, but it is most likely in this stage, since the mother, who must sleep sometime, is faced with total loss of control. Both parents, therefore, have to confront safety issues at a deeper level.

Step 7. Still moving step by step in carefully planned stages, the family moves to an increase in the number of overnight visits. The indicators that the family is ready for more than one overnight visit per week are:

1. The family has been successful at the previous stage.

2. The family as a unit and individually continues to progress in all areas of therapy.

3. Family functioning continues to be monitored through regular family and individual sessions.

4. The mother and father continue to participate in marital therapy.

Step 8. This step is full-time reunification for a trial period, with progress evaluated after one month. All family members, therapists, and officials should be involved in this reevaluation, and it should include individual session feedback as well as group session discussion.

Even after reunification, the work is not over; the post-reunification stage is the most critical. For this stage, a continuing plan of therapy should be developed, as the needs of the family dictate. Continuing family therapy is generally indicated. There are good legal and therapeutic reasons for the father to continue individual therapy, and parents are generally eager to continue marital therapy.

Successful reunification is not just a mechanical progression through steps but a process for eliciting and coping with issues as they arise. It is the norm for problems to arise as the family progresses through reunification, and the family's willingness to admit and address these problems healthily is vital to the process. Although this step-by-step structure does not necessarily mirror a family's actual psychological process or guarantee a lack of crises, fallbacks, or failures, according to the Chesapeake Institute, it is the best structure for ongoing assessment and healing of all family members involved.

GIARETTO INSTITUTE. The Giaretto Institute's Child Sexual Abuse Treatment Program is organized for fully integrated treatment, the heart of which is the self-help model. It is based on three primary tenets: the child-victim is best served by a return to a healthy family of origin; this return requires that the abusive family be entirely, indubitably healed; and accomplishing this level of family healing requires the integration and cooperation of all therapeutic, legal, and societal organizations involved in a case of incest.

Many nontherapeutic groups tend to respond emotionally to the subject of reunification. They do not believe in the treatability of offenders and the reparability of the family and feel that those who do are insensitive to child and community protection. Such groups focus almost entirely on punishment of offenders and spouses who failed to prevent the abuse. Victims are often actively discouraged from participating in treatment.

As a result, families coming into treatment have often experienced a variety of discouraging and negative official treatment that has increased their resistance, denial, and even hostility to treatment providers and programs. The Giaretto Institute's program is designed not only to cope with these conditions but also to actively address the doubts and biases of other professionals, convincing them to join cooperatively with treatment providers and families in the healthy resolution of incest cases.

The therapeutic regimen of a typical family of four in which the offender is the father and the victim is the daughter includes the following:

1. Mother and daughter are immediately provided individual therapy.

2. Dyadic therapy for child and mother is begun as soon as the child feels comfortable (based in part on the mother's preparedness to believe and support her).

3. The perpetrator is provided therapy when he has removed himself from the home and acknowledges responsibility for the abuse.

4. Siblings are given individual therapy to overcome "daddy's favorite" and other typical processes and feelings.

5. Conjoint family therapy, including the perpetrator, is started when it is deemed appropriate.

6. Marital therapy is begun if the wife wants to salvage her marriage and if the therapist be-

lieves that the two have progressed enough in individual treatment.

7. Dyadic victim-offender therapy is started in later stages of the program, provided the victim is ready and the father is able.

8. Conjoint family therapy, including all family members, becomes the principal treatment modality and continues through completion of the therapeutic program.

The therapist initially faces a difficult dilemma. In the best of circumstances, the first reaction of families is generally denial (often expressed in efforts to get the victim to recant, citing the dire consequences to family) and nonempathic urges. Some legal offices may even discourage victims from participating in treatment. Therapists are faced with the fact that they are likely to be putting the family and family members in real danger by encouraging the end of denial, yet denial eliminates any chance for healing and ensures further danger. The confrontation of denial offers some hope should the family do the healthy thing.

Parents United (PU) support groups help the therapist deal with a family in a state of crisis that has been increased by the possible negative contributions of other social agencies. Following the guidelines provided by PU training, the therapist presents the idea to a family in the first session and, if the members are amenable, gets them in touch with a family that has made significant progress toward reunification. The first contact is made by phone. Over time, the therapist builds up enough paired new-old families to constitute parents groups and victims groups. This peer support system greatly eases and accelerates the families' preparation for treatment. It also contributes to their progress through treatment, by increasing their confidence in treatment and themselves and by discouraging denial.

RESTORING THE FAMILY TO HEALTH

The authors hope that two purposes, both equally important, have been served by this chapter. Formally, the chapter is a source of information and guidelines on the application of family treatment methods to adult sexual offender treatment. But because the subject is still so provocative, the authors also attempted to demonstrate that the inclusion of a family component or at least a family perspective in adult sexual offender treatment offers enormous potential benefits to all those affected.

Traditional social attitudes toward child sexual abuse and abusers, as well as traditional treatment methods, have left many families with both scars and anger. The fact that a majority of sexual abusers are male and a majority of victims are female has prompted many of those concerned with sexual abuse, professionals as well as laypersons, to maintain a guilty-until-proven-innocent view of any perspective that is not punishment oriented. The recent recognition that some sexual abusers are female and that some sexual abuse victims are male either boggles the mind or offends the sensibilities to such an extent that the information is discounted or minimized. This response is not entirely unreasonable, given our social and professional history, even when the reactions are completely emotional rather than objective.

However, the health of all concerned—sexual abuse offenders, sexual abuse victims, their families, and society as a whole—depends on an objective response to sexual abuse, rather than a reactive one. The authors and all those cited here are steadfastly committed to the safety, protection, and healing of victims and communities and to the belief that treatment of sexual offenders is a vital contributing factor thereto.

The untreated sexual abuser is, by definition, responsible for harming others; without intervention, he or she is a continuing threat to the community at large. Incarceration may protect the community for a limited time, but incarceration ends, and nothing has changed. Treatment for the sexual abuser is critical if there is to be any change in cognitions or behavior, but treatment that does not involve those significantly impacted by the abuse offers no opportunity for healing or reunification. Therefore, we believe that the optimal treatment of adult sexual offenders considers not only the abuser but also his or her entire social support system, whenever this is possible or feasible. Everyone in the family of an adult sex offender, whether intrafamilial or extrafamilial, deserves the opportunity to achieve the healing that can result from involvement in the therapeutic process.

This opportunity for healing is precisely the possibility offered by the incorporation of family treatment methods within the overall treatment design for adult sexual abusers. Whatever the offense, sexual abuse is expressed, develops, and occurs within social environments. The abusers, their victims, and their families are likely to be connected not only by the act of the offense but also by the social dynamics preceding, following, and surrounding the offense. Therefore, the victims, the abusers, and all others harmed by the abuse are generally best treated in terms of the social context in which the abuse occurred. The only hard-and-fast requirement is that the specific circumstances of the people affected by the abusive behavior be addressed and that the therapist remain open to an inclusive approach. Everyone deserves to be offered the help that involvement in a family-oriented treatment program can provide.

REFERENCES

Allen, C., & Lee, C. (1992). Family of origin structure and intra/extrafamilial childhood sexual victimization of male and female offenders. *Journal of Child Sexual Abuse, 1*(3), 31–45.

Appelstein, C. (1993). Peer helping peer: Duo therapy with children in residential care. *Residential Treatment for Children and Youth, 10*(4), 33–53.

Ballard, D., Blair, G., Devereaux, S., Horton, A., & Johnson, B. (1990). A comparative profile of the incest perpetrator: Background characteristics, abuse history

and use of social skills. In A. Horton, B. Johnson, L. Roundy, & D. Williams (Eds.), *The incest perpetrator* (pp. 43–64). Newbury Park, CA: Sage.

Bear, E., & Dimock, P. (1988). *Adults molested as children: A survivor's manual for women and men.* Orwell, VT: Safer Society Press.

Bendicsen, H., & Carlton, S. (1990). Clinical team building: A neglected ingredient in the therapeutic milieu. *Residential Treatment for Children and Youth, 8*(1), 5–21.

Berliner, L., Schram, D., Miller, L., & Milloy, C. (1995). A sentencing alternative for sex offenders: A study of decision making and recidivism. *Journal of Interpersonal Violence, 10*(4), 487–502.

Blanchard, G. (1995). *The difficult connection: The therapeutic relationship in sex offender treatment.* Brandon, VT: Safer Society Press.

Bloom, R. (1994). Institutional child sexual abuse: Prevention and risk management. *Residential Treatment of Children and Youth, 12*(2), 3–17.

Bowden, K. (1994). "No control of penis or brain"? Key questions in the assessment of sex offenders with a learning difficulty. *Journal of Sexual Aggression, 1*(1), 57–63.

Burgess, A., Groth, N., Holmstrom, L., & Sgroi, S. (Eds.). (1978). *Sexual assault of children and adolescents.* Lexington, MA: Lexington Books.

Caliso, J., & Milner, J. (1994). Childhood physical abuse, childhood social support, and adult child abuse potential. *Journal of Interpersonal Violence, 9*(1), 27–44.

Cameron, C. (1994). Women survivors confronting their abusers: Issues, decisions, and outcomes. *Journal of Child Sexual Abuse, 3*(1), 7–35.

Carlo, P. (1991). Why a parental involvement program leads to a family reunification: A dialogue with child-care workers. *Residential Treatment for Children and Youth, 9*(2), 37–48.

Childress, B. (1992). Thinking about parents and rescuing children. *Residential Treatment of Children and Youth, 9*(4), 29–42.

Daly, D., & Peter, V. (1988). Promoting safe environments in residential care. In W. Small & F. Alwon (Eds.), *Challenging the limits of care* (pp. 55–64). Needham, MA: Trieschman Center.

Durkin, R., Becker, J., & Feuerstein, R. (1995). Can environments modify and enhance the development of personality and behavior? Toward an understanding of the influence of the modifying environment in group care settings. *Residential Treatment for Children and Youth, 12*(14), 1–12.

Edwards, J., & Alexander, P. (1992). The contribution of family background to the long-term adjustment of women sexually abused as children. *Journal of Interpersonal Violence, 7*(3), 306–320.

Edwards, S., & Lohman, J. (1994). The impact of "moral panic" on professional behavior in cases of child sexual abuse: An international perspective. *Journal of Child Sexual Abuse, 3*(1), 103–126.

Elias, H. (1994). The impact of "moral panic" on professional behavior in cases of child sexual abuse: Review, commentary and legal perspective. *Journal of Child Sexual Abuse, 3*(1), 137–139.

Elliot, M. (Ed.). (1993). *Female sexual abuse of children.* New York: Guilford Press.

Erooga, M. (1994). Where the professional meets the personal. In T. Morrison, M. Erooga, & R. Beckett (Eds.), *Sexual offending against children: Assessment and treatment of male abusers* (pp. 203–220). New York: Routledge.

Flomenhaft, K., & Sullivan, C. (1992). What happens to children after the acute-care hospital transfers them to state facilities. *Residential Treatment for Children and Youth, 10*(2), 13–22.

Foa, E., Rothbaum, B., & Steketee, G. (1993) Treatment of rape victims. *Journal of Interpersonal Violence, 8*(2), 256–276.

Garner, H. (1988). *Helping others through teamwork: A handbook for professionals.* New York: Child Welfare League of America.

Giaretto, H., & Einfield-Giaretto, A. (1990). Integrated treatment: The self-help factor. In A. Horton, B. Johnson, L. Roundy, & D. Williams (Eds.), *The incest perpetrator* (pp. 219–226). Newbury Park, CA: Sage.

Greene, J., & Holden, M. (1990). A strategic-systemic family therapy model: Rethinking residential treatment. *Residential Treatment for Children and Youth, 7*(3), 51–55.

Groth, N., Burgess, A., & Holmstrom, L. (1978). Crisis issues for an adolescent-aged offender and his victim. In A. Burgess, N. Groth, L. Holmstrom, & S. Sgroi (Eds.), *Sexual assault of children and adolescents* (pp. 43–58). Lexington, MA: Lexington Books.

Hanson, R., Lipovsky, J., & Saunders, B. (1994). Characteristics of fathers in incest families. *Journal of Interpersonal Violence, 9*(2), 155–169.

Heras, P. (1992). Cultural considerations in the assessment and treatment of child sexual abuse. *Journal of Child Sexual Abuse, 1*(3), 119–124.

Hess, A. (1990). Residential treatment: Beyond time and space. *Residential Treatment for Children and Youth, 7*(4), 41–56.

Horton, A., Johnson, B., Roundy, L., & Williams, D. (Eds.). (1990). *The incest perpetrator.* Newbury Park, CA: Sage.

Kaplan, L. (1986). *Working with multiproblem families.* Lexington, MA: Lexington Books.

Kapp, S., Schwartz, I., & Epstein, I. (1994). Adult imprisonment of males released from residential childcare: A longitudinal study. *Residential Treatment for Children and Youth, 12*(2), 19–36.

Kobayashi, J., Sales, B., Becker, J., Figueredo, A., & Kaplan, M. (1995). Perceived parental deviance, parent-child bonding, child abuse, and child sexual aggression. *Sex Abuse: A Journal of Research and Treatment, 7*(1), 25–44.

Krueger, M., & Drees, M. (1995). Generic teamwork: An alternative approach to residential treatment. *Residential Treatment for Children and Youth, 12*(3), 57–69.

Lamb, S., & Edgar-Smith, S. (1994). Aspects of disclosure. *Journal of Interpersonal Violence, 9*(3), 307–326.

Laws, D. (1994). How dangerous are rapists to children? *Journal of Sexual Aggression, 1*(1), 1–4.

Long, P., & Jackson, J. (1994). Childhood sexual abuse: An examination of family functioning. *Journal of Interpersonal Violence, 9*(2), 270–277.

Maddock, J., & Larson, N. (1995). *Incestuous families: An ecological approach to understanding and treatment.* New York: W.W. Norton.

Maletzky, B. (1991). *Treating the sexual offender.* Newbury Park, CA: Sage.

Mayer, A. (1983). *Incest: A treatment manual for therapy with victims, spouses and offenders.* Holmes Beach, FL: Learning Publications.

Mayer, A. (1988). *Sex offenders: Approaches to understanding and management.* Holmes Beach, FL: Learning Publications.

Meinig, M., & Bonner, B. (1990). Returning the treated sex offender to the family. *Violence Update, 1*(2), 3–11.

Menses, G., & Durrant, M. (1990). Contextual residential care: The application of the principles of cybernetic therapy to the residential treatment of irresponsible adolescents and their families. *Residential Treatment for Children and Youth, 7*(3), 11–32.

Minuchin, S. (1974). *Families and family therapy.* Cambridge, MA: Harvard University Press.

Mirkin, M., & Kolman, S. (Eds.). (1985). *Handbook of adolescents and family therapy.* New York: Gardner Press.

Morgan, S., Fulliton, W., & Nabors, L. (1993). Adolescents' perceptions of acceptability of inpatient treatments: Does exposure to the treatment make a difference? *Residential Treatment for Children and Youth, 10*(4), 85–99.

Morrison, T. (1994). Learning together to manage sexual abuse: Rhetoric or reality? *Journal of Sexual Aggression, 1*(1), 29–44.

Morrison, T., Erooga, M., & Beckett, R. (Eds.). (1994). *Sexual offending against children: Assessment and treatment of male abusers.* New York: Routledge.

Muram, D., Miller, K., & Cutler, A. (1992). Sexual assault and the elderly victim. *Journal of Interpersonal Violence, 7*(1), 70–76.

Mussack, S. (1994, September). The impact of family involvement on sexual offender treatment. Paper presented at the Association for the Treatment of Sexual Abusers National Treatment and Research Conference. San Francisco, CA.

Nelson, T., & Trepper, T. (Eds.). (1993). *101 interventions in family therapy.* New York: Haworth.

Petrik, N., Olson, R., & Subotnik, L. (1994). Powerless and the need to control: The male abuser's dilemma. *Journal of Interpersonal Violence, 9*(2), 278–285.

Pitsch, H. (1992). Children in residential care and their families: A systems perspective. *Residential Treatment for Children and Youth, 10*(1), 91–103.

Powers, D. (1990). Some medical implications of sexuality in residential centers. *Residential Treatment for Children and Youth, 8*(2), 83–96.

Renken, R. (1989). *Intervention strategies for sexual abuse.* Alexandria, VA: American Association for Counseling and Development.

Roesler, T., & Wind, T. (1994). Telling the secret. *Journal of Interpersonal Violence, 9*(3), 327–338.

Rose, M. (1992). The design of atmosphere: Ego nurture and psychic change in residential treatment. *Residential Treatment for Children and Youth, 10*(1), 5–23.

Ryan, G. (1991). Theories of etiology. In G. Ryan & S. Lane (Eds.), *Juvenile sexual offending: Causes, consequences and correction* (pp. 41–55). Lexington, MA: Lexington Books.

Ryan, G., & Lane, S. (1991). *Juvenile sexual offending: Causes, consequences and correction.* Lexington, MA, Lexington Books.

Schwartz, T., & Schultz, B. (1991). Teamwork as a function of treatment. *Residential Treatment for Children and Youth, 9*(2), 49–53.

Sgroi, S. (1978). Introduction: A national needs assessment for protecting child victims of sexual assault. In A. Burgess, N. Groth, L. Holmstrom, & S. Sgroi (Eds.), *Sexual assault of children and adolescents* (pp. xv–xxii). Lexington, MA: Lexington Books.

Small, R., Alwon, F., & Maier, H. (1988). *Challenging the limits of care.* Needham, MA: Trieschman Center.

Smith, G. (1994). Parent, partner, protector: Conflicting role demands for mothers of sexually abused children. In T. Morrison, M. Erooga, & R. Beckett (Eds.), *Sexual offending against children: Assessment and treatment of male abusers* (pp. 178–202). New York: Routledge.

Thomas, J. (1991). The adolescent sex offender's family in treatment. In G. Ryan & S. Lane (Eds.), *Juvenile sexual offending: Causes, consequences and correction* (pp. 333–376). Lexington, MA: Lexington Books.

Thomas, J., & Viar, W. (1994, September). *The familial roots of sexual aggression.* Keynote presentation for the 1994 National Organization for the Treatment of Abusers Conference, Durham, England.

Thomas, J., & Viar, W. (1995). *Modeling in therapeutic environments. Residential treatment staff manual and training packet chapter.* Memphis, TN: J. Thomas Consulting Services.

Thrasher, S. (1994). Psychodynamic therapy and culture in the treatment of incest of a West Indian immigrant. *Journal of Child Sexual Abuse, 3*(1), 37–52.

Trepper, T., & Barrett, M. (1988). *Treating incest: A multiple systems perspective.* Binghamton, NY: Haworth.

Ward, T., Hudson, S., & Marshall, W. (1995). Cognitive distortions and affective deficits in sex offenders: A cognitive deconstructionist interpretation. *Sexual Abuse: A Journal of Research and Treatment, 7*(1), 67–84.

Wherry, J., Jolly, J., Aruffo, J., Gillette, G., Vaught, L., & Metheny, R. (1994). Family trauma and dysfunction in sexually abused female adolescent psychiatric and control groups. *Journal of Child Sexual Abuse, 3*(1), 53–65.

White, W. (1986). *Incest in the organizational family.* Bloomington, IL: Lighthouse Training Institute.

Ziegler, R. (1990). Staff reactions in treating adolescents with borderline disturbances in a residential setting. *Residential Treatment for Children and Youth, 8*(1), 23–39.

11 Assessment and Treatment of Intellectually Disabled Sexual Abusers

Emily M. Coleman
James Haaven

To work with intellectually disabled sex offenders is to enter a different culture that embodies both the experience of being intellectually disabled and the particular context of sex offender therapy. To become acquainted with this culture, clinicians unfamiliar with those who are intellectually disabled must first consider and appreciate what that experience is like. For example, decisions that nondisabled persons make automatically can be puzzling to intellectually disabled persons. It is important to understand that intellectually disabled persons in some ways think differently from, not simply more slowly than, nondisabled persons. An intellectually disabled person is more likely to use categorical thinking rather than logical, inductive, or deductive thinking; therefore, labeling is a preferred teaching method. Whereas the nondisabled population is intent on making time on the superhighway of learning, the intellectually disabled population takes the back roads—a longer but often more scenic trip, and one that may take more signage along the way. The destination can be reached by either route. Finally, intellectually disabled persons have to master different adaptive skills, such as effectively faking understanding, to manage daily tasks in a world in which they often don't fit.

For clinicians inexperienced in sex offender treatment, understanding of the culture is also predicated on an appreciation of the many ways in which sex offender treatment is distinct from other therapies. The primary goal of relapse prevention is preset, not determined by the client. The actual identity of the client being served—the offender, the community, or the legal system—continues to be debated. Unlike with most other therapies, there may be serious consequences to the client, such as incarceration or the loss of family or job, if the client does not comply with treatment program requirements. Finally, the therapist plays more of a teacher role, with some police person thrown into the mix, than the usual therapist role embodying unconditional and nonjudgmental concern.

To work with intellectually disabled sex offenders, it is necessary to first appreciate the uniqueness of the sex offender therapist's role and the experience of the person who is intellectually disabled. An understanding of this particular culture facilitates effective intervention.

Much attention has been given to the appropriateness of the words used to describe persons who are intellectually disabled and to persons who sexually offend. Terms such as "mentally deficient" or "retarded" have been largely discarded, as has the term "sex deviant." The tendency to refer to a group of people as "whatever" rather than as persons who do "whatever" is frowned upon. This controversy is understandable in such emotionally charged areas. Language is especially powerful when the results provide a label with significant and limiting consequences for the individual. The term "intellectually disabled sex offender" used throughout this chapter is not meant offensively and is not intended to imply that the person is defined solely by those aspects. The therapeutic approach inherent in the program described in this chapter requires seeing the person in a holistic and respectful manner.

The focus of this chapter is on adult male sex offenders who are in the mild to borderline ranges of mental retardation. Therefore, the pronoun "he" is used throughout the chapter, although this usage is not meant to ignore the existence of female offenders. Much of the material is also applicable to adolescent intellectually disabled offenders, but it is beyond the scope of this chapter to address the differences and adaptations needed for that population. Finally, persons with more severe cognitive deficits may require a greater emphasis on environmental contingencies and operant-based techniques such as response-cost, time-out, and differential reinforcement of other behaviors (DRO) procedures. In contrast, the approach described in this chapter for persons with mild to borderline mental retardation can be regarded as being under the umbrella of self-control and relapse prevention models. It should be noted, however, that it is a mistake to overemphasize the role of IQ as an indicator of appropriate treatment strategies, since IQ alone does not adequately describe a person's abilities.

There are more similarities than differences between sex offenders who are intellectually disabled and those of average intelligence and above. Members of both populations typically hold cognitive distortions justifying sexual abuse, experience low self-esteem, have deficits in interpersonal skills (including difficulties in anger and stress management, a lack of empathy and perceptive skills, poor impulse control, and inadequate social and assertiveness skills), have incorrect or inadequate knowledge of sexuality, hold rigid attitudes regarding gender roles, and demonstrate deviant sexual arousal. However, differences do exist that need to be acknowledged and taken into consideration in designing effective assessment and treatment strategies.

For example, intellectually disabled sex offenders may use denial as a more generalized coping system to defend against anything threatening. An intellectually disabled sex offender may deny his cognitive deficits or any other difficulty in a wish to belong. To address denial of sexual offending in an intellectually disabled sex offender, then, is potentially to focus on an entire adaptive style rather than to change a more discrete defense as in a nondisabled offender. Another significant difference involves the level of low self-esteem. Although most sex offenders experience low self-esteem, an intellectually disabled sex offender may feel particularly inept because he has fewer areas of competency and because he has so often been the victim of ridicule. He may become very sensitive to critical remarks.

In working with intellectually disabled sex offenders, it is necessary to have a clear understanding of what constitutes normal, inappropriate, offending, and problematic sexual behaviors. More often than with the nondisabled population, an intellectually disabled person may be referred for sex offender treatment when he does not actually have a sex offending problem. This misreferral is related in part to societal attitudes. The media give the impression that only young, attractive, wealthy, fully able persons are sexually active. Unfortunately, because society is so uncomfortable with the sexuality of disabled persons, behavior that is acceptable among the nondisabled is deemed unacceptable among the disabled. For example, in some facilities, masturbation in private is a rule violation. Perhaps even more frequently, privacy is not provided, so there is no appropriate setting in which to engage in what is often the only sexual outlet available to an intellectually disabled person. Moreover, an intellectually disabled person may receive the same negative consequences for adult consenting sexual behavior as for sexually offending behavior. This lack of discernment by society, caretakers, and family teaches an intellectually disabled person to be nondiscriminative as well. Referrals must be screened to ensure that the problem resides with the intellectually disabled person rather than with the referral program structure or staff and administrative attitudes.

Care must also be taken to screen out persons evidencing inappropriate sexual behavior rather than sexually offending behavior. Inappropriate sexual behavior may appear to be the same as offending behavior but primarily reflects a history of environmental restrictions, social skills deficits, lack of limit setting, isolation, segregation, and/or lack of privacy rather than the desire to engage in sexually offending behavior. For example, an intellectually disabled person may leave his fly unzipped because he has not been reminded to finish dressing or because he has hopes of shocking a female staff member. Similarly, an intellectually disabled person may rush to hug a child upon meeting her because of a lack of limit setting in his upbringing or because he is physically attracted to the young girl. Although in both cases the person needs to be stopped and redirected in the immediate situation, the subsequent intervention is different. The person involved in the former situations may need a time-limited course of social skills training, whereas the person showing the latter motivations is more likely to require intensive sex offender treatment, including self-control techniques, empathy training, cognitive restructuring, and so on, in addition to social skills training.

Finally, another category involves problematic sexual behavior that is harmful to the person himself but not directly to others. This includes self-injurious autoerotic behavior such as asphyxiation and inserting objects in the penis, navel, or anus to achieve sexual gratification. Unfortunately, this behavior often goes unnoticed until severe physical damage occurs. Asphyxiation can unintentionally result in death. Other problematic behaviors may involve coprophilia, urolagnia, excessive masturbation, or fetish activity that interferes with the person's life to such an extent that he cannot work or engage in any other worthwhile activity. These behaviors may be the result of sexual or physical victimization, boredom, a perceived or actual lack of alternative sexual outlets, a lack of knowledge of sexuality, and/or difficulty achieving erection or ejaculation. A sex offender program is not appropriate for a person with these characteristics.

As noted previously, the focus of this chapter is on intellectually disabled men who engage in sex offending behavior, not inappropriate or self-harmful sexual behavior. The remainder of the chapter provides how-to information on the assessment and treatment of intellectually disabled sex offenders.

ASSESSMENT

Effective intervention begins with a sex offender–specific evaluation designed for the intellectually disabled person (Murphy, Coleman, & Haynes, 1983). The purpose of the assessment is to determine the nature and scope of the sexual problems and to consider risk level, therapy needs, and placement concerns in offering treatment recommendations. Evaluations may be conducted in an outpatient or residential setting and may occur in a day or over several weeks or months. Particular components may also vary from program to program, but the following is an outline of suggested evaluation practices.

THIRD-PARTY INFORMATION

Assessment begins before actually meeting the client. As with nondisabled offenders, obtaining and reviewing records is an essential first step

(Caparulo, 1991). However, unlike with most nondisabled clients, documentation of the sexual offenses may be nonexistent, scanty, or vague. If referred directly from the caretaking agency or family, the intellectually disabled sex offender may not be court mandated for treatment or not involved with the legal system in any way. The legal system is sometimes reluctant to become involved with intellectually disabled sex offenders, feeling that they are best served within the province of the social services, or mental health system. This presents many challenges to the treatment provider, but the relevant consequence here is that police reports, preinvestigation reports, and victim reports are often nonexistent or not available. Descriptions of inappropriate or deviant sexual behavior in the files of agencies or institutions are frequently absent, inconsistent, vague, and/or euphemistic. The clinician consequently often needs to take a more active role in obtaining information about the sex offending behavior by interviewing family members or staff.

Information on other aspects of the client's life, including family and placement history, annual reviews, psychiatric reports, and daily living skills assessments, may be abundant and far exceed the information available on nondisabled clients in these areas. This background information is a clear advantage in working with an intellectually disabled sex offender, as an understanding of the entire life history and current functioning of the client in all areas is helpful.

Before seeing the client, it is also important to assess the reasons for referral and to understand the expectations of the referral source and of the client. For example, a policy of not evaluating persons who have been charged with an offense but not yet convicted should be considered, because sex offender evaluations may be used inappropriately to attempt to prove guilt or innocence of a particular crime. In addition, a person charged but not yet convicted of a sexual offense is not in a position to be open and honest with the evaluator, knowing that the information will be forwarded to the court. The purpose of a sex offender evaluation is to determine treatment needs and is most valuable when conducted periodically over time to also evaluate treatment effectiveness. One should be wary of the results of a one-time evaluation that affects a major decision, such as release from prison. An intellectually disabled sex offender may under- or overestimate the impact of a sex offender evaluation on placement or treatment decisions. The clinician must take into account the extent to which the client is invested in a particular outcome and therefore may be influenced to adjust his self-report accordingly.

INFORMED CONSENT

Because intellectually disabled sex offenders may have more difficulty understanding the informed consent procedure, it is especially important to provide a simple but clear and thorough explanation of the evaluation process. This explanation should include a description of the evaluation procedure, its purpose, the benefits and risks, and the confidentiality limits. The client should be taken on a tour of the laboratory and shown the plethysmograph. The explanation of the confidentiality limits can be particularly complicated. Confidentiality limits in different programs vary from the complete privacy offered by a federal certificate of immunity to a total waiver of confidentiality. Many sex offender programs now require the client to sign a total waiver of confidentiality, whereas relatively few use a federal certificate of immunity. Sex offender programs may also offer partial confidentiality, in which releases to probation or parole officers, other therapists, or family members are required, and there may be certain exceptions to confidentiality, such as if the client identifies a specific future victim. Particularly crucial, but unfortunately also particularly confusing, are policies concerning state child abuse reporting laws: The clinician is required to report previously unreported cases of child abuse, but state agencies usually will not take information if the victim is unidentified. Reporting specific, previously undisclosed instances of child abuse may involve loss of freedom; it is paramount that the client understand this potential consequence. Understanding is not necessarily related to IQ. Clients who are "street savvy" may grasp the situation immediately; others who have been repeatedly threatened but never actually involved with the legal system may not believe that they will suffer any negative effects.

To aid in the client's understanding, role-plays in which various scenarios are acted out may be helpful. Do not simply ask if the client understands the information and accept a yes or no response. It may be necessary to spend several sessions explaining the evaluation process in order for the client to understand and then proceed with the assessment. In some cases, the client may need to be reminded of the confidentiality limits at the beginning of each session. If the client has a court-appointed guardian, the same care should be expended in explaining information to the client and the guardian. The guardian ad litem's signature on the evaluation consent form should be obtained as well.

GENERAL HISTORY AND MENTAL STATUS EXAMINATION

As noted previously, information about the nonsexual aspects of the client's life is often available through the referral source and agencies or departments that have been involved with the client. This is particularly helpful, as it may be difficult for the client to give concise, accurate information about his family background and general history because of his cognitive deficits. Through a combination of client self-report and referral information, the evaluator gathers information regarding the client's history of suicidal ideation and behavior, substance abuse and other addictions, education, employment, criminal behavior, psychiatric hospitalizations, placement, outpatient treatment, medication and medical history, and victimization, including physical, emotional, and sexual abuse or neglect.

The family genogram and history are obtained. His current life situation, including living arrangements, school or employment, daily activities, use of leisure time, physical health, and support network, is also assessed. The clinician also conducts a mental status examination in which the client's appearance, mood and affect, orientation, memory, cognitive functioning, judgment and insight, and thought process, content, and quality are assessed. All this information is important in itself and also for its potential impact on the sex offending problem.

SEXUAL HISTORY

The practitioner's skill in taking a sex history is perhaps most significant in the evaluation process. Particular questionnaires may vary. The plethysmograph may or may not be used, but the assessment necessarily involves being able to communicate clearly and accurately with the client about sex. This is true regardless of the practitioner's therapeutic orientation or the client's presenting sexual problem.

Obtaining an accurate sexual history from an intellectually disabled sex offender can be both more crucial and more difficult than obtaining one from a nondisabled sex offender. The accuracy of the sex history may be more crucial because of the increased likelihood of incomplete third-party information, as noted previously. In addition, review boards or human rights advocates may be less likely to allow use of the plethysmograph, further limiting relevant, objective data. In some cases, unfortunately, the sex history information may be the sole data available.

At the same time, an intellectually disabled sex offender may experience more difficulty being open about sexuality, and in particular the offending history, than a nondisabled offender. Initially, most clients, disabled and nondisabled, are in the early stages of denial and feel anxious, embarrassed, or angry in the interview session. These feelings obviously inhibit a client's forthrightness. An intellectually disabled sex offender experiences this inhibition as well as a general difficulty with the unfamiliar. For him, an appointment with an unknown person in an unfamiliar place can cause anxiety by itself. An intellectually disabled sex offender may be more likely to misinterpret the purpose of the evaluation and may also have created his own vocabulary for sexual terms. An intellectually disabled sex offender may have difficulty focusing and paying sustained attention, even when the subject is nonthreatening. Persons who are intellectually disabled have honed and frequently depend on their ability to discern and give what is expected. All these factors can interfere with the accuracy of information obtained in the sex history. With knowledge, training, and practice, however, the practitioner can learn to anticipate, identify, and cope with these factors.

To maximize the likelihood of obtaining correct information, attention to the setting, both physical and emotional, is important. The room in which the interview takes place should be private. A client will not be open if the interview takes place with the office door open or in the day room. Unplanned interruptions should be avoided. If the plethysmograph is going to be used, the laboratory should be considered as a potential interview site in order to adapt the client gradually to the plethysmograph. The clinician also wants to provide an emotionally safe and respectful place for the client. It is important to put the client at ease while pursuing the needed information. The exception to the rule is clients who are actively hostile, disrespectful, or sexualizing. This behavior is not to be tolerated. If, after a warning, the client continues inappropriate behavior, the interview should be terminated. This is an opportunity to set limits and teach appropriate behavior. To help reduce the client's anxiety, the clinician can acknowledge the difficulty in disclosing sexual offending and note the client's courage in choosing to do so. For a client who is making an effort to reveal information, the interview should be paced so that less threatening questions are interspersed with difficult questions when the client needs and deserves a break. For a client with a short attention span, contract a time period for work followed by a break of some kind. During the evaluation interviews, a therapy animal may be helpful in lessening the client's anxiety, increasing his self-esteem, developing a rapport with the therapist, and providing a relaxing diversion during the break.

Throughout the interview, the clinician should be calm, professional, respectful, and concerned. Embarrassment, shock, or laughter "at" the client is likely to stop any further disclosure. Discover and use the client's sexual vocabulary in order to maximize accuracy. The clinician may choose to add a more acceptable term to the client's term, but the primary goal here is to obtain accurate information. Drawings of body parts and sexual activities may be helpful in confirming correctness. Ask one question at a time without hesitancy, apology, or euphemisms while looking the client in the eye. Avoid rapid-fire questioning or relying on a fatigue factor. Although sometimes helpful with nondisabled offenders, these techniques unnecessarily confuse an intellectually disabled sex offender without producing valid data. Assume that the client has engaged in every sexual activity so that questions begin with "when" or "how often," not "did you ever." Ask the client about each and every sexual behavior.

One particular issue in working with intellectually disabled sex offenders is distinguishing between denial and actual cognitive deficit. When an intellectually disabled sex offender says "I don't know" or "I don't remember," he may be speaking the truth. Inconsistency in self-report of frequencies, time periods, ages, and so forth may be due to cognitive or memory deficits rather than denial. Compare the intellectually disabled sex offender's ability to recall other nonsexual life experiences as a marker. Use information already known to aid the client's memory. For example, it may be easier for a client to identify a specific period by where he was living rather than by his age.

The sex history interview is an opportunity for the clinician to teach the client to begin to take responsibility for his sex offending by revealing the needed information. The client can feel a sense of relief through unburdening himself, as well as a sense of accomplishment that he has taken a first step toward change. The clinician should frame it as such.

PSYCHOMETRIC TESTING

Unfortunately, few psychometric tests are designed specifically for intellectually disabled sex offenders. Most often, tests used to evaluate nondisabled sex offenders are adapted for use with intellectually disabled sex offenders. Depending on the nature of the test, the questionnaire can be more or less easily adapted by simplifying the language or changing the response style, for example, from a 1-to-5 rating to a yes-or-no response. Certain tests, such as the Deragatis Sexual Functioning Inventory (Deragatis & Melisaratos, 1979), although helpful with nondisabled clients, are too complicated for the majority of intellectually disabled clients. In all cases, it is desirable for the client to accurately complete as much of the questionnaire himself as possible. This participation both decreases the influence of the person assisting the client and gives the client the maximum responsibility possible. The type and extent of assistance needed vary. It may consist of reading the test to the client and the client marking the response, or simply having a person available to answer questions regarding the test. The test may be converted for use on an audiotape or computer to facilitate the client's involvement.

It is important to evaluate and monitor depression levels throughout the evaluation process, as it is often stressful for the client to be asked directly about his sex offending behavior. Additionally, when the client comes for the sex offender–specific evaluation, the disclosure of his offending has often just occurred. He may have just faced legal charges, been transferred to a more structured site, lost his job, or lost the respect of friends or family due to the disclosure of the sex offense. This increases the need to monitor depression, which can be difficult to identify in an intellectually disabled person. The Beck Depression Scale (Beck, 1967) is a commonly used, fairly simple, short questionnaire in which the client chooses the statement that best describes how he feels at the time.

Other questionnaires commonly used in sex offender evaluations that can be fairly easily adapted include the Adult Self-Expression Scale, the Sexual Interest Cardsort, and the Pedophile Cognition Scale. A questionnaire designed to evaluate interpersonal skills or assertiveness such as the Adult Self-Expression Scale (Gay, Hollandsworth, & Galassi, 1975) can be helpful as a supplement to behavioral observations during the interview. The Sexual Interest Cardsort developed by Gene Abel and Judith Becker is a 75-item questionnaire describing 15 different kinds of sexual activities, including adult consenting heterosexual and adult consenting homosexual behavior, as well as problem sexual behaviors. The client is asked to rate his sexual response to the items. The Pedophile Cognition Scale (Abel et al., 1984) is a 29-item questionnaire that lists common thinking errors or cognitive distortions justifying sexual abuse. The client notes his agreement or disagreement with the statements.

In contrast to these questionnaires, the Socio-Sexual Knowledge and Attitude Test (Edmonson, Wish, & Fiechtl, 1977) was specifically developed for persons who may not be verbally proficient or whose speech is unintelligible. Information regarding knowledge and attitudes in 14 areas, including body parts, masturbation, dating, and intimacy, is obtained. The client responds by pointing to one of four pictures presented to him by the clinician. Although not created specifically for intellectually disabled persons with sex offending problems, the information is often relevant and useful.

Psychometric testing offers the client another avenue by which to reveal sensitive information. Sometimes the client feels too embarrassed or ashamed to tell the clinician face-to-face but is able to disclose information through questionnaires. Assessment of depression, interpersonal skills, sexual interests, thinking errors, relevant attitudes, and sexual knowledge can and should be done through as many means as possible, including psychometrics, interviewing, third-party information, and plethysmograph.

PLETHYSMOGRAPH

The penile plethysmograph has been shown to be a useful assessment tool with nondisabled offenders (McGrath, 1991) and can be a valuable assessment component with intellectually disabled offenders as well. The penile plethysmograph can provide information with which to confront the offender's denial, identify arousal problems, develop a treatment plan, and perhaps most importantly, monitor treatment progress. Although research has been conducted comparing plethysmograph results of nonoffender control subjects with those of sexual offenders among the nondisabled population, no such research has occurred within the intellectually disabled population. Therefore, the data must be interpreted more conservatively. It is somewhat analogous to use of the plethysmograph with adolescent sex offenders, as there is no nonoffender adolescent comparison group.

Certain adjustments are needed in the use of the plethysmograph with intellectually disabled offenders. As noted previously, intellectually disabled sex offenders are likely to be more anxious than nondisabled offenders throughout the assessment process because of low self-esteem and difficulty facing change. Entering an unfamiliar laboratory room in which the client is expected to place the penile transducer on his penis can be particularly stressful. Conducting the initial interview sessions in the laboratory room may help the client relax in that setting. Having the client sit in the laboratory simply listening to relaxing music on the headphones may also adapt the client to the procedure. If the sex offender program is conducted on an inpatient basis, there are usually multiple opportunities to acclimate the client to the laboratory setting. In addition, other program participants who have experienced the laboratory procedure can reassure the client as to the usefulness and relative ease of the procedure. Initial laboratory data may be thrown out until the client feels more relaxed. As with nondisabled offenders, intellectually disabled sex offenders are usually anxious initially but then adapt to this assessment component. The process of adjustment may be somewhat slower, however.

Attention to the effect of medication on sexual arousal and the resulting plethysmograph data is particularly important, as intellectually disabled sex offenders may be more likely to be on medication. Changes in plethysmograph readings may be related to changes in medication regimens and need to be carefully monitored. Intellectually disabled sex offenders may have more difficulty sitting still during the assessment. Due to this problem and a shorter attention span, more laboratory sessions of a shorter duration may be indicated. Instructions for placing and removing the gauge must be simple, clear, and explicit. Without adequate instructions, expensive gauges may be accidentally damaged or destroyed by the client. Demonstrating placement of the gauge with a ceramic model of the male genitals may be helpful in this regard. The rating system for the client's self-report of degree of arousal and pleasure can be simplified as well, to match the understanding of the client.

Finally, more care must be taken in the choice of both visual and audio stimuli in the laboratory with an intellectually disabled sex offender. Currently, the use of slides depicting actual persons is controversial, as the rights of and potential harm to the persons in the slides must be weighed against the usefulness of the stimuli in ultimately preventing further sex abuse. It is hoped that the availability of computer-enhanced slides will resolve this issue. However, it should be noted that an intellectually disabled sex offender may need a clear visual cue if he has difficulty discerning the audiotape description of sexual activity. Whether the stimulus is an auditory or a visual one, however, simplicity and clarity are crucial. Slides should have a clear background, and the figure in the slide should not be complicated by unusual postures or clothing. The words used in the audiotape descriptions should be simple. After the stimulus presentation, the client can be asked to describe the stimulus in order to verify accurate understanding.

Other general caveats and limitations of the

plethysmograph are pertinent to its use with intellectually disabled sex offenders as well. For example, the plethysmograph cannot be used to prove guilt or innocence. This technology should be used in conjunction with a comprehensive sex offender evaluation. Those administering and interpreting the plethysmograph must be well trained. When these conditions are assured, the plethysmograph offers valuable information not otherwise obtainable, given offender denial and frequent lack of adequate third-party information.

COMMON DIAGNOSTIC ERRORS

It has been the authors' experience that several diagnoses tend to be unrecognized among the intellectually disabled, adversely affecting the therapeutic process. Because of societal attitudes toward the intellectually disabled, paraphilia is frequently underdiagnosed. Just as normal sexual behaviors can sometimes be seen as abnormal, truly offending behaviors among the intellectually disabled can be minimized. An intellectually disabled person can be viewed as innocent, asexual, and childlike and therefore incapable of purposefully committing a sexual offense. Also frequently underdiagnosed are character disorders, substance abuse, depression, organicity, and posttraumatic stress disorder. Obviously, such difficulties have clear and significant implications for treatment. For example, an active substance abuser is considered inappropriate for sex offender treatment. The substance abuse needs to be addressed first, and a period of sobriety must occur before the client enters sex offender–specific treatment. The possibility of depression should always be explored. It may be a precursor to sex offending but can be difficult to identify. Organic brain damage or dysfunction can cause hypersexuality or hyposexuality that is related to the sex offending problem.

In contrast to these problems, schizophrenia appears to be overdiagnosed. Because an intellectually disabled person may be more prone to illusions and sensory misperceptions, he may be inaccurately judged as hallucinating.

FEEDBACK

An often neglected part of the evaluation process is a final session in which the evaluation results and treatment recommendations are discussed with the client. The sex offender–specific evaluation is a lengthy and often stressful endeavor for the client. He has put much work and effort into the process and deserves the opportunity to understand as fully as possible the evaluation outcome. The plethysmograph and psychometric results are explained to the extent that the client can understand them. Overexplaining can overwhelm or confuse the client, but a simple, concise explanation involves the client from the beginning as an educated consumer and advocate in the treatment process. This session is a time to both emphasize the serious nature of the sexual problem and reassure the client that effective treatment is available if he applies himself.

Owing to the frequent lack of documentation of the sexual problem, it is also important to provide a written record of the evaluation results and treatment recommendation. A complete and comprehensive report is time-consuming to write, and doing so may be unrealistic, given clinicians' high direct-care productivity quotients and given that the cost of producing a written report is usually not covered by insurance. However, at least a brief letter summarizing the evaluation process, evaluation results, and treatment recommendations is in order.

TREATMENT

The efficacy of treatment for nondisabled sexual offenders is often questioned in both public and professional arenas (Quinsey, Harris, Rice, & Lalumiere, 1993). That skepticism increases when considering treatment efficacy with intellectually disabled sex offenders. However, the clinical experience of specialized treatment providers indicates that many intellectually disabled sex offenders are amenable to treatment

(Caparulo et al., 1988; Fried, 1986; Gafen, 1988). Objective data also reflect this conclusion. The recidivism rate (defined as committing a new sexual offense) for 62 sex offenders treated at the Social Skills Program at the Oregon State Hospital (Haaven, Little, & Petre-Miller, 1990) was 23 percent. Although more outcome data and research are needed, it is clear that treatment of intellectually disabled sex offenders is viable and that alternatives such as incarceration without treatment are not.

IMPACT OF SITE

Ideally, in each community, a comprehensive and coordinated continuum of services would be available for intellectually disabled sex offenders, from secure, highly structured, and treatment-intensive residential settings to high-quality outpatient services. Depending on his risk level and treatment needs and progress, the client would shift in either direction to the appropriate setting. Unfortunately, placement is all too often the luck of the draw and depends on the vagaries of societal attitudes, service availability, the legal system, and insurance coverage. The need to continue to advocate for services for intellectually disabled sex offenders is clear.

For high-risk clients, a secure residential treatment site or 24-hour supervision offers safety for both the client and the community. Additionally, this level of structure offers a significant advantage in providing a total environment whose purpose is to teach the client to control sexual offending behavior. The entire staff is committed to this goal so that the client hears this message from many different people at different times and in different places. All aspects of the client's environment, from wall hangings to clothes, can reflect treatment strategies and goals.

For clients who can be maintained safely in the community, an outpatient program has the advantage of working with the client in his home setting so that the actual problems he faces on a day-to-day basis can be addressed. The clinician needs to plan for considerable collateral time when the client is seen on an outpatient basis. It is necessary to coordinate with all the other significant players in the client's life, such as family members, probation or parole officers, employers, residence providers, and so on, in order to obtain an accurate picture of the client's functioning, ensure an adequate support system, avoid splitting among the involved caregivers, and develop a comprehensive and coordinated system of care. The outpatient therapist cannot work effectively independently and should consider all the relevant players as a vast network. Because generalization of learning is so difficult for an intellectually disabled sex offender, it is crucial that he have assistance in reentering the community. Residential programs should allow for transition through outpatient aftercare.

As with nondisabled offenders, group treatment is the treatment of choice for intellectually disabled sex offenders. Groups for intellectually disabled sex offenders are usually smaller (six rather than eight members), and sessions are usually shorter (one hour rather than one and a half hours). The power of the group is its ability to both support and confront the offender. An individual therapist, regardless of his or her skill and experience with this population, does not have the impact of a peer group to address denial, point out distortions, or develop a relapse prevention plan.

As in the assessment phase, it is crucial to have the client's and/or the guardian's informed consent to the treatment program. An outline of the entire therapy program can be described initially, and concise, simple explanations of each treatment procedure should be provided at the time of its implementation. The clinician or therapist clearly notes the risks and benefits of the procedure. Examples of specific treatment consent forms are available (Haaven et al., 1990).

TREATMENT STRATEGIES

Regardless of whether the program is residential or outpatient, certain treatment strategies or philosophies should be kept in mind and integrated throughout the therapeutic program. These strategies reflect the uniqueness of working with intellectually disabled sex offenders. Without attention to these issues, the efficacy of treatment is questionable or greatly reduced.

TEACHING EFFECTIVELY. An intellectually disabled person may be more hampered by the therapist's old-fashioned and inept teaching methods than by his own intellectual deficits. Therapists tend to teach the way they were taught, which usually means large rooms, teacher at distance, didactic presentations, and abstract, formal lectures. Schooling is too often a boring, draining process, a rite of initiation to be allowed into the ranks of the employed. Any doctoral intern will confirm this experience.

In fact, most people learn more easily and effectively when emotion is linked with the learning process. This teaching style may be uncomfortable initially for the therapist, but it also gives the therapist a license and a mandate to introduce creativity into the therapeutic process. The therapist should look for elements of fun, the dramatic, and even the bizarre in treatment. For example, rather than teaching use of a condom by stating the instructions repeatedly, a game such as condom relay races may be employed. Group members are divided into two teams, each coached by one of the co-therapists. The first man in line on each team is given a condom and races his opponent across the room to correctly put the condom on a plaster of Paris set of male genitals. He then removes the condom, returns to the line, and the next person does the same task. The first team to finish wins.

This kind of process can lend an air of excitement and fun that facilitates learning. Entertainment creates engagement. In contrast, talking while seated in a circle of eight quickly becomes monotonous. The therapist may feel more professional, but the client is half asleep. However, if the process is project-oriented, lively, and hands on, the interest of group members is more likely to be sustained and learning enhanced.

ENCOURAGING MOTIVATION. One of the reasons that an intellectually disabled sex of-

fender fails to change is that he does not have sufficient reason to do so. The problem behavior he is engaging in is self-reinforcing, and negative consequences are lacking or weak in comparison. He may be ignorant of other possible sexual outlets, or such outlets may not be available to him. An intellectually disabled sex offender is sometimes rescued from the legal system with the best of intentions. However, this rescue robs him of the motivation most people need to address a painful problem that requires considerable time and effort to learn to manage. Sex offenders who are not intellectually disabled find it almost impossible to change in today's society without the motivation provided by the legal system. The vast majority of all successfully treated sex offenders have been court-mandated into treatment, but professionals and caregivers in the mental retardation field are often reluctant (not without reason) to have an intellectually disabled person enter the legal system. Certainly, an intellectually disabled sex offender may be lost or ill treated in the legal system. However, with mutual education and coordination of legal and social systems, probationary status can be beneficial to an intellectually disabled sex offender. It is unrealistic to expect an intellectually disabled sex offender to change simply because it's the right thing to do.

If the legal system cannot be harnessed, other temporary external motivation must be found and used. Contingency management programs can be developed in which an intellectually disabled sexual abuser is rewarded for periods which he does not engage in the problem behavior or precursors to it (such as staring at children). With approval by the human rights committee, privileges and eventually unsupervised time can be contingent upon the client's progress in treatment. It is necessary to decide ahead of time what consequences can be levied by the agency if an intellectually disabled sexual abuser reoffends. For example, if an intellectually disabled sex offender abuses another resident within a program, the perpetrator must be removed from the site. Just as there are clear criteria for entry into a program, there need to be clear criteria for termination from the program. This can be difficult if the program is already considered the last stopping place. However, if the safety of the residents is not provided for, the treatment program is a sham. Vague threats or threats that are not followed through teach a person to ignore such admonitions; they unnecessarily complicate treatment.

CREATING FACILITATING ENVIRONMENTS. Perhaps one of the most neglected aspects of influence is the physical environment (Ferguson & Haaven, 1990). The physical environment is active 24 hours a day and can seriously hamper or facilitate healthy social interaction. Simply moving from the typical institutional setting to a large safe-home setting with color-coordinated furnishings, flowers, and pictures can have a dramatic effect on a person. The furniture can be arranged to encourage conversation. Rooms can be designed to provide soothing privacy or encourage active group interaction. Significant acting-out behavior can be reduced through this kind of environment. In fact, the most effective security comes from a culture in which the resident feels that this is not the kind of place in which people act inappropriately. This culture is established in part by its physical environment.

FOSTERING SELF-RELIANCE. Most intellectually disabled persons have been taught to be dependent on others. Whether an intellectually disabled person has grown up in an institution or a family, others often leap to do tasks that he is capable of performing. Families are tempted to overprotect. Staff find it quicker to do the job themselves. The intellectually disabled person's learned dependence further erodes his already low self-esteem and discourages active problem solving and personal accountability.

In contrast, the clinician can evaluate each task and delegate appropriate ones to the intellectually disabled sex offender. In a residential setting, this delegation of tasks may include daily operational, educational, or therapeutic roles. In an outpatient setting, homework assignments are the responsibility of the client, not his parent or program or residence manager. In all settings, self-charting should be employed so that the intellectually disabled sex offender learns to evaluate and appreciate his own progress. A buddy or sponsor system can be devised in which a more advanced offender helps someone who is newer to the therapeutic process.

Fostering self-reliance does not mean giving up dependence on the therapist too quickly in the clinical process. An intellectually disabled sex offender's dependence can be utilized early in the treatment process to engage with the therapist and then to maintain a therapeutic alliance.

TREATMENT COMPONENTS

The following treatment components should be integrated into all therapy programs for intellectually disabled sexual abusers in order to provide comprehensive and coordinated care. The sequencing of the components depends in part on the degree of risk and access to the community. In a long-term secure setting, it is an advantage to be able to concentrate initially on cognitive restructuring. If the client's thinking errors are addressed, he will be more amenable to learning and using other aspects of treatment. In an outpatient setting, the possibility for relapse is increased simply because the client is in the community; therefore, the client needs to learn self-control techniques as quickly as possible.

Components overlap. It is impossible to teach covert sensitization, for example, without running into the client's cognitive distortions. Distortions must be noted, but not necessarily dealt with at length, when they are voiced. Although it is usually useful to structure components discretely, interpersonal skills training is occurring in every group meeting as group members listen and give one another feedback. Opportunities to confront denial or minimization may appear anytime and should be utilized.

In a residential program, a client may be involved in many groups during a day or week. He may be working simultaneously on stress management, ammonia-assisted biofeedback, and sex education. In an outpatient program, the contacts vary from perhaps several times a week to a once-monthly support group, depending on the client's treatment status.

SELF-CONTROL SKILLS. In choosing from the multitude of self-control techniques available (Jensen, Laws, & Wolfe, 1994), the therapist should look for those that are or can be made concrete, immediate, and interesting and discard techniques that are primarily intellectual, abstract, and boring. For example, masturbatory satiation, although very effective in reducing deviant arousal in nondisabled sex offenders, has not been particularly useful with intellectually disabled sex offenders. Learning the technique itself is difficult. Concentrating and focusing on a purposefully boring process for an hour is more difficult. If an intellectually disabled sex offender is able to master the technique, it appears that many more than the usual 20 hour-long audiotapes are necessary to decrease deviant arousal. Unfortunately, the therapist usually becomes satiated critiquing the tapes much more quickly than the offender does making them.

In contrast, covert sensitization and minimal arousal conditioning have proved effective with intellectually disabled sex offenders without undue wear and tear on the therapist. The efficacy of covert sensitization is enhanced if the client creates relevant collages or the covert scenes are acted out within the group rather than only recording them on a tape recorder. There are obvious limitations to what can be acted out, but role-playing the deviant chain or sexual abuse cycle can aid in integrating the material. The aversive and escape scenes can also be role-played. For example, consider the following deviant chain: being bored, riding on the subway at rush hour, finding an exhausted-looking parent holding groceries and a child, offering to look after the child, and then molesting the child while he or she sits in his lap. To role-play this, the group room can be arranged as a subway. Group members choose roles, such as certain subway riders. A manikin can be dressed as the child. The client walks through the scene, saying aloud his planning process, which usu-

ally includes many thinking errors. Initially the client stops the scene as he begins to approach the exhausted parent and child, and an aversive scene such as being arrested, handcuffed by police, and jeered at by other passengers is role-played. Gradually, the role-played scene is moved back so that the aversive scene is contingent upon the client thinking about riding the subway. This can also be videotaped to allow the client to critique himself.

Ammonia-assisted biofeedback offers the client a means to identify his problem arousal and then reduce it. Many clients initially deny or are unaware of the presence of an erection response. The plethysmograph and a biofeedback device such as a light bar are used to alert the client to his developing problem arousal as he listens to audiotape descriptions of his problem behavior. At a prearranged point based on the client's arousal level, the client sniffs from a vial of ammonia. Both the biofeedback and the self-administered ammonia offer immediate and concrete data and consequences that are helpful.

INTERPERSONAL SKILLS. In addressing his sexual problem, the intellectually disabled sex offender is often giving up a central part of his life, an activity and interest that have been major reinforcers for him. It is crucial, therefore, that this problem behavior be replaced with the skills and the opportunity for healthy social and sexual relationships. Interpersonal skills training offers the client the means to establish and maintain relationships with others. Interestingly, social skills training is regarded as among the most acceptable treatments for both intellectually disabled and nondisabled sex offenders (Lundervold & Young, 1992).

Once basic social skills are learned, another obstacle to building friendships remains: Opportunities for an intellectually disabled person to meet potential friends or partners are often limited. Many communities do not have social groups or events that are developed for or welcoming to an intellectually disabled person. Also, an intellectually disabled person is sometimes disdainful of or reluctant to join groups identified as intellectually disabled. Some enterprising person will probably develop a computer dating service for the intellectually disabled, and certain communities have already begun personal ad newsletters for intellectually disabled people. More needs to be done to ease the way for healthy connections with both disabled and nondisabled persons.

"Interpersonal skills" covers a vast array of skills, including social, assertiveness, empathy, and leisure-time skills; stress management; anger control; and perceptive skills. To facilitate learning, role-plays, board games, and feelings charts can all be employed. Imaginative homework assignments are essential, for example, a scavenger hunt in which clients form teams to gather appropriate personal information from others. It is important to remember that social skills are situation- and person-specific: Someone who is able to give compliments easily may not be able to express anger appropriately. Someone may be able to express anger at a parent but not at the boss. Each person's strengths can be highlighted both to increase self-esteem and to provide a model to other group members.

Teaching the client how to "fake it," that is, how to cope in a situation in which he is not able to participate fully, is also helpful. For example, the client may want and need to attend Alcoholics Anonymous, but is understandably intimidated by speaking in that situation. Role-plays in which the client practices saying "I pass" or "I don't choose to speak right now" allow him the benefit of attending an AA meeting even though it is not designed specifically for the intellectually disabled.

Learning how to manage leisure time is especially important for an intellectually disabled person who has been institutionalized or who, for other reasons, is unaware of his interests or has difficulty initiating activity. Because boredom can be a precipitating factor in committing a sexual offense, hobbies and activities can aid directly in relapse prevention.

Perceptive skills and empathy skills often seem to elude sexual offenders, who frequently misperceive social cues in a manner that justifies their sexual offending. A lack of empathy then allows them to ignore the pain they are causing. Therapy animals can be particularly helpful in teaching perceptive and empathy skills: Clients are sometimes more motivated and more able to perceive and empathize with a therapy animal than with a human being. For example, a client can be asked to read the reaction of a dog greeting him or be asked what it feels like for a cat to lie in the sun. This interest and skill can then be transferred to persons.

SEX EDUCATION. Sex education for an intellectually disabled sex offender includes such traditional topics as male and female anatomy and sexual functioning, birth control, sexually transmitted diseases, safer sex, sexual dysfunctions, heterosexuality, and homosexuality. The primary emphasis, however, is on attitudes toward sexuality and values clarification. Facts, figures, and the names of internal organs quickly fade, but the ability to make healthy decisions about sexual options remains essential. Therefore, facilitating discussion of thoughts and opinions is important, rather than merely presenting predigested information. The importance of teaching effectively is as relevant in this treatment component as in the others. *Condom Sense*, a humorous movie with a serious message, is shown in the Oregon Social Skills Program. Staff impersonating Dr. Ruth or Joyce Brothers can answer questions in a talk-show format. In recent years, sex education resources specifically geared toward an intellectually disabled audience have become available (Kempton, 1993).

The main difference in teaching sex education to offenders versus nonoffenders is the continual emphasis on its relevance to sex offending. A lack of information about sexuality or sexual misconceptions can be contributing factors toward committing a sex offense. Feelings of sexual inadequacy based on such misinformation often act as a further precipitant. For example, if a heterosexual offender believes that women are only interested in dating a man with a Porsche, children become more appealing as sexual objects because they are less demanding.

COGNITIVE RESTRUCTURING. Unfortunately, an intellectually disabled sex offender is just as adept as a nondisabled offender in his ability to develop cognitive distortions or thinking errors justifying his sexual abuse behavior. Far from being immune to the impact of cultural social-ization, an intellectually disabled sex offender uses media messages normalizing violence and sexism to absolve himself of responsibility for sexual offending. Teaching that encourages rigid male and female stereotypes and conserva-tive sexual beliefs are absorbed by an intellectu-ally disabled sex offender. These beliefs and teachings can then become attitudinal precipi-tants to sexual offending. For example, a rapist who believes that "a man has to do what a man has to do" considers forced sexual behavior his entitlement, not an act of rape. Cognitive re-structuring is equally crucial for an intellectu-ally disabled sex offender as for a nondisabled offender. Self-control skills are useless if the per-son does not see a problem to control.

The framework of old me–new me offers a way for an intellectually disabled sex offender to understand and integrate cognitive restructur-ing. "Old me" represents the thinking errors or criminal self-talk that led to trouble for the in-tellectually disabled sex offender. Old-me think-ing may include ideas such as "me first" (feeling entitled and superior) and "poor me" (seeing oneself as the victim). Simple drawings illus-trating these concepts that can be worn on large buttons or put on the wall are used as reminders. In contrast, "new me" represents the type of per-son the intellectually disabled sex offender is striving to be. The new-me person uses smart self-talk, such as "it's okay to let others be first" and "sometimes I don't get what I want and that's life."

Cognitive restructuring can also be accom-plished through role-plays in which one group member takes on the persona and thinking er-rors of another group member. Everyone in the group has a role, such as the probation officer, the therapist, the victim, the victim's parent, or the friend of the offender. The person whose distortions are being expressed also acts in one of these roles; it is his task to talk the group member or therapist role-playing himself out of

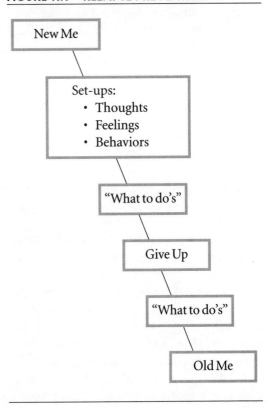

FIGURE 11.1   RELAPSE PREVENTION

New Me

Set-ups:
- Thoughts
- Feelings
- Behaviors

"What to do's"

Give Up

"What to do's"

Old Me

his own thinking errors. The rest of the group chimes in when the client can no longer success-fully argue the counterperspective. The process of understanding and accepting why a thinking error is a thinking error is much more difficult than simply intellectually identifying the distor-tion. Having to persistently counter one's own distortions being voiced by another also pro-vides a check on whether the client has indeed integrated the material.

RELAPSE PREVENTION. Relapse prevention is viewed as one of the most effective treatment approaches for sexual offenders (Laws,1989; Pithers & Kafka, 1990). Its usefulness applies to intellectually disabled sex offenders as well, but again, the concepts must be redesigned to be more user-friendly to an intellectually disabled sex offender. In Figure 11.1, the relapse preven-tion model has been both streamlined and sim-plified, but its rationale remains intact. "New me" carries the meaning of abstinence, the start-ing point in relapse prevention. Rather than seemingly unimportant decisions, the intellectually disabled sex offender looks for "set-ups." Set-ups may include set-up feelings, set-up thinking, set-up behaviors, and set-up situations. Adaptive coping responses translate into "what to do's," and the abstinence violation effect becomes "give-up." In group meetings or classes, each client practices identifying and coping with various set-up situations while other group members give feedback. Each client also develops a crisis card, sometimes in the form of a stop sign, which summarizes his set-ups and what to do's. This crisis card or stop sign can then be carried with him at all times.

Developing a support network outside the treatment setting, including a monitoring system, is also an important part of relapse prevention. An intellectually disabled sex offender should identify specific persons in the community, such as family members, friends, a minister, or graduate offenders, who would be willing to provide support as needed. The intellectually disabled sex offender explains his risk factors, sexual abuse cycle, and relapse prevention plans to these support persons. They are then in a position to help the offender be alert to risk situations, as well as to suggest or remind the offender of the appropriate "what to do." The probation or parole officer should also be well informed of these factors and support persons and should monitor the intellectually disabled sex offender as needed.

ONGOING CARE

The importance of transition and ongoing care cannot be overemphasized in treatment planning for intellectually disabled sex offenders. As noted previously, change is difficult for them. Without adequate preparation, transition out of a program makes an intellectually disabled sex offender particularly vulnerable to relapse. Attention to transition and ongoing care is also crucial because an intellectually disabled sex offender has difficulty generalizing learning to new situations.

As an intellectually disabled sex offender learns how to manage his sex offending problem, he should be progressing to a less structured setting with increasing opportunities to cope with his sexual problem and to form satisfying adult relationships. It is important that this change from one setting to another be gradual.

CONCLUSION

The field of treatment of intellectually disabled sex offenders is still very young. Its strength lies in our ability and willingness to remain open and flexible, continually incorporating new ideas as they show promise and empirically testing their effectiveness. Its downfall is remaining steadfast in preconceived notions. For example, not long ago, many practitioners scoffed at the notion of cognitive restructuring with intellectually disabled sex offenders. Yet the concept of "old me–new me" is now widely accepted and has been successfully incorporated into many programs for this population.

An intellectually disabled sex offender deserves the opportunity to change. The most efficient and effective means of accomplishing change must be continually sought and refined through careful clinical research. Research recommendations include determining the prevalence and incidence of sexual offenses among the intellectually disabled population, comparative studies of treatment efficacy, careful description of study samples, and the development and validation of assessment tools for intellectually disabled sex offenders (Schoen & Hoover, 1990).

REFERENCES

Abel, G.G., Becker, J., Cunningham-Rathner, J., Rouleau, J., Kaplan, M., & Reich, J. (1984). Abel and Becker Cognitions Scale. In A. Salter (Ed.), *Treating child sex offenders and victims* (pp. 278–280), Thousand Oaks, CA: Sage.

Beck, A.T. (1967). *Depression.* New York: Harper & Row.

Caparulo, F. (1991). Identifying the developmentally disabled sex offender. *Sexuality and Disability, 9*(4), 311–322.

Caparulo, F., Comte, M., Gafen, J., Haaven, J., Kaufman, K., Kempton, W., Sissala, L., Whitaker, J.M., & Wilson, R. (1988, March 25–27). *A summary of selected notes from the working sessions of the First National Training Conference on the Assessment and Treatment of Intellectually Disabled Juvenile and Adult Sexual Offenders.* Columbus, Ohio.

Deragatis, L.R., & Melisaratos, N. (1979). The DSFI: A multidimensional measure of sexual functioning. *Journal of Sex and Marital Therapy, 5*(3), 244–281.

Edmonson, B., Wish, J., & Fiechtl, K. (1977). *Development of a sex knowledge and attitude test for the moderately and mildly retarded.* Final report, HEW. Project G007500382. Columbus, OH: Nisonger Center, Ohio State University.

Ferguson, E.W., & Haaven, J. (1990). On the design of motivating learning environments for intellectually disabled offenders. *Journal of Correctional Education, 41*(1), 32–34.

Fried, E.R. (1986, May). *A multimodal treatment of developmentally disabled sex offenders.* Paper presented at the fourth National Conference on the Sexual Victimization of Children, New Orleans, LA.

Gafen, J. (1988, October). Taped interview by F.H. Knopp, Safer Society Program and Press.

Gay, M.L., Hollandsworth, J.G., & Galassi, J.P. (1975). An assertiveness inventory for adults. *Journal of Counseling Psychology, 22,* 340–344.

Haaven, J., Little, R., & Petre-Miller, D. (1990). *Treating intellectually disabled sex offenders.* Orwell, VT: Safer Society Press.

Jensen, S., Laws, R.D., & Wolfe, R. (1994, November). *Reduction of sexual arousal: What to do and not do.*

Paper presented at the 13th annual Research and Treatment Conference of the Association for the Treatment of Sexual Abusers, San Francisco, CA.

Kempton, W. (1993). *Socialization and sexuality: A comprehensive training guide for professionals helping people with disabilities that hinder learning.* Haverford, PA: Author.

Laws, D. (1989). *Relapse prevention with sex offenders.* New York: Guilford Press.

Lundervold, D.A., & Young, L.G. (1992). Treatment acceptability ratings for sexual offenders: Effect of diagnosis and offense. *Research in Developmental Disabilities, 13,* 229–237.

McGrath, R.J. (1991). Sex-offender risk assessment and disposition planning: A review of empirical and clinical findings. *International Journal of Offender Therapy and Comparative Criminology, 35*(4), 328–350.

Murphy, W.D., Coleman, E.M., & Haynes, M.R. (1983). Treatment and evaluation issues with the mentally retarded sex offender. In J.G. Greer & I.R. Stuart (Eds.), *The sexual aggressor: Current perspectives on treatment* (pp. 22–41). New York: Van Nostrand Reinhold.

Pithers, W., & Kafka, M. (1990). Relapse prevention with sex aggressors: A method for maintaining therapeutic gain and enhancing external supervision. In W. Marshall, D. Laws, & H. Barbaree (Eds.), *The handbook of sexual assault: Issues, theories and treatment of the offender* (pp. 343–361). New York: Plenum Press.

Quinsey, V.L., Harris, G.T., Rice, M.E., & Lalumiere, M.L. (1993). Assessing treatment efficacy in outcome studies of sex offenders. *Journal of Interpersonal Violence, 8*(4), 512–523.

Schoen, J., & Hoover, J.H. (1990). Mentally retarded sex offenders. *Journal of Offender Rehabilitation, 16*(1/2), 81–91.

12 Working with Culturally Diverse Populations

Alvin D. Lewis

Successful models for treating adult sex offenders have existed for the past 20 years, and treatment models have also been developed for adolescent sex offenders in recent years. These models have generally focused on treating offenders as a homogeneous population when, in fact, the population is heterogeneous. Sociocultural and gender issues must be considered in the assessment and treatment of sex offenders. Cultural differences are important variables that have been neglected for too long in the assessment and treatment of sex offenders. Jones (1983) notes that knowledge of the cultural base from which a client is operating is vital for all human service practitioners.

PREASSESSMENT CULTURAL CONSIDERATIONS

Clinicians must consider several factors before initial contact with the offender. Perhaps the first factor to consider is who should do the assessment. Characteristics of the evaluator are variables that can significantly affect how much information will be given by the offender and the family. For example, if the offender is an adult female, more information may be shared if the interviewer is female than if the interviewer is male. The gender of the offender and the gender of the interviewer represent important variables when determining who should conduct the assessment.

Some individuals or families may request an interviewer of a preferred gender. Others may request that the interviewer be of a certain ethnic or racial group. Whenever possible, such requests should be respected and efforts made to satisfy them; agency or facility staff can ask about the reasons for the request.

The acculturation of the offender and his or her family should be considered as well. Sometimes, based on information obtained about the offender, the interviewer determines how much acculturation the offender has experienced. A recent move from another country may be a clear indicator of the acculturation status of an offender and family. Children generally assimilate into new cultures more quickly than parents and grandparents. Therapists should consider this factor if the offender is an adolescent or sexually reactive child. Acculturation may become a dynamic factor in the assessment and treatment process.

A decision should be made whether an interpreter is needed before the initial interview with the offender and the family. Sometimes, the referral source may clearly articulate the need for an interpreter. Other times, language fluency may not be known, so the therapist should perhaps contact the offender and/or family about this matter. Language concerns are discussed in detail later in this chapter.

Many factors must be considered when deciding who should attend the initial interview. The people who attend the interview would be different for an adult client than for an offender who is an adolescent. Meeting with the offender and family members separately may be appropriate in some situations. This may increase everyone's comfort level and the quality of information obtained from the offender and family. Willis, Dobrec, and Sipes (1992) point out, for example, that sex or sexuality is not an acceptable topic to discuss openly among Native Americans. The therapist should consider gender, race and ethnicity, religion, history, and degree of acculturation when determining participants in the assessment interview.

A final issue that should be considered is what should be modified or not done in the assessment process. A staff member who is a member of the client's racial or ethnic group can help determine what aspects of the assessment should be modified or eliminated. A specialist who knows the culture could be consulted as an alternative.

CLINICAL ASSESSMENT AND DIAGNOSTIC ISSUES

The cultural context of behavior is an important element in a comprehensive evaluation. The offender's family and the family's experience must

be considered. Vargas and Koss-Chioino (1992) assert that therapists are often not aware of the cultural content and context in their work. Clearly, what is considered acceptable and unacceptable sexual behavior varies from culture to culture and from one period in time to another (Zastrow, 1993).

The belief that all clients have the same measure of "normal" behavior is a common assumption in the assessment and treatment process. Treatment professionals must be aware of an implied assumption that "normal" is almost universal across social, cultural, and economic or political backgrounds. Behavior that is considered normal differs according to the situation, the cultural background of the person being judged, and the time during which a behavior is displayed or observed (Pedersen, 1987).

The notion of traditional culture and mainstream culture must be examined. Some ethnic and racial groups maintain much of their traditional culture, but others may identify more with mainstream culture. This varies within cultural groups and families as well. McGoldrick, Pearce, and Giordana (1982) emphasize the importance of assessing how much connection a minority client has with the culture of origin. Vargas and Koss-Chioino (1992) point out to therapists that individuals and families are often caught between the conflicting pulls of traditional practices of their own cultural groups and those of the mainstream culture.

CASE EXAMPLE

B's family came to the United States from Cambodia two years ago. He would have been expected to have very little contact with young women until his early 20s in his country of origin. Much of his free time would have been spent with other young adult males. In Cambodia young adult males often hug, hold hands, and sit close together.

B was enrolled in a large university in his sophomore year after his family's immigration to Detroit. B immediately found himself caught between traditional values and practices and the practices of mainstream culture. His new peers made fun of him for sitting close to other males and wanting to hold their hands. He was in two physical altercations during his first three months at the university. The fights occurred because two classmates thought that B was trying to harass them sexually. Soon, he was being called a "fag" by his peers at the university.

Several months passed, and B began to show an interest in young women. He began sneaking out to meet a young woman because his parents did not approve of his dating, in accordance with traditional practices. Several males at the university told B that if he wanted to prove he was not gay, he had to have sex with the young woman he was seeing. This created much conflict for B.

Eventually, B decided he would try to have sex with the young woman. He pushed to visit the girl's house when her parents were out one evening. B later admitted to date rape. He had done what he thought all young adult American males did. His family felt great shame and wanted to keep his crime a secret. B became depressed and tried to commit suicide. He begged his parents to move back to Cambodia.

BICULTURALITY

Persons of color in America must learn to function in two environments: their own culture and that of the mainstream society. Biculturality, the ability to function in two worlds, is adaptive (Anda, 1984). It is different from assimilation, which implies total immersion in mainstream culture and having all needs met based on mainstream norms, values, beliefs, and perceptions. The therapist must understand and accept the importance of biculturality for the offender of color. For example, an offender who is Chinese American may celebrate Chinese New Year as a holiday but may also appreciate Christmas.

A young adult offender who is Asian may make eye contact with the therapist during an assessment, but not with his or her parents. The offender who is bicultural understands the im-

portance placed on eye contact in mainstream culture. However, the offender may not make eye contact with his or her parents out of respect, as determined by the culture of origin. The therapist would then need to be culturally sensitive in his or her evaluation of eye contact in the assessment and treatment process.

FAMILY TRADITION AND STRUCTURE

Family structures vary considerably among ethnic and racial groups. Much intragroup diversity exists. Some groups are more patriarchal, and others are matriarchal. Still others are egalitarian. Minnuchin (1974) did extensive research on family structure and emphasized the importance of understanding family structure and respecting it in the therapeutic process.

Mistakes can be made that lead to the offender and family dropping out of therapy, if a therapist does not understand the importance of family structure. Understanding the father's special role in a patriarchal family structure is very important. The therapist must be careful not to stereotype. The therapist must not hold on to an assumption if the experience with the offender or the family differs. Boyd-Franklin (1989) asserts:

> The clinician must test hypotheses and accept and discard them according to his or her experience of the individual and family. Knowledge about culture is a flexible hypothesis and not a rigidly held thesis. (p. ix)

Role flexibility is an important aspect of some family structures. Many African-American families, for example, maintain more role flexibility between spouses than do White families. Parenting by the oldest child may be accepted in other families of color. He or she may function as a surrogate parent and may be in charge when neither parent is home or available. The child does not carry out this role when a parent is available. Minnuchin (1974) points out that role flexibility is seen as a strength in some racial groups. However, he goes on to say that the extended family structure is quite vulnerable to boundary and role confusion.

Family composition is another aspect of family tradition. I grew up in a home inhabited by parents, siblings, grandparents, nephews, and nonbiologically related adults. The grandparents and unrelated adults had authority to discipline the children.

Parents expect married adult children to live at home for several years before getting their own places in some Asian and Hispanic cultures. I lived with a Chinese family while serving as a Peace Corps volunteer in Malaysia. The family's oldest daughter and her family lived at home. The daughter was a nurse, and her husband owned his own business. At age 40 and 42, respectively, they finally moved into their own home with their two children. The couple had owned two houses for more than 10 years but rented them to tenants. A therapist working with this family would need to be sensitive to this factor and not see the adult children as dependent and irresponsible.

DEGREE OF ACCULTURATION

The therapist, as part of the assessment, must understand acculturation. Acculturation may be defined as the degree to which a person of color meets his or her needs in the mainstream culture. Degree of acculturation varies from one individual to another and from one family system to another. The therapist must be careful of bias there. That is, the therapist must realize that an individual or family may be bicultural by choice. Needs are met in both the mainstream culture and the culture of origin. For example, some East Indians may stop wearing saris after living in the United States for a few years. Other Indian women may have lived here for 20 years and wear saris but also wear Western clothes. Biculturality may similarly occur regarding holidays. Some individuals or families may celebrate their traditional holidays, but others may celebrate only American holidays.

The therapist can make some preliminary hypotheses during the assessment based on family members' dress, language, and roles. Often, conflicts arise between young adults and parents and grandparents. Young adults frequently want to identify wholly with the mainstream culture, but parents and grandparents might want to be bicultural sometimes. Minnuchin (1974) further stresses that the family structure must change shape, with rules and roles modified to fit their new context.

LANGUAGE

The clinical assessment should be conducted in the preferred language of the offender and the family, if possible. Before the assessment, the therapist should have determined what language the offender and family want to use. Arrangements should then be made to use an interpreter who, ideally, is a mental-health professional. The interview is then less cumbersome, and the chances of miscommunication are decreased.

The therapist should *never* use a child to interpret. Often, this is viewed as disrespectful to the family, especially the parents. Other reasons why a child should not interpret include that (1) the family hierarchy is not being considered, (2) children may distort what the therapist says, (3) children may distort what the parents or other family members say, (4) children can be triangulated in the communication process, and (5) exposure to sexual information may be inappropriate for a child.

The therapist must be sensitive to cultural nuances when it is necessary to use an interpreter. The following factors should be considered: (1) gender of the interpreter, (2) comfort level of the interpreter with the nature of the interview and the use of sexual words and phrases, (3) background of the interpreter — professional or layperson — in mental health, (4) inappropriate use of family members as translators, (5) the speed of the therapist's speech to ensure that the interpreter can easily understand, and (6) preliminary meetings with the interpreter to devise a plan to ensure clear communication.

According to Baker (1981):

The "ideal" interpreting style falls between the extremes of translating every word versus a summary and varies according to the client, circumstances, and the personalities of the worker and interpreter. The key to effective interpreting is for the worker and interpreter to become a close team in their enterprise, using the best qualities of each to help clients more effectively. Thus, the working relationship between them is crucial. (p. 393)

HELP-SEEKING BEHAVIOR

Asking for help from a mental-health professional, in many cultures, is a last resort. The offender may feel that he or she will "lose face" because of the evaluation, if the assessment is mandated. When I was a Peace Corps volunteer, I was aware that any individual or family who met with me was doing so as a last resort. In other words, everything else had failed, including seeing a traditional healer.

The therapist may need to ask the individual or family members how they have already tried to resolve the problem. Also, the therapist may want to find out how the problem would be dealt with within the culture. Lappin (1983) notes that conducting cross-cultural assessments and therapy is a balance.

The balance has to do with the attitude the therapist conveys — one of asking for the individual or family's help while, at the same time, offering help. Cultural questioning is the start of a process that can begin to challenge old rules, roles, and narrow definitions of self. (p. 125)

Ho (1987) points out that clients' lack of knowledge of help-seeking behavior could cause many therapists to misdiagnose something that is actually a cultural difference as something that is pathological.

EYE CONTACT

In mainstream Anglo-American culture, eye contact is highly valued. Many people use a handshake and eye contact to negotiate multi-million-dollar transactions. Much is written about eye contact and other nonverbal behavior in the field of mental health. The evaluator often mentions in clinical assessments whether the client made good or poor eye contact during the interview. Some people associate innocence or guilt with eye contact or the lack of it. However, eye contact is culturally mediated. Adult children in the Chinese culture are not expected to make eye contact with their parents. To do so is considered disrespectful to the parents and elders. A teenager in the African-American culture should not look directly at the parent, especially during a father-son talk when the son is being disciplined or receiving a lecture.

Some cultures hold professionals in very high regard. In other cultures (e.g., India), people of one class or caste cannot look directly at someone from a different socioeconomic class or caste. The therapist must take this factor into consideration in the evaluation process. An offender may not make eye contact with the professional based on his or her cultural background. In some Asian cultures, the client is expected to refrain from eye contact with the therapist out of respect.

SPIRITUALITY AND RELIGION

Spirituality is seen as a complex notion. The therapist needs to have some knowledge of spirituality as it pertains to a culture to do a comprehensive assessment. African Americans, for example, consider spirituality a very important dimension of the community. Many people believe that African Americans endured and survived slavery and other oppressions because of their strong spiritual foundation.

The therapist must try to understand that spirituality may be a guiding factor for the offender and his or her family. Also, the therapist must be able to differentiate between religion and spirituality. Frequently, even mental health professionals see religion and spirituality as the same. Boyd-Franklin (1989) asserts that the role of spirituality has received much attention in the mental-health literature in recent years.

The therapist attempts to understand what the offender is saying with respect to spirituality and religious belief during the assessment. Even before the interview, the therapist may want to do some reading about spirituality or consult with a specialist on the culture who can offer some expertise in this area.

HOW PRIVACY IS TREATED IN THE FAMILY AND CULTURE

Privacy is both cultural and contextual. A Muslim woman covers her body to be modest. This custom is an effort not to appear attractive or provocative toward males. A common belief among Muslims is that Western females dress provocatively and, as a result, increase the chance that they might be sexually abused or raped.

I observed, during service in the Peace Corps, various East Indian family members sleeping on the floor together. Sleeping next to her 16-year-old grandson was common for a grandmother. The culture saw no need for the grandson to have privacy with respect to sleeping arrangements. Muslim families, in the same culture, allowed adult and adolescent males to swim with shorts or trunks but required females to be fully clothed in the water.

I have observed many situations in which Asian adult males and children cover themselves with sarongs or use locked stalls to change clothes in a public rest room. Most American males change clothes and allow their genitalia to be briefly exposed in similar situations.

Many males from Asian and East Indian cultures find it difficult to work with female therapists from the West. The male may be distracted by or uncomfortable with the way the therapist is dressed. This circumstance would make it difficult to create trust and develop a constructive clinical relationship (McGoldrick et al., 1982). Iranian men, in particular, have difficulty following a female therapist's directives and recommendations. They avoid discussing painful

issues, including sexual matters (Zastrow, 1993). Therefore, a male therapist probably would need to do the assessment and therapy.

SOCIAL TOLERANCE FOR DEVIANCE AND DYSFUNCTIONAL BEHAVIOR

Tolerance for deviant and dysfunctional behavior varies from culture to culture. What is viewed as abhorrent in one society may be socially sanctioned in another society.

Much of the sexual abuse in Native American families involves father-daughter and stepfather-stepdaughter incest. Frequently, the offender is not convicted of a sexual crime and does not receive treatment for a psychosexual disturbance. Instead, he is treated for alcoholism or other substance-abuse problems. The offender's spouse and the community then accept that the "problem" has been addressed.

The African-American culture allows little open discussion about homosexual lifestyles. A person who is lesbian or homosexual is viewed as "sick," and community members think that homosexuals will be "punished by God." A large segment of the population that is highly religious sees AIDS as God's punishment of gays and thinks that if gays "gave up their lifestyle and repented, then they could be saved." Although the mainstream culture no longer views homosexuality as an illness or as deviant behavior, it is still viewed this way in the African-American culture. Although there is no documented connection between homosexuality and sexual offending, this punitive attitude becomes relevant to sex offenders who molest victims of their own gender, decreasing the likelihood that victims or offenders will voluntarily report the incident.

Gagnon and Henderson (1975) found some cultures that accept and others that encourage homosexuality. Today, all males among the Siwans of North Africa are expected to engage in homosexual relationships throughout their lives. Sullivan, Thompson, Wright, Gross, and Spady (1980) reported that among the Aranda of central

Australia, relationships take place between young boys and unmarried men, with these liaisons generally ending at heterosexual marriage.

PAPER-AND-PENCIL TESTING

The assessment process often includes administration of a series of paper-and-pencil tests. However, the therapist must be careful in the interpretation of the results. Most psychological tests and psychosexual instruments were normed on White populations in the United States. Therefore, administering these tests to a person of color may not reveal much useful information.

Although many "culture-fair" or "culture-free" tests have been developed in recent years, few such tests are actually used. The Cattell is a culture-sensitive test of intellectual abilities used with and administered to offenders of color. No studies are available concerning outcomes in use of the Cattell versus the WISC-R or III.

CHOICE OF THERAPIST

The choice of a therapist is vitally important in cross-cultural counseling. An offender may ask for a therapist of a specific race or gender. If meeting this request is possible, it should be done. However, the offender should be given a choice. All Mexican Americans should not be assigned to Mexican-American therapists, even if this were possible. The offender (not to mention the treatment provider) may consider it patronizing to be automatically assigned a therapist of the same race.

The interactions between White therapists and minority clients may be more restrained than are those between therapists and clients of the same race (Atkinson, 1983). The same may be true when a male client is working with a female therapist or vice versa. Parloff, Waskow, and Wolf (1978) conclude that cultural matching of a therapist and client is not clearly preferred. Other research also suggests a lack of support for the preference of matching clients

and therapists by culture. Helms (1985) reports that clients with the strongest commitment to their own ethnic group are more likely to prefer therapists from the same ethnic background.

Research by Carkhuff and Pierce (1967) shows that counselors who are different from their clients in ethnicity, social class, and gender have the greatest difficulty effecting constructive changes. Atkinson (1983) reports that the preference for counseling style may be more important than racial match between the therapist and African-American, Asian-American, and low-income White clients, but less important with middle-class White clients.

Lambert (1981) suggests the possibility that cross-cultural therapy may be contraindicated in most circumstances. He goes on to say that there are many complications in understanding and communicating with culturally different clients. Client-counselor relationship correlates with therapy outcome (Peoples & Dell, 1975). Therefore, it is extremely important that the therapist is confident and competent to work with the offender and that the offender views the therapist as competent and culturally sensitive.

CHOICE OF TREATMENT MODALITIES AND METHODOLOGIES

Some aspects of mainstream sex offender treatment may be contraindicated when working with clients from a specific cultural background. Aspects that are contraindicated vary from one culture to another. The constructs of "healthy" and "normal" that guide the delivery of mental-health services are not the same for all cultures. Group therapy may not work well for Asian offenders, for example, who often believe that they will "lose face" by discussing their problems publicly; being in a group would be viewed as "public." Group treatment could be considered if the offender was born in a Western culture or has lived in the West for several years.

Family therapy may not be useful with some minority offenders. Family therapy with Asian families, for example, may be ineffective because of the importance placed on family reputation. Family members often attempt to protect one another and the good reputation of the whole family. Although the family will not question any directives or instructions given by the therapist, little or no work will be done toward implementation because of discomfort and other issues that the family considers inappropriate or shameful to discuss with the therapist.

The therapist may have to meet with the offender and/or family several times to determine appropriate treatment modalities and methods in particular cases. Pedersen (1988) states that the application of standard methods and modalities indiscriminately across cultural groups creates problems. Kavanagh and Kennedy (1992) note:

> Providers are often unfamiliar with appropriate intervention and communication strategies in situations that involve persons or groups dissimilar from themselves or that involve circumstances beyond their own experience. Discomfort based on unfamiliarity can threaten personal integrity and encourage resistance and defensiveness. (p. 50)

Research findings have generally shown that many people of color are inappropriately or inadequately served by mental-health services. Traditional counseling theory and methods may often run counter to important developmental aspects of indigenous helping models found in various cultural groups. Traditional counseling practices have often failed to meet the needs of people from diverse cultural backgrounds (Sue & Sue, 1990).

Therapists have usually been taught generic techniques in graduate school. These techniques may work well with clients from the mainstream culture. However, they may be ineffective in work with clients of color (Pedersen, 1988). Minnuchin and Fishman (1981) found that many minority clients terminate therapy early because they have no frame of reference for the therapeutic techniques used by the therapist.

The more a therapist knows about a client's culture, the greater the opportunity for success in the therapeutic relationship. Clients are more likely to stay engaged in treatment when they are comfortable with the techniques used. Boyd-Franklin (1989) notes that spiritual reframing is a useful technique with African-American individuals and families. Spiritual beliefs clinically manifest themselves in many different forms and can be used as part of the reframing by a therapist who is aware of them.

Discussing sex offenses with a therapist is difficult for most people. The therapist must understand that for some offenders of color, little disclosure will occur in the first few sessions. The therapist may have to employ the rituals of social amenities between himself or herself and the offender for a longer time than usual, particularly with Native Americans and Asians. The therapist may still need to base the pace on the offender, even when the presenting problem is already known.

A therapist will hear something about traditional healers and/or traditional medicine at some point in therapy. The therapist may lose the offender and the family if the importance of the traditional healer is negated. McGoldrick et al. (1982) assert that the therapist must recognize that therapy may have to include traditional healers as co-therapists or consultants. The nontraditional technique of including elders and traditional healers in therapy can change the course of treatment constructively (Coutoure, 1980).

Using personal experience as a technique takes on a new meaning in work with Asian Americans. The individual and family may expect the therapist to engage in self-disclosure as a way to develop trust. Most therapists have been trained to reveal little about themselves in the therapeutic process. However, if the therapist expects to develop a relationship with an Asian client, revealing a little personal information may be necessary to give the client some perspective about the therapist.

Therapists may have to adapt their communication style in working with Hispanic and Asian clients. The pace for gathering needed information may have to be much slower than with dominant-culture clients. McGoldrick et al. (1982) note that if the client sees the therapist as aggressive, pushy, and insensitive, the client may feel stressed and disengage from treatment.

CASE EXAMPLE

The Wu family consisted of the parents in their mid-30s, an 11-year-old daughter, and a 16-year-old son. The therapist had a background in work with Asian families and a solid foundation in sex offender treatment. The therapist, therefore, did not insist that the daughter openly express anger toward her father for sexually abusing her. For the daughter to have done so would have been disrespectful.

Even with educational restructuring, the victim, especially a child, probably would not be able to express negative feelings easily. The therapist should not push the victim or family too hard; some families never feel comfortable deviating from this cultural style of expression (Pedersen, 1988).

STORYTELLING

Storytelling is a nontraditional technique that has utility for some cultures. In particular, this technique has been used effectively with African Americans and Asian Americans. Storytelling is nonthreatening and especially helpful early in therapy when trust and rapport are being established. Boyd-Franklin (1989) notes that establishing the relationship can be the most difficult aspect of therapy with some clients. Storytelling can be used as a joining tool and can be used throughout therapy. Storytelling is a part of Native American culture. Stories are often passed down from one generation to the next. Understanding the importance of storytelling to a culture and being able to recite some well-known stories will serve the therapist well. In African-American and Native American cultures, history was passed on to others through storytelling (Boyd-Franklin, 1989).

RITUAL

Therapists can also employ rituals as a nontraditional technique. There are rituals unique to each culture and some that transcend many cultures. During my training at the Philadelphia Child Guidance Clinic, I observed rituals being used effectively by many therapists in cross-cultural work. Sue and Sue (1990) note that clients become "stuck" when they cannot adapt effectively to the experiences that influence their lives. Rituals can help get a client "unstuck" and move them to a functional level.

RACISM, PREJUDICE, AND POVERTY

Any therapist working with an offender of color must understand the historical and current context of a particular group's experiences with racism and poverty. Robinson (1989) "believes that the initial phase of therapy is the point at which the clinician must assess both the impact of race and racism on the process of therapy" (p. 323). If, for example, the offender includes race as a relevant factor in the presenting problem, the therapist must be sensitive to this. Whether overt or covert, racism is often the apparent basis for decisions and actions that will profoundly affect the lives of people of color. By choosing not to elicit or acknowledge the client's perspective regarding race, the therapist risks disrupting the formation of an alliance that the client experiences as empathic (Robinson, 1989).

The experiences of persons of color with racism and prejudice vary from one culture group to another. African Americans, for example, came to this country primarily from West Africa as slaves. Jews were persecuted in Germany and many other European countries. Native Americans were placed on reservations after years of strife with the mainstream culture. The therapist must know the history of the culture and have an understanding of racism, prejudice, and poverty to treat sex offenders of color effectively. Robinson (1989) notes four issues that may significantly affect the effectiveness of treatment: (1) racial congruence of the client,

(2) influence of race on the presenting problem, (3) the therapist's racial awareness, and (4) the therapist's therapeutic strategies (p. 323).

CASE EXAMPLE

J is a 30-year-old African-American male who was convicted of sexual abuse of his girlfriend's 10-year-old daughter. Early in treatment, a session focused on safe sex practices. J and the therapist had very different views about the use of condoms. J admitted that he had sex and did not use condoms, although he sometimes had sex with females other than his girlfriend. J felt that condoms were mainstream culture's way of limiting the population growth of African Americans. J spoke of involuntary sterilizations of African Americans that occurred in the 1930s and 1940s. In J's view, this practice was racist and was done to reduce the African-American population systematically. The therapist was unable to appreciate what J was saying. The therapist did not know the history of African Americans, so he continued to tell J that he would die of sexually transmitted diseases if he did not use condoms.

Pedersen (1987) concludes that therapists display 10 frequent assumptions resulting in cultural bias in counseling. His ninth assumption relates to the importance of history for a proper understanding of contemporary events. Pedersen notes that counselors are more likely to focus on crisis-precipitating events, and if clients talk about their own history or the history of their "people," the counselor is likely to stop listening and wait for clients to "catch up" to current events, which the counselor considers more salient than history. The client's perspectives may require historical background knowledge that the client feels is relevant to the complete description of his or her problem from his or her point of view. In many cultures, the connection between past and present history makes it necessary for counselors to understand clearly a client's historical context to understand his or her present behavior.

The therapist in the preceding case example had little knowledge of the offender's past and therefore could not understand his views about condoms. In that case, even if the therapist were uninformed, he could have consulted someone familiar with the culture or brought it up as an issue with colleagues on the treatment team.

SPIRITUALITY, RELIGION, INDIGENOUS HEALERS, AND OTHER BELIEF SYSTEMS

The issues concerning spirituality and religion in cross-cultural treatment are similar to those described in the assessment section of this chapter. Little emphasis has been placed on religion and other belief systems in sexual abuser treatment. However, multicultural counseling practice may be enhanced if therapists consider the influence of religion or spirituality to be a crucial dynamic in the helping process (Lee, 1991; Boyd-Franklin, 1989). Religious institutions are important sources of psychological support in the cultural traditions of many groups. The therapist must understand the religious and spiritual influences of the abuser and his or her family. Spiritual beliefs are part of a survival system in some cultures. For example, an offender might state that "God will take care of my problem." Therapists need to be sensitive to offenders' belief systems while also requiring them to take responsibility for their abusive behaviors and address their psychosexual problems.

CASE EXAMPLE

Mr. H is a 42-year-old, married father of two children. He is receiving sex offender counseling for abusing two prepubescent boys. The treatment team has recommended to the therapist that masturbatory satiation be part of the treatment protocol. Mr. H tells the therapist that he does not masturbate due to his religious beliefs. Consequently, he says that masturbatory satiation will not help him. The therapist has provided multicultural treatment to sex offenders and their families for several years. Rather than challenge the offender, the therapist validates the offender's religious beliefs. However, over the next several weeks, he also helps the offender understand the efficacy of the treatment. Mr. H eventually agrees to masturbatory satiation for a three-month period. The therapist and the offender monitor his arousal through monthly phallometric assessments. Mr. H is encouraged by the results and therefore agrees to continue beyond the three months.

At times, the therapist must elicit the help of a religious leader or traditional healer to work effectively with an offender and his or her family. African-American families who are very religious often turn to their ministers for support during emotional crises such as divorce, suicide, death, substance abuse, or the impending imprisonment of a loved one (Broadfield, Lewis, & Davis, 1991). The therapist can develop a relationship of trust and respect with the offender and the family if a link is established with their minister.

The therapist needs to have some familiarity with traditional healers of an offender's culture. The offender probably has had contact with a traditional healer, even when an offender is referred for court-ordered treatment. Lemoine (1986) notes that "exploring how a family has used a traditional healer, when to call one, or whether or not to consult one are questions the western psychotherapist has only recently learned to be of value" (p. 171). The therapist may have to delve deeper into the culture to be effective, depending on how the offender and his or her family use the traditional healer.

CULTURAL VIEW OF SEXUAL ABUSE AND INCEST

The definitions of sexual abuse vary from one culture to another. Also, incest, though taboo in most Western and Eastern cultures, is viewed differently in remote and less-developed cultures. Zastrow (1993) points out that what is acceptable and unacceptable sexual behavior varies from culture to culture and from one period to another. The sexual relationships be-

tween the young boys and unmarried men of the Aranda, as previously described, are a clear example of such differences among cultures.

The therapist must view incest and other sexually abusive behaviors from both cultural and legal contexts. What may have been acceptable in one culture is a crime in another culture. The therapist must help the offender and the family understand that a sexual crime was committed based on laws and statutes when conflicts arise between cultural and legal standards. The therapist needs to help the offender in accepting responsibility for the sexual offense and making a commitment to treatment.

The Native American offender living on a reservation poses a unique challenge. This situation is often complicated if the offender has a substance-abuse problem as well. He or she may well plead for substance-abuse counseling, and the sex-offending behavior may never be addressed. When the offender returns home, the child is then at risk of being sexually abused again.

The therapist needs to be aware that it is common in Native American families for the victim to recant the abuse. Open discussion of sexual issues in these families, including sexual abuse, is a cultural taboo, especially when the family resides on a reservation (S. Paddock, personal communication, 1995).

In many Asian cultures, treatment can be complicated in incestuous families. Often, the incest goes unreported unless the family seeks treatment as a last resort for another problem. If exposed, the Asian offender and family may contend that he or she suffered with "amok" or psychotic violent rage. Therefore, the offender and the family believe that the offender cannot be held accountable for the sexual abuse (Sullivan et al., 1980). One pitfall in working with Asian offenders and families noted earlier was the likelihood that victims may consider it disrespectful to express negative feelings to parents. The cultural traditions might also be such that the offender cannot talk about his or her behavior in the presence of the victim and other children (Chao, 1992).

OTHER CULTURALLY MEDIATED MATTERS

The Western-trained therapist doing cross-cultural work will come to realize that certain techniques and social gestures are not appropriate or acceptable and are, in fact, culturally dystonic. Silence as a technique is effective with some offenders but not with others. Intensity and confrontation are other techniques that are culturally mediated. Most Asian cultures would find confrontation offensive, resulting in the client providing even less disclosure and dropping out of treatment.

The appropriateness of social touch, including handshakes, is culturally determined. Shaking the hands of Asian women is frequently considered inappropriate. Also, the open expression of affection in public is unacceptable. This factor would affect family and marital counseling when the therapist wants to use experiential therapies. The couple would probably be very uncomfortable with any instruction requiring a public display of affection.

The culturally sensitive therapist is mindful of things such as manners, eye contact, laughter, gestures, and body language. Lappin (1983) notes that, to be effective, therapists should know nuances of group and intragroup differences. While cultural qualities and patterns cannot be reduced into neat categories, forming a knowledge base about the culture with which therapists work is essential. It means becoming attuned to the macro and micro aspects of therapy and the culture. Characteristics such as body posture, voice tone, and facial expressions carry a greater meaning in cross-cultural work.

Therapists working with offenders and their families need to become more knowledgeable about the culture because of the increase in cultural diversity in most Western countries. The therapist must be comfortable with learning about cultural nuances from the offender, the family, and others.

CULTURALLY BASED BELIEF SYSTEMS ABOUT PHARMACOLOGY

The use of pharmacotherapy with sex offenders has increased in recent years. Medication has been used with sex offenders when other therapies have not decreased the intensity of their deviant arousal. Depo-Provera has been used for several years and, more recently, Depo-Lupron. Medical research has shown some efficacy with Prozac and Paxil.

Many offenders refuse to take such medication because they think that it will prevent them from having a normal sex drive or will make them impotent. Use of medication becomes even more complex in cross-cultural situations. There is a demarcation between Eastern and Western medicine in most Asian cultures. Tung (1980) points out that "as a rule, western medicines are all hot and herb medicines possess more cooling properties" (p. 6). Usually, Asians are cautious about Western medicines because they think the medicines are too potent for their constitutions.

Studies of dosages among Asian and Latino populations have been conducted. Lee (1982) has worked with Asian Americans and states:

> Clinical reports from Asian countries and sporadic reports in the United States suggest that dosages based on Caucasian patient populations may not be readily applicable to Asian populations. Very detailed explanations and clarification of appropriate dosages are necessary. The mixing of Eastern and Western medicines is a concern to many therapists. It is advisable to get a detailed medical history from the client and to advise against the use of internal herbal medicines in conjunction with psychotropic or other drugs. (p. 549)

The therapists and physicians who believe that offenders can benefit from hormonal therapy must consider the cultural implications of such medicine. Clinicians must move slowly to try to help offenders understand the potential benefit of the treatment in the management of sexual problems.

MAINTENANCE AND AFTERCARE

Offenders must accept that maintenance or aftercare is an essential part of their treatment. The therapist who is treating a person of color must take into consideration cultural factors that affect the offender's participation in maintenance and aftercare. Some factors include (1) offenders' belief systems about maintenance, (2) choice of a therapist, (3) choice of modalities, and (4) language and need for an interpreter.

STRATEGIES FOR PROVIDING CULTURALLY SENSITIVE AND RELEVANT SEX OFFENDER TREATMENT

McGoldrick et al. (1982) point out that no therapist can become an expert on all racial and ethnic groups. What is essential is to develop an openness to cultural variability. Recommended strategies include:

1. Be an explorer; be willing to form hypotheses and test them.

2. Be open to consulting with colleagues who are familiar with an offender's culture.

3. Understand that the offender and his or her family will need to teach the therapist about some aspects of their culture.

4. Ask about the obvious if you do not understand it (e.g., why do Muslim women cover their bodies?).

5. Use an interpreter, if necessary, to help with the language and as an expert on the culture.

6. Remain aware that some communication styles and therapeutic techniques will be more effective than others in cross-cultural work.

7. Be aware of subjects that are taboo and bring them up only when the client seems ready to discuss them.

8. Learn to appreciate and work with the offender's natural helping system and indigenous healers when appropriate.

9. Honor and respect cultural diversity and differences.

10. Increase awareness and understanding of the contributions of various cultures.

Incorporation of more knowledge about diversity and culture into the current model is needed. Using a generic model to treat sex offenders of color is no longer acceptable as sex offender–specific treatment develops. Therapists must adapt their skills and increase their knowledge base to serve minority offenders effectively. This improvement can be achieved through training, consultation, and a willingness to learn from the offender and his or her family.

REFERENCES

Anda, D. (1984, March/April). Bicultural socialization factors affecting the minority experience. *Social Work*, 101–107.

Atkinson, D. (1983). Ethnic similarity in counseling psychology: A review of research. *The Counseling Psychologist, 11*(3), 79–92.

Baker, N. (1981, September). Social work through an interpreter. *Social Work*, 391–397.

Boyd-Franklin, N. (1989). *Black families in therapy: A multi-systems approach.* New York: Guilford.

Broadfield, C., Lewis, A., & Davis, J. (1991). Substance abuse in the African-American community. *Forum*, pp. 5–7.

Carkhuff, R., & Pierce, R. (1967). Differential effects of therapist race and social class upon patient depth of self-exploration in the initial clinical interview. *Journal of Counseling Psychology, 31*, 632–634.

Chao, C. (1992). The inner heart: Therapy with Southeast Asian families. In L. Vargas & J. Koss-Chioino (Eds.), *Working with culture* (pp. 157–181). San Francisco: Jossey-Bass.

Coutoure, J. (1980). *Next time try a medicine man.* Unpublished manuscript.

Gagnon, B., & Henderson, J. (1975). *Human sexuality: The age of ambiguity.* Boston: Little, Brown.

Helms, J. (1985). Cultural identity in the treatment process. In P. Pedersen (Ed.), *Handbook of cross-cultural counseling and therapy* (pp. 239–245). Westport, CT: Greenwood Press.

Ho, M. (1987). *Family therapy with ethnic minorities.* Newbury Park, CA: Sage.

Jones, R. (1983, September). Increasing staff sensitivity to the Black client. *Social Casework: The Journal of Contemporary Social Work,* 419–425.

Kavanagh, K., & Kennedy, P. (1992). *Promoting cultural diversity: Strategies for health care professionals.* Newbury Park, CA: Sage.

Lambert, M. (1981). The implications of psychotherapy. In A. Marsella and P. Pedersen (Eds.), *Cross-cultural counseling and psychotherapy* (pp. 126–158). New York: Pergamon Press.

Lappin, J. (1983). On becoming a culturally conscious family therapist. In L. Jones (Ed.), *Cultural perspectives in family therapy* (pp. 122–136). New York: Guilford Press.

Lee, C. (1991). Cultural dynamics: Their importance in multicultural counseling. In C. Lee & B. Richardson (Eds.), *Multicultural issues in counseling: New approaches to diversity* (pp. 11–16). New York: Wiley.

Lee, E. (1982). A social systems approach to assessment and treatment for Chinese-American families. In M. McGoldrick, J. Pearce, & J. Giordana (Eds.), *Ethnicity and family therapy* (pp. 527–551). New York: Guilford Press.

Lemoine, J. (1986). *Shamanism in the context of H'mong resettlement.* In G.L. Hendricks, B.T. Downing, & A.S. Deinhard (Eds.), *The H'mong in transition* (pp. 82–98). New York: Center for Migration Studies.

McGoldrick, M., Pearce, J., & Giordana, J. (1982). *Ethnicity and family therapy.* New York: Guilford Press.

Minnuchin, S. (1974). *Families and family therapy.* Cambridge, MA: Harvard University Press.

Minnuchin, S., & Fishman, C. (1981). *Family therapy techniques.* Cambridge, MA: Harvard University Press.

Parloff, M., Waskow, L., & Wolf, B. (1978). Research on therapist variables in relation to process and outcome. In S. Garfield & A. Bergin (Eds.), *Handbook of psychotherapy and development* (pp. 82–102). New York: Wiley.

Pedersen, P. (1987, January). Ten assumptions of cultural bias in counseling. *Journal of Multicultural Counseling and Development,* 16–23.

Pedersen, P. (1988). *A handbook for developing multicultural awareness.* Alexandria, VA: American Association for Counseling and Development.

Peoples, V., & Dell, D. (1975). Black and White student preferences for counselor roles. *Journal of Counseling Psychology, 22,* 234–259.

Robinson, J. (1989, July). Clinical treatment of Black families: Issues and strategies. *Social Work,* 323–328.

Sue, D.W., & Sue, D. (1990). *Counseling the culturally different: Theory and practice* (2nd ed.). New York: Wiley.

Sullivan, T., Thompson, K., Wright, R., Gross, G., & Spady, D. (1980). *Social problems.* New York: Wiley.

Tung, T. (1980). *Understanding the differences between Asian and Western concepts of mental health and illness.* Unpublished manuscript.

Vargas, L., & Koss-Chioino, L. (Eds.). (1992). *Working with culture.* San Francisco: Jossey-Bass.

Willis, D., Dobrec, A., & Sipes, D. (1992). Treating American Indian victims of abuse and molestation. In L. Vargas & L. Koss-Chioino (Eds.), *Working with culture* (pp. 276–299). San Francisco: Jossey-Bass.

Zastrow, C. (1993). *Introduction to social work and social welfare.* Pacific Grove, CA: Brooks/Cole.

13 Aftercare Programming

Steven E. Mussack
Mark S. Carich

R esearch clearly supports aftercare as a critical element in helping offenders maintain recovery (Carich,1991a; Carich & Stone, 1993; Green, 1995; Ingersoll & Patton, 1990; Steele, 1988). The purpose of this chapter is to discuss aftercare as a component of sexual offender treatment in both inpatient and outpatient settings. Components, methods of application, rationales, and specific goals are offered for consideration from a utilitarian, practitioner-oriented perspective. Similarities and differences between aftercare programming developed for post-inpatient treatment and post–community-based treatment are considered. Potential outcome measures, both objective and subjective, are offered. The components discussed are not intended to limit the practitioner. They are offered to provide a foundation or guidelines for the development and maintenance of aftercare as part of an effective sexual offender treatment program.

WHAT IS AFTERCARE?
(There's more? I thought you said I was done.)

Aftercare is a designated period of continued support and supervision after an offender's formal participation in therapy is completed. It is a transitional therapeutic process. A primary focus is on the maintenance of changes made during the active phase of sexual offender therapy rather than the development of new life changes.

The primary goal of aftercare is to ensure an offender's continued success in maintaining himself or herself safely within the community. Support and monitoring are provided at reduced levels of intensity and frequency from those provided during active therapy. Clients are encouraged to use and expand in an increasingly independent manner the support networks and life skills developed during therapy. Throughout the course of aftercare, community-based professional support and monitoring remain immediately available to constructively intervene when behavioral lapses or other difficulties occur.

Aftercare programming is generally based on several assumptions, including:

1. Sexual offenders have the potential to relapse into offending or reengage in sexual offense behaviors after treatment (Green, 1995; Laws, 1989, 1995; Schwartz & Cellini, 1995).

2. Excessive use of cognitive distortions, lack of empathy, self-centeredness, destructive entitlement beliefs, poor impulse control, and dysfunctional relationships are common characteristics in the lives of sexual offenders (Carich & Adkerson, 1995). Coping with and ameliorating the destructive influences of these characteristics are an important focus in both active treatment and aftercare.

3. Offenders frequently engage in multiple deviancies, ranging from sexual harassment, voyeurism, exhibitionism, and pedophilia to rape and serial murder (Abel, Becker, Cunningham-Rathner, Mittelman, & Rouleau, 1988; Carich & Adkerson, 1995). They also vary in their levels of obsession and compulsion focused on sexually deviant behavior. The presence of other abnormal psychological variables also varies. The clinician must consider all these factors when developing an aftercare plan.

4. Offenders retain the potential for reoffense even though they have developed a new lifestyle based on nonoffending behaviors (Laws, 1989; Thompson, 1989).

5. There is no known "cure," defined as a permanent absence of potential for committing sexually deviant acts, for sexual offenders (George & Marlatt, 1989). Ongoing safety is attained through the effective maintenance of self-control strategies and support networks developed during the course of treatment.

6. Treated offenders, especially those who have been released from incarceration, have been dependent on a highly structured environment and therefore need to be slowly weaned toward independence. This wean-ing process enhances the likelihood of long-term reoffense prevention.

7. For aftercare to be effective, there must be ongoing cooperation and communication among all components of the offender's support and intervention network (Carich, 1991b; Green, 1988, 1995).

AFTERCARE FOR INPATIENT OFFENDERS
(It's a big bad world out there)

Aftercare for sexual offenders making the transition from inpatient to outpatient care is more complex and intensive and potentially more lengthy than aftercare for offenders treated in outpatient settings. Residential clients have been engaged in an intensive treatment process that surrounds them with other individuals who are all engaged in similar treatment activities. Essentially, they have been living in a much less diversified and much more regimented culture than is available to them when they return to the community. The diversity and complexity of choices available can at first be overwhelming.

Many inpatient treatment programs require offenders to begin developing their support networks prior to leaving treatment. But it is often necessary for such clients to begin developing support networks as part of their relapse prevention plan only after being released to the community. This process is generally part of the active treatment phase for offenders treated in outpatient settings.

These formerly incarcerated offenders or residentially treated abusers face the difficult and necessary process of learning to interact in "real-life" situations while continuing to employ the skills they have rehearsed in a relatively protected, highly supportive inpatient treatment setting. They must now begin to interact with people who are not educated or trained in the skills the offender has developed and who either have no clue about the importance of avoiding high-risk situations or actively invite the offender to lapse into old, unhealthy patterns. Follow-up by the treating agency to ensure that effective aftercare programming is established is essential. Without adequate follow-up, offenders tend to falter (Green, 1988, 1995; Steele, 1988). These offenders quickly discover that there are many influences in the community that are not supportive of their continued success and safety.

Transition into the community can result in "culture shock." More intensive aftercare support and supervision are needed initially, regardless of the level of preparation, for offenders treated as inpatients compared with those treated as outpatients. In its early stages, this intensity may be similar to the levels of support and supervision offered to clients first entering outpatient treatment. The focus of such intensity is to aid the offender in successfully applying all he or she has learned in the controlled inpatient setting in an essentially hostile and less supportive community environment. Once the client has successfully made the transition to community living, the tasks common to outpatient aftercare can be addressed.

Placement in a transitional residential facility, such as a halfway house, is helpful and is often needed by offenders treated in inpatient programs. This is particularly true for offenders with histories of significant sexually abusive pathology, those who have demonstrated histories of a broad range of antisocial and narcissistic behaviors, or those entering the community with no social ties and no support network. Many offenders reentering the community need a more structured environment than independent living can provide. Ideally, such offenders would progress from a halfway house to supervised independent living (Carich, 1991a, 1991b; Carich & Stone, 1993).

The primary purpose of a structured residential environment is to facilitate the offender's successful integration back into society. Food and lodging, as well as emotional support, are provided while the offender obtains gainful employment, develops support networks, and works out constructive means of coping with influences to return to a destructive lifestyle (Carich, 1991a, 1991b, 1992). Offenders enter into a behavioral contract that focuses on general rules

of the house, their behavior within the community, and involvement in various treatment and/or aftercare services. Supervision and monitoring are accomplished through a variety of means, including direct supervision, intermittent checks on the offender's whereabouts by supervising corrections officers or house staff, buddy systems, telephone check-ins, curfews, daily activity logs completed by the offender and monitored by polygraph, urinalysis and Breathalyzer testing to monitor for drug or alcohol use, and other measures (Carich, 1991a, 1992). Consequences for failure to follow behavioral contracts can range from verbal reprimand through restriction of movements within the community to reincarceration.

The halfway house staff becomes an integral component of aftercare for clients who are provided such services. Integration of all aftercare services through active, ongoing communication is essential. Specially trained halfway house managers may be best suited to coordinate the aftercare programming. It is the aftercare provider's responsibility to initiate and facilitate contact among halfway house staff, parole agents, other treating agents or agencies, and other members of the offender's relapse prevention network, including family, friends, religious advisers, and employers.

Finally, when considering the aftercare needs of offenders transferred from inpatient to outpatient settings, the receiving program must complete a thorough assessment of the client's progress in treatment (Carich, 1999). There are many instances in which an inpatient program releases an offender into the community prior to the completion of treatment. There are multiple reasons for such decisions, many of which are due to overcrowding and economic considerations. As part of this assessment, the outpatient therapist needs to have access to a treatment summary and recommendations from the transferring program, as well as complete an entry-phase evaluation. It may be necessary to simply enter the transferring offender in active outpatient treatment rather than moving him or her directly to aftercare. Taking care to conduct a careful assessment with any transferring client is strongly recommended.

Clients in outpatient treatment are generally expected to have developed and successfully used a relapse prevention network prior to making the transition to aftercare. They face fewer but still significant challenges as they transfer into the aftercare phase of their therapy program.

MAKING THE TRANSITION INTO AFTERCARE
(It ain't over until the therapist, parole officer, client, and support network sing)

An important treatment consideration is the message the offender is given by the treating agency or professional when moving into the aftercare phase of treatment. Many programs, including the CHOICES program, used the term "graduation" or "completion" to refer to an offender's completion of the active phase of treatment. Offenders reported that they felt "done" with treatment when they were told that they had "graduated" or "completed" treatment. Thus, when faced with aftercare, offenders often felt frustration or resentment, which led to increased lapses, relapses, lack of compliance, and higher dropout rates during aftercare. Defining the offender's graduation or completion of the treatment program as including the completion of aftercare can clarify expectations. CHOICES now provides clients with a certificate of "transition" upon entering aftercare and a subsequent certificate of "completion" once the client has successfully completed one year of aftercare. This revised procedure has reduced client frustration and confusion about program completion requirements and has decreased the frequency of lapses and relapses during the aftercare phase of treatment. Recovery is emphasized as a lifelong process, not something that ends with "graduation." Many offenders need to remain in some form of ongoing treatment.

LAPSES AND RELAPSES
(Better now than later)

Identifying areas of lapse and relapse is another goal of aftercare. A lapse is defined as an offender's failure to recognize that he or she has entered into the assault cycle and is maintaining cognitive distortions in the service of continuing the cycle. A lapse can be thought of as any slide or movement toward relapse. A relapse is defined as the culmination of a series of thoughts, feelings, and behaviors that results in the offender, another person, or both, experiencing either sexual or nonsexual harm.

Aftercare is a time of difficulties and mistakes for offenders. It is a time when they may become less vigilant or begin to withdraw from their support networks, trying to make it "on their own." Recognizing lapses and preventing relapses are important factors in the process of safely stabilizing offenders within the community. After the completion of active treatment, identifying situations in which offenders are still prone to lapse or relapse is extremely important. Areas of potential risk that were not adequately addressed during active treatment can be identified. This process creates the opportunity to further strengthen offenders' resources in the identified areas and to increase the likelihood of continued personal and community safety. During nonsexual lapses and relapses, offenders' thoughts, feelings, and actions often mirror sexual offense patterns. Aftercare creates the opportunity for lapses and relapses to occur due to the decrease in support and supervision. Sufficient monitoring and support must be available, however, to identify when such lapses and relapses occur and to help offenders refrain from progressing to sexual assault.

Lapses, or failure to recognize "red flags," can occur in the lives of even the best-prepared offenders. They may return to a level of secretiveness about these events as a result of multiple variables: fear of disappointing the therapist, family members, probation or parole officers, or others; fear of sanction; desire to continue a deviant lifestyle; shame, guilt, or confusion; or concern that therapy may be prolonged if they report the events.

Aftercare is a time of polishing and solidifying the safety, support, nondestructive coping, and self-monitoring strategies developed by offenders during active therapy. It is also a time to clarify areas needing further therapeutic focus. Identifying these areas of concern — situations that occur prior to sexual reoffense and during aftercare — further clarifies environmental triggers in offenders' assault cycles. Offenders can then get help in developing additional constructive coping strategies to increase the likelihood of long-term safety.

SUPPORT NETWORKS
(Even the Lone Ranger had Tonto)

Aftercare is a time of extricating the offender from the therapeutic and legal systems in a safe, systematic, monitored, and structured manner. It is a time of ensuring that each client has met the goal of developing a positive and trustworthy support system whose members are aware of the abuser's sexual assault history and cycle. Members of this support system must be both willing and trusted to confront the offender when they observe lapses or relapses. They need to be available in all settings in which the offender functions. Ultimately, they need to be part of a network the offender has developed and included in his or her therapeutic process. It is this network that takes over when aftercare ends.

Clients often struggle with the development of such a support system or with the desire to become less involved in and dependent on it as they move through aftercare. Reinforcing the importance of this network through the inclusion of its members directly in the aftercare process is extremely important. Bringing these individuals directly into the therapeutic setting and establishing specific roles for them in supporting the offender can be invaluable. Providing opportunities for supported interaction and identifying specific tasks that each member of

the offender's support network can perform will help the offender maintain a safe, abuse-free lifestyle.

SANCTIONS AND SUPPORT
(I can [almost] do it by myself)

Sanctions and support are ongoing components of any aftercare program. The availability of sanctions is clearly a motivating factor for the majority of sexual offenders during treatment. Sanctions serve at least three functions: as punishment for wrongdoing, to motivate the offender to change currently harmful behaviors to avoid implementation of the sanction, and to motivate the offender to develop and display specific behaviors to avoid implementation of the sanction.

One important component of sexual abuser treatment is immediately available sanctions. Reducing the abuser's dependence on external sanctions and increasing his or her use of internal controls is an important goal of therapy. Ultimately, within the therapeutic context, another goal of aftercare is to further reduce an abuser's potential dependence on external sanctions as a method of behavioral control. Significant focus is placed on the abuser's development of internalized controls. These new internalized controls are maintained through the abuser's interaction with a support network and a desire to constructively maintain self-respect and the respect of others.

A common goal of therapy is the development of self-respect as an internal guide to help abusers prevent further abuse by recognizing potential risk situations. It is hoped that the experience of self-respect becomes self-reinforcing and is maintained through consistently responsible, accountable, nonabusive behaviors. Aftercare presents many additional opportunities for abusers to experience and identify situations in which they are likely to act or react in ways that damage their self-respect. Monitoring the emergence of such situations and encouraging the development of more self-respecting alternatives are also goals of aftercare.

The goal of using and reinforcing self-respect as an internal motivating force is not realistic for some offenders. These offenders seem to exhibit behavioral control only through their continued heightened awareness of potential sanctions. In such cases, a goal of aftercare is to aid the offender in establishing a support network that will work to remind him or her of potential sanctions.

In all cases, the goals of offender and community safety are best met when both support and sanctions are provided from a place of modeling respect. The offender may make decisions to lapse or relapse at any point. These choices are not a direct affront to either the therapist or the parole or probation officer. They are self-destructive actions that are also destructive to others, and they may occur during both active treatment and aftercare.

By the time an offender reaches aftercare, it is hoped that the offender will maintain appropriate behavior through his or her focus on self-respect. Lapses in this focus need to be dealt with by modeling respectful approaches during interactions with the offender. A return to active therapy to more thoroughly address the issue is warranted should an offender exhibit behaviors that necessitate more severe sanctions.

MONITORING OF THE OFFENDER (Don't you trust me yet?)

Monitoring strategies can take two forms: external and internal (for a specific, detailed explanation of supervision of sex offenders, see Cumming & Buell, 1997).

EXTERNAL MONITORING

External monitoring strategies involve supervision from elements or sources outside the individual offender. These sources can include the parole or probation officer, halfway house staff, family members, employers, friends, and thera-

pists. In addition, psychophysiological assessments may provide a dimension of external monitoring (Carich, 1991a, 1992; Cumming & Buell, 1997).

Two commonly used psychophysiological assessment instruments are the polygraph (lie detector) and the penile plethysmograph. The photo-plethysmograph is employed as an assessment instrument for women but has received much less clinical focus than its counterpart for males.

The polygraph is a biofeedback device used to monitor changes in specific physiological responses: heart rate, blood pressure, respiration, and galvanic skin response. These responses are recorded graphically on a continuous strip of paper while an individual is asked questions that can be answered with a yes or no response. A trained examiner can assess, with a significant degree of certainty, whether the client's response is truthful or deceptive. Clearly, when the questions focus on whether an offender is maintaining himself or herself safely within the community, this assessment device can be invaluable in promoting safety and validating an offender's positive efforts.

Polygraph assessments are usually conducted semiannually, at a minimum, in programs that employ this technology. They are used both to ensure that an offender has made full disclosure of all sexually deviant history and to validate that the offender is conducting himself or herself safely within the community. During aftercare, a continued pattern of semiannual assessments can continue to serve a constructive purpose.

The penile plethysmograph is a biofeedback device that provides information about a male's sexual arousal and interest response (Murphy & Barbaree, 1994; Roys & Roys, 1999). Information is gathered through the direct measurement of changes in the circumference of the client's penis as he is exposed to potentially sexually arousing pictures, videos, or audiotapes depicting a variety of deviant and nondeviant sexual activities. The change in penile circumference is measured by having the client place either a mercury-in-rubber strain gauge or a Barlow gauge around his penis while sitting in a private room. The gauge is then attached to a remote instrument that records changes in gauge size on a continuous strip of graph paper. As each stimulus is presented, a technician records the stimulus on the graph paper, and the relative level of sexual arousal response to a specific stimulus can be assessed.

For female offenders, the photo-plethysmograph can be employed to obtain similar data. The female client is placed in a similar setting and is asked to place a device, approximately the size of a tampon, in her vaginal canal. This device is remotely connected to the plethysmograph and measures changes in vasoconstriction (blood flow) in the blood vessels of her vaginal canal. These changes measure female sexual arousal response, which is then recorded on a continuous strip of graph paper. Stimuli are presented in the same formats as with male clients, and the data can be assessed to determine the types of sexual activity depicted by the stimuli that elicited the greatest sexual arousal response.

When plethysmographic assessment technology is available in a program, it is frequently part of an initial assessment battery used to develop a treatment plan. Specific behavioral interventions can be initiated to aid the client in reducing sexual responses to deviant stimuli when it is determined that he or she experiences a significant deviant sexual arousal response. The plethysmograph can then be utilized to measure changes in sexual arousal and interest response over time to evaluate the effectiveness of behavioral interventions. It is both valuable and important to continue such assessments at 3-, 6-, or 12-month intervals, after the completion of behavioral therapy to ensure that the gains made remain stable over time. Continuation of such assessments during aftercare can help determine the ongoing effectiveness of the offender's deviant sexual arousal control efforts as therapeutic contact and support decrease. Then behavioral interventions can be reinstituted, if needed, to aid the offender in living successfully and safely within the community. It is important to consider that no psychophysiological assessment is foolproof, so it should not be relied on in the face of conflicting information.

As stated earlier, one goal of aftercare is to enhance the likelihood that an offender has attained sufficient information, skills, and desire to interact safely within the community after aftercare. At the aftercare stage, it is hoped that each of these tools will validate the offender's ongoing gains rather than the need for further intervention. Aftercare has also served its purpose if a need for further intervention is assessed and the identified need receives appropriate therapeutic focus.

INTERNAL MONITORING

Internal monitoring refers to the abuser's development of effective self-monitoring skills or, as one offender described it, "I need to become my own probation officer and therapist." Both active treatment and aftercare have goals of aiding the sexual abuser in developing effective self-monitoring strategies. Aftercare presents a supported and supervised opportunity for the offender, therapist, and probation or parole officer to assess the effectiveness of those skills prior to the offender's applying them with full independence.

Self-monitoring is often enhanced if it is coupled with some form of structure or ritual. Several useful strategies include writing autobiographies, maintaining journals, and tracking deviant urges and fantasies (Bays & Freeman-Longo, 1989; Bays, Freeman-Longo, & Hildebran, 1990; Carich & Stone, 1993, 1996; MacDonald & Pithers, 1989; Pithers, 1990).

Offenders are frequently required to complete an autobiography during active treatment (Long, Wuesthoff, & Pithers, 1989). Offenders are instructed to write in detail about significant life events, including past traumas, past offenses, triggering events, high-risk situations and factors, and offense behaviors. They are also told to describe specific details about offense behaviors, including personal thoughts, perceptions, and feelings during their offenses. Autobiographies provide information concerning abuser defenses, triggering events, patterns of abuse, and lapse and relapse patterns. Additionally, information about an abuser's early history, which can affect both treatment and aftercare decisions, can be obtained. During aftercare, continuation, repetition, or review of this process can assist the abuser in remaining cognizant of both the negative events of his or her past and the positive changes that are occurring now. Carich and Stone (1996) also developed a "future autobiography" in which the abuser writes about his or her history, including coping strategies employed and the risk of reoffense. The abuser then specifically identifies new coping strategies he or she has developed in treatment and how these strategies will be employed in relationships in the future.

Journals and diaries are other types of self-monitoring methods that can provide ongoing information concerning an offender's current state and level of functioning (Bays, et al., 1990; Schwartz & Cellini, 1988, 1995). Entries are made describing triggering events (high- and low-risk situations, interpersonal conflicts), feelings, thoughts, behaviors, urges, and fantasies. Tracking deviant fantasies, thoughts, and behaviors can occur as part of keeping a journal or diary. Details such as time, place, location, and mood can be important and useful in aiding the offender in maintaining effective, safe coping strategies.

MEDICATION
(There are no magic bullets)

Medroxyprogesterone acetate, commonly called Depo-Provera, Provera, or MPA, has been found to be effective in aiding offenders who struggle with extremely frequent, intrusive sexual fantasies coupled with compulsive or impulsive acting out. Originally developed as a method of birth control, this drug was later used to temporarily stop the developmental progression in young females who were experiencing the early onset of secondary sexual characteristics. It is also used to mitigate the effects of menopause. Provera is often administered intramuscularly, although oral dosage is possible. Its effect in males is to reduce testosterone levels. This decrease is often found to result in a reduction in the intensity of sexual urges, which can help the offender focus on cognitive-behavioral components and other treatment tasks. When given in appropriate dosage levels, Provera will not prevent sexual functioning in males. Cyproterone acetate, a chemical relative of Provera, has also been used to treat offenders, with similar effects.

Prozac, Zoloft, and Paxil are part of a newer class of commonly prescribed antidepressants called selective serotonin reuptake inhibitors. Members of this drug family have also been used in the treatment of obsessive-compulsive disorders with some success. Some sexual offenders whose offense behaviors have obsessive-compulsive qualities have gotten relief from their feelings of sexual compulsion through the use of Prozac or similar-acting antidepressants (Kafka, personal communication, 1995).

The medications discussed in this section are not meant to be an exhaustive list. The purpose here is to highlight the importance of considering a variety of interventions and coordinating the most effective resources when developing an aftercare plan. The use of medications is discussed as a part of the focus on aftercare because it may be necessary to continue them once their administration is started during active therapy. There are risks of side effects with each of these medications, and their administration should be monitored by a physician familiar with their application to sexual offender populations. Sudden discontinuance of any prescribed medication is not recommended unless ordered by the prescribing physician. Administration of such medications for the purpose of assisting a sexual offender in controlling deviant behaviors and urges is recommended only with appropriate psychotherapeutic support.

AFTERCARE METHODS
(There are many roads to Mecca)

Generally recommended and preferred methods of sexual offender treatment involve group therapy supplemented with individual and, when possible, family therapy components. Aftercare, as an extension of treatment, functions within these same modalities. Typically, an offender is involved in a specific aftercare group, or the offender continues to attend the therapy group he or she attended prior to making the transition, but on a less frequent basis. During aftercare, the frequency of therapeutic contact is often individually contracted. A rule of thumb for offenders in community-based treatment is to begin by reducing the frequency of contacts by no more than 50 percent. Consideration of any further reduction in the frequency of therapeutic contact can be made over time. Involvement of all supportive and monitoring resources in decision making is still of paramount importance. Continuation of polygraph and plethysmograph assessments, when available, is recommended.

As part of their aftercare upon release to the community, formerly incarcerated offenders often need direct involvement in an ongoing community-based therapy program consisting of weekly group therapy with individual and/or family therapy at biweekly intervals. As previously noted, aftercare for such offenders often resembles the ongoing therapy provided to offenders who have been treated on an outpatient basis throughout their therapy, because of their need to develop a functioning support network as well as to become self-supporting. These offenders often need additional social skill building and support for such issues as reentering the community, maintaining a sense of self-worth, coping with loneliness and boredom, seeking employment, and developing new relationships and leisure activities. These offenders will face risk factors for which they could only mentally prepare while incarcerated. Much of the skill building that takes place in institutional programs will need further refinement and reinforcement upon the offender's release into the community.

It is also important to remember that many institutional programs now focus on helping an offender develop sufficient safety strategies and skills so that he or she can effectively and safely participate in a community-based program, rather than focusing on completion of a thorough sexual offender treatment program. Still, the offender may arrive in the community with the impression that he or she has completed treatment rather than simply completed a process that has readied him or her to complete treatment at a community level. Thus, as previously stated, a thorough assessment of a formerly incarcerated offender is strongly recommended upon referral for aftercare in a community-based setting.

Areas of assessment for post-incarceration aftercare candidates are similar to those identified in the chapter on assessment in this handbook. Carich (1999) uses 15 factors of recovery. These and additional issues to be assessed include:

- awareness of offense cycle, with specific lapse and relapse prevention alternatives

- communications skills and/or deficits and interpersonal issues

- employment skills and deficits

- level of employment of cognitive distortions and responsibility issues

- difficulties with authority figures and other key issues

- overall presence of antisocial and other personality disorder characteristics

- current support network and its members' availability to participate in aftercare treatment.

- substance abuse history and need for specialized support such as Narcotics Anonymous, Alcoholics Anonymous, or more direct substance abuse treatment

- levels of deviant sexual arousal and need for specific behavioral interventions (when ascertainable)

- completion of a disclosure polygraph (when needed and available)

- need for further academic training

- level of denial and responsibility

- presence of psychiatric disturbance

- presence of ongoing medical concerns or need for medication management

- current and planned living arrangements

- development of specific risk-management plans for living in the community and the viability of such plans

- nature and type of therapeutic interventions the offender has participated in, along with the offender's level of participation and success

- history of personal victimization, degree to which this issue has been addressed in previous treatment, and presence of any posttraumatic stress symptoms that may be exacerbated by contacts with specific individuals or situations in the community

- presence of any other psychological disorders that need to be a focus of intervention

- level of deviant sexual arousal and arousal management skills

Many contemporary treatment and aftercare programs have a cognitive-behavioral focus, with the inclusion of a relapse prevention model. It is important to clarify with formerly incarcerated clients the type of treatment they have had. If their previous programs followed models that are significantly different from the community-based programs they will be entering, the therapist should take the time to understand the previous models and to educate the offenders about the models of intervention in the groups they will be joining.

It is important to emphasize the value of familial involvement in both active treatment and aftercare phases of sexual offender therapy. The success of the relapse prevention model has demonstrated the importance of the development of support networks as part of therapy and aftercare. Familial involvement can be a major contributor to sexual offenders' success in treatment, as well as to the maintenance of

long-term safety. Mussack (1994 & 1995), in a 20-month study, found markedly reduced treatment dropout rates for offenders whose family members were engaged in their community-based treatment. Approximately 86 percent of the offenders in treatment who had no family member involvement dropped out of treatment, compared with a 35 percent dropout rate for offenders whose family members were involved in their therapy.

GRADUATION AND DISCHARGE (Is it ever safe to quit?)

It is recommended that aftercare continue for a minimum of one year after transition. There are many "hard-core" sexual offenders (e.g., those with significant personality disorders or ongoing, inadequately controlled deviant sexual obsessions or compulsions) who need to remain in aftercare programming for the rest of their lives. Sexually sadistic offenders and offenders who have engaged in sexual or serial murder fall into this category. The decision to terminate or graduate a client from aftercare must be based on multiple considerations that are examined by several resources. Criteria to consider include:

- regular attendance at aftercare sessions

- regular attendance at meetings with a parole or probation officer

- maintenance of behaviors that were part of the decision criteria to move the client into aftercare

- recognition of lapses or relapses, either through self-observation or through the observation of others, with immediate efforts to use healthy coping strategies

- maintenance of the support network

- maintenance of stability within the community in areas of employment, education, relationship, and family

- two or more consecutive plethysmograph assessments indicating no significant deviant sexual arousal and interest response[1]

- two or more consecutive polygraph assessments (when such assessments are part of the treatment program) with no significant deceptive responses

- agreement among therapist, parole or probation officer, offender, and members of the support network that termination is appropriate

A CONTINUUM OF CARE

Sexual offender treatment and recovery are best viewed as part of a continuum ranging from intensive treatment through aftercare and lifelong maintenance.

Aftercare is a necessary component of any sexual offender treatment program. Failure to provide aftercare increases the likelihood that lapses and relapses will go unattended and progress in intensity. Therapy is an intensive process that encourages a significant amount of offender dependence on both sanctions and support. Aftercare provides a period of "decompression" during which the offender is monitored with decreasing frequency and intensity without full withdrawal of these supportive resources. It is a period when offenders begin to "kick up their heels" as they reexperience freedom, with all its attendant invitations to return to old behaviors.

Aftercare is also a time when lapses and relapses can be expected. Support and monitoring are maintained at levels that can "catch" such lapses and relapses before sexual harm is done to another human being. It is hoped that issues that were either not recognized in active therapy

or given insufficient focus will present during aftercare. This timing creates an opportunity to aid the offender in establishing additional healthy alternatives and further strengthen his or her resources in the development and maintenance of a nonabusive and fulfilling lifestyle.

The type and intensity of aftercare programming need to be designed to meet the specific needs of the individual offender. Assessing each offender's level of risk to reoffend and ongoing needs is part of effective aftercare planning. Some offenders need more structured and intensive care than others. The level of aftercare support needed depends on the offender's pathology, the presence of abnormal psychopathology, the type of treatment provided to the offender, and the offender's skills, resources, and commitment to remaining nonabusive.

REFERENCES

Abel, G., Becker, J., Cunningham-Rathner, J., Mittelman, M. & Rouleau, J. (1988). Multiple paraphiliac diagnoses among sex offenders. *Bulletin of the American Academy of Psychiatry and the Law,* 16, 153–168.
Bays, L., & Freeman-Longo, R. (1989). *Why did I do it again? Understanding my cycle of problem behaviors.* Orwell, VT: Safer Society Press.
Bays, L., Freeman-Longo, R., & Hildebran, D. (1990). *How can I stop? Breaking my deviant cycle.* Orwell, VT: Safer Society Press.
Carich, M.S. (1991a). Aftercare programs: An essential element for post-incarcerated sex offenders. *INMAS Newsletter,* 4(1), 15–18.
Carich, M.S. (1991b). Some notes on individualized aftercare programming. *INMAS Newsletter,* 4(2), 9–11.
Carich, M.S. (1992). Developing a sex offender aftercare program. *INMAS Newsletter,* 6(1), 12–13.
Carich, M.S. (1999). Evaluation of recovery: 15 common factors or elements and 15-factor sex offender recovery scale. In M. Calder (Ed.), *Assessing risk in adult males who sexually abuse children* (pp. 279–287). Dorset, England: Russell House.
Carich, M.S., & Adkerson, D. (1995). *Adult sexual offender assessment packet.* Brandon, VT: Safer Society Press.

[†] It should be noted that some offenders have difficulty responding to any behavioral interventions focused on reducing deviant sexual arousal and interest response and thus are not able to meet this criterion for termination. In such cases, consistent maintenance of the other criteria should be depended on, with additional focus on the offender's use of avoidance strategies.

Carich, M.S., & Stone, M. (Eds.). (1993). *Offender relapse prevention*. Chicago: Adler School of Professional Psychology.

Carich, M.S., & Stone, M. (1996). *Sex offender relapse intervention workbook*. Chicago: Adler School of Professional Psychology.

Cumming, G., & Buell, M. (1997). *Supervision of the sex offender*. Brandon, VT: Safer Society Press.

George, W.H., & Marlatt, G.A. (1989). Introduction. In D.R. Laws (Ed.), *Relapse prevention with sex offenders* (pp. 1–31). New York: Guilford Press.

Green, R. (1988). Community management of sex offenders. In B.K. Schwartz & H. Cellini (Eds.), *A practitioner's guide to treating the incarcerated male sex offender: Breaking the cycle of sexual abuse* (pp. 141–145). Washington, DC: NIC.

Green, R. (1995). Community management of sex offenders. In B.K. Schwartz & H.R. Cellini (Eds.), *The sex offender: Corrections, treatment, and legal practice* (pp. 21-1–21-8). Kingston, NJ: Civic Research Institute.

Ingersoll, S.L., & Patton, S.O. (1990). *Treating perpetrators of sexual abuse*. Lexington, MA: Lexington Books.

Laws, D.R. (Ed.). (1989). *Relapse prevention with sex offenders*. New York: Guilford Press.

Laws, D.R. (1995). Central elements in relapse prevention procedures with sex offenders. *Psychology, Crime and Law, 2*, 41–53.

Long, D.J., Wuesthoff, A., & Pithers, W.S. (1989). Use of autobiographies in the assessment and treatment of sex offenders. In D.R. Laws (Ed.), *Relapse prevention with sex offenders* (pp. 85–95). New York: Guilford Press.

MacDonald, R.K., & Pithers, W.D. (1989). Self-monitoring to identify high-risk situations. In D.R. Laws (Ed.), *Relapse prevention with sex offenders* (pp. 96–104). New York: Guilford Press.

Murphy, W.D., & Barbaree, H.E. (1994). *Assessment of sex offenders by measure of erectile response: Psychometric properties and decision making*. Brandon, VT: Safer Society Press.

Murphy, W.D., Barbaree, H., & Eccles, A. (1991). Early onset and deviant sexuality in child molesters. *Journal of Interpersonal Violence, 6*, 323–336.

Mussack, S. (1994 & 1995). *The impact of family involvement on sexual offender treatment*. Papers presented at Association for the Treatment of Sexual Abusers National Treatment and Research Conferences, San Francisco, 1994, and New Orleans, 1995.

Pithers, W.D. (1990). Relapse prevention with sexual aggressors: A method of maintaining therapeutic gain and enhancing external supervision. In W.L. Marshall, D.R. Laws, & H.E. Barbaree (Eds.), *Handbook of sexual assault: Issues, theories, and treatment of the offender* (pp. 343–361). New York: Plenum Press.

Roys, D.T., & Roys, R. (1999). *Protocol for phallometric assessment: A clinician's guide* (2nd ed.). Brandon, VT: Safer Society Press.

Schwartz, B.K., & Cellini, H.R. (Eds.). (1988). *A practitioner's guide to treating the incarcerated male sex offender: Breaking the cycle of sexual abuse*. Washington, DC: NIC.

Schwartz, B.K., & Cellini, H.R. (Eds.). (1995). *The sex offender: Corrections, treatment, and legal practice*. Kingston, NJ: Civic Research Institute.

Steele, N. (1988). Aftercare treatment programs. In B.K. Schwartz & H.R. Cellini (Eds.), *A practitioner's guide to treating the incarcerated male sex offender: Breaking the cycle of sexual abuse* (pp. 117–122). Washington, DC: NIC.

Thompson, K.J. (1989). Lifestyle interventions: Promoting positive addictions. In D.R. Laws (Ed.), *Relapse prevention with sex offenders* (pp. 219–226). New York: Guilford Press.

14 Perspectives on the Future

Steven E. Mussack
Mark S. Carich

The primary purpose of this book is to provide an overview of contemporary sex offender treatment, along with specific applications and methods for assessment, treatment, and aftercare. Program development and maintenance, cultural issues, family involvement, and developmental disabilities are areas that require special concern if effective intervention is to occur.

Sexual offender assessment, treatment, and aftercare are continually interrelated. Effective treatment begins with the completion of a comprehensive assessment. The initial assessment provides the foundation for ongoing assessments of risk, amenability, and progress. Aftercare begins when sufficient progress has been made in treatment, providing the opportunity to assess the offender's ability to engage in effective self-maintenance, as well as the need for additional treatment.

Family and community involvement and the development of additional resources in an offender's relapse prevention network are extremely important if treatment is to remain effective in the long term. Sexual deviancy is not curable, and the risk of reoffending increases without extensive external support for the offender.

It is important that all interventions model the behaviors offenders need to reduce the risk of relapse. Sexual offender treatment is extremely demanding on both the offender and the therapist. Therapists need to focus on maintaining effective self-care and making themselves available to members of the support network and coworkers if they are to remain effective.

The effectiveness of sex offender treatment has been supported throughout the literature (Barbaree, Marshall, & Hudson, 1993; Greer & Stuart, 1983; Knopp, 1984; Laws, 1989; Marshall, Laws, & Barbaree, 1990; Ryan & Lane, 1991; Schwartz, 1988). To date, our success has been measured primarily as a reduction in the number and frequency of offenses. It remains frightening to communities that we cannot guarantee a "cure" for individuals who do such heinous, offensive acts. Sadly, when a sexual offender relapses and reoffends, the result is the sexual transgression or violation of another human being. Such violations raise moral outrage, produce a loss of hope, and heighten concerns that any effort to intervene is doomed to fail.

The future of sex offender treatment depends on our continuation of efforts to look at ourselves critically, acknowledging both what we have learned and the limitations of this knowledge. As a discipline, we are emerging from our adolescence and continually developing more innovative and effective intervention techniques, strategies, and approaches. The focus of treatment has been on helping the offender initiate and maintain recovery or gain the skills to maintain abstinence from offending (Carich, 1991, 1997, 1999).

The field of sexual offender treatment has developed organizations throughout the world that are promoting effective research and treatment. The Association for the Treatment of Sexual Abusers (ATSA) has over 2,000 members in the United States and Canada and has several state affiliates and affiliations with similar organizations around the world. ATSA published *Ethical Standards and Principles for the Management of Sexual Abusers* (1997), which provides guidelines for phallometric assessment, standards of clinical practice, and a code of ethics for its members. Similarly, the National Task Force on Juvenile Sexual Offending, representing the Adolescent Perpetrator Treatment Network, developed standards for the assessment and treatment of adolescent perpetrators (1993). In addition, the U.S. National Institute of Corrections (NIC) (Schwartz, 1988) and the Safer Society Foundation support our efforts to formulate better research. It has now become our additional responsibility to speak out about what we have accomplished, to be willing to leave our offices and go into the public arena to educate the public about our successes and what we have learned and continue to learn from our failures.

The public's fear and rancor concerning sexual crimes, especially those committed against children, appear to be on the rise. Some skeptics hold the opinion that treatment should be abolished, that incarceration is an effective solution. As a discipline, we have developed strong evidence that untreated offenders reoffend with much greater frequency than treated offenders. The solution of incarceration is clearly only temporary, and it costs more per offender than most treatment programs. This cost comparison does not take into consideration emotional and psychological costs, which will simply be delayed by the current trend toward incarceration and away from treatment. Some of our most effective treatment and research programs have been closed or downsized due to "budget considerations" or political pressure in favor of punishment. Prisons are being enlarged with the belief that incarcerating offenders of all kinds will keep the public safe.

All this concern and attention are due, in part, to our success in bringing to public awareness the enormity of the problem of sexual abuse. The attention we have gained has brought needed support and recognition for the victims of sexual abuse. For a time, it also brought support for the treatment of sexual offenders. Our mistake (if it is one) was focusing on research, learning, and direct treatment. We paid too little attention to providing ongoing information concerning our efforts and successes to the public. Some of this neglect may have been due to fear that such attention would invite further attacks.

We have much to be proud of in all that we have done and continue to do. Many who support our efforts simply need our encouragement and leadership to speak out with us. We must place before the public the research and data that provide strong support for our continued efforts. To ensure that we retain the position and respect our discipline has achieved over the past 25 years, each of us needs to contribute to an ongoing community education effort involving local communities and state and national policy makers.

The field of sexual abuser treatment represents the front line of sexual abuse prevention. We have expanded our efforts to include both early intervention and extensive family and community involvement. What we can continue to accomplish depends on our receiving continued support from one another, our communities, and our governments. We all need to add another task—continued community education—to the burdens we have accepted if we are to continue meeting our goal of making society safer.

REFERENCES

Association for the Treatment of Sexual Abusers. (1997). *Ethical standards and principles for the management of sexual abusers.* Beaverton, OR: Author.

Barbaree, H., Marshall, W., & Hudson, S. (Eds.). (1993). *The juvenile sex offender.* New York: Guilford Press.

Carich, M.S. (1991). The recovery of sex offenders: Some basic elements. *INMAS Newsletter, 4*(4), 3–6.

Carich, M.S. (1997). Towards a concept of recovery in sex offenders. *The Forum, 9*(2), 10–11.

Carich, M.S. (1999). Evaluation of recovery: 15 common factors or elements and 15-factor sex offender recovery scale. In M. Calder (Ed.), *Assessing risk in adult males who sexually abuse children* (pp. 279–287). Dorset, England: Russell House.

Greer, J., & Stuart, I. (Eds.). (1983). *The sexual aggressor: Current perspectives on treatment.* New York: Van Nostrand Reinhold.

Haaven, J., Little, R., & Petre-Miller, D. (1990). *Treating intellectually disabled sex offenders: A model residential program.* Orwell, VT: Safer Society Press.

Knopp, F.H. (1984). *Retraining adult sex offenders: Methods and models.* Syracuse, NY: Safer Society Press.

Laws, D.R. (Ed.). (1989). *Relapse prevention with sex offenders.* New York: Guilford Press.

Marshall, W., Laws, D.R., & Barbaree, H. (Eds.). (1990). *Handbook of sexual assault: Issues, theories and treatment of the offender.* New York: Plenum Press.

National Task Force on Juvenile Sexual Offending. (1993). *Juvenile and Family Court Journal, 44*(4).

Ryan, G., & Lane, S. (Eds.). (1991). *Juvenile sexual offending: Causes, consequences and corrections.* Lexington, MA: Lexington Books.

Salter, A. (1988). *Treatment of child sexual abuse.* Beverly Hills, CA: Sage.

Schwartz, B. (Ed.). (1988). *A practitioner's guide to treating the incarcerated male sex offender.* Washington, DC: NIC.

Index

Abel Assessment for Sexual Interest, 14
Abel, Gene G., 13, 66, 69, 72, 199
Abel-Becker Cognition Scale, 66–67, 69, 70
Abel Screen II, 55
Abrams, S., 61
Abstinence violation effect (AVE), 83, 93, 98
Academic history in sexual offender evaluation, 16
Acculturation, 211–12, 214
Addictions and indulgences in sexual offender evaluation, 17
Adjunctive therapy groups, 178; couples therapy, 181; multifamily groups, 178–79; multifamily psychoeducation group, 179; multifamily therapy group, 179–81; parent support group, 179; siblings and children's group, 181; spouses and significant others group, 181
Adkerson, D., 6–7, 25
Adolescent Offender Treatment Contract, 45, 127
Adolescent Perpetrator Treatment Network, 111, 238
Adult Offender Treatment Contract, 45, 127
Adult Self-Expression Scale, 199
African Americans, working with, 213, 215, 216, 218, 219, 220
Aftercare programming, 225; aftercare for inpatient offenders, 226–28; aftercare methods, 232–34; continuum of care, 235; graduation and discharge, 234–35; lapses and relapses, 228–29; making the transition into aftercare, 228; medication, 232; monitoring of the offender, 230–32; sanctions and support, 229–30; support networks, 229; what is aftercare?, 225–26
Amenability to treatment in sexual offender evaluation, assessing, 24
Ammonia-assisted biofeedback, 205
Anal sex, 156
Anchored Clinical Judgment risk assessment instrument, 24
Anger management, 152–53
Antiandrogen medications, 113
Antidepressants, 113, 232
Anxiety management techniques, 151
Armstrong, J., 152
Arousal. (*see also* Sexual arousal disorders): psychophysiological, 13–14
Arrest therapy, 106
Asian Americans, 218, 221, 222
Assertiveness training, 60, 152
Assessment: assessing denial, 54–55; common assumptions in sexual offender, 12–13; comprehensive psychosexual, 14–25; and evaluation defined, 170; and evaluation in family therapy, 170–74; of intellectually disabled sex offenders, 195–201; issues in treatment program develop-

ment, 40–41; polygraphic, 14; progress assessments, 27; of sexual interests, 13–14
Assisted covert sensitization, 107, 111
Association for the Treatment of Sexual Abusers (ATSA), 1, 4, 238
Atkinson, D., 217
Attachment styles in adults, 154, 155
Autobiographies, writing, 73, 231–32
Aversive behavioral rehearsal (ABR), 59–60
Aversive techniques for controlling sexual arousal, 108–11

Baker, N., 214–15
Bandura, A., 144
Barbaree, Howard, 53, 70, 71
Barlow gauge, 13–14
Barrett, M., 173–74
Bartholomew, K., 154, 155
Baumeister, R. F., 94
Bays, L., 19–20, 120, 121
Beal, L. S., 152
Beck Depression Scale, 199
Becker, Judith, 13, 199
Beech, A., 85
Behavioral interventions, relapse prevention and, 96–97
Biculturality, 213, 214
Biofeedback, 205
Biographical information in sexual offender evaluation, 15
Bird, S., 1, 13
Boredom therapy, 111
Bowman, S., 67
Boyd-Franklin, N., 213, 215–16, 218, 219
Bradshaw, John, 121
Bumby, K. M., 69, 70
Burgess, Ann, 121
Burt, Martha, 66
Burt Rape Myth Scale, 69, 70
Burt Scales, 68–69
Busconi, A., 79

Campbell, T., 24
Carich, M. S.: aftercare programming, 233–34; assessing amenability to treatment, 24; defining sexual abusers, 3, 4; future autobiography, 232; guidelines for interviewing sexual offenders, 25; recommendations for therapists in sexual offender treatment, 6–7; relapse prevention, 94; risk assessment, 24; sexual assault cycle, 87–88; sexual assault profile, 18–20, 238

Carkhuff, R., 217
Cattell (test), 217
Chesapeake Institute, 185–88
Child Behavior Checklist, 79
Child molesters: cognitions and implicit theories in, 94–95; indirect methods for arousal control, 113; social behavior of, 150
Child Sexual Abuse (Finkelhor), 121
Child Sexual Behavior Inventory, 79
Children: as language interpreters, 214; relapse prevention for, 79; siblings and children's group, 181; state child abuse reporting laws, 196–97; theories concerning children as sexual objects, 95; treatment in child sexual abuse cases, 175
CHOICES program, 228
Clarke Sex History Questionnaire, 54
Classical conditioning, 96
Closed Adolescent Treatment Center (CATC), Colorado, 88
Cognitive-behavioral approaches, abuser group therapy and, 4
Cognitive-behavioral interventions, relapse prevention and, 97
Cognitive-behavioral model of relapse, 80–83
Cognitive deconstruction, theory of, 94, 95
Cognitive disorders, 6
Cognitive Distortions and Immaturity (CDI) Scale, 66, 67–68, 69
Cognitive distortions in relapse prevention, 82
Cognitive distortions and restructuring in sexual abuser treatment, 65, 73–74; assessment approaches and empirical literature, 66–70; treatment approaches, 70–73
Cognitive interventions, relapse prevention and, 94–97
Cognitive restructuring, 94, 206–7
Collaborative teamwork in family therapy, 169–70
Communication skills, 159, 160
Community-based treatment: aftercare programming, 227; for intellectually disabled sex offenders, 202; sexual abusers in, 6
Composite cycle (sexual assault cycle), 90
Condom Sense (movie), 206
Confidentiality issues: in sex offender group process, 127; in treating intellectually disabled sex offenders, 196; in treatment program development, 40
Conflict resolution skills, 160
Constructive entitlement, 9
Content cues, 84
Contingency management programs, 203

Contracts: lapse, 97; treatment, 45, 127–29
Conversational skills, 96, 151–52
Coping strategies in relapse prevention, 99, 208
Correctional sex offender programs, 125
Correctional Sex Offender Treatment Agreement, 45, 127
Cosmopolitan, 47
Couples therapy, 181
Covert interventions, 96
Covert sensitization, 96, 107, 108–11, 205
Cox, W. M., 78, 79
Criminal history in sexual offender evaluation, 17
Cues, 84, 99
Culturally diverse populations, 211, 222; acculturation, 214; biculturality, 213; choice of therapist, 217; clinical assessment and diagnostic issues, 212–23; eye contact, 215; family tradition and structure, 213–14; help-seeking behavior, 215; language, 214–15; maintenance and aftercare, 223; paper-and-pencil testing, 217; pharmacology, 222–23; preassessment cultural considerations, 211–12; privacy, 216; racism, prejudice, and poverty, 219–20; ritual, 219; sexual abuse and incest, 221; social tolerance for deviance and dysfunctional behavior, 216–17; spirituality and religion, 215–16, 220–21; storytelling, 219; strategies for providing culturally sensitive and relevant sex offender treatment, 223; treatment modalities and methodologies, 217–19
Culture-fair/culture-free tests, 217
Cumming, G. F., 85
Cunningham-Rathner, J., 13
Cyproterone acetate, 232

Dangerous world implicit theory, 95
Davis, M. H., 141–42
Day, D. M., 70
Denial in sexual abusers, 47–48, 50; absolute deniers, 53; assessing denial, 54–55; aversive behavioral rehearsal, 59–60; breaking through and emerging from denial, 40, 55–56, 62; common patterns and methods of denial, 51–53; defensive denial in family therapy, 176; denial in intellectually disabled sex offenders, 194; externalizers, 52; group pressure, 59; internalizers or disassociators, 52–53; rationale for breaking through denial in therapy, 53; rationalizers, 52; relinquishing denial, 50–51; sexual abusers' denial, 48–49; specific techniques, 56–61; understanding denial, 49–50; why is denial a problem?, 48
Depo-Lupron, 222

Depo-Provera, 222, 232
Deragatis Sexual Functioning Inventory, 199
Developmental sexual experiences in sexual offender evaluation, 18
Deviant fantasies to confront distortions, 73
Diagnoses in sexual offender evaluation, 24–25
Diagnostic and Statistical Manual of Mental Disorders (DSM-IV), 3, 11, 18, 24–25
Disclosure in family therapy, 164, 168, 169
Disinhibitors, 82
Dobrec, A., 212
Doren, D., 23
Dormancy, 90
Dwyer, M., 67

Education history in sexual offender evaluation, 16
Emotional Empathy Scale, 141
Emotional loneliness, 161
Empathy Scale, 141
Empathy training, 141–42; emotional expression and recognition, 143–44; for intellectually disabled sex offenders, 206; treatment components, 142–46; victim empathy, 146; victim harm, · 144–46
Environmental controls for arousal control, 113
Ethical Standards and Principles for the Management of Sexual Abusers (ATSA), 238
Evaluation, defined, 170
Evaluation, sexual abuser, 11–12, 27; collateral interviews, 27; common assumptions in sexual offender assessment, 12–13; comprehensive psychosexual assessment, 14–25; guidelines and tactics for interviewing sexual offenders, 25–27; progress assessments, 27; specialized assessment methods, 13–14
Extended family history in sexual offender evaluation, 15
Extrafamilial abuse, 164
Eye contact, 215

Facilitators, recovering sex offenders as, 121–22
Family of origin section in sexual offender evaluation, 15
Family treatment of adult sexual abusers, 163–65; abuse of power, powerlessness, empowerment, 177; adjunctive therapy groups, 178–81; assessment and evaluation, 170–74; blurred boundaries, 178; co-therapist teams, 167–68; comprehensive agency treatment, 185–89; denial, minimization, projection of blame, 176; developing a family treatment plan, 174–78; divided

loyalty, 176–77; engaging the family, 168–70; family intervention in psychoeducational group process, 138; family reunification, 182–83; family secrets and hidden agendas, 177; family therapy for culturally diverse populations, 217–18; goals of family treatment, 175; innovative programs, 184–89; intergenerational abuse, 177–78; restoring the family to health, 189–90; sexuality, 178; social isolation, 178; therapist issues, 165–66; therapist modeling, 166–67; treatment issues and interventions, 175–78

Fantasies: masturbatory, 3; orgasmic reconditioning and masturbatory fantasy change strategy, 107–8; use of deviant fantasies to confront distortions, 73

Female-offenders, photo-plethysmograph for, 230, 231

Finkelhor, David, 121

Fischer, S., 24

Fishman, C., 218

Fiske, J., 1, 13

Fon, C., 94

Fordham, A. S., 85

Forensic Mental Health Associates, 121

Foul odors in assisted covert sensitization, 111

Four-Stage Cycle (assault cycle model), 89

Freeman-Longo, R.: assessing amenability to treatment, 24; assessments of sexual interest, 13; empathy training, 141; relapse prevention, 90; sex offender treatment, 120, 121; sexual assault profile, 19–20; treatment programs, 1, 4

Freud, Sigmund, 105

Future of sex offender treatment, 237–39

Gagnon, B., 216

Gang history in sexual offender evaluation, 17

Geographic stability in sexual offender evaluation, 16

Giaretto, H., 69

Giaretto Institute, 188–89

Giordana, J., 212

Gordon, Thomas, 121

Gore, D. K., 66, 69, 70

Graduated treatment, 228

Grapp, P., 15

Gray, A. S., 25, 79, 87

Gross, G., 216–17

Groth, A. Nicholas, 121

Group interventions to confront distortions, 71–73

Group pressure to confront denial, 59

Group process, sex abuser treatment, 117–18; family intervention, 138; group composition and assignment, 123–24; the group process, 129–31; group staffing patterns, 126–27; group structure, 124–25; importance of long-term group treatment, 138; the ongoing sex offender treatment group, 123–38; psychoeducational group process, 119–23; suspension and termination, 136–37; task groups, 126; treatment contracts, 127–29; treatment phases, 131–36; treatment philosophy and goals, 118–19

Group treatment: abuser group therapy, 4; for culturally diverse populations, 217; deniers' group, 60; for intellectually disabled sex offenders, 202; relapse prevention group process, 98–100; treatment programs and group structure, 42–44

Groups, adjunctive family, 178–81

Guberman, C., 146

Haaven, J., 3

Hanson, R. K., 23, 24

Harm reduction, 85

Harris, A. J. A., 23

Hayashino, D. S., 66

Healing the Shame that Binds You (Bradshaw), 121

Helms, J., 217

Henderson, J., 216

Henderson, M. C., 67

High risk offenders, 123–24

Ho, M., 215

Homosexuality, 216

Houchens, P., 79

Hudson, S. M., 83, 85, 86–87, 94, 95

Humbert, P.E., 60

Hypotheses, relationship, 160–61

Imagery and futuristic interventions, relapse prevention and, 97–98

Inappropriate sexual behavior vs. sexually offending behavior, 195

Incest, cultural view of, 221

Incestuous families, 173–74, 184–85, 216

Infatuation, 159

Informed consent, 114, 196–97

Initial risk assessment, 24

Instrumental hypotheses, 161

Intellectually disabled sexual abusers, 193–95, 208; assessment, 195–201; treatment, 201–8

Interpersonal Reactivity Index, 142

Interpersonal skills, 96, 205–6
Interviews: collateral, 27; guidelines and tactics for interviewing sexual offenders, 25–27; motivational interviewing, 85
Intimacy training, 154–55
Intrafamilial abuse, 163–64
IQ, 194, 197

Jealousy, 157–58
Jensen, S. H., 111
Johnston, L., 94
Jones, R., 211
Journaling: in aftercare programming, 232; daily journals in sex offender group process, 129–30; journaling techniques to confront distortions, 73; writing techniques for relapse prevention, 97
Justifications Scale, 66, 67–68, 69
Juveniles: assault cycle and juvenile offenders, 88; relapse prevention for, 79; in sex offender group process, 123

Kalichman, S. C., 67
Kavanagh, K., 218
Kear-Colwell, J., 85
Keenan, T., 95
Kennedy, P., 218
Klebe, K. J., 66
Knopp, F. H., 141
Koss-Chioino, L., 212
Kubler-Ross, E., 48

Lambert, M., 217
Lane, S., 87, 88
Language issues: in culturally diverse populations, 212, 214; in treating intellectually disabled sex offenders, 194
Lappin, J., 215, 222
Lapse contracts, 97
Lapses and relapses, 228–29
Larson, N., 173, 174
Laws, D. R., 79, 85, 100
Lee, E., 222
Legal system and treating intellectually disabled sex offenders, 203
Lemoine, J., 221
Lie detectors, 230
Lie Scale, 54
Life histories, writing, to confront distortions, 73
Listing techniques for relapse prevention, 97
Loneliness, 161–62

Losing face, 215
Loss, Peter, 117
Love at first sight, 158–59
Lowe's modification of the relapse process, 84–85

McCormack, J., 94
McFall, R. M., 149
McGoldrick, M., 212, 218, 219, 223
McGrath, R. J., 23, 25
Maddock, J., 173, 174
Maletsky, B. M., 111
Marital and significant relationship history in sexual offender evaluation, 16–17
Marital therapy, 181
Marlatt, Alan, 78, 80
Marlowe-Crowne Social Desirability Scale, 66, 69
Marques, Janice K., 70, 78, 84
Marshall, W. L., 70, 71, 83, 94, 150
Masturbatory acts, 3
Masturbatory satiation, 113, 205, 220
Medical history in sexual offender evaluation, 18
Medications: aftercare programming, 232; for arousal control, 113, 200; and culturally based belief systems, 222–23
Medroxyprogesterone acetate (MPA), 232
Meinig, Mary, 184–85
Men Who Rape (Groth), 121
Mental health status assessment: in sexual offender evaluation, 20–21; in treating intellectually disabled sex offenders, 197
Military history in sexual offender evaluation, 17
Miner, M. H., 70
Minimal arousal conditioning, 111, 205
Minnesota Multiphasic Personality Inventory (MMPI), 22, 67, 68
Minnuchin, S., 213–14, 218
Mittleman, M., 13
Model of Dysfunctional Cognitions (MDC), 94–95
Modeling, 166–67
Molinder, I., 67
Motivational interviewing, 85
Multifamily groups, 178–79
Multifamily psychoeducation groups, 179
Multifamily therapy groups, 179–81
Multiphasic Sex Inventory (MSI), 54, 66, 67
Murphy, W. D., 4, 71, 73–74
Mussack, Steven E.: aftercare programming, 234; defining sexual abusers, 3; family support in sex offender treatment, 164; guidelines for inter-

viewing sexual offenders, 25; polygraphic assessment, 14; psychosexual assessment, 15; working with sexual offenders, 7

National Adolescent Perpetrator Network, 111, 238
National Catholic Reporter, 47
National Institute of Corrections (NIC), U.S., 238
National Task Force on Juvenile Sexual Offending, 238
Native American offenders, 212, 221
Nature of harm theory, 95
Nelson, C., 70
Networks and support groups, 96
Newsweek, 47
Nichols, H. R., 67
No Safe Place: Violence Against Women and Children (Guberman and Wolf), 146
Nonconsent, defined, 3–4
Nonsuicidal self-destructive history in sexual offender evaluation, 21
Normality concept, abuse cycle and, 90

Observation, defined, 170
Olfactory conditioning, 111
Operant conditioning, 96
Orgasmic reconditioning, 106–8
Overt aversive stimulus, 111
Overt/covert events, 83

Paraphilias, 3, 13, 18, 61
Parent Effectiveness Training (Gordon), 121
Parent support groups, 179
Parents United (PU) support groups, 189
Parloff, M., 217
Partial confidentiality, 196
Passive planning process, 82
Patterns, defined, 170
Paxil, 222, 232
Pearce, J., 212
Pedersen, P., 218, 220
Pedophile Cognition Scale, 199
Peer networks, 96
Personality characteristics in sexual offender evaluation, 22
Petty, J., 152
Phallometry: in confronting abusers about denial, 61; phallometric assessment, 13–14
Pharmacological interventions: for arousal control, 113; culturally based belief systems about pharmacology, 222–23

Photoplethysmograph, 14, 230
Physical attractiveness, 158
Pierce, R., 217
Pithers, William D.: anger management, 152; cognitive distortions, 70; relapse prevention, 78, 79, 80, 81, 82, 84, 85, 87, 90
Plethysmograph, 14, 197, 198, 200–201, 205, 230–31
Pollock, P., 85
Polygraph, 230
Polygraphic assessment: for breaking through denial, 60–61; in sexual abuser treatment, 6, 14
Prior treatment and psychiatric history in sexual offender evaluation, 21
Privacy, 216
Problematic sexual behavior, 195
Program development, treatment, 37; assessment issues, 40–41; burnout prevention, 42; client population, 39; confidentiality, 40; creating the atmosphere for change, 41; group structure and content, 42–44; implementing the program, 38–41; preimplementation, considerations, 37–38; program goals and direction, 38–39; staff selection and training, 41–42; staff self-care and professional support, 45; treatment contracts, 45; voluntary or involuntary participation, 39–40
Proud loner style, 161
Provera, 232
Prozac, 222, 232
Psychological assessment in sexual offender evaluation, 20–22
Psychological testing in sexual offender evaluation, 21
Psychometric testing in treating intellectually disabled sex offenders, 199
Psychophysiological arousal, 13–14
Psychosocial history in sexual offender evaluation, 15–17

Rape cycle, 88
Rape and Molest Scales, 66, 69, 70
Rapid Risk Assessment for Sex Offence Recidivism (RRASOR), 24
Rapists: rape offenders view of themselves, 123; sexual arousal control, 113; social behavior of, 150
Rational emotive therapy (RET), 70
Reactive jealousy, 157
Reasonable doubt, denial and, 50
Recovery-based risk assessment, 24
Relapse cues, 84

Relapse minimization, 85

Relapse Prevention with Sex Offenders (Laws), 79

Relapse prevention and the sexual assault cycle, 77–78; assault cycle, 87–90; clinical application of relapse prevention and offense cycles, 93–100; cognitive interventions, 94–97; determinants of relapse and the cognitive-behavioral model of relapse, 80–83; evolution of relapse prevention, 100–101; goals of relapse prevention, 79–80; history of adapting relapse prevention for sex offenders, 78–79; integration of relapse prevention and assault cycle models, 90, 92; modifications of offense precursors: risk factors and relapse cues, 83–84; modifications to traditional models of relapse prevention, 84–85; relapse interventions, 93–98; relapse prevention for intellectually disabled sex offenders, 193, 207–8; self-regulation model of the relapse process, 85–87

Relapse reduction, 85

Relapses and lapses, 228–29

Relationship skills. *see* Social and relationship skills

Relationships dynamics in sexual offender evaluation, 22

Religion: role of religion in sexual offender evaluation, 15–16; spirituality and religion in culturally diverse populations, 215–16, 220–21

Repetitive listing for relapse prevention, 97

Residential-based treatment: aftercare programming, 226–27; for intellectually disabled sex offenders, 202, 204; residential sex offender programs, 125; staff management, 44

Responsibility and disowning behaviors in sexual offender evaluation, 21–22

Rinck, C. M., 67

Risk assessment in sexual offender evaluation, 22–24

Risk factors in relapse prevention, 83–84, 99–100

Robinson, J., 219–20

Role flexibility in family structures, 213

Role playing: role-plays in cognitive interventions for relapse prevention, 94; role-plays in sex offender group process, 134; social skills, 151, 153, 159; in treatment of intellectually disabled sex offenders, 197, 205, 206; in victim harm scenario, 144–45

Ross, Jonathan E., 117

Rouleau, J., 13

Safer Society Foundation, 121, 238

Salter, Anna, 53

Samenow, S. E., 67

Seemingly insignificant decisions (SIDs), 83

Seemingly unimportant decisions (SUDs), 83, 84, 92, 98

Segal, Z. V., 66, 67

Selective serotonin reuptake inhibitors, 232

Self-disclosure, 159–60

Self-esteem: enhancement, 151, 152; in intellectually disabled sex offenders, 194

Self-induced aversive conditioning, 96

Self-monitoring methods, 231–32

Self-respect, developing, 229–30

Sex education for intellectually disabled sex offenders, 206

Sex Offender Treatment Evaluation Project, 78

Sexual abuse: cultural view of incest and, 221; defining sexual abusers, 3–4

Sexual abuse/assault profile in sexual offender evaluation, 18–20

Sexual abuser treatment, defining: common treatment objectives, 4–5; how sexual abuser treatment differs from other therapies, 5–6; key areas and elements of treatment, 4; recommendations for therapists working with sexual offenders, 6–9

Sexual arousal disorders, controlling, 105, 115; addressing special problems and issues, 113–15; assisted covert sensitization, 107, 111; conducting treatment, 106–13; covert sensitization, 107, 108–11; developing a treatment plan, 105–6; integrating other types of treatments, 113; orgasmic reconditioning, 106–8; verbal satiation, 107, 111–13

Sexual assault cycle. *see* Relapse prevention and the sexual assault cycle

Sexual assault victims, 127

Sexual dysfunction data in sexual offender evaluation, 18

Sexual history: in sexual offender evaluation, 18–20; in treating intellectually disabled sex offenders, 197–98

Sexual Interest Cardsort, 199

Sexual relations, 155–57

Sgroi, Suzanne, 121

Shealy, L. S., 67

Significant others: marital and significant relationship history, 16–17; spouses and significant others group, 181

Silence, 222

Simkins, L., 67, 68, 69, 70

Sipes, D., 212

Six-Stage Cycle (assault cycle model), 89–90, 91

Skills and knowledge testing in sexual offender evaluation, 21
Smith, Gerrilyn, 175
Social interest assessment in sexual offender evaluation, 21
Social interventions, relapse prevention and, 96
Social isolation in families, 178
Social loneliness, 161
Social and relationship skills, enhancing, 149–50; anger management, 152–53; conversational skills, 151–52; development of relationship skills, 158–61; general social skills component, 150–53; intimacy training, 154–55; jealousy, 157–58; loneliness, 161–62; relationship skills component, 153–62; sexual relations, 155–57
Social relationships and activities in sexual offender evaluation, 17
Social Sexual Desirability Scale, 54
Social tolerance, 216–17
Social touch, 222
Socio-Sexual Knowledge and Attitude Test, 199
Spady, D., 216–17
Spouses and significant others group, 181
Stepped care approach for relapse prevention, 85
Stermac, L. E., 66, 67
Stevenson, W., 1, 13, 141
Stickrod, A., 25
Stimulus control techniques, 96–97
Stitzer, M. L., 78, 79
Stone, M., 19–20, 232
STOP (stop, think, options, practice), 94
Substance use or abuse history in sexual offender evaluation, 17
Sue, D., 219
Sue, D. W., 219
Sullivan, T., 216–17
Support groups, 96, 179, 189
Support networks, aftercare, 229
Supportive confirmation, 6
Suspicious jealousy, 157
Synanon model for drug abuse treatment, 4

Task groups: in sex offender group process, 126; in treatment programs, 42
Temporal cues, 84
Terminal hypotheses, 160
Theory knitting, 96
Theory of mind in sex offenders, 95–96
Thinking errors, 6, 204, 205
Thompson, K., 216–17
Thornton, D., 23, 24

Thought suppression, 94
Three-Phase Cycle (assault cycle model), 88–89
Treatment contracts, 45, 127–29
Trepper, T., 173–74
Triggering events, 83
Trust in sexual abuser treatment, 6
Tung, T., 222

Vargas, L., 212
Verbal satiation, 107, 111–13
Vermont Treatment Program for Sexual Aggressors, 78
Victim empathy, 146
Victim harm, 144–46
Victims of sexual offenders, defined, 3–4
Videotapes: for psychoeducational group process, 121; for relapse prevention, 79; video of victim's statement, 61
Voices, a Collection of Writings by Survivors of Sexual Abuse (Woods), 146

Wallace, R., 25
Ward, T., 83, 85, 86–87, 94, 95, 96
Ward, W., 67
Waskow, L., 217
West, M. A., 70
Who Am I and Why Am I in Treatment? (Freeman-Longo and Bays), 120
Willis, D., 212
Wolf, B., 217
Wolf, M., 146
Woods, G., 146
Work history in sexual offender evaluation, 16
Workbooks: for psychoeducational group process, 120; and treatment manuals for relapse prevention, 79
Wright, R., 216–17
Writing techniques: in aftercare programming, 231–32; hypothetical victim/offender letters, 145–46; for relapse prevention, 97; written assignments in psychoeducational group process, 122
Wurtele, S. K., 66

Yochelson, S., 67

Zamora, P., 87, 88
Zastrow, C., 221
Zoloft, 232

Select Safer Society Publications

Healthy Thinking/Feeling/Doing from the Inside Out: A Middle School Curriculum and Guide for the Prevention of Violence, Abuse & Other Problem Behaviors by Jack Pransky and Lori Carpenos (2000). $28.

The Adult Relapse Prevention Workbook by Charlene Steen (2001). $22.

Roadmaps to Recovery: A Guided Workbook for Young People in Treatment by Timothy J. Kahn (1999). $20.

The Secret: Art & Healing from Sexual Abuse by Francie Lyshak-Stelzer (1999). $20.

Outside Looking In: When Someone You Love Is in Therapy by Patrice Moulton and Lin Harper (1999). $20.

Web of Meaning: A Developmental-Contextual Approach in Sexual Abuse Treatment by Gail Ryan & Associates (1999). $22.

Feeling Good Again by Burt Wasserman (1999). A treatment workbook for boys and girls ages 6 and up who have been sexually abused. $16.

Feeling Good Again Guide for Parents & Therapists by Burt Wasserman (1999). $8.

Female Sexual Abusers: Three Views by Patricia Davin, PhD, Teresa Dunbar, PhD, & Julia Hislop, PhD (1999). $22.

Cultural Diversity in Sexual Abuser Treatment: Issues and Approaches edited by Alvin Lewis, PhD (1999). $22.

Sexual Abuse in America: Epidemic of the 21st Century by Robert E. Freeman-Longo & Geral T. Blanchard (1998). $20.

Personal Sentence Completion Inventory by L.C. Miccio-Fonseca, PhD (1998). $50, includes ten inventories and user's guide. Additional inventories available in packs of 25 for $25.

When You Don't Know Who to Call: A Consumer's Guide to Selecting Mental Health Care by Nancy Schaufele & Donna Kennedy (1998). $15.

Tell It Like It Is: A Resource for Youth in Treatment by Alice Tallmadge with Galyn Forster (1998). $15.

Assessing Sexual Abuse: A Resource Guide for Practitioners edited by Robert Prentky and Stacey Bird Edmunds (1997). $25.

Impact: Working with Sexual Abusers edited by Stacey Bird Edmunds (1997). $20.

Supervision of the Sex Offender by Georgia Cumming and Maureen Buell (1997). $25.

STOP! Just for Kids: For Kids with Sexual Touching Problems adapted by Terri Allred and Gerald Burns from original writings of children in a treatment program (1997). $15.

Shining Through: Pulling It Together After Sexual Abuse (Second Edition) by Mindy Loiselle & Leslie Bailey Wright (1997). $16. A workbook for girls ages 10 and up.

Back on Track: Boys Dealing with Sexual Abuse by Leslie Bailey Wright and Mindy Loiselle (1997). $14. A workbook for boys ages 10 and up.

A Primer on the Complexities of Traumatic Memories of Childhood Sexual Abuse: A Psychobiological Approach by Fay Honey Knopp & Anna Rose Benson (1997). $20.

The Last Secret: Daughters Sexually Abused by Mothers by Bobbie Rosencrans (1997). $20.

When Children Abuse: Group Treatment Strategies for Children with Impulse Control Problems by Carolyn Cunningham and Kee MacFarlane (1996). $28.

Adult Sex Offender Assessment Packet compiled by Mark Carich & Donya Adkerson (1995). $8.

Adolescent Sexual Offender Assessment Packet by Alison Stickrod Gray & Randy Wallace (1992). $8.

The Relapse Prevention Workbook for Youth in Treatment by Charlene Steen (1993). $18.

Pathways: A Guided Workbook for Youth Beginning Treatment by Timothy J. Kahn (Third Edition 2001). $22.

Pathways Guide for Parents of Youth Beginning Treatment by Timothy J. Kahn (Third Edition 2002). $10.

37-to-One: Living as an Integrated Multiple by Phoenix J. Hocking (1996). $12.

The Brother/Sister Hurt: Recognizing the Effects of Sibling Abuse by Vernon Wiehe, PhD (1996). $10.

Man-to-Man, When Your Partner Says NO: Pressured Sex & Date Rape by Scott A. Johnson (1992). $7.50.

From Trauma to Understanding: A Guide for Parents of Children with Sexual Behavior Problems by William D. Pithers, Alison S. Gray, Carolyn Cunningham, & Sandy Lane (1993). $5.

When Your Wife Says No: Forced Sex in Marriage by Fay Honey Knopp (1994). $7.

Female Adolescent Sexual Abusers: An Exploratory Study of Mother-Daughter Dynamics with Implications for Treatment by Marcia T. Turner & Tracey N. Turner (1994). $18.

Protocol for Phallometric Assessment: A Clinician's Guide, Second Edition, by Deloris T. Roys & Pat Roys (1999). $10.

Adults Molested as Children: A Survivor's Manual for Women & Men by Euan Bear with Peter Dimock (1988; 5th printing). $12.95.

Family Fallout: A Handbook for Families of Adult Abuse Survivors by Dorothy Beaulieu Landry, MEd (1991). $12.95.

Embodying Healing: Integrating Bodywork and Psychotherapy in Recovery from Childhood Sexual Abuse by Robert J. Timms, PhD, and Patrick Connors, CMT (1992). $15.

The Safer Society Press is part of The Safer Society Foundation, Inc., a 501(c)3 nonprofit national agency dedicated to the prevention and treatment of sexual abuse. We publish additional books, audiocassettes, and training videos related to the treatment of sexual abuse. To receive a catalog of our complete listings, please check the box on the order form (next page) and mail it to the address listed or call us at (802) 247-3132. For more information on the Safer Society Foundation, Inc., visit our website at www.safersociety.org.

ORDER FORM

Date:_____

All books shipped via United Parcel Service.
Please include a street location for shipping
as we cannot ship to a Post Office address.

SHIPPING ADDRESS:

Name and/or Agency _____

Street Address (no PO boxes) _____

City _____ State_____ Zip_____

BILLING ADDRESS (if different from shipping address):

Address _____

City _____ State_____ Zip_____

Daytime phone (_____)_____   P.O.#_____
                                             (must be submitted)

Visa or MasterCard # _____ Exp. Date _____

Signature (for credit card order) _____

☐ Please send me a catalog.   ☐ Do not add me to your mailing list.

QTY	TITLE	UNIT PRICE	TOTAL COST

SUBTOTAL	
VT RESIDENTS ADD 5% SALES TAX	
SHIPPING (SEE BELOW)	
TOTAL	

No returns.
All prices subject to change without notice.
Bulk discounts available, please inquire.
All orders must be prepaid.

Phone orders accepted with MasterCard or Visa.
Call (802) 247-3132 or fax (802) 247-4233

Make checks payable to:
SAFER SOCIETY FOUNDATION, INC

Mail to:

Shipping and Handling

1–5 items	$5	26–30 items	$20
6–10 items	$8	31–35 items	$23
11–15 items	$12	36–40 items	$26
16–20 items	$14	41–50 items	$31
21–25 items	$17	51+ items	call for quote

call for quote on rush orders

Safer Society Press
PO BOX 340 • BRANDON • VT 05733
A program of The Safer Society Foundation, Inc.
www.SaferSociety.org

Notes

Notes

Notes

Notes

Notes

Notes

Notes